Philosophic Inquiry

AN INTRODUCTION TO PHILOSOPHY

PRENTICE-HALL PHILOSOPHY SERIES

Arthur E. Murphy, Ph.D., Editor

LEWIS WHITE BECK

Professor of Philosophy
The University of Rochester

Philosophic Inquiry

AN INTRODUCTION TO PHILOSOPHY

PRENTICE-HALL, INC.

Englewood Cliffs, N. J.

First Printing.........March, 1952
Second Printing......January, 1953
Third Printing.......October, 1953
Fourth Printing........April, 1957
Fifth Printing........January, 1958
Sixth Printing...........July, 1958
Seventh Printing........May, 1959
Eighth Printing......January, 1961
Ninth Printing .... June, 1961
Tenth Printing..... September, 1962
Eleventh Printing...... June, 1963

66250—C

For C. H. B. and B. H. B.

Preface

The problems of philosophy are the most natural, the most human, and the most perennially perplexing problems that confront thinking people. Philosophy is a persistent attempt to think things through. Only secondarily is it a study of the writings of philosophers, or a technical field with an obscure terminology. Philosophy is not the exclusive concern of professors of philosophy, but is the rigorous and responsible effort of intelligent men and women to examine their life, the universe, and their place in it.

The writings of great philosophers of the past and of today are important in carrying through that examination of life without which, Socrates said, life is not worthy of man. But the basic problems of philosophy do not grow out of these writings or out of disputes among philosophers; they grow out of the bafflement and confusion that every intelligent person experiences when he wonders what man is, why he is here, and what his destiny is. Though answers to these questions may be demanded of that group of extraordinary men we call great philosophers, the questions themselves emerge in daily life, in science, in religion, in art, in morals, in politics, and in other deeply felt concerns of men.

This conception of the relation of philosophy to life and to other fields of inquiry has guided the writing of this book. Chapter 1 describes philosophy from this point of view and tries to show how some of the commonest questions require the kind of inquiry traditionally called philosophic. The remainder of the book is devoted to inquiries into four of them: What are the best ways of knowing, by which we may perhaps get intelligible and defensible answers to our other questions? How can we find the characteristics of what is familiarly called "the good life," which might constitute standards and goals of moral effort? What is man? And what, if anything, can we know about the general characteristics of the universe and man's place in it?

The first of these questions is discussed in Chapters 2, 3, and 4. These chapters describe and evaluate various "substitutes" for inquiry, the function of reason and experience in knowing, and the method of hypothesis so distinctively and successfully used in the sciences. Chapter 5 discusses the implications of scientific knowledge expressed as laws of nature for understanding man and the status he claims as a free agent. Chapter 6 deals with problems that arise from the interrelations of the sciences, and especially with those encountered in efforts to extend scientific inquiry to man himself and society.

The second of the questions, which concerns the method of ethical inquiry, is taken up in Chapter 7. The various ways of knowing previously discussed as ways of discovering facts are brought to bear upon decisions concerning goals and ideals.

Chapter 8 introduces the kind of speculative inquiry attempted in efforts to answer the questions that have the broadest import: What is man, and what is the universe in which he lives? This chapter points out its importance, its procedure, and its limitations.

The last five chapters then present some of the typical answers given by great philosophers, in which many people still find intellectual and also emotional satisfaction. The first of these, in Chapter 9, is that man is primarily a spiritual being dependent upon a supernatural God. Chapters 10 and 11 give the answers of the great idealists: all existence is a manifestation of spirit or mind. Finally, the last two chapters give the answers of naturalists (materialists, dialectical materialists, and "critical naturalists") whose program is to explain all things in terms analogous to those used in the sciences.

This approach to philosophy differs in significant ways from that of many other books. Some of them present one historic "school" after another, each with its own message. I am convinced that the great metaphysical schools and traditions are important and are among the most interesting parts of philosophy. But I have deferred a survey of them and of their polemics until the last part of the book, to a time when the student will have gained some facility in the analysis of philosophical problems. Some other books are more systematic and encyclopedic; but their weakness, as I see it, is to lay before the beginner a series of answers to technical questions he does not understand.

Nevertheless, much of the material included in either a historical or encyclopedic introduction appears also in this book, but with motivation and context changed. Great historical traditions and classical works are discussed here, but they are presented as attempts to answer pressing questions in science, ethics, and religion as well as in philosophy; they are not regarded primarily as answers to technical questions proposed by one philosopher to another. Similarly, the systematic problems of philosophy—those of perception, of universals, of the *a priori*, of the relation of the mind to the body, of the criteria of truth and value, of freedom and determinism, of mechanism and purpose, of objective vs. subjective status of contents of consciousness, and so on—are here. But here they are seen in a context of tentative inquiry and not in such a form that a student might feel, "Here is philosophy; learn these terms, these questions, these answers, and three objections to each, and you will know philosophy."

No problem is included simply because a great philosopher has discussed it. All are problems about which thinking men who are not philosophers are troubled, or questions suggested by the breakdown of their ready-made and often conflicting answers to these problems—this break-down constituting the original and continuing occasion for philosophic inquiry.

The book is designed for use as a basic text in either a one-semester or a two-semester introductory course. In a two-semester course, the entire book can be used in conjunction with assignments to source materials. To facilitate use of classical writings in philosophy, I have, wherever possible, cited inexpensive editions instead of standard editions, since the former are more likely to be readily available to students. Several anthologies, notably that by D. J. Bronstein, Y. H. Krikorian, and P. P. Wiener (*Basic Problems of Philosophy*, New York, Prentice-Hall, Inc., 1947), can be conveniently used as sources of extra assignments. In the bibliographies at the end of each chapter I have cited many recent writings, especially articles in philosophical journals, to help students avoid the common feeling that all philosophical literature is old. Works cited in the chapters have, with a few exceptions, been omitted in the bibliographies.

In a one-semester course the entire book can be used, or selections from it can be combined with collateral assignments. To permit flexibility in selection, each chapter, with a few obvious exceptions, has been made almost entirely independent of the others, and almost any combination of chapters will form a meaningful program. If selection is made, however, Chapters 1, 4, 7, and 8 will probably be the most suitable nucleus.

Dr. Martin Allen Greenman, Dr. William D. Geoghegan, and Mrs. Janis T. Dowd, my colleagues in the University of Rochester, have given expert and generous assistance in the writing of the book, and I am happy to express my gratitude to them. I thank also the following publishers for permission to quote from works covered by their copyrights: Abingdon-Cokesbury Press; Appleton-Century-Crofts, Inc.; Benziger Brothers, Inc.; Burns Oates & Washbourne Ltd.; *The College of the Pacific Publications in Philosophy;* Columbia University Press; Thomas Y. Crowell Company; Dodd, Mead & Company, Inc.; Doubleday & Company, Inc.; E. P. Dutton & Co., Inc.; *Encyclopaedia Britannica;* Harper & Brothers; Harvard University Press; The Humanities Press; International Publishers; *Isis; The Journal of Philosophy;* John Lane The Bodley Head, Ltd.; The Liberal Arts Press; Longmans, Green & Company; The Macmillan

Company; W. W. Norton & Company, Inc.; Oxford University Press; *The Philosophical Review;* Charles Scribner's Sons; University of California Press; University of Chicago Press; and Yale University Press.

LEWIS WHITE BECK

Table of Contents

MATERIALISM; MATERIALISTIC THEORIES OF THE MIND. DIA-
LECTICAL MATERIALISM—THE "MATERIALISM" OF DIALECTI-
CAL MATERIALISM; "DIALECTIC" IN DIALECTICAL MATERIAL-
ISM; THE MATERIALISTIC PHILOSOPHY OF HISTORY. CRITICISM
AND CONCLUSION.

Philosophic Inquiry

AN INTRODUCTION TO PHILOSOPHY

1

On Philosophy and Philosophizing

What is man? "What a novelty! What a monster, what a chaos, what a contradiction, what a prodigy! Judge of all things, imbecile worm of the earth; depositary of truth, a sink of uncertainty and error; the pride and refuse of the universe!"

These are some answers given by Blaise Pascal.[1]

What *is* man? Is he a being a little lower than the angels, or a little higher than the apes? Is he the darling of the gods, their puppet, or a heroic rebel against them? Is he the center of things, or is his birth on a middle-sized planet of an insignificant star just a queer accident in a planless universe? Is his little life rounded with a sleep, or is it his birth that is but a sleep and a forgetting? Is he best described as the only rational animal, as the only animal that laughs, as the only animal that makes and uses tools, or as "the only animal that eats when it isn't hungry, drinks when it isn't thirsty, fights when it isn't angry, and makes love all the year 'round"?

The question of what he is must have troubled man from the first dawn of thought. It is a question that has challenged poets,

---

[1] Blaise Pascal, *Pensées* (1656-1657), translated by W. F. Potter, page 121, § 434. New York: E. P. Dutton & Co., Inc., 1931, Everyman's Library.

preachers, prophets, historians, and philosophers from the beginning. It is just under the surface of the typical college "bull session," and probably was not far below the surface when our ancestors gathered around the fire 10,000 years ago.

The question has been answered in part, at least, by the scientific investigations of medical men during the past 3,000 years. More recently it has been intensively studied in the newest of the sciences, psychology, anthropology, and sociology. We know that man is a physico-chemical being, an animal, and a part of a social group; many think that he is a spiritual being, a being with rights, duties, aspirations, and a destiny that cannot be completely discovered or explained in scientific terms. Neither the sciences nor religion tell us what is the bearing of some of these answers on the others. Their answers are fragmentary and need to be weighed, analyzed, and integrated.

Intellectual analysis and integration are the tasks of the philosopher. Philosophy has been defined as "a persistent attempt to think things through." The characteristic attitude of the philosopher is, or ought to be, patient and open-minded inquiry in a serious, disciplined, and ambitious effort to find the general traits of reality, the significance of human experience, and the place of man in the universe as a whole. Philosophy is a vigorous attempt to think about the ultimate questions that are usually "answered" by our emotions and vague hopes and fears. It is a reasoned effort to see facts and ideals, emotions and truths, man and the universe, in such a way that they will, when taken together, make more "sense" than when taken piecemeal.

PHILOSOPHY OF LIFE

The philosopher does what we all do from time to time when we face great problems and try to trace out their ramifications in our lives as a whole; but he does it more seriously, more persistently, and more skillfully than most of us who save our best efforts for dealing with more immediate problems.

Every man has opinions on the subjects the philosopher investigates. Therein lies both the importance of philosophy to the common man and the chief difference between the common man and the technically trained philosopher. While both have opinions, the philosopher makes inquiries; but both are interested ultimately in the same questions. There is a little of the philosopher in all of us, and much of the common man in the greatest philosophers. Both the philosopher and the common man are interested in why we should be moral. Both would like to know whether there is an ideal of justice binding on every man and on every state. Both want to know what, if any, are the limits of human knowledge, beyond which our minds can never go. Both believe in, disbelieve in, or have doubts about the existence of God. Both speculate on the question of freedom of the will and on the limits of human responsibility. Both think they have, or are looking for, some satisfactory answer to the question of what man is and what is his place in the scheme of things.

On questions like these, every thinking person has opinions. Most of us have not formulated our ideas very concisely, so that the bearing of our beliefs about some one of these questions upon our opinions about the others is not usually clear. Our answers to these questions do not hang together very well. Instead of having some large view that might help us to see answers to all these and still other questions, most of us hold one opinion about one of these questions and other perhaps incompatible opinions about the others. The common man dislikes theories, but someone has aptly described him as "that wildest of all possible theorists," for he has *many* theories, a different theory about each of these questions, instead of *one* theory that will cover them all. The theories he has, to be sure, are not usually *called* theories; they are regarded simply as opinions, attitudes, beliefs. He has picked them up from his parents, his church, books, newspapers, friends, and enemies.

Many a man, if he had the wit of Dean Acheson, could rightly say, "All I know I have learned at my mother's knee, or some other joint."

It is not surprising, therefore, that such beliefs do not usually hang together very well. The unity they have, such as it is, is not a logical unity, with one belief implying or strengthening the others. Their unity is due simply to the fact that they are the beliefs that are congenial to a given man, beliefs that fit in with his own character, sentiments, and needs. Taken together, this complex of beliefs and attitudes is what is usually called one's "philosophy of life." One can agree with the statement of the German philosopher, Fichte, who said: "Tell me what your philosophy is, and I shall tell you the sort of man you are."

The relevance of philosophy to character and conduct has been emphasized by the English essayist, G. K. Chesterton, who wrote that he is among those people

> . . . who think that the most practical and important thing about a man is . . . his view of the universe. We think that for a landlady considering a lodger, it is important to know his income, but still more important to know his philosophy. We think that for a general about to fight an enemy, it is important to know the enemy's numbers, but still more important to know the enemy's philosophy. We think the question is not whether the theory of the cosmos affects matters, but whether, in the long run, anything else affects them.[2]

Motives in the study of philosophy

We all have a philosophy of life; why, then, should anyone study philosophy? If we all have our beliefs and are ready to defend them—as we are, by argument if possible, and by force, if necessary—why subject ourselves to the labor of learning the history of metaphysics or reading Aristotle?

The reason is this: having opinions on philosophical questions is one thing, and philosophizing is something more. Phi-

---

[2] G. K. Chesterton, *Heretics* (1905), pages 15-16. New York: Dodd, Mead & Co., 1927. Used with the permission of John Lane. The Bodley Head, Ltd., London.

losophy is a thinking and an inquiring attitude, while what we call philosophy of life is generally a mixture of unexamined opinions taken on faith and frequently acquired in early childhood, almost invariably on insufficient evidence. A philosophy of life, if it consists simply of what we believe almost "by instinct," is not consistently worked out, and may not be intellectually worth defending at all. It usually does not come up to certain specifications of coherence, scope, and precision that the technical philosopher demands of his ideas. Philosophy of life is so much a matter of glands and environment, and so little the product of a persistent attempt to think, that the man in the street frequently does not know what he does believe or how to justify what he thinks he does accept.

Most people, however, do not feel the inadequacy of their world-view. It is generally shared by their fellows, and it is seldom talked about by adults bent upon the business at hand. Smaller questions occupy so much of our energies that the perennial issues of life are shut out or are left to preachers and poets. In our century, Chesterton says,

> We are more and more to discuss details in art, politics, literature. A man's opinion on tramcars matters; his opinion on Botticelli matters; his opinion on all things does not matter. . . . Everything matters—except everything.[3]

These words of Chesterton, however, were written many years ago; since then, wars have been fought, and other wars have threatened, partly because individuals and peoples *have* taken different views of "everything." Complacency about "everything" has been violently shocked by changes in political systems, educational goals, and science. Percentagewise, perhaps, the number of people interested in studying philosophy is still small, but philosophical books have been best-sellers, and since World War II, philosophy classes in American colleges have been larger and livelier than ever before. Why do students take courses in philosophy? Apart from the obvious

---

[3] *Ibid.*, page 13.

reason that some college curricula require it, I think there are three reasons.

1. *People suspect the inadequacy of their own philosophy of life*—Most people, even if they do not talk about their philosophy of life, act as if it were one of their dearest possessions, one that they will hold on to longest and modify as little as possible. A man may change his opinion on a scientific question by doing a single experiment; a single exposé may change his politics; but he will hold to his view of life as a whole with a tenacity more characteristic of a bulldog than of an impartial investigator. Even so, in view of the world situation and the acquaintance many people now have with other divergent views of life, few people are quite as dogmatic as they once were. About philosophical matters, they now preface their remarks with such telltale evidence of sneaking doubt as, "Well, as I see it . . ." or "This is only my opinion, but. . . ." Even while defending their beliefs, they are frequently ready to listen to those of others to see if they can either find better ways to defend their own or (at least, sometimes) get a view of things that may be more adequate than the one they had before. Philosophy classes are at least supposed to raise the questions, to put things into proper perspective, and to provide an opportunity for intelligent discussion of the things that matter most. Hence students are willing now, in larger numbers than ever before, to submit themselves to the "shock treatment" administered by the professor of philosophy who questions what has previously been unquestioned.

2. *People recognize that there is a high rate of obsolescence among ideas*—The world has changed much since many accepted ideas were formulated. It may well be, as many people believe, that the ideas they and their fellows have are becoming useless for making the modern world really intelligible and for guiding us through its complexities. Copernicus upset more than astronomy; he changed men's ways of looking at "everything," and one task of philosophy from his time until the end of the seventeenth century was to repair the damage that he

had done to older views of life. But the damage was repaired by changing men's views, not by attacking the astronomers. The formulation of Darwin's theory of evolution in 1859 delivered another profound shock, from which many institutions and the minds of many men have not yet fully recovered. Similar revolutions in thought have been started by Freud and by Einstein. Because intellectual revolutions are slow and seldom complete, the minds of many men are filled with inconsistent ideas. Some of these ideas go back thousands of years, others a few hundred, and a few, challenging all the rest, come from contemporary movements in religion, the arts, science, and politics.

Alfred North Whitehead has defined the function of philosophy with reference to this incongruity: "Philosophy is an attitude of mind towards doctrines ignorantly entertained." [4] Self-examination and the examination of society are human necessities; the study of philosophy and the earnest attempt to philosophize provide an opportunity for and a challenge to personal and social examination.

3. *People find it important to understand ideas they do not accept*—The present political split in the world reflects a long-run philosophical or ideological conflict between peoples who not only have different forms of government, but also, different philosophies of life. One of the most urgent needs today is that the peoples of the Orient and of the Occident understand one another, and this means understanding the philosophies of life that reign in other parts of the world. This is difficult. It is hard enough to formulate and elaborate our own beliefs; it is far more difficult to do this for beliefs held by people we have never seen, especially if we look down upon them or fear them.

Philosophers have expressed the aspirations, ideals, and ideas of their cultures. It is commonly admitted that our understanding of Greek civilization is helped by understanding the thoughts of its greatest philosophers; and now, people are

---

[4] Alfred North Whitehead, *Modes of Thought*, page 233. New York: The Macmillan Company, 1938.

coming to believe that one way, and perhaps the best way, of understanding our contemporaries, our potential allies or enemies, is by reading and understanding the thoughts of their greatest thinkers.[5]

Each of these reasons for studying philosophy indicates that we need and sometimes want to make a persistent attempt to think things through. In this, we should be grateful for any help that we can get. We need this help especially when we face some far-reaching problem—moral, political, religious, scientific, artistic—that our presupposed ideas do not help us to solve, or that these ideas may have helped create. Philosophy begins in a natural curiosity that will not be satisfied with what we already know or think we know; according to Aristotle, it begins in wonder. "Hast any philosophy in thee, shepherd?" The answer is, Yes, but it needs cultivating.

The personal and the historical in philosophy

All of this brings out two important truths about philosophy. First, *it is personal*. It is a world-view constructed out of a person's own experience and what he can learn from others, and it is aimed at rendering intelligible the problems that beset him as a man. Each man sees the world from his own perspective, is confronted by his own perplexities, and makes his own demands for meaningfulness. Each man, by the necessities of his own nature, must be his own philosopher.

But no man is alone in this endeavor. Philosophy of life is personal, but—and this is the second important truth—*"technical" philosophy is social and historical*. Philosophy, as intellectual inquiry and discipline, has its own techniques, answers, traditions, and history. The answers have emerged from the thoughts of philosophers, who were, of course, beset by all the human challenges, but who rose above the merely personal. Men do not cease to be men when they become philosophers. Each continues to some extent to see the world with his own

---

[5] This is argued in detail in a philosophical best-seller, F. S. C. Northrop's *The Meeting of East and West*. New York: The Macmillan Company, 1946.

"refractive index." But a philosophy that is wholly private and unique is incommunicable and useless in the struggle for intelligibility and intellectual survival. It is one world that men are trying to cope with, and each philosopher teaches a lesson which, he believes, will serve for more than to rationalize his own frustrations. Philosophers do indeed disagree, but there is some glimmer of agreement among them that careful study can bring out and that can serve as a standard for evaluating our own answers. Brand Blanshard has expressed this faith in the philosophic tradition:

> If in Elysium Aristotle and Dewey ever meet over their ambrosia with St. Thomas, Hegel, and Bertrand Russell, the complaint of the attendant spirits is not likely to be that, finding each other unintelligible they sat in silence and parted early, but rather that they found an understanding so long awaited that talk and laughter went on incontinently till after dusk fell over Olympus.[6]

Just as important as the fact that each man is his own philosopher, then, is the other fact that types of questions and groups of answers tend to recur in the history of philosophy. They recur because the number of important and meaningful questions that arise and the number of sound answers that can be given to these questions are limited. Each thinker can therefore learn from those who have thought well on the same problem. Each one can stand on the shoulders of earlier thinkers and survey a more distant horizon, a more spacious landscape; and he may be warned by their examples from falling into their errors. In this sense, philosophy has a history and has made progress. A person, however intelligent, who attempts to wrestle with the deep problems without the aid of a Plato, a Descartes, a Kant, is wasting his strength, perhaps conquering intellectual lands already conquered, and certainly making mistakes already made and regretted.

The history of philosophical ideas, like novels and dramas,

---

[6] Brand Blanshard, in *Philosophy in American Education*, page 106. New York: Harper & Brothers, 1945.

tends to exhibit repeated plots. Each idea has its own history, origin, and development; a philosophical idea has its natural friends and natural enemies among other ideas, and a natural growth. Just as it has been said that every short story has one of a small number of basic plots that authors use over and over again with different characters in different locales, so also there are some natural intellectual plots in the life-history of philosophical ideas. Even a student of ordinary gifts is likely to formulate for himself some philosophical thesis that seems to him to be original and new. He may say, "I believe all my knowledge comes from experience," or "I believe that the purpose of life is to get as much pleasure as possible." This is all very fine; no reading of philosophy books can take away the glory he feels when he enunciates an idea he calls his very own. But it takes rare philosophical talents to see without help what these ideas mean and where they would lead if developed consistently. Most people will have one or two such ideas, and be oblivious to the fact that, if they are going to accept one of these beliefs, there are other statements they have never even thought about that they *must* believe if their philosophy is to be logically consistent. This is where a knowledge of the thought-patterns that have emerged in the works of great philosophical thinkers is of most help. Philosophizing is not at all the same thing as reading books on philosophy; but reading books on philosophy is one of the most important steps in each individual's inquiry after answers to philosophical questions.

Serious philosophizing is work; and the more help we have in doing it, the better for us and the further we may go. That is why just thinking one's own thoughts, irreplaceable and exciting as it is, is no excuse for failing to think through the thoughts of others to see where our ideas and theirs must lead.

WHAT QUESTIONS ARE PHILOSOPHICAL?

We have mentioned and given illustrations of certain questions that are of concern to men in general but of preeminent interest to philosophers. These are rightly called *philosophical questions*. What do they have in common? We shall describe five features shown by most, if not all, questions usually considered to be philosophical.

Philosophical questions are not primarily questions of fact

In asking philosophical questions, we are not asking for facts; at least, not for the sort of facts that we get when we ask a historian or a physicist a question. There are indeed facts *about* philosophy, such as the fact that Plato wrote the *Republic* and that Kant died in 1804, and the student of philosophy usually wants to know some of these facts. But when someone asks you what your philosophy is, you answer not in terms of what definitions or historical facts you know or what specific information you have. Rather, you try to express the *meaning* of what you know and believe.

Philosophy, from the etymology of the word, is not "love of knowledge" (facts), but "love of wisdom." Wisdom is more than accumulated knowledge; the wise man may or may not be highly educated. Wisdom is an attitude toward what we know or toward what we know we are ignorant of. It is an attitude of balanced judgment, of sound evaluation, of long-range perspective. Many men of great learning never achieve it; many a man or woman who is illiterate has achieved it. But, of course, wisdom is richer if it is based on broad experience and deep learning. One difference between the philosopher (as this term is used to praise and commend men of broad vision in whatever walk of life) and the *professional* philosopher at his best, is the wider knowledge that the latter is expected to be able to survey and integrate. The philosopher strives for wisdom as the main goal of his life; for most of us, if it comes, it comes as a by-product of our experience and character.

But philosophy makes no promises. Philosophy is not wisdom, but the *love* of wisdom. The philosopher is not always a wise man; he is the man who professes to *seek* wisdom. But the questions philosophy asks are questions that only a truly wise man could answer. The modest man will not presume to call himself wise; but there is no boast in professing to seek after wisdom—although there may be hypocrisy in it. Diogenes Laertius, in his *Lives of the Eminent Philosophers*, one of the chief sources of our knowledge about ancient philosophers, tells us of the history of the word *philosophy:*

Pythagoras was the first person who invented the term 'Philosophy', and who called himself a philosopher. . . . For he said that no man ought to be called wise, but only God. For formerly what is now called philosophy was called wisdom, and they who professed it were called wise men, as being endowed with great acuteness and accuracy of mind; but now he who embraces wisdom is called a philosopher.[7]

Philosophical questions are related to decisions about values

This is, perhaps, another way of saying that philosophy is a search for wisdom instead of information about facts (knowledge). For wisdom, as we have seen, is an attitude of valuing and weighing courses of action so that they will fit into a reasonable interpretation of the human situation. Arthur E. Murphy has said,

The subject-matter of philosophy is the things that men take seriously, not for limited purposes, but in the basic commitments which determine, on the whole, what they make of their lives and of the world they live in.[8]

Except within very narrow limits, science does not tell men what they should do. Granting that certain ends are desirable, science can, in many cases, tell them what they must do in order to achieve these goals. Science tells us that hydrogen cyanide is a very good poison and that penicillin is a very good germ-killer; but science alone cannot tell the scientist or anyone else whether euthanasia is morally justified or not. By

---

[7] Diogenes Laertius, *Lives of the Eminent Philosophers* (C. D. Yonge, trans.), pages 9-10. London: H. G. Bohn, 1853.

[8] Arthur E. Murphy, *The Uses of Reason*, page 288. New York: The Macmillan Company, 1943.

virtue of science alone, we do not know whether we ought to use the penicillin or the cyanide.

What the ordinary man is interested in is not just how to accomplish a certain purpose, important as that knowledge is. He wants to know what purpose to choose from among those open to him. The ends and purposes to be chosen usually stem, directly or indirectly, from religion. But the religious answer, rightly or wrongly, now satisfies fewer people than heretofore. Many people in our society have doubts about the truths claimed by religion. These people are not sure that the standards of conduct that religious teachers set up long ago are the best ideals for conduct today. Others grant the truth of these teachings, but do not see how they can be applied in our complex society. It is not our place here to examine and evaluate these doubts and hesitancies; but they do exist, and they cry out for resolution.

One of the purposes of philosophy is to evaluate this kind of doubt. Philosophers do discuss questions of ultimate value, and most philosophical questions raise, either explicitly or implicitly, the issue of the nature of values. Philosophical conclusions about the universe and the place of ideals and values within it eventually lead to decisions as to which of our conflicting ideals are most worthy of pursuit. Even philosophical discussions that are not explicitly about values have a bearing on the value decisions we make. For instance, how one answers the question, "Does God exist?" may determine his answer to questions concerning the standards to be used in judging conduct and guiding choices. Similarly, questions about the relation of the mind to the body or of the best ways of knowing will, when answered one way or another, suggest attitudes and theories about values and about the obligations of men.

Philosophers also deal explicitly with questions of value. Moral questions are studied in that part of philosophy called *ethics.* In *aesthetics,* philosophers discuss the nature of beauty and the standards used in criticizing and appreciating works of art. *Logic* deals with the formal principles of reasoning and with relations between propositions that can be taken as norms for judging the validity of various ways of thinking. *Philosophy of religion* discusses the values in religion; *philosophy of history* deals with the meaning and value of the historical process and of the methods for discovering the facts of history. *Philosophy of law* and *political philosophy* seek to establish reasonable criteria for judging the aims and functions of government and law. *Philosophy of science* questions and evaluates the methods of scientific thinking and tries to determine the value and significance of the scientific enterprise as a whole. There are also philosophies of business, of education, in fact, of every field of experience about which men think deeply. Whenever men, no matter what work they are doing, stop to inquire into that work from the standpoint of its ultimate values and significance in the whole scheme of things, they are then philosophizing.

Philosophical questions are critical

Philosophy is, in part, an analysis of conceptions and meanings that are usually, at least in some field of endeavor, taken for granted. Every field of experience—science as much as religion—bases its attitudes and inquiries on assumptions that are accepted as starting points. They are accepted, as it were, on faith, and they are generally used without much critical examination. One of the principal tasks of the philosopher is to examine them and to evaluate them, to make their meaning explicit, to determine the limits of their application, to see the grounds on which they may be justified. Moritz Schlick, an Austrian philosopher who believed that criticism was the whole duty of philosophy, emphasized the bearing of philosophy on the concepts and presuppositions of other intellectual pursuits when he wrote,

There are not specific "philosophical" truths which would contain the solution of specific "philosophical" problems, but philosophy has the task of finding the meaning of all problems and [of] their solutions. It must be defined as *the activity of finding meaning*.[9]

Many of the greatest philosophers of the past are remembered now not so much for the great systems and world-views that they propounded as for their painstaking analysis of problems and of techniques for solving them. David Hume's analysis of the concept of cause, for instance, which we shall examine in Chapter 5, is a permanent part of philosophical analysis, acknowledged to be such even by those who disagree with Hume's conclusions. Philosophers have made some of their most important contributions when they first discerned an assumption or learned to ask a new question that had been overlooked by their predecessors. Their questions were frequently more important than the answers they were able to give.

We shall see many illustrations of philosophical criticism of accepted but vague meanings; the discussion of common sense in Chapter 2 is such an analysis. We cannot answer a question such as "Is common sense dependable?" until we know what it means. Or consider the common philosophical question, "Has life any meaning?" I suppose everyone's philosophy of life includes some sort of answer to this very vague question. But the philosopher analyzes the question before he speculates about an answer to it. Such questions must be made precise, or they cannot be intelligently discussed at all. Thus Spinoza and Hegel and Augustine tried to answer the question of the meaning of life after they had inquired into what it meant; while the same question asked by Job was not a precise question so much as an expression of puzzlement or intellectual bafflement. The man who asks the question usually wants consolation or some message that will satisfy him and either justify or still his rebellion against things. The philosopher quietly begins, "What do you mean by 'meaning'?"

---

[9] Moritz Schlick, "The Future of Philosophy," *The College of the Pacific Publications in Philosophy*, 1932, page 58.

Philosophers by profession and amateur philosophers usually sin in opposite directions with respect to philosophical analysis and criticism. Some philosophers, like Schlick, think that analysis and criticism are the entire task of philosophy; they are certainly, to many professionally trained philosophers, the most interesting part of their work, and some never get beyond them. When a pupil once objected to Morris R. Cohen's having criticized his beliefs but not having given him anything to take their place, Cohen is said to have replied, "Hercules was required to clean the Augean stables; it is not said that he had to refill them."

Students and amateurs, like Cohen's pupil, frequently become impatient with the fine-spun analyses given by teachers and textbooks in philosophy. "After all," a student once said to me, "I came into this class wanting to find out how to make my life richer, and I heard long discussions about the concept of life and value and even an analysis of the word 'how', but I'm not a bit nearer to answering my main question than when I began." I imagine, however, that the student was closer than he thought; for at least he had given up the naive notion that the question he was asking was a simple one that I could answer or whose answer he could find in a book. I think he will never again be satisfied with facile answers of which the only recommendation is that they have a perhaps specious obviousness about them.

The philosopher does sometimes get so interested in his technique that he forgets the human interest that may first have led him and his students to philosophy; the student suffers from impatience to get to the main point. Some philosophers are like pianists who play only scales; on the other hand, some students are like beginners in music who are so anxious to play Beethoven that they resent having to learn scales. Each has exaggerated one aspect of the process of music-making or philosophizing.

Philosophical analysis and criticism are not ends in themselves, but they are a very important means to the working out of intelligible solutions to the deepest philosophical problems:

> By removing prejudice and confusion, by spreading enlightenment through the clarification of basic ideas, [the philosopher] occupies an indispensable role as a guide on the however tortuous path of human progress.[10]

Philosophical questions are speculative

The questions asked by philosophers push us *past the limits of established knowledge,* asking what might lie beyond. Philosophers have made some of their most important contributions by making intelligent guesses about what lies beyond the knowledge of their time. Democritus suggested the existence of atoms long before there was clinching scientific evidence for accepting their existence; Empedocles suggested some kind of evolution long before biologists came to similar conclusions on the basis of their much greater knowledge; many scientific discoveries in psychology and sociology vindicate suggestions made long ago by philosophers. Of course, philosophers have made an even larger number of guesses that have been refuted by the further accumulation of facts. But because the critical scientist usually accomplishes more by staying fairly close to the level of what he can observe, and rightly hesitates before making broad generalizations and sweeping hypotheses, he is often helped by remembering the freer speculations of philosophers.

Philosophers also speculate *beyond the limits of all possible scientific knowledge.* Questions as to whether God exists or not, whether there are any ultimate values, whether there is a final purpose of existence, are not questions for which we look to science for answers. They are not questions about facts that the scientist will perhaps eventually get around to answering; they are questions about value and meaning—including even

---

[10] Herbert Feigl, in *Readings in Philosophical Analysis* (H. Feigl and Wilfred S. Sellars, eds.), page 26. New York: Appleton-Century-Crofts, Inc., 1949.

the value and meaning of science itself. Any answer to these questions requires imaginative speculation, a readiness to go beyond all the facts with the hope of formulating some hypothesis that will make them all more intelligible than if they were looked at scientifically:

It is part of the business of philosophy to continue the consideration of such questions, to make us aware of their importance, to examine all the approaches to them, and to keep alive that speculative interest in the universe which is apt to be killed by confining ourselves to definitely ascertainable knowledge.[11]

Human beings want and need answers to the great philosophical issues, and they expect—rightly or wrongly—that philosophers shall help them to find intelligible, even if not demonstrable, answers to them. For it is certain that if philosophers do not deal with these questions, others less responsible and less disciplined in thought will do so. Most philosophers, fully cognizant of the obstacles in the way of establishing any speculative conclusions, do try to make out the general features of things by speculating beyond the facts. Scientific knowledge is not enough; intelligence can and ought to be used in trying to see the bearing of the facts we know on ideals and hopes and on that much greater drama of which we can never really know more than a small part. Some reasonable guesses about the drama as a whole, and also about the stage, the backstage, and the wings, are needed by the actors in the human drama. The most reasonable guesses can be made by men whose imagination is disciplined by analysis and criticism, not by wild theorists, by dogmatic seers, or by men who never look beyond what is at the other end of the microscope, but by philosophers who try, at least, to see things whole. They are the responsible and disciplined speculators.

[11] From *Problems of Philosophy,* by Bertrand Russell, pages 241-242. New York: Home University Library, Oxford University Press, 1912.

Philosophical questions are synoptic

By synoptic vision we mean "seeing things whole," seeing everything in its bearing upon everything else, seeing things in their integral togetherness. This characteristic of philosophy really sums up all the others. Whereas science and many of the special branches of philosophy deal with only particular aspects of things or narrow "universes of discourse," philosophy itself is an attempt to remain keenly aware that we live in *one* world. Our knowledge breaks awareness of this world into bits and studies each aspect or part piecemeal, or, at most, the relations holding among a few of its parts. In this way, our knowledge gains certainty and clarity. Any attitude that goes beyond this is speculation, and is sometimes criticized as "mere mysticism." The mystic immerses himself in The Whole or The One and what he gains in scope and depth, he loses in detail and logical rigor. But, says Whitehead, "The purpose of philosophy is to rationalize mysticism," [12] that is, to render intelligible the view of the whole that comes from imagination, speculative flights, and what Whitehead calls "direct insight into depths as yet unspoken." Synoptic philosophical questions are questions about "everything."

The synopsis that is the aim of philosophy is one of the features that make it of great importance in education. Modern education requires specialization, and universities have departments that make specialization in teaching and research possible. Most schools leave "generalization" of the student to be a matter of precept and acculturation in an intellectual atmosphere provided by libraries, laboratories, lecture rooms, and association with scholars. Philosophy, although it is usually a special department in a university, fails to do its whole job if it remains simply a curriculum for training expert technicians in logical analysis and erudite students of the history of philosophical ideas. The philosophy department and philosophy

---

[12] Alfred North Whitehead, *Modes of Thought,* page 237. New York: The Macmillan Company, 1938.

classes, at their best, provide a center of gravity for the educational program which is somewhere near the center of experience instead of off to one side. Philosophers seek to generalize, to synthesize, to criticize, and to integrate. As teachers, their task is not only to make Ph.D.'s in philosophy, or to give students of accounting a nodding acquaintance with Plato; their task is also to develop the student's ability to gain a synoptic view of himself and his place in the world, to show him that he is really one person in one world—not a Christian on Sunday, a chemist one hour, a classicist the next, an athlete in the afternoon, and a wolf in the evening.

This cannot be taught in the same way that skills and even some knowledge are imparted. It is something that the student must teach himself by trying to make and to examine his own philosophy. This was the method of Socrates, who said that he acted as midwife for others who were trying to bring their own ideas to birth; it was the method of Kant, who said, "I cannot teach philosophy, I can only teach philosophizing." By such a method, the study of philosophy can help the student to work out his own problems through showing him that he is not alone in his perplexities; the greatest minds in history have faced the same problems and have used their genius in trying to solve them. The world is full of problems for all of us. The task of a course in philosophy is not to tell the student the answers—as if the teacher or the author of the textbook knew them!—but to make him fully aware of the ramifications of his questions, of some possible answers to them, and of his stake in each.

These, then, are the distinguishing traits of philosophy at its best. Philosophy grows out of the need of each thinking person to find an intelligible order in his life so that he can think and feel that things "make sense." Philosophy is not an accumulation of facts, although it uses all the facts that it can get and that the individual can master. It deals rationally with values and ideals; it tries to see the most general contours of the world, which is not merely a world of brute fact but also a stage on which ideals are pursued and values are, in fortunate moments, appreciated; and it tries to integrate all the partial views we have into a reasonable picture of the whole. Its inquiry is detailed analysis and disciplined speculation. It goes critically beneath and speculatively beyond established facts. There is a place in it for individual beliefs and ideals; there are many rooms in the mansion of philosophy. At the same time, however, its problems recur from age to age, and from the masters each of us can learn which solutions are promising and which ways of dealing with our own puzzles are futile. We feel, perhaps, that our problems of coming to terms with ourselves and discovering our place in things are personal problems; but the ones that most perplex us are the most human and perennial of all.

BIBLIOGRAPHY

Baldwin, Robert C., and McPeak, James A. S., *An Introduction to Philosophy through Literature*. New York: The Ronald Press Company, 1950. Chapter 1.

Blanshard, Brand, "Education as Philosophy." *Swarthmore College Bulletin*, Vol. XLII, (July, 1945), pages 1-19.

—— et al., *Philosophy in American Education*. New York: Harper & Brothers, 1945.

Bronstein, D. J., Krikorian, Y. H., and Wiener, P. P. (eds.), *Basic Problems of Philosophy*. New York: Prentice-Hall, Inc., 1947. Chapter 9.

Cohen, J. W., "The Role of Philosophy in General Education," *Journal of Philosophy*, Vol. XLIV, No. 18 (August 28, 1947), pages 477-485.

Dewey, John, *Reconstruction in Philosophy* (1920). New York: New American Library Mentor Books, 1950.

Edman, Irwin, *Four Ways in Philosophy*. New York: Henry Holt and Company, Inc., 1937.

Hoernlé, R. F. Alfred, *Idealism as a Philosophy*. New York: George H. Doran Company, 1927. Chapter 1.

Robinson, Daniel S. (ed.), *An Anthology of Recent Philosophy*. New York: Thomas Y. Crowell Company, 1929. Part 1.

Virtue, Charles F. S., "Hast any Philosophy in Thee, Shepherd?"

Bulletin of the American Association of University Professors,
Vol. XXXV, No. 4 (Winter, 1949), pages 698-706.
Whitehead, Alfred North, *The Aims of Education* (1929). New
York: New American Library Mentor Books, 1950. Chapters 1
and 8.

QUESTIONS AND TOPICS FOR DISCUSSION

1. Read a few autobiographical essays by recent philosophers in
   Contemporary American Philosophy (Adams and Montague,
   eds.), *Contemporary British Philosophy* (Muirhead, ed.), or
   American Philosophy Today and Tomorrow (Hook and Kallen,
   eds.). Write a brief essay on the personal factors that led some
   of the men to take up philosophy as their life work.
2. Make a list of topics that you think a philosopher should deal
   with. Which of them seem to you to be most interesting? Does
   an answer to any of them seem to presuppose answers to any of
   the others? Try to arrange the questions in the order in which
   you think they might best be studied.
3. State carefully the difference between a philosophical and a psychological inquiry into beliefs and standards of value. What contributions, if any, would one of these inquires make to the other?
4. Discuss the place that philosophy has, and the place you think it
   ought to have, in the college curriculum. It has been suggested
   that some course in philosophy ought to be given to high school
   students. Do you agree with this suggestion?
5. What are some reasons given for *not* studying philosophy? How
   sound do you think they are?

2

Some Substitutes
for Inquiry

Disciplined and responsible inquiry as a way toward knowing the truth and deciding among conflicting ideals is laborious and often irksome. Men who genuinely desire the truth are frequently unwilling to exert themselves in a persistent attempt to think through their problems, and they fall back upon some supposed substitute for inquiry, tacitly asserting that they already know the truth or that there is some easy way to its discovery.

In this chapter we shall discuss and evaluate three ways of knowing that are uncritical in the sense that their use does not entail much thinking or careful weighing of evidence. These three ways of knowing are: the appeal to common sense, the appeal to private faith, and the appeal to authority. They are commonly employed in many of the practical affairs of daily life, and they cannot be wholly avoided in any serious attempt at deciding which of our beliefs are dependable and which should be held in suspicion. But they are not without weaknesses and even dangers, and they may lead men astray as often as they guide them correctly.

By a "way of knowing" is meant a method or a procedure.

It has psychological roots that can be explained by the scientist. We are concerned with each method, however, not simply as a psychological phenomenon, but from the standpoint of (a) how dependable it is as a *source* of knowledge about the world, and (b) how trustworthy it is as a *criterion* for deciding which beliefs we have about the world are true.

THE APPEAL TO COMMON SENSE

Common sense is sometimes facetiously thought of as a power or faculty that *we* have, but that most other people seem unfortunately to lack. Many men readily admit that they are ignorant of history or higher mathematics, but few if any will concede that they do not have their full share of common sense. Countless jokes on long-haired professors and intellectuals turn on the assumption that these people, in spite of their learning, lack that one precious capacity for using common sense which the most ignorant man may have.

Like many household phrases, "common sense" is not easy to define. But there seem to be three kinds of belief or attitude that go under this name. Common sense may mean beliefs we have as a result of the nature and constitution of the mind itself, which therefore can be expected to be found in every normal mind regardless of its lack of special training and experience. Or common sense may mean a common "turn of mind," not the *content* of beliefs that are universally held, but a "way of thinking" followed by all minds by their very nature. Or, lastly, common sense may mean the shared beliefs of men, or of a fairly large group of men, without implying that these beliefs are "born" in their minds or are present in every man's mind.

Common sense as beliefs belonging to the nature of the mind

According to the first meaning of the word, common sense comprises all those beliefs that men have "by nature." Some philosophers have believed that in addition to the ideas we get from our experience (the idea of red, for instance) and the ideas we form in our own mind by combining such ideas (as the idea of a winged horse is constructed by the imagination from the experience we have of horses and wings), there are yet other ideas that are *innate*. Some philosophers have argued that these ideas are placed in the mind by an act of God, and are worthy of respect for that reason; other philosophers have argued that they are inherited from our ancestors, who discovered them by experience. Plato, in the *Meno*, suggests that they are remembered from a previous life of the soul. Still other philosophers, not caring to indulge in such speculation, say simply that certain ideas, principles, or beliefs are present in all minds because they are a part of the mind's intrinsic nature. In each of these theories, ideas of this sort are deemed especially trustworthy, since they are due either to faith in God as a being who would not deceive His creatures by giving them false beliefs, or to a conviction of our dependence upon the past experience of the race, or to what is regarded as the self-evidence of the principles that the mind is able to intuit or apprehend immediately.

Inasmuch as it is doubtful if any ideas (in contrast to *abilities* of the organism) are inherited, and since we cannot be sure that the soul existed prior to birth or that there is a God who put certain ideas in our mind, let us confine our attention here to the view that the mind by its nature immediately apprehends self-evident principles. Sometimes the term "common sense" is used to refer to the mind's *ability to grasp self-evident principles,* and sometimes it is used to refer to the *self-evident principles themselves,* which the mind possesses by nature. (The ability and the kind of knowledge seem to imply each other, and accepting one requires accepting the other; but it is well to be aware of this dual meaning of the word, and to make sure in which of the two meanings "common sense" is being employed in any particular argument.)

There are, says Jacques Maritain, a leading contemporary French philosopher,

> . . . certainties which arise spontaneously in the mind when we first come to the use of reason [and] are thus the work of nature in us, and may therefore be called an endowment of nature as proceeding from the natural perception, consent, instinct, or natural sense of the intellect. Since their source is human nature itself, they will be found in all men alike; in other words, they are common to all men. They may therefore be said to belong to the common perception, consent, or instinct, or to the *common sense* of mankind.[1]

Among the principles that, Maritain says, are parts of common sense are "the data of the senses" (for example, "that bodies possess length, breadth, and height"), "self-evident axioms" (such as, "every event has a cause"), consequences immediately deducible from these axioms (like the theorems of geometry, which depend upon the axioms of geometry), and finally, "the great truths without which man's moral life is impossible" (for example, "knowledge of God's existence, the freedom of the will, etc.").

If it is true that all men inevitably accept these beliefs or principles, it might be argued that they are more likely to be true than beliefs or principles accepted only by some men. Of course, it is possible to find some people who do not understand and accept these principles—infants, certain types of mental patients, unlettered primitive peoples, and so on. That is not important here, however. What is meant is that these principles are invariably accepted by minds that are sufficiently intelligent to understand these principles and their alternatives, and to accept the former and reject the latter. It is reasonable to suppose that the principles on which all competent men agree are more dependable than those on which there is still dispute among men of understanding and knowledge.

Even so, however, it is hard to find principles that meet the requirement. For instance, mathematicians and physicists are not now quite so sure as they once were that bodies can be adequately described as three-dimensional. In many problems

---

[1] Jacques Maritain, *An Introduction to Philosophy*, page 134. Quoted by permission of the publisher. New York: Longmans Green & Company, Inc., 1931.

in physics and astronomy, there are theoretical reasons for considering Euclidean three-dimensional geometry as only a "first approximation" to the geometry of the real world.[2] One cannot say dogmatically that the principles claimed by Maritain as belonging to common sense are *wrong*, but these disputes suffice to show that they are not quite so indubitable as his statement might lead one to suppose.

This is even clearer with respect to the last of the common sense principles mentioned, namely, the existence of God. It is by no means certain that without knowledge of the existence of God the moral life is impossible, unless we *define* the moral life in such a way that belief in the existence of God is *itself* a moral principle. But this seems to be an arbitrary way of considering the "moral life," since many men have lived what is regarded as a moral life and have had acute awareness of their duties, but have doubted or denied that God exists. Such men are too numerous for us to say that a particular theological principle *must* be accepted as a basis for morality.

Maritain, of course, is aware that in spite of his definition of common sense, there are men who do not share his belief that God's existence is indubitable. So he says, "All men, unless spoiled by a faulty education or by some intellectual vice, possess a natural certainty of these truths." [3] But, we may ask, how are we to decide whether one's education is "faulty," and who it is that is guilty of "intellectual vice"? These are terms of abuse, not of description. Some philosophers, after all, have argued that it is the *belief* in God that is the result of a "faulty education." Unless one believes in some way that God *does* exist, he might think that the education that teaches that God does exist is the education that is faulty.

Let us grant for the sake of the argument that *most* men who seem to be competent, who are suffering from no obvious

---

[2] The question of geometry is introduced here only to illustrate views that are incompatible with Maritain's examples. It is to be discussed in its own terms later (pages 65-70).

[3] Jacques Maritain, *op. cit.*, page 135.

"intellectual vice," and who have had what seems to be an adequate education do accept the principles that Maritain claims are directly apprehended as self-evident, but let us give up the claim that *all* men of this class accept them. Does this show that they are true? Or that they belong to the nature of the mind instead of to the "climate of opinion" in which they are accepted? It does not. The history of thought is full of incidents where almost everybody—including those considered at the time to be most competent and best educated—has accepted a given belief or principle, and only a few persons have held the opposite belief, yet the few have subsequently been found right and the others wrong. One thinks, for instance, of Galileo's being forced to renounce the doctrine that the earth moves. In view of such incidents, the appeal to the common sense of mankind (now watered down to an appeal to the opinion of most men who, we say, have a good education and no "intellectual vice") is not likely to be very effective in evaluating the disputed beliefs.

For these reasons, we may doubt whether any of the principles Maritain cites are self-evidently true and come to us as an "endowment of nature." This does not imply, of course, that there are not some indubitable principles; it only suggests that we cannot be sure *what* principles are indubitable. Every system of knowledge, from geometry to theology, is based upon some unproved assumptions *taken to be* true. Within the framework of that knowledge, they are both indemonstrable and indubitable. But the certainty and necessity we ascribe to these principles is relative to the system they support and to the degree of credence we give to that system as a whole. If one claims to know anything or any truth, however recondite, with absolute certainty, somewhere along the line he must assume that some truths are self-evident and are evidence for the principles he accepts as certain but not *self*-evident. But just what these truths are must be a matter of dispute among men working in different systems of ideas that they claim as knowledge. In other words, fundamental truths seem to be discoverable, if at all, by examining the position of principles within a related body of statements that one takes to be knowledge; they are not found by inspecting principles in isolation, or by studying the nature of the mind that knows them. And because different men of equal competence do accept diverse and incompatible systems of statements as constituting their own "best knowledge," it is not likely that disputes between them can be resolved by pointing out any indubitable principles that they must all accept.

There is one exception to this. There is, indeed, one class of propositions that are indubitable and are used in the construction of all consistent systems of propositions, principles, and beliefs. They are tautologies—propositions that repeat or make explicit the meaning of their terms. Examples of these are: "a is a," "if $a=b$, $b=a$," "every effect (not every event) has a cause," "every wife has a husband," and the like. Without adhering to principles of this kind, no consistent thought or communication is possible. It is no objection to these principles that careless thinkers and speakers sometimes infringe them even when they do not deny them. When they do infringe them, what results is never valid argument and knowledge.

But a more serious objection to considering them to be a natural guarantee of knowledge is that, singly or collectively, they cannot serve as sufficient foundation for any knowledge of the real world. They are empty. They do not lead beyond themselves. They do not tell us anything specific about the world, for they apply equally to every thinkable thing, real or unreal. When we know indubitably that "a rose is a rose," we know not a bit more about reality than we know indubitably (as we do) that "a snark is a snark." When we know indubitably that "every wife has a husband," we know a truth that would remain true (though it would lose its importance) even if men and women were to become extinct.

We cannot have knowledge of the world made up exclusively of this kind of statement, or depending upon it alone. But such statements, *when combined with propositions about the real world,* do give us further knowledge as valid consequences of the propositions about the real world. Any body of knowledge must contain some propositions that are not tautologies and not self-evidently true in the sense in which we have admitted that *these* are self-evident propositions. The propositions that make any body of knowledge refer to the real world—to objects in space, to the causal relations among things, to the existence of God—are not the self-evident tautological principles, but the *other* propositions whose truth is not self-evident. Logic is concerned with the analysis of relations among propositions, so that we are helped to see what propositions "self-evidently follow" from other propositions, but logic cannot show that any factual propositions about reality are self-evident.

Common sense as a common "turn of mind"

That the minds of most men, or perhaps even of all sane men, act in more or less the same way is hardly disputable. Though we might cavil at the "more or less," which can cover a very great variety of differences, it nevertheless seems reasonable to suppose that our minds, like our bodies, have a tendency to behave in much the same way under similar conditions. If we follow this assumption, we need not say that all men hold the same specific beliefs irrespective of their experience and education, but we can say that the "normal" human being is likely to think and behave like other "normal" human beings and to draw similar conclusions from similar experiences. This might be so regardless of the special beliefs and knowledge that each one of us has and that differentiate one person's attitude and information from those of another.

Through the advances of comparative anthropology, even this may appear to some to be an extravagant claim. Primitive peoples who believe in magic, we are told, neither think the same thoughts nor think the same way as we, whose minds have been to some extent formed by science. "Patterns of thought," it seems, vary with the "patterns of culture." It has even been argued that different races have different "ways of thinking." If these arguments are correct, then there is no such thing as common sense in the second meaning of the word.

But let us grant, for the sake of the discussion, that there are patterns or turns of thought that are universal throughout mankind. Would that recommend them as ways of thought that can be depended upon to give us true beliefs? That the commonness or universality of a turn of mind does not guarantee that it will produce correct beliefs is argued by Francis Bacon (1561-1626) in his *Novum Organum*, which is sometimes said to have ushered in the modern age by challenging the medieval modes of thinking.

Bacon asks us to consider the "idols and false notions which are now in possession of the human understanding and have taken deep root therein." Among the idols he finds those which he calls the "Idols of the Tribe," which "have their foundation in human nature itself, and in the tribe or race of mankind." They seem to be precisely what we have just called common turns of mind. He gives a list of these idols, which, although widespread or common to all men, nevertheless lead us astray in the search for truth:

The human understanding is of its own nature prone to suppose the existence of more order and regularity in the world than it finds. . . . Hence the fiction that all celestial bodies move in perfect circles.

The human understanding when it has once adopted an opinion . . . draws all things else to support and agree with it. And though there be a greater number and weight of instances to be found on the other side, yet these it either neglects and despises, or else by some distinction sets aside and rejects.

The human understanding is moved by those things most which strike and enter the mind simultaneously and suddenly, and so fill the imagination; and then it feigns and supposes all other things to be somehow, although it cannot see how, similar to those few things by which it is surrounded.

The human understanding is unquiet; it cannot stop or rest, and still presses onward, but in vain. Therefore it is that we cannot conceive of any end or limit to the world; but always as of necessity it occurs to us that there is something beyond.

The human understanding is no dry light, but receives an infusion from the will and affections.

But by far the greatest hindrance and aberration of the human understanding proceeds from the dulness, incompetency, and deceptions of the senses; in that things which strike the sense outweigh things which do not immediately strike it, though they be more important.

The human understanding is of its own nature prone to abstractions and gives a substance and reality to things which are fleeting.[4]

Bacon points unmistakably at fallacies that are as natural and common now as in his own day. "We feign more order and regularity. . . ." Is that not the basis of much of the unwillingness to believe that physics must give up the principle of "same cause, same effect" in its sub-atomic research? [5] We are all certainly guilty of adopting an opinion and then neglecting evidence against it. This is known in logic as the fallacy of "neglect of negative instances," and we commit this fallacy whenever we make a judgment such as "All Germans are militaristic," or "All Chow dogs are vicious." The third of the turns of mind on Bacon's list is still among us, as witness the enthusiasm with which the strange, the new, and the spectacular are accepted in popular science, politics, and religion. Propagandists especially profit from this common fallacy by frightening us into agreement with them. The next of the idols is the one that misleads us when we demand or claim detailed knowledge beyond the scope of our experience, when, for instance, we demand or claim the same kind and degree of certainty in matters of history or politics as we find in mathematics or science. The "infusion from the will and affections" gives rise to what is commonly done, but universally condemned, under the name of "wishful thinking." The last of the idols mentioned

---

[4] Francis Bacon, *Novum Organum* (1620), Aphorisms 45-51. (*Bacon Selections*, Mathew Thompson McClure ed. New York: Charles Scribner's Sons, 1928, pages 290-294.)

[5] Cf. page 143.

here by Bacon is present whenever we think, for instance, that a body falls to the earth because of "gravity" instead of saying that the law of gravity is the name we give to the generalization that bodies do attract each other, or say that an animal takes care of her young because of the "maternal instinct." This is known in logic as the "fallacy of reification," which means confusing a concept with a real object or cause. We commit this fallacy whenever we confuse an abstraction with a reality—and our tendency to do this is responsible for much of our gullible acceptance of propaganda, by which we are skilfully seduced into taking words for realities.

If our argument is valid, then, we cannot say that a belief is correct simply because it is a consequence of some common or universal turn of mind or natural tendency of thought. For it is just as natural and common for the mind to fall into error as it is for it to discover true beliefs; the only difference, perhaps, is that it is harder to discover the errors that most of our fellows make just as "naturally" as we do. But if the truth is hard to find, would we not be more likely to discover it by exercising unusual and uncommon discipline in our search for it, than by just depending upon our "human nature" to lead us all to it by an easy path? [6]

Common sense as shared belief

In spite of the fact that our inquiry has not brought to light any universally held beliefs or given us any reason to believe that a common turn of mind is more likely to lead to truth than to error, it may be said that there *is* such a thing as common sense, that we all depend upon it, and that generally it does not lead us astray. This is undoubtedly true if by common sense we mean something much more modest than Maritain suggests. Let us call common sense those beliefs, however they arise and whether they are true or false, that are shared by a

---

[6] Cf. Bacon's essay, "On Truth." *The Works of Francis Bacon*, Vol. XII, pages 81-84 (James Spedding, R. L. Ellis, and D. D. Heath, eds.) Boston: Brown and Taggard, 1860.

group of men in intellectual and practical intercourse with one another. Then common sense will contain the beliefs that people do not have to be formally taught; our common sense beliefs are those that we get almost by a process of "social osmosis." We "absorb" beliefs in all our dealings with our fellows. We all believe that the earth goes around the sun; but it might be hard for many of us to give any very cogent reason why we are so sure of it; after we "learned" it, we forgot the reasons and remembered only the fact. Similarly, most people, whether they say so or not, believe in some sort of God, but they would have considerable difficulty in describing their belief or in showing that it is justified.

We would say, "These beliefs are just a part of common sense; you don't have to be an expert, or have any special college degree, to know that sort of thing." The reason we accept such beliefs without knowing or remembering the reasons for them is that they are not ordinarily challenged; the people we talk with share them, and they do not ask us why we believe just as they do.

That such beliefs as this are often useful is quite certain. Without such a community of opinion, practical agreements could not be reached. Like Archimedes, who said, "Give me a place to stand and I can lift the earth," so also we need a "place to stand," a set of opinions we do not have constantly to defend, so that we can go about practical concerns or get some special knowledge that is *not* shared by our fellows. These common beliefs have been called the "emotional cement" that holds society together in spite of differences of opinion about more specific questions of science, politics, religion, and morality.[7] The man who lacks common sense, in this ordinary meaning of the word, is the man whose ideas and beliefs on these everyday matters diverge so widely from those

---

[7] For descriptions of American common sense, see Robert S. Lynd and Helen M. Lynd, *Middletown*, Chapter XX, (New York: Harcourt Brace and Company, Inc., 1929), and Thurman Arnold, *The Folklore of Capitalism*, (New Haven, Conn.: Yale University Press, 1937).

of the general run of his fellows that he is not able easily to cooperate with them and to share their common hopes, truths, and illusions.

In his own field, dealing with rather poorly defined and unspecific questions of considerable practical importance, there is much to be said for the man of common sense. He is perhaps wise in not setting up his own experience against what is sometimes called the "wisdom of his race." His acceptance of the common standards of morality without personal experimentation to see if, for instance, honesty *is* the best policy, is almost essential for the existence of a harmonious society of cooperating individuals.

But there are dangers present in too facile an appeal to common sense, especially when it is backed by the authority of public opinion and the threat of ostracism for those who disagree. In his famous essay *On Liberty,* John Stuart Mill emphasized the danger that lies in *any* kind of interference with freedom of individual thought. While we are especially cognizant of the threat from some powerful agency like a totalitarian state, even in a democracy there is an insidious but pervasive interference with the freedom of thought and inquiry. It is the force of public opinion against the man who seriously questions the common sense, the basic assumptions and conventions of his society. Some brave thinkers will resist this force, and a few of them, at great personal cost, will finally convince the public or posterity that their views are correct. But common sense too often lays the dead hand of tradition on the individual's mind and prevents him from even entertaining original ideas. Such a mind is held in invisible bonds by dogmatism; common sense is often only a polite name for the dogmatism of ignorant minds that will not listen to argument. It takes originality and rare courage to go against the social pressure of common sense, even when this pressure is not expressed through "thought police." But advance in knowledge and civilization depends upon the possibility that unpopular ideas will be thought of and can gain a hearing. That is why freedom of thought, speech, and religion is not merely a luxury for the individual who enjoys it, but, in the long run, a necessity for the welfare of the society itself. Mill says,

> If all mankind minus one, were of one opinion, and only one person were of the contrary opinion, mankind would be no more justified in silencing that one person, than he, if he had the power, would be justified in silencing mankind. . . . The peculiar evil of silencing the expression of an opinion is, that it is robbing the human race.[8]

We have spoken of the social uses and dangers of shared beliefs. What of their truth? Is a belief any more likely to be *true* because our fellows share it with us? Here we must draw a distinction between the proper sphere of common sense and what lies beyond its scope—although often in specific cases, the line is hard to draw. Common sense is in its sphere when it deals with decisions of a fairly immediate practical nature: it is right to feed the hungry, to heal the sick, to clothe the naked; it is right to treat a man as innocent until he is proved guilty, and the like. But is common sense a recommendation for the widespread belief that "war is inevitable because man is naturally aggressive"? That paintings ought to look like the things they are paintings of? That God created the world? That everything has a cause, even if some physicists seem to doubt it? That we can do nothing about improving the human race? That the soul is immortal? These are matters where the common, shared opinions may very well be wrong, if still (although perhaps only in the short run) quite useful for the harmonious relationships among men in a particular society. Common-sense beliefs are those that fit the "lowest common denominator" of the minds in a society; but if truth is difficult to find, we cannot expect to hear it on every street corner.

There are other reasons for questioning common sense as the touchstone of truth. The most obvious objection is that common sense varies from time to time and from place to

---

[8] John Stuart Mill, *On Liberty* (1859), Alburey Castell, ed. New York: F. S. Crofts & Co., 1947, page 16.

place, from one culture to another and even from one social class to another. Previously we alluded to the earth's movement as a matter of common sense, because among us it is a shared belief not dependent upon expert knowledge or special education. But 400 years ago a man was punished for teaching it, and certainly the crowd was against him. If it was common sense in 1616 that the earth is stationary, and common sense (in Europe and America, at least) in 1952 that it moves, common sense certainly exhibits a variability that we do not expect the truth to show. I may believe that the earth moves because everyone I know believes it; I may just passively accept the beliefs of my fellows. But if I have a *good* reason for believing it, it cannot be merely that the majority believes it—for the majority has often been as wrong as it was in 1616 when it punished Galileo.

John Stuart Mill, in discussing the way in which men appeal to the "collective authority" of their fellows to back up their own beliefs, concludes by saying,

> It is as evident in itself, as any amount of argumentation can make it, that ages are no more infallible than individuals; every age having held many opinions which subsequent ages have deemed not only false but absurd; and it is as certain that many opinions, now general, will be rejected by future ages, as it is that many, once general, are rejected by the present.[9]

Again, common sense varies from country to country; a common sense view in America concerning the function of government would be condemned not merely by the government but probably also by the common sense of the people of Russia. But what sort of criterion of true belief is it that sanctions one answer this side of the Iron Curtain and another beyond it? Certainly not a trustworthy one.

In spite of all this, we may be warned, "Don't lose your common sense." Indeed, it is wise not to lose any sense we have, common or uncommon. But there is probably more

---

[9] *Ibid.*, page 18.

danger in taking common sense too seriously than in losing it altogether. Its effects on our thought are pervasive even when unnoticed. The following is a sound maxim in trying to judge the claims of our common-sense beliefs: do not make it a principle to ask at every point, "How does this view conform to common sense?" For this question will usually have been tacitly and favorably answered before we ever seriously entertain the new belief, and the danger of being too far "off base" is not nearly so great as the danger of never leaving the base.

THE APPEAL TO PRIVATE FAITH

Suppose a man has believed all his life that absolutely unrestrained economic competition is characteristic of American capitalism, or that the sun goes around the earth, or that men are by nature evil, and that someone shows him reasons to doubt his belief. If his appeal to common sense does not satisfy his need to justify his beliefs, or if he is unable to find common-sense agreement with his views, he may respond, "Well, I can't prove it is true, but I know it is, all the same," or "If you don't agree, so much the worse for you. I just feel it in my bones that I am right." In such a case, he is appealing to his own feelings as a source and warrant of true belief. We say that he is depending on a "private faith." (Of course many other people may have the same faith, but that is not here the reason for his certainty; he has the touchstone of truth, he believes, in himself.) Something similar to this appeal to faith is found in a woman's "intuition" that a man is in love with her, or a man's "hunch" that a certain horse is "bound to win."

Usually such an appeal is made only for beliefs that involve our emotions. A person is not likely to "feel it in his bones" that water consists of oxygen and hydrogen, although indeed he may do so if his fame and reputation depends upon his answer to a scientific question. But wherever this kind of appeal is made, the person who makes it is, as it were, retreating from the public forum or laboratory where beliefs can be impartially examined, and is claiming that he, and perhaps he alone, possesses the standard of truth. He behaves in this way to avoid the inconvenience and pain of doubt. By insulating himself from criticism and from the danger of having to admit that he is wrong, he preserves his peace of mind. It cannot be denied, says Charles S. Peirce,

. . . that a steady and immovable faith yields great peace of mind. It may, indeed, give rise to inconveniences, as if a man should resolutely continue to believe that fire would not burn him, or that he should be eternally damned if he received his *ingesta* otherwise than through a stomach-pump. But then the man who adopts this method will not allow that its inconveniences are greater than its advantages. He will say, "I hold steadfastly to the truth, and the truth is always wholesome." And in many cases it may very well be that the pleasure he derives from his calm faith overbalances any inconveniences resulting from its deceptive character. . . . When an ostrich buries its head in the sand as danger approaches, it very likely takes the happiest course. It hides the danger, and then calmly says there is no danger; and, if it feels perfectly sure there is none, why should it raise its head to see? [10]

But beliefs held for no better reason than emotional need are by no means guaranteed to be true. False beliefs have been held as tenaciously as true beliefs; the unfortunate patient in the mental hospital who tenaciously believes he is Henry of Navarre and who preserves this illusion by regarding the doctors and nurses as his courtiers, does not make his belief one bit truer by the profundity of his faith.

Bacon, in the work from which we have already quoted, calls such beliefs arising from the "peculiar constitution, mental or bodily, of each individual, and also in education, habit, and accident," the "Idols of the Cave." (The name comes from the famous "Myth of the Cave" in the seventh book of Plato's *Republic*, which is an account of the errors into which we fall

---

[10] Charles S. Peirce, "The Fixation of Belief" (1878). Reprinted by permission of the publishers from Charles Hartshorne and Paul Weiss, editors, *Collected Papers of Charles Sanders Peirce*, Volume 5, pages 234-235. Cambridge, Mass.: Harvard University Press, 1935.

in our judgments of what is real.) Because each one of us loves
his own little idol so dearly that he does not examine it ("Love
is blind," as Chaucer and Shakespeare noted), many false beliefs are established that would not stand the cold light of
criticism. So far is private faith from being a warrant for a
belief that Bacon argues that we ought to be especially critical
of our dearest beliefs:

> Let every student of nature take this as a rule,—that whatever his
> mind seizes and dwells upon with peculiar satisfaction is to be held
> in suspicion, and that so much the more care is to be taken in deal-
> ing with such questions to keep the understanding even and clear.[11]

Recognizing and checking tenacious beliefs

Such caution as Bacon recommends is difficult; frequently
we do not even know what our most deep-seated beliefs are,
or at least we do not recognize them as our own private beliefs
but think that they are so obviously true that everyone should
grant them without question. Psychoanalysis has thrown much
light on the deep emotional needs that are manifest to consciousness as fixed ideas, obsessions, systematized delusions,
and fanatically held religious, political, and moral beliefs. According to the teachings of psychoanalysis, our childhood desires are so thwarted and repressed that they are driven from
consciousness, only to appear again in disguised but acceptable form as tenacious belief or compulsive action, having only
a symbolical relation to the underlying need.

Whether one accepts the views of the psychoanalysts or not,
it is now commonly recognized that much of our thinking is
determined by our emotional needs, and that frequently we
are not aware of the extent to which the wish is father to the
thought. To discover the emotional foundation of many beliefs,
a carefully conducted psychoanalysis may be necessary. But

---

[11] Francis Bacon, *Novum Organum* (1620), Aphorism 58. (*Bacon Selections*, Mathew Thompson McClure, ed. New York, Charles Scribner's Sons,
1928, page 297.)

much of our wishful thinking can be controlled and disciplined by less drastic measures.

There are four steps (short of a psychiatric treatment) involved in examining and, if necessary, correcting our tenaciously held beliefs.

1. *We must find out specifically what our prejudices or tenaciously held beliefs are*—It does not suffice to be just "against prejudices" any more than to be "against sin." It is necessary to know *specifically* what our prejudices are; they do not come before us labeled "prejudice," but they are accepted as truths.

One way of identifying our prejudices is by observing our "emotional temperature." Does someone's saying, "All races are equally good and intelligent" make our blood boil? Do we have a warm glow of satisfaction when someone says, "My country, right or wrong!"? Do we feel a cold anger when someone says, "God does not exist"? These emotional reactions show that something more than an intellectual judgment is being challenged.

2. *We must try to find out why we hold the beliefs with such emotional fervor*—As mentioned above, this sometimes can be done only by psychoanalysis; but it can frequently be done by mere self-observation. Is one an ardent Republican because his family has always been Republican? Does one earnestly believe in God because, as a child, reciting a prayer kept him from being afraid of the dark?

To recognize the source of the emotional "kick" in our beliefs is a great step towards lessening it, so that the belief can be examined. Just as the electrician cuts off the current before he examines a defective socket, so also we need to cut off some of the "emotional current" before we can safely examine our beliefs.

3. *We must determine what are the alternatives to our tenaciously held beliefs*—Strong emotional commitments are usually made as if there were only one alternative to our belief: *either* capitalism *or* communism, *either* belief in the literal truth of the Bible *or* absolute atheism, *either* white *or* black,

with nothing in between. Such sharp dichotomies, however, are gross oversimplifications. Between one extreme and another there may be many intermediates, and recognizing their existence will give more opinions to choose among; our rejection of atheism, for instance, might not then force us into fundamentalism, our hatred of communism might no longer blind us to the faults in capitalism. Getting rid of the habit of thinking in simple "black and white" terms may make the consequences of modifying our beliefs not so nearly as fatal as they would be if we had to choose only between two extremes.

4. *We must try to weigh the evidence for and against each belief, so that we can choose among them; and then we must begin to act on the best belief as if we believed it*—Sooner or later we may substitute an intelligently examined and intellectually valid belief for a prejudice.

THE APPEAL TO AUTHORITY

No man is sufficient unto himself, no matter how strong his faith in his own beliefs. Our experience is too limited for any of us to be able to test every one of his beliefs by "first-hand experience." Because human beings have language, they are able to profit by the experience of their predecessors and contemporaries; and the man who attempted to find out *everything* for himself without listening to the testimony of others would put himself almost on the level of the animals, each generation of which has to begin not where the preceding generation left off, but almost where it began. Only because we learn not merely by our own experience but by that of others can human experience be cumulative from generation to generation.

Of course, no man believes everything that he is told. He selects, perhaps unconsciously and unintentionally, the "authorities" whose opinions he will accept. Each of us tends to believe more of what he reads in one newspaper than of what he reads in another; many have their favorite encyclopedias, favorite radio commentators, favorite preachers, and favorite professors; they accept their favorites' opinions as true and pattern their own beliefs after those of authorities they admire. The child begins on this path when he asks his parents his first questions, and to a great extent, even the most skeptical man continues on the path throughout his life.

We all make use of authorities every time we look at a map, find the pronunciation of a word in a dictionary, or check the atomic weight of some element in a chemical handbook. This use of authority is sensible and unavoidable. But the appeal to authority is easily abused. If the authority I appeal to is not competent, the appeal spreads error instead of truth. If I believe whatever I am told by some authority I respect, I may often gain true beliefs; but it is certain that my gullibility will often lead me astray. If I do not form an opinion until I know what decision has been reached by some editorial writer, what shall I do in cases that he does not decide for me? How shall I decide when two authorities to whom I ordinarily defer contradict each other? These are serious questions for anyone who believes that the wisest course is to put his faith in the opinions of some authority.

Since we all depend upon authorities for many of our beliefs, since authorities may disagree with each other, and since each individual cannot make himself an authority on all disputed subjects, it would be well to have some kind of test by which to decide which alleged authorities are most dependable. If we do not have and apply such a test, we shall be confused by opposing authorities and "experts," and we shall certainly be victimized by some of them if we are not on our guard.

Tests for alleged authorities

In a court of law, expert testimony is accepted as authoritative only if the man who is offering it is able to meet certain requirements; if he cannot do so, he is not allowed to testify as an expert witness. Similarly, the "authority" we appeal to in matters of science, politics, religion, or morality might well be subjected to searching questions that would establish his competency or incompetency. There are four questions that may suitably be asked of any man or institution claiming such authority that one is tempted to give up his private judgment and accept the judgment of the "expert."

1. *Does the alleged authority have any credentials as an expert on the matter in question?*—The credentials we are asking for are not diplomas or college degrees, although these may sometimes be of help in deciding the worth of an authority. We are asking: has the authority any preeminent "right" to his opinion on this special subject? If it is a scientific question, has the man been trained in science? If it is a religious question, has the man thought deeply and critically along these difficult lines?

It is surprising how many so-called authorities do not pass this test. A great scientist expressing an opinion on politics or religion may not himself claim that he is an authority on these matters, but the general public and the editors of magazines and newspapers frequently treat his pronouncements on these subjects with the same respect that they would properly accord to his scientific opinions. The Catholic Church, which claims infallibility only in questions of "faith and morals," nevertheless pronounces on matters of art, politics, and science. Although it disclaims infallibility in these matters, except insofar as they are thought to affect faith and morals, how many of the faithful draw the distinction between the sphere where the church claims infallibility and the many spheres where it speaks without making such a claim, and where its competence to speak is, at least in principle, open to question?

Certainly the right to an opinion on any subject should not be taken from one man just because he is an eminent scientist, or from another because he is a respected theologian. But let the public be on guard not to confuse a man's authority in one field with his competence to deal with quite different questions. When a theologian speaks on scientific subjects, or a scientist on religious subjects, each is speaking as a private citizen to whom we may well listen; but to neither is due the respect we owe to an "authority." If we do not remember this, we have only ourselves to blame, but propaganda and an authority's very human love of dogmatizing may contribute to our forgetting it. Press agents advertise a new book on religion by "a great mathematician," a political treatise by "a great logician," a philosophy of science by "the distinguished theologian and divine, the Rev. ——." These are effective advertising devices, giving the authors an aura of authority they do not have in the subject matter of their books. And human beings *do* love to dogmatize. If you accept my opinion on historical matters as authoritative, it may not be long before I try to influence you to accept my religion, my politics, or my morals.

Remember, then, in applying this first test: there are no experts or authorities in general, but only experts or authorities on special subjects; do not let an authority in one field pose as an authority in all the others.

2. *Does the authority attempt to persuade you by appeals to your reason and to acknowledged facts, or by emotional and propagandistic appeals?*—Men are often not rational animals, and an appeal only to men's reason probably would not sell many cigarettes or much of a particular kind of soap, or get thousands of people to vote for Senator *X* in an election. That is a regrettable fact about human nature, but it is fully exploited in propaganda. Here we are trying to find out whether certain beliefs or opinions are *true*. I want to know, for instance, whether there is going to be a depression. The man who answers my question with charts and graphs and statistics may be wrong, may even be intentionally fooling me, but other things being equal, at least he seems more dependable than one who "soft-soaps" me, appeals to my vanity and fear, or abuses "that man in the White House."

Men are not always guided by reason, and hence, to get a good idea widely accepted it is sometimes—indeed usually—necessary to enlist their emotions. But the inquiring mind should not confuse an emotional appeal, which can just as well be made for a false belief as for a true one, with a reasoned argument that bears on the subject at hand.

3. *Does the authority permit examination of his reasons and disagreement with his decisions, or does he condemn and punish those who dare to question?*—An argument may be "won" by a big boy who tells a little fellow, "Believe me, or I'll pound you soft." This kind of argument, known in logic as the *argumentum ad baculum* ("appeal to the big stick") may "win" by quieting opposition and forbidding disagreement; but it does not decide the truth of the matter. It can be used just as well to gain a reluctant acceptance for a false belief as for a true one; indeed, its use raises a serious suspicion in the mind of an observer that perhaps the belief enforced in this way is not true and can be established *only* through appealing to force.

One reason why we are usually ready to accept the statements in science made by an authority is that the scientist does not publish just his conclusions but also his reasons for holding his opinions. By describing his experiments and calculations, he invites others to check his conclusions; this gives us more confidence in him than if he merely announced his results.

A belief is more dependable if it can be checked in an atmosphere of freedom—when it appeals to our knowledge and good sense and not merely to our blind loyalty to some great name. Only in the open market of ideas, where different beliefs are offered for comparison and examination, can we have confidence in those who are reputed to be authoritative or expert.

4. *Does the alleged authority stand to gain by my believing him?*—In other words, is he an "impartial witness" to the truth? It may be true that everyone gains something by being believed; a scientist will receive more promotions, and a historian may sell more of his books, if his conclusions are believed than if they are disregarded or doubted. But this is not sufficient to impugn their objectivity, for their beliefs can be checked (Question 3, above) and a mistake may cause them to lose their standing. But one may very rightly doubt some of the assertions a politician makes in the heat of a campaign, for he

stands to gain from our believing what he says regardless of whether it is true or not.

Often a man does not claim authority in his own name, but in the name of some great book (say, the Bible), great man (for example, Jefferson), or great institution (for instance, a church, a political party). In these cases we should apply our questions to the man who claims to speak for the authority, as well as to the authority itself. One of the most tragic instances of the prostitution of authority is found in the medieval attitude toward Aristotle. Bacon calls errors into which we fall through an uncritical acceptance of authority the "Idols of the Theatre." [12] Most of the errors he opposes under this rubric derive from a blind acquiescence to the philosophy and science of Aristotle. Certainly, there were many errors in Aristotle (although perhaps not so many as we are led to believe by the modern revolt of thought against him). But Aristotle was not himself an authoritarian dogmatist; the real *bête noire* of Bacon was not Aristotle—they were in many respects comparable figures—but the "Aristotelians," who regarded Aristotle as "the master of those who know" and consulted his books instead of the "great book of nature." Aristotle would successfully have passed our four "tests," but the same cannot be said for the disciples, whose blind subservience to Aristotle was an obstacle in the search for truth.

Dangers in the appeal to authority

Because so many "authorities" do not pass these very reasonable tests, there is often a *prima facie* case against acceptance of their decrees. But sometimes an authority meets these tests; should we then accept his conclusions as true? The answer is often that we should, for, as stated above, none of us can have first-hand knowledge of everything he is interested in knowing. But even where authority is justified, a passive acceptance

---

[12] Francis Bacon, *Novum Organum* (1620), Aphorisms 44, 61-63. (*Bacon Selections*. Mathew Thompson McClure, ed. New York: Charles Scribner's. Sons, 1928, pages 290, 300-302.)

of it may be dangerous. There are three reasons for this: Authorities, even the "best" authorities, often disagree with one another. A man who is in the habit of blindly seeking authority for every belief he has will be lost and helpless when they disagree.

Secondly, authorities, especially in religious, moral, and political questions, are likely to be revered now simply because they have been revered for a long time. It is easier to think of great men of the past as having some distinction and preeminence over those of the present; political writers are more likely to cite Jefferson than Roosevelt, religious writers more likely to appeal to the authority of Luther or Thomas Aquinas than to the leading theologians of today. The reason for this lies partly in the fact that the thought of these men has survived a long time; their writings are "classic." But this attitude neglects the valid discoveries and insights of a later day. For this reason, the appeal to authority is often hidebound and frequently out of touch with present-day problems. An instructive illustration of this is seen in legal disputes, where the "conservative" calls for a "strict interpretation" of the authority of the Constitution, and is opposed by the "progressive," who argues that legal thinking should take into account present-day views in science, economics, sociology, and psychology.

But perhaps the greatest danger in unbounded respect for and dependence upon authority is its effect upon character. The man who always appeals to authority does not, and finally cannot, think for himself. He loses his originality, initiative, and intellectual courage. Mill well says,

The price paid for this sort of intellectual pacification, is the sacrifice of the entire moral courage of the human mind. . . . No one can be a great thinker who does not recognize, that as a thinker it is his first duty to follow his intellect to whatever conclusions it may lead. Truth gains more even by the errors of one who, with due study and preparation, thinks for himself, than by the true opinions of those who only hold them because they do not suffer themselves to think.[13]

---

[13] John Stuart Mill, *op. cit.*, pages 32-33.

The social setting of the appeal to authority

The appeal to authority is a social necessity in a highly diversified and specialized society like our own. A society with complex industrial, social, scientific, and governmental tasks, each of which requires expert training and knowledge, could not function without respect for expert authority. One may hope to become an authority whose judgment in a fairly narrow field is justified, respected, and accepted; but the specialization that enables one to become such an authority requires that he accept the authority of others trained in other fields. The day of the "scientist" is almost past; this is the day of psychologists, chemists, geologists, botanists, physicists, but not of the encyclopedic scientist or scholar. (There are some rare exceptions, fortunately.) There are those who wish to turn government itself over to narrow specialists, or who think this step is inevitable.[14]

One of the chief aims of a liberal education, including the study of philosophy, is to keep this splintering of the intellectual life from disrupting the society itself. In addition to knowing a specialty required in his vocation, each of us, if he is to be a good citizen, needs to have some synoptic view of the whole. A danger of the appeal to authority, we have said, is that it will weaken the intellectual fiber of the man who constantly makes this appeal. A liberal or general education frees each of us from the narrow bounds of his own specialty and gives him at least some intelligent insight into other specialties and their bearing on one another. Mutual respect, not blind subservience to the voice of some authority, is one of the fruits of an educational system that does not try to produce more and more men who know more and more about less and less, so that while their knowledge grows along one line their ignorance in all others makes them victims of the unjustifiable claims of unscrupulous "authorities." It is perhaps significant that the

---

[14] Cf. James Burnham, *The Managerial Revolution*. New York: John Day Company, 1941.

most highly educated and specialized nation in Europe fell victim to a fanatical "authority" in the field of politics. Authority over men's minds brings with it great power over their entire life. The blind appeal to and acceptance of authority, therefore, always entails a threat to freedom. Obviously it threatens freedom of thought. But equally certainly it threatens welfare and life itself. Peirce says,

> Wherever there is an aristocracy, or a guild, or any association of a class of men whose interest depend, or are supposed to depend, on certain propositions [beliefs] . . . cruelties always accompany this system; and when it is consistently carried out, they become atrocities of the most horrible kind in the eyes of any rational man.[15]

Peirce wrote this in 1877; the events of the past 20 years have tragically confirmed his words. To think our own thoughts and to put them forth in an atmosphere of freedom for intelligent criticism and evaluation is the first line of defense of everything that reasonable men hold dear. Reasonable men should be aware of all the forces in their own society and in the world that threaten "the first freedom." [16]

In advancing our knowledge and welfare and wisdom, *there is no substitute for inquiry.*

BIBLIOGRAPHY

Bury, John, *A History of Freedom of Thought.* New York: Oxford University Press, 1913.
Commission on Freedom of the Press, *A Free and Responsible Press.* Chicago: University of Chicago Press, 1947.
Drake, Durant, *Invitation to Philosophy.* Boston: Houghton Mifflin Company, 1933. Chapters 1 and 2.
Isaacs, Nathan, *The Foundations of Common Sense.* London: Routledge & Kegan Paul, 1949.
Laski, Harold J., *Liberty in the Modern State* (1930). London: Penguin Books, 1937.

---

[15] Charles S. Peirce, *op. cit.,* page 236.
[16] For an account of some of the less obvious but insidious threats to freedom of thought, see Morris L. Ernst, *The First Freedom.* New York: The Macmillan Co., 1946.

Lippmann, Walter, *Public Opinion*. New York: The Macmillan Company, 1927.

Milton, John, *Areopagitica* (1644). Many editions.

Montague, William Pepperell, *The Ways of Knowing*. New York: The Macmillan Company, 1925. Chapters 1 and 2.

Murphy, Arthur E., *The Uses of Reason*. New York: The Macmillan Company, 1943.

Plato, *The Apology*. Many editions.

Stebbing, L. Susan, *Thinking to Some Purpose* (1939). London: Penguin Books, 1948.

QUESTIONS AND TOPICS FOR DISCUSSION

1. Contrast the "common sense" of our own society with that of some foreign country, or with that of some primitive tribe described in books on anthropology.
2. To what extent, if at all, can a false belief be psychologically useful to a person?
3. Is the author of this book guilty of an illicit appeal to authority in quoting Bacon against the appeal to authority?
4. Observe about a dozen advertisements and decide what sorts of appeal to belief they employ.
5. Make a list of some beliefs of your own that fall in the general field of philosophy. Why do you accept them?
6. Make a list of some beliefs that you once held tenaciously, but have now given up. Why did you surrender them?
7. What are some of the outstanding social forces that make impartial thought difficult?

3

Experience and Reasoning

In attempting to answer the question, "How do we know that so and so really exists?" or, "What justification is there for the belief that such and such a statement is true?" we are forced beyond the appeals to common sense, authority, and private faith. Perhaps the simplest answers to the questions would be, "Because I see it," or "Because it would be illogical not to believe it."

Each of these answers is dependable to some extent, yet we seldom take them in isolation from each other. The first alone is not adequate, because we know that our senses can delude us, as when we see a mirage in a desert. And the second alone is inadequate, for we know that we can think quite logically about things that we admit never existed, such as a perfect gas. But how do we bring these two answers to bear upon each other? And if they conflict in some specific case, as they do, for instance, when we see a mirage in the desert but say, "It cannot be water," how do we decide between them?

These are among the most controversial problems in the history of epistemology, which is the part of philosophy that deals with the methods, scope, and validity of our knowledge.

They turn upon the relative dependability of reasoning and sense experience as sources and criteria of knowledge. Few philosophers, if any, have said that either alone can give knowledge, but some have insisted upon the primacy of one over the other. Those who emphasize the basic role of sense experience are called *empiricists,* and those who emphasize the role of reason are called *rationalists.* By studying some of the most important expressions of the empiricist and the rationalist epistemologies, perhaps we can see how both sensing and thinking are involved in knowing. For the empiricist doctrine, we shall consider a work by Plato,[1] and for the rationalist doctrine, one by Descartes.

THE EMPHASIS UPON SENSE EXPERIENCE

Plato (427-347 B.C.), one of the greatest of the Greek philosophers, wrote his works as dialogues. His dialogues are really little dramas of ideas, with opposing ideas brought into conflicts that have their plots and climaxes. In most of the dialogues, including the one we are about to study, the chief speaker is Plato's teacher, Socrates. Some of the dialogues as we have them probably never took place exactly as Plato describes them, and Socrates is probably used primarily as the spokesman for Plato's own views. But Plato was a great writer, and all through the dialogues, he is able to show the character and personality of his teacher and his associates. Sometimes these personal glimpses of them and of the life around them are among the most interesting parts of his works, and lend color and impact to the most technical discussions.

That is true of the *Theaetetus.*[2] Theaetetus is a young Athenian who shows great promise as a mathematician, and his

---

[1] Please note that Plato was not himself an empiricist; the work that we are about to consider is an exposition, not a defense, of empiricism.

[2] There are many editions. Perhaps the most convenient is that of Irving M. Copi (New York: Liberal Arts Press, 1949 [The Little Library of Liberal Arts, No. 13]). Citations are made to the *standard* pagination, however, which is the same for all good editions.

teacher wants Socrates to talk with him. Socrates says that he himself cannot teach Theaetetus anything, for he has no knowledge; he compares himself to a barren midwife who helps another woman to have her child, then examines the infant and (according to the Greek custom) destroys it if it is weak and deformed. Hence, instead of telling Theaetetus what he himself might believe, he helps Theaetetus to bring his own ideas to birth. The method he uses is question-and-answer, a kind of intellectual midwifery known to this day as the Socratic method of instruction.

The question he asks Theaetetus is: *What is knowledge?* This is an important question. It was especially important at that time. Plato lived in the period after the Peloponnesian War in which Athens was defeated and the old order of things was upset. Thinking men were confused by the variety of beliefs prevalent in the sciences, religion, morality, and politics of the day. Believing that sound knowledge was the only valid basis for conduct, and believing that the popular myths and conflicting ideologies were inadequate as a foundation for intelligent behavior, Socrates' circle was anxious to find a definition and criterion of knowledge.

After being flattered and cajoled by Socrates, Theaetetus attempts to answer his question. He says: "He who knows perceives what he knows, and therefore I should say that knowledge is perception" (page 151). It is easy to see the plausibility of this answer when we remember the endless disputes that were in the air concerning the existence of the gods, opposing political ideas, and the structure of the universe. Theaetetus is denouncing vain theorizers; he will accept only what his senses show him and not trouble himself about speculations and theories on things he cannot see. Theaetetus, in fact, sounds like an ancestor of the man from Missouri who has to be shown, or of doubting Thomas.

Socrates seems at first to grant that this answer is plausible, but then he asks: are the qualities that we perceive in things qualities that belong to them absolutely, or only in their relation to us? "Is the wind, regarded not in relation to us, but absolutely, cold or not?" Remembering that some will feel the wind as cold and others will feel it as warm, according to their own bodily state, Theaetetus answers that the wind does not have a quality intrinsically or absolutely, but only relatively to the person who perceives it. In other words, he grants that we perceive things not as they are but as they appear to us. "Appears to us" means exactly the same thing as "we perceive."

Socrates now shows that this is the doctrine of another Greek philosopher, Protagoras, who affirmed that we cannot know anything absolutely, but only in relation to ourselves. Protagoras said, "Man is the measure of all things." In other words, the test of the quality of a thing is simply whether you observe that quality, and as different people observe different qualities in the wind, each must be the judge himself. This doctrine, sometimes called the theory of *homo mensura* ("man the measure") and sometimes epistemological relativism (truth is relative to the individual), is expressed in the following argument:

Whatever I perceive is relative to me (to my warmth or cold, whether I am color-blind or not, my illness or health, and so on).
But knowledge is perception (by definition).
Therefore knowledge is relative to me or to the man who has it, and there is no objective knowledge the same for all men.

This argument seems plausible to Theaetetus, and he says, "My perception is true to me, and is always a part of my being; and, as Protagoras says, to myself I am the judge of what is and what is not to me" (page 160).

But while it is certainly true that perception varies from person to person and even from moment to moment for the same person, difficulties arise if we say the same thing about knowledge. If each man's sensing is the sole evidence for the existence or the qualities of a thing, according as he perceives it or does not perceive it, how shall we ever say, as we do, that one man's knowledge is better or more accurate than another's?

If both have perceptions, as they do, and if perception is knowledge, why do we accept one man's report on the qualities a thing has but reject another's? Why accept the judgment of a physician instead of that of the patient? After all, the patient is probably having a more vivid experience of pain than the physician has. Why, indeed, let man instead of the dog-faced baboon be the measure of all things? For each species of animal has its own pattern and mode of perception.

Theaetetus flounders helplessly in attempting to answer these and other questions Socrates puts to him. Whenever Theaetetus' common sense leads him to draw a distinction between truth and error, he implictly admits that there is some difference between mere perceiving and knowing, for the man who is making a mistake and therefore lacks knowledge is none the less having perceptions about which he judges. Unless knowledge is something more than mere perception, we could not draw a distinction between knowledge and ignorance. A mirage, which looks like water, is perceived just as surely as a real lake is perceived, but one of these perceptions is a part of or foundation of an illusory belief while the other is a part of knowledge. What, in a word, justifies us in drawing the common distinction between correct and incorrect perception? If nothing justifies it, we do not have a theory of knowledge at all.

Much of Plato's philosophy is an attempt to answer this question, and we shall return later (in Chapters 5 and 7) to some aspects of his answer. We shall not pursue the argument further at this point (it runs to about page 187 in the *Theaetetus*) except to draw the conclusion to which Socrates gently leads the boy: perception, while essential to knowledge, is not the whole of knowledge. *Whenever I state a belief or make a sentence that I think is true of the real world or an object, I am stating more than I perceive.* ("I believe this wine is sweet," or "This wine is sweet," says more than "This wine tastes sweet to me," or "I perceive a sweet taste when I drink this wine.") Indeed, in stating our beliefs we sometimes have to go against what we do perceive. (I may rightly say,

"This is a sweet wine, but because I've just eaten some candy it tastes rather bitter to me.")

Theaetetus' definition of knowledge thus shows that it cannot meet the tests Socrates puts to it, and must be "exposed and destroyed."

THE EMPHASIS UPON REASONING

Mathematics, unlike zoology, for instance, is a *rational science*. By this we mean that the mathematician is not interested in describing facts of observation, except perhaps incidentally for some practical purpose. When the mathematician demonstrates a theorem in geometry, for instance the theorem that the area of a triangle equals $\frac{1}{2}ba$, he does not actually measure triangles drawn on the blackboard, and he readily admits that the figure he uses in his proof is not actually a perfect triangle with perfectly straight legs. If he did measure it, he would find that its area is *not* exactly $\frac{1}{2}ba$. Rather, his procedure is to show that, granted certain definitions and assumptions, it follows logically and necessarily that, "If T is a triangle whose base is represented by a number b and whose altitude by a number a, then the area of T is represented by a number $= \frac{1}{2}ba$." This kind of knowledge is called *a priori*, because it is not derived from the observation of particular figures such as those drawn on a blackboard. Knowledge that could be gained only from the observation of such particulars, such as "This triangle was drawn with blue chalk," is called *a posteriori* knowledge, for it is knowledge that we can have only after the sense perception of particular things. A *posteriori* knowledge is never logically necessary or known to be universally applicable; we can always imagine, and frequently find, some exception to any statement made only on the basis of particular observations we have made.

Mathematics was taken by the rationalists as the ideal kind of knowledge. It is certain, logical, and indisputable. The rationalists believed that the hitherto endless dispute of philosophers and theologians could be settled by adapting the procedures of mathematics to the needs of the study of nature, the mind, and God.

In the first half of the seventeenth century, scholasticism, the philosophy of the Church, was challenged from two sides. Bacon, as we have seen, objected to its Idols of the Theatre, to what he regarded as its slavish acceptance of ideas based on authority, and against it he insisted upon the importance of new observations of nature and man. In this respect, Bacon was an empiricist, objecting to the authoritarianism and the empty logic by which many of his opponents believed they could demonstrate scientific and philosophical truths *a priori*. About the same time, René Descartes (1596-1650), the French philosopher and mathematician, attempted to put philosophy on a new footing by adapting to it the method of reasoning he had learned and used in mathematics.

Descartes' *Discourse on the Method of Rightly Conducting the Reason and Seeking for Truth in the Sciences* [3] was published in 1637. It describes a "method of gradually increasing my knowledge and of improving my abilities as much as the mediocrity of my talents and the shortness of my life will permit" (page 2). He discovered this method after he had become disillusioned with the study of philosophy, which seemed never to settle any of its questions, and of the sciences, which, as he said, took their first principles from the speculations of philoso-phers. His personal life also brought him to search for a new method, for he traveled widely and discovered such a variety of opinions tenaciously held by different peoples that he could not "select anyone whose opinion seemed to me to be preferable to those of others, and I was thus constrained to embark on the investigation for myself" (page 11).

Mathematics, in which he had already distinguished him-

---

[3] The most accurate and convenient translation is that of Laurence J. La- fleur (New York: Liberal Arts Press, 1950. [The Little Library of Liberal Arts, No. 19].) All quotations are from that edition, by permission of the publisher.

self, provided Descartes with the guide he needed in thinking for himself:

> Those long chains of reasoning, so simple and easy, which enable the geometricians to reach the most difficult demonstrations, had made me wonder whether all things knowable to men might not fall into a similar logical sequence. If so, we need only refrain from accepting as true that which is not true, and carefully follow the order necessary to deduce each one from the others, and there cannot be any propositions so abstruse that we cannot prove them, or so recondite that we cannot discover them. It was not very difficult, either, to decide where we should look for a beginning, for I knew already that one begins with the simplest and easiest to know.[4]

So after the model of the mathematician, he set up four rules of method for himself:

> The first rule was never to accept anything as true unless I recognized it to be evidently such: that is, carefully to avoid precipitation and prejudgment, and to include nothing in my conclusions unless it presented itself so clearly and distinctly to my mind that I had no occasion to doubt it.
>
> The second was to divide each of the difficulties which I encountered into as many parts as possible, and as might be required for an easier solution.
>
> The third was to think in an orderly fashion, beginning with the things which were simplest and easiest to understand, and gradually and by degrees reaching toward more complex knowledge, even treating as though ordered materials which were not necessarily so.
>
> The last was always to make enumerations so complete, and reviews so general, that I was certain that nothing was omitted.[5]

The second rule tells us simply to analyze complex questions into simpler ones; the fourth tells us to review our work to make *sure* that nothing has been omitted and that we have not been guilty of any error in reasoning. But the really original and distinctive parts of Descartes' method are given in the first and third of these rules.

---

[4] René Descartes, *Discourse on the Method of Rightly Conducting the Reason and Seeking for Truth in the Sciences*, pages 12-13.
[5] *Ibid.*, page 12.

The first is the really decisive one. "Clearness and distinctness" are the marks of a true idea. A clear idea is one that is indubitable to an attentive mind, such as the idea that a three-sided figure has three angles. A distinct idea is one that an attentive mind will not confuse with any other idea, such as the idea of a triangle in contrast to the idea of a square. Mathematics is full of such clear and distinct ideas; they are stated in axioms and definitions, from which, in accordance with the third rule, all other true propositions in mathematics can be deduced step by step.

The attainment of the same degree of certainty in science and philosophy that has been reached in mathematics will be possible if we can find axioms or simple, clear, and distinct ideas, from which we can draw certain conclusions *a priori*. Descartes therefore begins his search for clear and distinct ideas outside the field of mathematics. For a while, he thinks like a skeptic, following a method of doubting every idea that can be doubted. His purpose is to doubt every idea that *can* be doubted even though no sane man *would* seriously doubt it; he is trying to find ideas which are not merely not dubious, but indubitable. He finds that he can doubt what is ordinarily considered common sense and he can doubt authorities; he can doubt his sense experience and memories; he can doubt the sciences, which are based upon them; he can, in fact, doubt everything except the fact that he is doubting. There is at least one indubitable truth: *Cogito, ergo sum*—I think, therefore I am. "This was so firm and assured that all the most extravagant suppositions of the skeptics were unable to shake it" (page 21). This, then, was the sought-for axiom, and whatever could be deduced from it would be as certain as the axiom itself. (Actually, in his demonstrations Descartes also used other axioms that he regarded as clear and distinct, such as the causal principle that everything must have a cause which is at least as real and perfect as its effect.)

With his indubitable axioms, Descartes then proceeds to prove some of the other beliefs that he had previously found dubitable. He gives several proofs for the existence of God and demonstrates the existence of the external world corresponding to his clear and distinct sense perceptions of it. In this way he believes that he can establish *a priori* knowledge in both theology and science. For purposes of illustration, let us consider only two steps in his argument.

1. I have an idea of God, that is, of a perfect being. This idea may be false; at least its truth can be doubted. But the existence of the idea, whether true or not, cannot be doubted and is not, in fact, disputed even by atheists. Now, by the second axiom, this idea must have a cause, and the cause must be as perfect or real as the effect; hence the idea of perfection must have a perfect cause. But I am not the cause of this idea, for I am imperfect, since I have doubts instead of knowledge. Therefore, a being outside me which is perfect must cause this idea. And a perfect being is God, by definition. Hence, God exists.

2. I have clear and distinct ideas of the external world, which I accept as true. I accept them as true by my nature, for which not I, but God, is responsible. But God is a perfect being, and a perfect being would not deceive his creatures. Hence, I am not deceived in thinking that there is an external world.

To sum up: Descartes, distrusting authority, common sense, and the testimony of his senses, tries to model philosophy after mathematics, and to take mathematics as the ideal for all knowledge. He searches for indubitable first principles or axioms that can be known intuitively or directly to be true. From these he makes demonstrations independent of sense experience; experience serves only to pose the problem and is referred to again only in the final stage (Rule Four) in order to make sure that no aspect of the problem has been overlooked. The results will be: (a) beliefs that are not self-evidently true can be shown to be true if they can be deduced from those that are self-evident; (b) beliefs can be shown to be false if their contradictories can be deduced from the axioms; (c) beliefs can be shown to be unfounded, so that a prudent man will withhold his judgment, if neither they nor their opposites can be deduced. In a word, all beliefs of which we can rightly be confident will be either self-evident, or demonstrably evident by virtue of being deduced from those which are self-evident. Demonstrable certainties shine by a light reflected from the certainties of the axioms and the logical rigor with which the deductions are made. When this program of searching for self-evident principles and then deducing their consequences is rigorously and exhaustively pursued, all knowledge will approach the certainty and rigor of mathematics.

By this approach, Descartes believed that he had found an answer to the skepticism rooted in conflicts of authority and opposing systems of common sense, without falling into a worse sort of skepticism, like that of Theaetetus, which does not give reason its proper due. Reasoning is under logical rules, which are the same for all men. Knowledge is not private to each knower, as Theaetetus had reluctantly to conclude, but is an ideal that men can achieve in common because of their possession of common principles. However much sense perceptions may vary from man to man, we can, by thinking critically, discover common principles like those of mathematics and the metaphysical principle of causation. These will give us a basis for agreement and insight into things as they are and not merely as they appear to each of us.

IMPLICATIONS OF NEWER VIEWS OF MATHEMATICS

Mathematics, for centuries before and after Descartes, was considered to be the most certain knowledge available. Beginning with self-evident principles that could not be denied and proceeding by logical inferences that could be checked and rechecked, it seemed to lead to indisputable results.

But in the nineteenth century, a new view of mathematics grew up. Mathematicians found that an assumption that Euclid had made could be replaced by alternative and incompatible assumptions, with the result that a whole family of new geometries, called non-Euclidean, could be constructed. Each of them is as logically cogent as Euclid's, but there are some theorems in them that are incompatible with some of Euclid's theorems because they are based on an assumption different from his.

Euclid states as a postulate, or unproved assumption, that in the following figure if the angle α is smaller than the angle β,

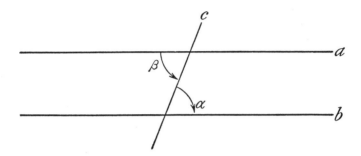

the lines a and b will meet if extended on the same side of line c as the angle α; and from this it follows—in fact, we say the same thing when we say—that if angle α is equal to angle β, the lines a and b are parallel, that is, they will not meet if extended infinitely in either direction. Lobachevski, and Riemann, in the nineteenth century, denied that this assumption was logically necessary or self-evident, and constructed systems of geometrical propositions in which it was not true. In Riemann's geometry there are *no* parallel lines. Many theorems that are true within the Euclidean system of geometry are therefore not true within the Riemannian. For instance, the sum of the interior angles of a triangle is not, for Riemann, equal to two right angles, for if the lines do meet when angle $\alpha =$ angle β, then $\alpha + (180° - \beta) = 180°$ while there is still to be counted the angle between lines a and b, which is necessary if they are to be legs of a triangle.

Such a non-Euclidean geometry was regarded for a long

time as merely a mathematical curiosity, its rules being no more applicable to reality than are, say, the rules of chess. Non-Euclidean geometry was a harmless but difficult mathematical game, while no one doubted that Euclid's geometry was the geometry of the real world.

Some mathematicians and philosophers, however, began to have doubts of this. After all, they said, the physical world does not contain absolutely straight lines, and the most accurate measurements we can make with a protractor do not give the sum of the angles of a triangle as absolutely equal to two right angles. Even Euclidean geometry seems to apply only approximately to the world of observation; and while we may think that any slight divergences from it are due to errors of observation and measurement, we cannot be absolutely sure that greater and greater accuracy in measurement will confirm this belief. The differences in the consequences between Euclidean and non-Euclidean geometries for the measurement of things in the real world would be so slight that they probably could not be discovered by any observations that we might make. Hence, one of the non-Euclidean geometries might apply to our observations with as much accuracy as Euclidean geometry, and the only reason we would have for preferring Euclid's geometry would be, not that we know it to be more true than the others, but that it is simpler and more familiar to us.

About 40 years ago, however, Einstein gave reasons for believing that the facts of astronomy were more conveniently described in terms of a non-Euclidean geometry than in terms of Euclid's. Some very careful observations by others and a great deal of theorizing by him led to the belief that very large triangles, such as those whose base line is a ray of light going from one star to another, are triangles whose measurable properties are those of non-Euclidean triangles instead of those of triangles as dealt with by Euclid.

Be that as it may, at least one conclusion of philosophical importance followed from the startling scientific innovation:

*some statements may be "mathematically true," yet not apply
to the real world or the world we experience and observe.* From
this it can be reasonably argued that the physical truth of
mathematical propositions cannot be guaranteed by their self-
evidence or "clearness and distinctness," as Descartes believed.
They are, on the contrary, *a priori* simply because they are the
logically necessary consequences of assumptions that the
mathematician has made. "Mathematically true" means merely
"logically implied by a set of mathematical assumptions or postulates." Just as I can logically infer that "If today is Sunday,
tomorrow must be Monday," in accordance with the rules of
the calendar and definitions of days of the week, whether today *is* Sunday or not, so also I can logically conclude from the
rules of non-Euclidean geometry that the sum of the angles of
a triangle is not equal to two right angles, whether the real
world of physical objects is really non-Euclidean or not. The
mathematician makes assumptions that are internally consistent
and draws logical inferences from them; but it is no part of
mathematics to show that these conclusions will apply to objects in the real world or whether the assumptions describe
what actually exists.

It is at this point that the modern interpretation of
mathematical knowledge differs most markedly from that of
Descartes. Descartes believed that principles he took as axi-
omatic were not just useful or interesting assumptions that
could be logically elaborated into interesting theorems; he believed that they were *true*, accurately describing the real
world. Recent philosophy of mathematics, in the light of the
work of Einstein, is not objecting to the *mathematics* of Descartes, but to the assumption he makes about the relation of
mathematics to physical reality. It says, in effect, that the
question of the applicability of a set of mathematical principles
to physical reality is an *empirical* question: are physical objects
of such a character that they can most conveniently be described, or their behavior best computed, in terms of mathematics based on Euclid's axioms, or in terms of some other

axioms? For everyone, mathematics itself remains purely rational; but the applicability of any particular set of mathematical principles is an empirical matter. This theory of mathematical knowledge has had wide repercussions in the study of epistemology and the philosophy of science. For if we cannot be sure that specific axioms of mathematics apply to the real world, how much less certain can we be that "self-evident" principles like "Same cause, same effect" apply to it! Encouraged by this theory of mathematics, many scientists and philosophers have claimed the right to assume quite different principles in place of those used by Descartes. For it is not a question of which assumptions are self-evidently true; they are interested in which ones—whether self-evident or highly recondite and artificial—will give them a basis for drawing "interesting" or "useful" conclusions in their study of nature.

If reason cannot decide even in these questions, how can we meet the views of peoples in different cultures who make quite different assumptions from ours on which they base their conduct? The communists argue that the assumptions one makes are determined not by reason but by the economic factors of his society or class; the Nazis used to say that the assumptions were determined by race; some evolutionists say that they are due to instinct, habit, or "inherited modes of thought."

If this is the whole story, it seems that reason is unable to save us from a skepticism even more profound than that implied in Theaetetus' relativism, for he relativized only our sense experience, while this view relativizes our reasoning itself. But fortunately, the existence of alternative mathematical systems does not imply that reasoning is merely a process of arbitrary assumption, although it does suggest that reason is not a super-psychological factor able by its own power alone to discover eternal verities. There is still a great difference between reasoning arbitrarily and reasoning responsibly.

Reason is not able to discover eternal truths about reality

simply by thinking its own clear and distinct thoughts. Its function is to organize our experience in such a way that it hangs together and makes sense, to interpret it in such a way that we can distinguish within it the true from the false and the basic, pervasive patterns from the trivial and the accidental. When experience is so organized that this is possible, we cannot but think that we have knowledge. However arbitrary or daring some of the assumptions may at first seem to be, we check them by reference to how they help us to understand what we observe. Sometimes we have to reject the assumptions or principles if experience doggedly stands against them, but sometimes we modify our specific beliefs about what we have observed to make them congruent with the reasonable principles that have satisfactorily served this organizing function.

Reasoning performs two tasks in knowing. First, it is concerned with drawing logical inferences from statements we make on whatever grounds, regardless of whether they are true or even assumed to be true. It is the task of reason, not of sensing, to show us that "If T is a Euclidean triangle, the sum of its angles must be equal to two right angles," "If there is a God, then there is some necessary being," or "If today is Sunday, tomorrow must be Monday." But reasoning does not tell us whether the premises are true or not, and hence does not tell us whether the conclusions are true. Although these examples of the inferences that reasoning permits us to draw are simple and straightforward, the real work of reason in establishing complex logical relations among propositions is intricate and requires much ingenuity. This work of reason in establishing logical relations among assumed propositions is called the "formal mode of thought," and it is studied in logic and mathematics.

The other task of reason is to elicit propositions from our experience (and imagination) which, while not known indubitably and not demonstrable simply by reference to the rules of formal thought, are capable of explaining what we observe.

Observation and imagination give rise to many "ideas" or "hunches" concerning the explanation of things. We can formulate them as propositions, and by logical inference from them we can predict what else we should expect to observe if these propositions are true. Propositions that function in this way are called hypotheses [6] or postulates, not indubitable and self-evident axioms. Reason alone would never discover or demonstrate them, but without reasoning we should never be able to formulate, test, and organize them. Our next chapter is devoted to showing their role in more detail.

BIBLIOGRAPHY

Boas, George, "Learning by Experience," *Journal of Philosophy,* Vol. XLIII, No. 17 (August 15, 1946), pages 466-471.

Bronstein, D. J., Krikorian, Y. H., and Wiener, P. P. (eds.), *Basic Problems of Philosophy.* New York: Prentice-Hall, Inc., 1947. Part 3.

Cassirer, Ernst, *The Problem of Knowledge* (W. H. Woglom and C. W. Hendel, trans.). New Haven, Conn.: Yale University Press, 1950. Chapters 1-3.

Cohen, Morris R., *Reason and Nature.* New York: Harcourt, Brace and Company, Inc., 1931.

Churchman, C. West, and Ackoff, Russell L., *Methods of Inquiry.* St. Louis, Mo.: Educational Publishers, Inc., 1950. Chapters 2 and 3.

Cornford, Francis M., *Plato's Theory of Knowledge.* New York: Harcourt, Brace and Company, Inc., 1935. (This is a commentary on and translation of Plato's *Theaetetus.*)

Descartes, René, *Descartes Selections* (R. M. Eaton, ed.). New York: Charles Scribner's Sons, 1927.

Einstein, Albert, *Sidelights on Relativity.* New York: E. P. Dutton & Co. 1922. Chapter 2.

Gewirtz, Alan, "Experience and the Non-Mathematical in the Cartesian Method," *Journal of the History of Ideas,* Vol. II, no. 2 (April, 1941), pages 182-210.

---

[6] There are, as we shall see, many kinds of hypotheses. We are referring at this point to the kind that we shall later call "collateral hypotheses" (page 94), although what is said here is true to some degree of all the various kinds to be discussed.

Kant, Immanuel, *An Inquiry into the Distinctness of the Principles of Natural Theology and Morals* (1764), in *Critique of Practical Reason and other Writings in Moral Philosophy* (Lewis W. Beck, trans.). Chicago: University of Chicago Press, 1949.

Lavine, Thelma Z., "Knowledge as Interpretation. An Historical Survey," *Philosophy and Phenomenological Research,* Vol. X, No. 4 (June, 1950), pages 526-540, and Vol. XI, No. 1 (September, 1950), pages 88-103.

Reichenbach, Hans, *The Rise of Scientific Philosophy.* Berkeley and Los Angeles: University of California Press, 1951. Chapters 3 and 8.

Walsh, W. H., *Reason and Experience.* Oxford: Clarendon Press, 1947.

QUESTIONS AND TOPICS FOR DISCUSSION

1. Read the *Theaetetus.* How does Theaetetus attempt to answer Socrates' criticism of his definition of knowledge?

2. Evaluate Descartes' argument for the existence of God. Do you think that it is logically valid? (That is, granting his premise, is the conclusion justified?)

3. Read Locke's *Essay Concerning Human Understanding,* Book I. Do you think Locke is criticizing a belief that Descartes held?

4. Discuss this definition of mathematics: *a game played with marks on paper, during which the mathematician doesn't know the meaning of the marks or whether what they say is true.*

5. Mathematics is sometimes called "the queen of the sciences," and is at other times said not to be a science at all. Discuss.

6. Comment on Einstein's statement: "As far as the laws of mathematics refer to reality, they are not certain; and as far as they are certain, they do not refer to reality."

7. Comment on Kant's statement that any body of knowledge is scientific to the degree that it makes use of mathematics.

8. Discuss the following statement by a prominent scientist: "Geometry is a descriptive science. If it does not describe the physical world, then it describes the way geometers think."

9. Read an account of Descartes' discovery of analytical geometry. Does this suggest why Descartes might be expected to be a rationalist in science and philosophy?

4

The Role of Hypotheses
in Inquiry

To see better the part that making and testing hypotheses plays in getting knowledge, we shall begin with several examples of how animals and men solve their problems. We shall begin with a cat, then go on to what happened to some of us this morning, and finally come to the case of a great scientist solving a problem in astronomy.

1. A psychologist puts a cat in a puzzle box and latches the door. The cat gives every indication of confusion, helplessness, and anger; she cries, tries to gnaw her way through the bars, and lashes her tail about. After a while, she accidentally touches the latch on the door and the door flies open and releases her.

The next day the psychologist puts her in the box again. Again she lashes about and eventually lets herself out. Gradually, as the experiment is repeated, she makes the right move sooner and sooner, until in a few days she quickly lets herself out without any random motion or wasted activity at all. We say that she has learned to solve the problem by "trial and

72

error": she tries this, that, and the other activity until finally, after many errors, she hits upon the right way.

If we like, we may say she now *knows* something, namely, how to get out of this box. But she knows very little; put her in another box with the latch at a different place, and she is as helpless as before and has to learn again by trial and error.

2. A man awakens in the morning and, while still sleepy, carries out a highly intricate bit of behavior without paying any attention to it: he ties his shoes laces. (That *is* an intricate operation, as anyone can see if he tries to explain how it is done to a person who doesn't know.) He is able to do this because he has learned it so well that his fingers do it almost automatically; he has done it so often that it requires no thought.

Now imagine that some morning his shoelace breaks as he is tying it. This disrupts the routine; suddenly all his attention is directed to the operation that, just a moment before, was below the level of consciousness. His habitual behavior is blocked, just as the puzzle-box blocks the cat's habitual behavior.

But the man does not behave as the cat does. To be sure, there may be a moment of non-adaptive floundering around; just as the cat lashes her tail in anger, the man may swear. The man, however, does something the cat cannot do, he thinks.[1]

Thinking is a process of learning by trial and error in which the trials and errors are not made in overt bodily behavior but in imagination. The man's thinking takes the form of trying out certain lines of action or plans without openly committing himself to them. Though his thinking may go so rapidly that it is hard to separate it into stages, probably something like this is going through his head: "I can wear that other pair of shoes, but if I do I mustn't wear this suit; perhaps I can tie this broken string, but no, it is too frayed; I believe there is another

---

[1] The following analysis of problem-solving is based on John Dewey's now classical *How We Think* (New York: D. C. Heath and Company, 1910, 1933).

pair of brown shoes in that closet; perhaps I can take the laces out of it and use them." In a moment he has thought of three lines of action he might take. He has found out where two of them would lead if he actually followed them (changing his suit, risking another break). He sees nothing against the third, so he overtly acts upon it.

He has solved his problem; he has gained (a little) knowledge in doing so, he has used knowledge he already had about his shoes and clothing, and he has judged each plan in advance of execution in the light of his other knowledge. If he has surveyed all of the possibilities and chooses the best, he has used an intelligence that the cat did not possess.

3. John Couch Adams, one of the discoverers of Neptune,

. . . while still an undergraduate . . . read of certain unexplained irregularities in the motion of the planet Uranus and determined to investigate them, with a view to ascertaining whether they might not be due to the action of a remote undiscovered planet. Elected a fellow of his college in 1843, he at once attacked the problem. It was this: from the observed [irregularities] of a known planet to deduce by calculation, assuming only Newton's law of gravitation, the mass and orbit of an unknown disturbing body. By September 1845 he obtained his first solution.[2]

Guided by his calculations, astronomers searched for the unknown planet and discovered it by telescopic observations in 1846. "Its mathematical prediction," says the Encyclopedia, "was an unsurpassed intellectual feat."

This "unsurpassed intellectual feat," like the actions of the cat and of the man with the broken string, was a response to a problematical situation. Although no habit was broken into by the discovery of the irregularities of Uranus, they gave an intellectual stimulus and aroused a questioning attitude. Predictions as to where Uranus could be seen at specified times had not been verified; what were the reasons for it, which, if they could be discovered, would make future predictions of

---

[2] Reprinted by permission from *Encyclopaedia Britannica,* fourteenth edition, Volume 1, page 155.

its position more accurate? All sorts of hypotheses about the motions of planets had been held in the history of astronomy. But Adams worked on the basis of one: all the planets go around the sun, and if their velocities are irregular, the irregularity is due to their alternate approach to and recession from some other body that attracts them. His problem, then, was to find out where such an unknown attracting body had to be in order to produce the observed irregularities. Having calculated where it would be if his guess about it was correct, it was a simple matter to look for it with a telescope. When it was found where Adams said it would be, his guess was "verified."

Now let us examine our three examples of problem-solving to see their similarities and differences.

1. *Problem-solving is occasioned by the new, the unexpected, which arouses or thwarts some interest*—If the cat had not wanted to get out of the box, she would not have had a problem to solve; if Adams had not become interested in understanding some aspects of Uranus' motions, he would not have devoted two years to explaining them.

2. *When a problem arises for a thinking man, it appears in an "unsettled area" surrounded by knowledge that is not unsettled*—The man whose shoelace breaks does not at the moment know how to solve the problem it puts to him, but he does not doubt that it is good to wear shoes, that he has other shoes, that shoes and suit ought to match, and the like. Adams did not know how to explain the motions of Uranus, but he did not doubt that planets go around the sun, that planets attract each other, that every event has some cause, that mathematics applies to astronomical facts, and so on.

The more intelligent a man is, the better able he will be to see the problem in the light of the relevant settled facts of his experience. The cat, perhaps, does this little or not at all.

3. *In the light of the relevant settled facts, a guess is made as to the best or only way of solving the problem*—Solving a problem is settling the unsettled. The guess is made about some unknown factor which would bring about this settlement

of doubt or frustration. For instance, in the second example, the laces the man believes he can get from another pair of shoes are the object of such a guess, and if they really are there, his problem is solved. In the third example, Neptune at such and such a place in the sky is the object of a guess. The cat, because she does not think, presumably does not make such guesses.

That which we suppose (but do not know) to exist so that it will provide a solution to a problem is called a *hypothetical object*, and the guess is called a *hypothesis*. The word "hypothesis" is used in many senses, and it is sometimes advisable to call the hypothesis that is applied in a specific case of this kind a *working hypothesis*.

4. *If a hypothesis helps us to solve a problem, it does so because from assuming the hypothesis we can draw conclusions which will have a bearing on our subsequent experience—If* the other shoes are in the closet, then their laces can be used in place of these; *if* the planet exists, then what would previously have been called an "irregularity" can be predicted to have such and such a magnitude in the future.

Acting upon the hypothesis may, of course, not solve the problem. If the other shoes are at the repair shop, acting on the hypothesis by looking for them will not get the man's shoe tied. If Neptune could not be found by aiming the telescope where Adams' hypothesis said it would be found, Adams would not have explained the irregularities of Uranus, could not predict its motions in the future, and would not have solved his problem.

The cat does not have sufficient intelligence to anticipate the results of her actions in a new and strange situation. She therefore has to try out many actions before she hits upon the right one. The men can anticipate and thus avoid the necessity of performing many overt trials, because they can try them out "in their minds" and anticipate what their consequences would be if they actually acted upon them.

THE ORIGIN OF HYPOTHESES

Hypothetical objects are things that we do not observe but that, if real, explain what we do observe. The line between hypothetical object and fact (which we do observe) is often indistinct. Strictly speaking, the legs of the table on which I am now writing are hypothetical; I do not now observe them but I assume that they are still there, and presumably I could observe them again by moving my chair. But an electron is a hypothetical object that we probably can never observe; the virus that some scientists believe causes a cancer is a hypothetical object that we may be able to observe someday. Observation alone does not suffice for formulating statements about those kinds of objects. In making hypotheses or guesses about them, we have to go beyond the facts; the hypothetical objects are at first conjured up by a disciplined creative imagination. Probably no rules can be given for this conjuring, although rules can be given for observing facts and drawing inferences from the hypotheses once they have been stated. Native wit, intelligence, lively imagination, a willingness to "go out on a limb," and perhaps even genius may be required for making significant hypotheses; the greatest thinkers are not the men who have made new observations or drawn logical conclusions from given axioms, but the men who have made new and unexpected guesses about hypothetical objects, guesses that explain what we observe but do not understand. The great thinker is not the mere collector of facts; he is more like a creative artist, who gives us a new and unexpected insight into things and permits us to anticipate new facts that we would not have discovered if he had not found what underlay the facts we already had.

But although no rigid rules can be given so that anyone by simply obeying them can be sure to formulate new and valuable hypotheses, a study of the lives and minds of great thinkers does suggest some of the ways in which good guesses about the unknown or unexplained have originated. Graham Wallas [3] believed that he had found a kind of "natural history" of discovery. He said there are four stages that many thinkers have gone through.

1. *Preparation*—Intelligent guesses about the unknown come only to minds prepared by knowing the available facts. *Examples:* Darwin collected facts about the variations of animals for years before he arrived at the hypothesis of evolution by natural selection; Newton knew many facts of mechanics and astronomy before he formulated his hypothesis of universal gravitation.

2. *Incubation*—The ideas we have must be allowed to incubate or mature. Close and persistent application to learning brute facts may inhibit the imagination; we need to "back away" from them before we can explain and understand them. *Examples:* Poincaré, the French philosopher and mathematician, worked on a problem and then dropped it during his military service, but solved it one day after not having thought of it for years; Helmholtz climbed hills on a sunny day after accumulating the "facts of the case," so that his ideas could mature; we advise our friends, "Sleep on it; it will be clearer tomorrow."

3. *Intimation*—After a period of incubation, we sometimes feel that we can now solve a problem that previously baffled us, although we do not fully know what the solution is. There is a feeling of readiness. *Example:* a famous German philosopher and psychologist, William Stern, said that he collected all the data on a problem, then let them incubate until he felt, "Now I can write it up," although when he began writing, he still did not know in detail what he was going to say.

4. *Illumination*—This is the most dramatic part of thinking, and is variously referred to in such expressions as: "It dawned on me that . . . ," "The idea burst upon me . . . ," "I saw in a flash . . . ," or "I had an inspiration." *Examples:* Archimedes

---

[3] Graham Wallas, *The Art of Thought,* Chapter IV. New York: Harcourt Brace and Company, Inc., 1926.

discovering the principle of specific gravity and dashing naked down the streets of Syracuse shouting, "Eureka!" Darwin's sudden discovery of the principle of natural selection while idly reading Malthus on the human struggle for a diminishing food supply. Kekulé suddenly seeing the ring-formula of benzene in the burning soot of his fireplace.

Such illumination, because its occurrence is so dramatic, is sometimes taken as a guarantee of the truth of what seems to have been revealed in it. For this reason it may sometimes seriously mislead us; it must be followed by careful and painstaking efforts at verification, and on further examination, it sometimes turns out that our most brilliant ideas are, unfortunately, not true. The vividness with which a new idea or hypothesis springs upon us is not at all a guarantee that it is true. False hypotheses come as dramatically as true ones. But because of the liveliness of the experience and because of one's natural love for his own "brain-child," we often are not as critical of them as we are of those ideas that come to others or that come to us with less impact. The wise and careful thinker will not give credence to a belief because of its inspirational occurrence; he will still require that it pass the test of verification.

The imagination is a tricky thing. It cannot be forced, and it is hard to discipline. So many unconscious and subconscious conditions affect it, and chance and apparently trivial experiences and events direct and inhibit it, that it would be silly to say that one ought to do this or that in order to make it work for advancing our knowledge or understanding. One person needs silence in order to do the thinking and dreaming from which his best ideas spring; another may want excitement and noise. Helmholtz said that even the slightest amount of alcohol stopped the process for him; Kekulé, on the other hand, had most of his best ideas over beer and cigars.

Perhaps the only counsel one can give towards improving the imagination for hypotheses—and it is counsel that makes

no promises—would be: try to find your own best way of hypothesizing. It involves five bits of advice:

1. Observe yourself; under what conditions—social, emotional, and so on—have your own best ideas come? Then when
you need to make a serious attempt to figure something out,
try to get yourself into that favorable state.

2. Getting a new idea, formulating some guess or hypothesis,
always means going beyond or against some of the ideas you
already have. The tenaciously held beliefs we have inhibit our
getting new ones; try to examine and suspect the Idols of the
Mind so as to give new and unfamiliar imaginings a chance to
enter.[4]

3. Draw a careful distinction between "facts" and "hypotheses." Many so-called facts are really a little factual observation plus a great deal of hypothetical interpretation. Ordinary
descriptions of things—and many scientific descriptions—involve the acceptance of hypotheses that may or may not be
correct. The physician, for instance, says, "The patient has
typhoid fever," but he usually observes only a few symptoms,
which might be caused by something else than the typhoid
germ. Hence, even here he is not simply reporting a fact but,
rather, making a conjecture, and the conjecture may be wrong
though the observation be correct. It is important to remain
aware of the hypotheses that we are using; when we remember
that they are hypotheses, it is easier to be critical and skeptical
of them than if we think they are hard facts. Often, unless we
are skeptical of old explanations, it is difficult to formulate
new and better ones.

4. Give special attention to the unusual facts, the apparent
exceptions. These are called "renegade instances," [5] but that is
a poor name for such valuable facts. They are "renegade" only
in the light of some accepted hypothesis that they do not fit.

---

[4] Einstein was once asked how he had made his great discoveries. He is said
to have replied, "I challenged an axiom."

[5] The name was suggested by V. C. Aldrich (*Philosophy of Science*, Vol.
III, No. 4 [October, 1936]), but is here used in a broader sense than Aldrich's.

Frequently we ignore them. Sometimes we content ourselves with the statement, "Well, the exception proves the rule," as if this statement meant that the rule or hypothesis is proved "true" by the exception. (Actually, this statement means, "It is the apparent exception to a rule that *tests* it, and if the hypothesis cannot apply to the apparent exception, then we should be suspicious of the hypothesis and try to find a better one.") Many a rejected stone has become the keystone of the arch; many a neglected or rejected fact—rejected because "it just couldn't be so"—has given the start to looking for a better hypothesis that will fit *all* the facts. To go back to our old illustration: many men had observed the irregularities in the motions of Uranus, but had neglected them, thinking that they must be the result of observational errors or mistakes in calculation.[6] But Adams took them seriously.

5. Be on the watch for analogies. An analogy is a comparison in which the relationship between two things is said to be the same as the relationship between two others. For instance, "The relation between a ruler and his people is the same as that between father and children" expresses an analogy. It may be wrong, of course, but frequently an analogy is very revealing even if it is wrong, for it directs us to look for previously unnoticed similarities and differences. In science, we see a good analogy in the work of atomic physicists of a generation ago, who thought of the atom as resembling a little solar system: the electrons were to the nucleus as the planets are to the

---

[6] Indeed, one of the most striking examples of missing an important scientific discovery because it just "couldn't be so" is found in the history of the discovery of Neptune. Long before Adams and a French astronomer, Leverrier, had predicted the existence and position of the planet, another French astronomer, LaLande, had actually *observed* Neptune itself telescopically. He was not looking for a planet and had no reason to suspect that a planet was in that part of the sky; hence he disregarded the discovery and attributed his measurements of a change in position of a "star" (as he thought) to an error in observation. James B. Conant (*Science and Common Sense*, pages 120-121. New Haven, Conn.: Yale University Press, 1951) gives some interesting illustrations from chemistry of discoveries that were missed because the mind of the scientist was not focused upon them when he observed the facts that later served to prove a new hypothesis.

sun. Darwin's theory of evolution is based on an analogy: nature, through the struggle for survival, selects those animals that are to survive and reproduce, as an animal-breeder selects animals for breeding purposes.

An analogy is like a mathematical ratio and proportion. If we know three terms in a proportion, we can calculate the fourth. From 2:4 as 6:x, we can determine that x is 12. Outside mathematics, we cannot be so certain of our analogies, but we can be guided by them in looking for some factors we do not now know. For example, if we believe that smallpox can be cured by vaccination, we might reason—correctly—that if we could induce a slight case of still other diseases by inoculation, we could give a person immunity from them; this analogy set scientists to work to find ways of weakening germ-cultures to produce slight attacks of disease and thereby prevent more virulent attacks. A good analogy by itself, of course, proves nothing; but it does open new paths of inquiry.

These bits of advice will not guarantee that new and enlightening ideas will come; but they may improve the chances.

MARKS OF A GOOD HYPOTHESIS

Anybody, of course, can make an indefinitely large number of guesses about anything. What is the cause of cancer? About this, with very little thought, one can guess: a germ, a virus, night air, evil spirits, the wrath of God, something in tobacco smoke, something in beer, the effects of too much study, hereditary factors, and so on. It takes no genius, or even much intelligence, to spin theories if one does not care what sort of hypotheses one is dealing with.

The competent thinker must have a *rich* imagination, or from the list of hypotheses to be considered he may omit precisely the right one. But it is a waste of time just to think of all conceivable hypotheses (as in our list of the possible causes of cancer, which might be indefinitely extended); the imagination must also be *disciplined*. By a disciplined imagination, we mean one that is able to discover *good* hypotheses,[7] hypotheses that are worth investigating. Epistemologists have discovered that good hypotheses have certain specific characteristics. Study of these can save labor by eliminating the necessity of trying to test poor hypotheses.

1. *A good hypothesis is adequate to and consistent with all the relevant known facts*—No matter how attracted we may be to a new hypothesis, we *cannot take it seriously if there are known facts that are inconsistent with it.* For instance, the hypothesis that cancer in general is caused by something in tobacco smoke is clearly a poor one, because men had cancer before tobacco was smoked.

Of course, what we think are facts may not actually be facts at all. For instance, in a detective story it may seem that *X is the murderer of Y* is a poor hypothesis, for it is a "fact" that *X* was *Y*'s best friend. But as every reader knows, that may not be a fact at all, though *X* wants the detective to believe it is.

In general, however, we can eliminate many hypotheses as worthless because they are incompatible with what we already know.

2. *A good hypothesis is (usually) consistent with other previously established hypotheses*—For instance, Adams accepted the Newtonian hypothesis that gravitational force was exerted by every body upon every other; he therefore did not have to consider the poor hypothesis that Uranus' motions were independent of other planets and due, say, to sunspots.

As we shall see later, we never establish a hypothesis without making use of other hypotheses that have previously been proposed. It is obvious, then, that we cannot test a hypothesis if it is incompatible with other hypotheses we have to assume in order to test it.

This rule of a good hypothesis is not absolute, for the other hypotheses *may* be wrong. But in general, a hypothesis con-

---

[7] A "good" hypothesis is not to be confused with a "true" one. We shall discuss true hypotheses in the next sections.

sistent with other hypotheses that have already been tested is more likely to be correct than one that is not.

3. *A good hypothesis is as simple as possible*—Other things being equal, the simplest among a set of hypotheses that meet the first two requirements is the best. This is known as the *law of parsimony* and sometimes, as "Ockham's razor," after William of Ockham (1290-1349), who is reputed to have said, "Entities [causes] are not to be multiplied beyond what is necessary."

It is very important to understand the meaning of "simple." "Simple" does not necessarily mean "easy to understand." It means *having a minimum of independent assumptions.* For instance, the Newtonian theory of physics is easier to understand than Einstein's, but it is not as good a hypothesis because it includes more independent assumptions. Again, a mathematical theorem may be proved in several ways, and sometimes the one that "goes the long way 'round" is easier to grasp than the proof the mathematician considers most elegant. But it is not the simplest explanation in the present sense for it uses more axioms, postulates, and steps than the shorter, more direct proof.

There is, of course, the danger that a hypothesis may be too simple. For instance, an explanation of human behavior in terms of one drive (sex or egoism, for instance) is simpler than one that uses a long list of "instincts." But it might be too simple in that it might not adequately deal with the variety of human behavior, and thus force the psychologist to supplement it with too many other hypotheses.[8] It is often a matter of dispute whether a very simple hypothesis is adequate, that is, whether it meets Criterion 1. But it is often rather easily decided that some particular hypothesis is more complicated than necessary. For example, astronomers now use only the hypothesis that bodies attract each other instead of the hy-

---

[8] Such additional hypotheses for dealing with cases neglected in a major hypothesis, or with renegade instances, are called *ad hoc* hypotheses.

pothesis suggested in the eighteenth century that they may also repel each other.

Sometimes it is said that the world is not really simple, and hence, the rule of parsimony will mislead us. This, of course, is a valid warning against using hypotheses that are so simple that they are not adequate to deal with the variety of actual facts. But given two hypotheses each of which fits all the known facts, we choose the simpler; we are as cautious as possible. Newton states the rule:

> We are to admit no more causes of natural things than such as are both true and sufficient to explain their appearances. To this purpose the philosophers say that Nature does nothing in vain, and more is in vain when less will suffice. For Nature is pleased with simplicity, and affects not the pomp of superfluous causes."

4. *A good hypothesis is fruitful and testable*—By this requirement, we mean that a hypothesis must have consequences at least some of which can be subjected to empirical test. The best hypotheses are those that lead us to expect something that we would not have expected, and presumably would not have found, unless the hypothesis had led us to look for it. In the case of Adams, his hypothesis led him to tell an astronomer where he should look if he wanted to see "a new planet swim into his ken," as Keats puts it. Only if the hypothesis has consequences that we can observe can we find out whether it is true or false. The hypothesis that the moon is a perfect sphere and its apparent hollows are really filled with some invisible glass-like substance is a hypothesis that Galileo could not refute. But it was not worth refuting because it was fruitless and untestable. A hypothesis must make a difference in our expectations about what can be detected in further experience; otherwise it is barren.

As mentioned before, a good hypothesis is not necessarily a true one. Often a hypothesis is good in that it guides us effectively in the discovery of new facts, although the facts that it leads us to observe are not the ones we expected on the assumption that the hypothesis was a true one. Perhaps the most famous illustration of a false hypothesis leading to valuable new facts is Columbus's discovery of America; according to his hypothesis, he should have got to India. Little examples of this fruitfulness of false hypotheses are found every day. A physician believes that a patient has a certain disease. On this hypothesis he predicts what conditions will be found on further examination; the further examination does not show these conditions and thus refutes his hypothesis. But in refuting the original hypothesis, he is not pushed back to his starting point, for the facts he has observed may set going a new line of thought that may lead to a true hypothesis. But without some good hypothesis, he would not know what tests to make or what facts and symptoms to look for.

A poor hypothesis does not have this directing function. The belief that a disease he is treating is due to the will of God may be true, but even if it is, the hypothesis is not a good one, for it does not lead to the discovery of further facts about the disease. Thus Spinoza, who believed that all philosophical explanation eventually takes us back to the ultimate reality he called God, nevertheless said, "The will of God is the refuge of ignorance," because it is the explanation the most ignorant man gives when he has no good hypothesis that will help him to understand a particular fact in nature.

A good hypothesis is frequently called a "working hypothesis," for it may guide us to further important observations regardless of whether it is true or not; sometimes, indeed, an hypothesis that we know quite definitely to be false can be good in this sense and is often used with full consciousness of its falsity.

5. *A good hypothesis must be explanatory*—By explanation is meant relation of apparently unrelated facts to one another in such a way that they can all be seen to have a common cause or to illustrate the same general principle. For instance, we explain the medicinal properties of an organic chemical compound by reference to its structure. Its structure is a hypo-

thetical characteristic that explains both its medicinal and its chemical properties, for from saying, "It has a hydroxyl group in such and such a position," we can compare it to other drugs that *look* quite different but behave the same way in the body or in a test-tube reaction. But a hypothesis that "opium puts people to sleep because of its dormitive power" is not explanatory; reference to its dormitive power explains nothing but only says again what we already knew. When Newton explained the fall of the apple, he did so not by invoking some mysterious power, but by showing that its fall was a special case under the general law that applied also to the motion of the moon around the earth. The hypothesis of gravitation does not explain *why* bodies attract each other, and as to this *why*, Newton himself said, "I make no hypothesis." To say "gravity" is the cause is like saying an animal cares for her young because of the "maternal instinct," the *only* evidence for which is that she does care for her young. But Newton's hypothesis does explain the falling apple and the revolution of the moon and the irregularities of Uranus' motion in the sense that it shows that whatever law accounts for one of these phenomena also accounts for the others.

An explanatory hypothesis is one around which a great deal of apparently diverse evidence converges, so that by assuming the hypothesis, we can interrelate what was apparently unrelated and see order and connection where previously we saw only brute fact and confusion.

THE LOGIC OF HYPOTHESES

Logic is the study of the laws and principles that give validity and correctness to thought, argumentation, and inference. Whenever we draw a valid conclusion from some statement, we are following, usually unconsciously, some law of logic. The laws of logic are for this reason sometimes called "laws of thought." They are not laws that tell us how thinking does always proceed, as Kepler's laws tell us how the planets actually do move. They are more like traffic laws, which tell us what we ought to do if we want to achieve certain results, such as a safe arrival. The laws of logic tell us the ways in which we must direct our thoughts *if* we want to make a correct inference from one statement to another. Each kind of sentence expressing a belief is under specific laws of logic, and to be sure that we do not go astray in complicated reasonings, it is well to know some of the guiding principles of the logic of the kind of sentence we are using.

In working with hypotheses, our beliefs are generally expressed in *hypothetical propositions* and *hypothetical syllogisms*. A few definitions are needed:

A *syllogism* is an argument with two premises and a conclusion. An example of a syllogism is: "All birds are warm-blooded; a canary is a bird; therefore a canary is warm-blooded." (We do not usually express our thoughts in syllogisms, but frequently omit one of the premises. We should be likely to say, "A canary is warm-blooded, because all birds are warm-blooded," leaving it unsaid that the canary is a bird. However, we can and sometimes do need to complete the argument, especially if we are being very careful, by supplying the missing premise.)

A *categorical proposition* is a statement that does not contain within itself any conditions or alternatives.[9] All of the propositions in the syllogism just given are categorical propositions, and that syllogism is called a *categorical syllogism*.

A *hypothetical proposition* is a statement that contains a conditional clause ("if so-and-so") and a resulting clause ("then so-and-so"). We call the "if-clause" the *antecedent,* and the "then-clause," the *consequent.* For example, "If germs cause diphtheria, there should be germs in the throat of this patient," is a hypothetical proposition. Its antecedent is "germs cause diphtheria," and its consequent is "there should be germs in the throat of the patient."

---

[9] Cf. any standard textbook of logic, for example, R. M. Eaton, *General Logic,* page 325. New York: Charles Scribner's Sons, 1931.

Hypothetical propositions are often not expressed in the "if . . . then . . ." form. Rather, we say, "Since the sun is coming out, it will probably stop raining," or "Napoleon lost the battle of Waterloo because he did not have enough men." But for logical exactness, it is better to "translate" them into strict logical form: "If the sun is coming out, then it will probably stop raining," and "If Napoleon did not have enough men, then he lost the battle of Waterloo." This often sounds artificial, but it improves the clarity of thinking, making it quite explicit what are the stated conditions and what are the consequences if these conditions are or were fulfilled.

A *hypothetical syllogism* is a syllogism whose major premise is a hypothetical proposition and whose minor premise and conclusions are categorical propositions. For instance, "If germs cause typhoid fever, then this water will probably give you typhoid fever; germs do cause typhoid fever; therefore this water will probably give you the disease."

An argument that obeys all the relevant laws of logic is called *valid*. One that does not do so is called a *fallacy* and is said to be *invalid*. A valid argument may have a false premise and still be valid. For example, "All men are Americans" is false, but it validly implies that "Some Americans are men," which is true. "All Americans live two hundred years" is false, but it validly implies, "Some Americans live two hundred years," which is also false. *But true premises and valid arguments always and in every case lead to true conclusions.* That is why it is so important to have both true premises and valid arguments; otherwise we cannot be sure that our conclusions are true.

It is possible to decide what kinds of hypothetical syllogisms are valid, that is, what combinations of hypothetical and categorical propositions will validly imply a conclusion. We shall, for the purposes of illustration, assume a rather silly major premise and evaluate the various ways in which it might be thought that a conclusion could be drawn.

CASE I: If wishes were horses, | Major premise.
beggars could ride.
Wishes are horses. | Minor premise, affirming the antecedent of the major premise.

Therefore beggars can ride. | Conclusion, affirming the consequent of the major premise.

This is valid. The major premise tells us under what condition beggars can ride, and the minor premise tells us that this condition is met. This is known as "affirming the antecedent," or *modus ponens*.

CASE II: If wishes were horses, | Major premise.
beggars could ride.
Beggars can ride. | Minor premise, affirming the consequent of the major premise.

Therefore wishes are horses. | Conclusion, affirming the antecedent of the major premise.

This is invalid. There might be, and there are, other reasons why beggars can ride. This is known as the fallacy of "affirming the consequent."

CASE III: If wishes were horses, | Major premise.
beggars could ride.
Wishes are not horses. | Minor premise, denying the antecedent of the major premise.

Therefore beggars cannot ride. | Conclusion, denying the consequent of the major premise.

This is invalid, for there might be other reasons why beggars can ride. This is known as the fallacy of "denying the antecedent."

CASE IV: If wishes were horses,   Major premise.
           beggars could ride.
           Beggars cannot ride.   Minor premise, denying the
                                           consequent of the majoɪ
                                           premise.

           Therefore wishes are   Conclusion, denying the an-
           not horses.   tecedent of the major
                                           premise.

This is valid, for if the antecedent implies the consequent and the consequent is false, then the antecedent under which the consequent would be true must itself be false. This is known as "denying the consequent," or *modus tollens.*

Thus there are two and only two valid modes of hypothetical syllogisms: that in which the minor premise affirms the antecedent and that in which the minor premise denies the consequent. Any other combination of hypothetical and categorical propositions is not a valid argument.

In science, of course, we are not interested in the rather fanciful kind of major premise that we have used in our illustration. We are interested in hypothetical major premises whose antecedents are presumably about some existing things that, if they really do exist, will explain the occurrences we actually observe. The antecedent is usually about a hypothetical object, something whose existence is not observed as a fact, but which is thought to exist as the cause or explanation of something we can observe as fact. To take a more serious illustration, Adams said, "If there is another planet at such-and-such a place, then the irregularities of Uranus' motion would be so-and-so." The man with the broken shoelace says, "If there is another pair of shoes, then I can use its laces." The chemist says, "If this liquid is acid, it will turn litmus paper red."

If the hypothesis [10] is fruitful and testable, its consequent

---

[10] It is necessary to call attention to the ambiguity of the word "hypothesis." The author cannot lay down a hard and fast rule as to how the word should be used, as people do use the word in a variety of senses; all he can do is to point out the ambiguity, and put the reader on guard against confusions that may result if the word is used in various senses without attention being called

will be a statement that refers to some observation, so that we can see whether the consequent is true, that is, whether it states an observable fact or not. If we know that the antecedent is true and that the consequent really follows from it, we can be sure of the consequent fact before observing it (method of affirming the antecedent). If we know that the consequent of the hypothetical premise is false by observing the facts it refers to—for instance, that in a specific case the litmus paper does not turn red—then we can conclude that the antecedent is also false (method of denying the consequent) and that the liquid was not acid.

It might seem that this little lesson in logic gives us a way of finding out which of our good hypotheses are true and which are false. In simple cases, like that of a man tying his shoe, this is correct. In such a simple example, we can affirm the antecedent by finding the other shoe. In much scientific work we can affirm the antecedent by using some more powerful instrument of observation. An X-ray may convert the hypothetical object (say, a stone in the kidney) referred to in a diagnosis or hypothesis into an observed fact. The telescope made visible the existence of a body in the part of the sky where Adams said a new planet would be found. But, unfortunately, in most inquiry something more is required than merely observing the object that we have made the antecedent about, and in many cases (for instance, in sub-atomic physics) we cannot do this at all.

---

to its exact meaning in each context. The following seem to be denoted by the word "hypothesis":

1. *The entire major premise.* For instance, "It is my hypothesis that if wishes were horses, beggars could ride." "It was Adams' hypothesis that if there were another planet, he could predict the motions of Uranus."

2. *The antecedent of the major premise.* For example, "Adams' hypothesis was that there was another planet."

3. *The object itself referred to in the antecedent,* a real object if the hypothesis (in Sense 2) is true. For instance, "The missing planet was not a known fact, but only a hypothesis, until it was observed telescopically."

I use the name "hypothetical object" instead of "hypothesis" when referring to "hypothesis" in Sense 3. The danger of confusion between Senses 1 and 2 is slight, since the context will usually show which is meant.

A common, but nevertheless erroneous, notion about science is that we verify a hypothesis by observing the consequent. It is often believed that this is the essence of the "experimental method"—never accept a hypothesis until it is verified by observation. But consider a simple example.

One might say, "If atoms exist, then chemical compounds will illustrate a specific law, say, the law of definite proportions. Dalton showed that chemical compounds follow this law. Therefore atoms exist." This seems to illustrate the process of verifying the hypothesis that atoms exist by referring to a fact of observation. But it breaks the logical laws of the hypothetical syllogism, since it is a case of affirming the consequent (Case II). We can no more logically verify the existence of atoms in this way than we could validly infer (in the example given as Case II) that wishes were horses simply because I have seen beggars ride.

We must conclude either that such scientific work is based on a logical fallacy, or that scientific verification is somewhat different from what it appears to be on the surface. Fortunately, the latter is the case.

Scientific verification is a more complex process than simply drawing a conclusion from a hypothesis, observing to see if the conclusion is a fact, and, if it is, accepting the hypothesis. We shall now see what more is involved.

There are two processes, both of which must be carried out if a hypothesis is to be verified. The first is the process of drawing a conclusion from a *family of hypotheses;* the second is the process of choosing among rival hypotheses.

Drawing conclusions from a family of hypotheses

One of the requirements of a good hypothesis is that it must be fruitful. It must lead us to search for some observable facts that we would not have expected without the hypothesis. But how does it do so? How does the antecedent, which is about something we do not observe, lead to a consequent about something that we can observe?

The answer to this question appears to be difficult only because we usually think that at any moment we are dealing with only one hypothesis. Actually, we are always dealing with a *family* of related hypotheses that mutually support one another and help to bridge the gap between any one hypothesis and the realm of observable fact. For instance, Adams was using not merely the hypothesis that there was another planet; this hypothesis alone would never have led to the other hypothesis: "If you look at such-and-such a part of the sky, you will find another planet." Adams was considering at least two hypotheses:

1. A hypothesis that there is between planets an attractive force that varies in the way stated by Newton and accepted by all astronomers.

2. A hypothesis that the irregularities of Uranus can, in the light of 1, be explained by the existence of another planet at the precise place and having the precise mass required to account for these irregular motions.

Notice that Adams was not interested in verifying the former, but used it because it was already sufficiently established. The first is related to the second in somewhat the same way that financial backing is related to a specific business venture, and we can properly call it a *collateral hypothesis*. It is sometimes called a *postulate*, since it is assumed to be true. The collateral hypothesis is a hypothesis about the "settled area of our experience," which is not questioned when the problem calling for Hypothesis 2 occurs. It functions in science somewhat like a postulate in geometry, from which we deduce the particular theorems. But because it is not self-evidently true and might, indeed, be wrong, we do not call it an axiom and thus make it appear utterly certain and not susceptible of correction.

On the basis of his collateral hypothesis, Adams calculated where the unknown planet would be if the hypothesis about it were true and if the existence of the unknown planet would, under the Newtonian hypothesis, adequately explain the observed motions of Uranus. He told astronomers, "If you point your telescope to such-and-such a place at such-and-such a time, you will observe a new planet." Notice that this is a third hypothesis.

This hypothesis, in the form "If you do so-and-so, you will observe such-and-such a fact," is an *operational hypothesis*. It is so called because its antecedent is an operation, a manipulation, something we can actually do. The operational hypothesis has a peculiar merit: its antecedent *can* be affirmed. The performance of an experiment or the taking of an observation is just this process of actually affirming the operational antecedent to see whether its results are those predicted.

Taking the process of scientific verification of hypotheses as far as we have now pursued it, the scheme is this: if the collateral hypothesis and the hypothesis to be tested are true (and we assume the first is true as a result of earlier inquiries), then if such-and-such operations are performed, such-and-such facts will be observed.

Or, to use our former illustration from Adams' work, we can outline the process of verification as far as we have now examined it:

Major premise: Family of hypotheses	If the hypotheses about gravitation are true	Collateral hypothesis
	And if the hypothesis about the unknown planet is true	Hypothesis to be tested; "working hypothesis"
	And if a telescope is pointed at Position p at Time t	Antecedent of operational hypothesis
	Then: a new point of light will be seen at p	Consequent
Minor premise: Experiment	The telescope is pointed at Position p at Time t	Affirming the antecedent of the operational hypothesis
Conclusion:	The point of light is seen	Observed fact, and the consequent of the entire family of hypotheses

The process schematically presented here is ordinarily called "testing a hypothesis by a fact," or the "observational or experimental verification of a hypothesis." The question to be considered now is: does the conclusion, the actual observation of the expected fact, justify the inference that the hypothesis we wanted to test is true? Can we be sure that the point of light that the astronomers did observe indicates the existence of a previously unknown planet, and that this planet is the cause of the observed irregularities in the motions of Uranus?

Reluctantly we must admit that we cannot be sure on the basis of the procedure outlined. For we are still affirming the *consequent* of the *family* of hypotheses as a whole. The antecedent we affirmed was merely the antecedent of the *operational* hypothesis, which is only one member of the entire family of hypotheses. We still do not know but that some other hypothesis might be consistent with the operational hypothesis and might better explain the facts to which we are led by it. To make sure that our hypothesis about the unknown planet is true, we must go through still another process, the process of elimination, by which we refute rival hypotheses that might be members of the family, or rival families of hypotheses.

The process of elimination considered logically

First, the process of elimination will be outlined schematically so as to give an over-all, logical picture of it. The next section will show how experiment is used in the process, and the appendix to this chapter will give an actual example of its successful application, in which we can see the connection among all the steps of scientific method.

In most problem-solving, there is one set of collateral hypotheses accepted without question, and a few rival, incompatible hypotheses to be tested. Each of these hypotheses we may assume to be consistent with the known facts and with the collateral hypothesis, for otherwise we do not need to trouble ourselves about them. But they are inconsistent with one another, so our problem is to see how to choose among them if they are equally good.

Let us call the collateral hypothesis or set of collateral hypotheses H_c; the rival hypotheses to be tested, H_1 and H_2; the operational hypotheses O_1, O_2, and so on; and the facts observed as consistent with both H_1 and H_2 by the letters f_1, f_2, f_3, and f_4.

Our present state of knowledge, in which we cannot choose between H_1 and H_2 in the light of the facts that we know, can be summarized in the following statements:

$$H_c \text{ and } H_1 \text{ and } O_1 \text{ imply } f_1 \text{ and } f_2$$
$$H_c \text{ and } H_2 \text{ and } O_1 \text{ imply } f_1 \text{ and } f_2$$
$$H_c \text{ and } H_1 \text{ and } O_2 \text{ imply } f_3 \text{ and } f_4$$
$$H_c \text{ and } H_2 \text{ and } O_2 \text{ imply } f_3 \text{ and } f_4$$

In other words, the operational hypotheses of experiments we have made do not help us choose between H_1 and H_2. But if H_1 and H_2 are good hypotheses, then they are fruitful, and that means that each should imply some new facts when conjoined to some new operational hypothesis O_3, and some new fact implied by H_1 and O_3 should be observably different from the new fact implied by H_2 and O_3. O_3 is called a *crucial experiment*. Then we predict:

$$H_c \text{ and } H_1 \text{ and } O_3 \text{ will lead to } f_5,$$
$$H_c \text{ and } H_2 \text{ and } O_3 \text{ will lead to } f_6$$

where f_5 is observably different from f_6. In words, when submitting the two hypotheses to a crucial experiment, we expect one fact if one hypothesis is true, and another fact if the other is true. Only observation will show which of the expected facts actually occurs. Suppose we do the experiment and observe f_5. Now in this case, we are no longer merely affirming the consequent of the family of hypotheses containing H_1 (which alone is invalid ground for affirming its antecedent), but at the same time, we are denying the consequent of the family containing H_2. This is a sufficient logical ground for saying that H_2 is refuted. And if H_2 is the only alternative to H_1 in the family of hypotheses consistent with H_c, this is sufficient logical ground for saying that H_1 is true.

It should be noted, however, that we do not usually know

for sure that H_2 is the only alternative to H_1; so the most we can say is that up to now we know of no other equally good hypothesis against which there is no refuting evidence, and hence we accept H_1.

In verification, therefore, we do not confirm a hypothesis simply by showing that it passes a specific observational test. We must, to be sure, show that it does pass all the tests we put it to, and evidence of widely divergent kinds ought to converge upon it. But we must also show that the other hypotheses do *not* pass all the tests we put to them. Convergence of evidence $(f_1 \ldots f_n)$ and elimination of alternatives, therefore, are the two prerequisites for accepting a hypothesis as true.

THE ROLE OF EXPERIMENT IN ELIMINATING HYPOTHESES

One of the outstanding traits of modern science is its emphasis upon experimentation. "Experimental science" is often taken as a synonym for "modern science," under the erroneous impression that ancient scientists did not perform experiments. Although ancient science was by no means wholly non-experimental, and although there are some highly rigorous modern sciences like astronomy that are not experimental in the ordinary meaning of this word, it is nonetheless true that the laboratory, where experiments are performed, is the typical institution of modern science.

In this section we shall discuss the nature of scientific experimentation to see how experiments are done and why they are so important. All sciences dealing with nature appeal to facts in the verifications of their hypotheses. That is to say, they are observational. Experimentation is only a way of observing things. An experiment is an observation made without having to wait for nature to produce the thing or event we want to observe. It is a technique of forcing nature to answer our questions by setting up artificial conditions (conditions that might not be met with at all in the normal course of nature or at the

time and place where they might conveniently be observed).
The scientific experiment forces nature to answer our questions
and does not wait for her to volunteer the information we want.
It was in this respect that Bacon compared experimentation to
the torture of a witness who might not divulge the information
we want unless forced to do so.

We shall briefly compare a scientific study in which experimentation was used with the same scientific study prior to the
introduction of experimentation. Physicians had long been
interested in the causes of pellagra. By observing many cases,
they found that it was a disease of high incidence among the
poorer classes of the population but was very rare among the
better-off. This might be due to any number of causes. Hypotheses about the unsanitary conditions, poor food, or wrong
diet prevailing among the very poor, or the crowded conditions
that might make a disease endemic among the whole population very prevalent among the poor appeared to be good
hypotheses, some or all of which might be true. But no one
knew which one was correct. It was not possible to find out
which was the true cause unless an experiment could be done
that would hold some conditions (food, exposure, unsanitary
conditions, and so on) constant while varying the condition
cited in the remaining hypothesis.

Most people in a society like our own will not voluntarily
submit themselves to the inconvenience and danger of being a
guinea pig for a scientist. You will not find the wealthy, who
get adequate food, volunteering to eat their good food under
unsanitary conditions just to prove some hypothesis about
diet. Dr. Joseph Goldberger, of the Rockefeller Institute for
Medical Research, however, found an ideal experimental situation: a group of men in prison having a high rate of pellagra-
incidence. Their living conditions and diet were more or less
identical. He could, therefore, experiment with one of these
conditions at a time, while holding the other constant. He
found in a very short time that the disease did not spread from
person to person, for the solitaries got it as often as the others;

improving the sanitary conditions did not lead to lowering the incidence-rate; but changing the diet so as to include fresh fruits and vegetables did cause the number of cases to decline.

Both before and after the situation was subjected to experiment, of course, observations were required. But earlier, the physicians did not really know what they were observing. By simply looking at a man with a disease, you cannot tell whether the important fact is that he is a dirty man, or a poorly nourished man, or a man who has been exposed to the disease. But with an experiment, in which you can find a man who is clearly an instance of one of these types but not of the others, you can eliminate the false hypotheses.

To normalize and control the possible causal factors and then to vary them one by one is the technique of experiment. In this way, we find relatively "pure" cases that nature and society do not present to us ready-made. The illustration, simple as it is, brings out many important aspects of the experimental testing of hypotheses.

1. *An experiment must be planned*—It has been said, "The armchair is mightier than the laboratory." Without planning the experiment, setting up proper controls, and knowing what factors it is worth while to vary and observe, an experiment is no more than just monkeying around in hopes of stumbling upon an interesting fact. Sometimes this is successful, and there are cases of accidental discoveries in the laboratory. But it is wasteful to count on making them, and when we do get results in this way, we have to repeat the experiment under more carefully controlled conditions to learn what our results really mean.

2. *In an experiment, we must know what conditions to hold constant*—The factors to be held constant are those considered in the collateral hypotheses and in the alternative hypotheses we are not now testing. The one to be varied is chosen on the basis of the hypothesis we are interested in testing at the moment. If our collateral hypotheses are wrong, or if we have overlooked some plausible alternative to the hypothesis we are

testing, we fail to control a relevant factor. When this happens, the experiment will not mean what it seems to mean. We shall get wholly surprising results that cannot be obtained again when we repeat the experiment, or the results will be so variable and "scattered" that we shall not know how to account for them.

3. *An experiment must be performed on an isolated system* —By an isolated system is not meant one that is absolutely isolated from everything else. We can never have isolated systems in this sense. All physical experiments, for instance, are performed in a gravitational field, and we cannot shield our experimental situations from all effects from the outside. But we do not need that extreme and unattainable degree of isolation. By isolating a system is meant arranging it in such a way that the factors that might affect it but that we are not interested in now testing will remain constant throughout a series of experiments. Which facts are to be held constant throughout a series are determined by the collateral hypotheses. Which ones are to be held constant in some experiments but altered in others are determined by the set of alternative hypotheses from which the elimination is to be made.

4. *A good experiment usually need not be repeated*—If we have actually controlled all the relevant conditions and have accurately observed the results of carefully controlled variations in the possible causes, there is no need to repeat the experiment. Not all experiments are good in this sense. It is always possible that we are not dealing with an isolated system, and it is always possible that there is some mistake in observation. But a single well-conducted experiment is far more revealing than a large number of uncontrolled observations. We need and have many observations of earthquakes and still do not know very much about their causes; we have only one experiment on the constitution of some chemical compound and no one feels the need to repeat it.

We have here what might appear to be a paradox to those who believe that science is largely inductive, going from many instances to a single generalization. The sciences that collect countless observations do not usually get the neat laws and results obtained in a science that can base its conclusions on a few well-conducted experiments.

5. *An experiment may not mean what it seems to mean—* The facts observed may not actually be relevant to the hypothesis being tested. This happens when the experiment is not properly planned, not carefully performed, or its results not accurately observed. It is, of course, true that some result will be obtained even from a careless or misguided experiment, but the results of such an experiment are not facts that can properly be used as evidence for or against a hypothesis. We might say that they are facts about some experimenter's work, but not facts that belong to the body of a science as evidence for or against a specific hypothesis. One example of a poor experiment shows the insignificance or misleading character of the results obtained when precautions in performing an experiment are not taken.

In a series of experiments in pathology, the purpose was to ascertain whether a certain chemical compound *A* causes cancer in rats. The experiment seemed to show that *A* did have this effect, but the observations were so surprising to other investigators that they repeated the experiments. Sometimes they duplicated this result and sometimes they found that the compound did not have this effect. Then it was discovered that in the original experiments, and in some of the subsequent ones, the reagent used had not been pure. The original experimenter had believed that it was a fact that *A* was a cause of cancer; the real fact was, "These rats, treated with the material in the bottle marked 'A,' developed cancers." It was not a fact that the compound that is *really A* was the cause of the cancers, although this was the conclusion drawn from the experiment; it was suspected and finally rejected because repetitions of the experiment gave different results.

In experiments that cannot be repeated with the same results, we say that there has been some "experimental error."

Such an error is insidious in its effect on the process of verification because we do not usually know when or in what experiments it occurs. We suspect the existence of experimental error only after some quite unexpected or otherwise unexplained results have been obtained. When an experiment produces results irreconcilable with hypotheses already well established, it is always wise to recheck and, if necessary, to repeat the experiment with greater care before saying that the hypothesis has been refuted. In cases where no well-established hypothesis exists to occasion strong expectations of some specific result, it is much more difficult to know when to suspect and how to detect experimental error. Sir Arthur Eddington made a neat paradoxical turn in a common statement to call attention to the uncertainty of observation and experiment: "Never accept a fact," he said, "until it has been verified by a theory."

This advice is important, and is actually followed. Suppose you do an experiment in a chemistry class and "discover" that the formula for water ought to be H_8O_3 and tell the instructor that you have "refuted" the textbook's hypothesis that it is H_2O. Without even going over your experiment in detail, he will rightly say that you must have made a mistake. Instead of giving you a good mark for having overturned some ancient error, he will give you a bad mark for being clumsy in the laboratory.

There is always the outside possibility, of course, that you may be right and all the other chemists wrong. Hence Eddington's advice is not quite perfect. If we *never* accepted a fact until it had been verified by theory, we should never have to change any of our hypotheses and would never be able to test any of them. The advice, however, warns us not to be overly confident that anything that seems to be a fact is really the kind of fact that the scientist is interested in—a fact that is decisive for or against some hypothesis or generalization.

6. *Not all problems can be dealt with experimentally*—The astronomer cannot produce an eclipse at will in order to see

what causes eclipses; the geologist cannot shift the continents about to see how they fit together; the psychologist cannot bring up a child in complete isolation in order to see how it would react at the age of 18 to the first sight of another person. Society as a whole does not allow itself to be experimented upon by anthropologists, geneticists, and sociologists.

In such instances as these, we have to work on observations that are given to us in the normal course of things. But in many of these cases, we have a valuable substitute for the controlled single experiment: statistical control. In an experiment, *we can control or neutralize the irrelevant factors.* In a statistical situation, we take as many cases as we can find with the hope that *the irrelevant factors will cancel each other out,* leaving only the relevant factors or real causes.

To take a simple illustration: you wish to know whether television in the home has any effect on children's school work. There are almost countless factors that probably do affect their school work—their I. Q., their relations to their parents, their affection for their teacher, their diet, their health, and so on. We might suppose, however, that if we take carefully selected groups of children with varying I. Q.'s, different diets and conditions of health, and differences in other respects that we think may have a bearing on school work, but all of whose parents have television sets, and compare them with other groups of varying I. Q., health conditions, and so forth, whose parents have no television sets, then in each group the high I. Q.'s will statistically cancel out the low I. Q.'s, the good diets and their effects will statistically cancel out the poor diets and their effects, and so on. If the groups have been chosen with proper regard to the rules of statistical inference, the factor that is not canceled out in each group will be the possession of or lack of television sets, and then we can see if the marks of these two groups differ significantly. If they do not, then we can consider the hypothesis that television affects school work as refuted.

Unfortunately, statistical control is seldom as perfect as

experimental isolation, so that we are often not able to draw from statistical studies conclusions as definite as we could draw if a laboratory experiment were possible.[11]

7. *It is not always safe to generalize from an experimental to a non-experimental situation*—The cautious scientist is always aware of the fact that the conditions he has experimentally controlled or eliminated may not be controlled or eliminated when someone attempts to use his result to make predictions about new cases. A drug may cure a disease in a rat, but be valueless against the same germs in a human body, where other conditions are not the same. Some chemical reactions may work well in a test tube, but before the chemical engineer builds a factory to perform this reaction on a large scale, he builds a "pilot plant" to discover and work out the "bugs" that show up in large-scale work. It is a mark of lack of scientific discipline to generalize the results from a few experiments and expect that like results will be obtained in all future cases.

An experiment that does not lead us to expect one thing rather than another in future cases is, of course, utterly worthless. Experiments are not done merely to bring new facts under observation; they are done in order that we may choose among hypotheses so that we can foretell facts that have not yet been observed. But the hypothesis that is confirmed by a series of carefully controlled experiments may not be—indeed, is usually not—the only hypothesis needed for more complex cases where the previously controlled factors are no longer controlled.

---

[11] Three other uses of statistics should be mentioned: (1) by studying a small sample, under some conditions it is possible to judge something about the whole group; (2) when experimental results are "scattered" so that the experiment must be repeated, it is possible by use of certain statistical methods to determine which of a set of numerical values is the most acceptable and which are most infected with experimental error; (3) as an experimental short-cut, statistical analysis permits inference from a series of experiments in each of which a *group* of variables (instead of a single one) have been systematically varied in specified ways.

CONCLUSION

Bacon, who is sometimes incorrectly considered to be a narrow empiricist, rightly saw how reasoning and observing are connected and how feeble science would be if it depended on either alone. He wrote,

Those who have handled sciences have been either men of experiment [observation] or men of dogmas [reason]. The men of experiment are like the ant: they only collect and use; the reasoners resemble the spiders, who make cobwebs out of their own substance. But the bee takes a middle course, it gathers its material from the flowers of the garden and the field, but transforms and digests it by a power of its own. Not unlike this is the true business of philosophy [science]; for it neither relies solely or chiefly on the powers of the mind, nor does it take the matter which it gathers from natural history and mechanical experiments [brute facts] and lay it up in memory whole, as it finds it; but lays it up in the understanding altered and digested.[12]

Brute facts are rendered intelligible by reason, and reason draws its sustenance and support from experience. To paraphrase a famous statement of Kant, reason without experience is empty, and experience without reason is blind. The method of science, which is by no means restricted to those fields of knowledge we all agree in calling the sciences, is a method of responsible hypothesizing for the sake of rendering intelligible the facts we have and for guiding us to facts as yet unobserved.

Our lengthy study of science has attempted to show two things. One is the way in which scientific method can be considered quite apart from the techniques of the laboratory; one can use the scientific method whether he ever gathers a statistic or works in a laboratory or not. Because this method has reached its highest precision in the sciences and has given us probably the most dependable knowledge we possess or can

---

[12] Francis Bacon, *Novum Organum*, Aphorism 95. (*Bacon Selections*, Mathew Thompson McClure, ed. New York: Charles Scribner's Sons, 1928, page 341.)

possess, it is a challenge to us to make use of such a method as far as we can in non-scientific inquiry.

The second thing our study of scientific method has shown is its limits. Science is not an exercise of pure reason leading to the discovery of absolute and indubitable truths. Science never rises above the level of hypothetical explanation, or explanation based on assumptions whose only justification is that they enable the scientist to predict future observations in the particular field of experience he claims as his own. Dogmatism, or the belief that we possess absolute assurance, is alien to the spirit of science and has no place in its method. We never indubitably know whether a particular hypothesis is true or not. There may always be some better or truer hypothesis waiting to be discovered by some future genius, some "nasty little fact," as Huxley remarked, "ready to kill the most beautiful hypothesis." In either case we shall have to modify or reject our hypothesis—not because our new knowledge will rest on some foundation that is better than science, but because the new hypothesis is called for by more rigorous and extensive use of the scientific method. All that we can ever say about a hypothesis that has been "verified," even one that has been "verified" so often that we think of it as an obvious truth and not as a conjecture at all, is this: it has worked better than any other hypothesis we now know; up to now we have found nothing against it; and it will probably continue to fit and foretell facts and guide us in our efforts to understand the world. If and when we have to reject or modify it, that will not be an intellectual defeat, for we shall be able to say of the one that takes its place: the new hypothesis is more nearly the truth than the old one was.

Even hypotheses so firmly established that we tend to think of them as being immutable and ultimate—that the earth goes around the sun, that Euclidean geometry applies to astronomical phenomena, that atoms exist—are, in the final analysis, only hypotheses that have been gradually confirmed without our finding anything against them. Absolute demonstration, with no if's, and's, and but's, is not the business of science or of any enterprise that makes use of the methods of science.[13]

This fact can make little or no difference to our modest attempts to add a little to the store of knowledge. Acknowledging it is by no means equivalent to skepticism. Recognizing that our best and most dependable knowledge is hypothetical in its structure need not make us withhold our judgment that Milton was born in 1608, or that water expands when it freezes, or that the sun will rise tomorrow. It may make some difference, as we shall see in Chapter 8, to the decision we make concerning how much assurance we can properly feel in the philosophers' attempts to "explain everything." But at this stage of our analysis, one task of philosophy with respect to the organization and scope of knowledge is clear. It is to keep us aware of the hypothetical status of the knowledge we have, and to forbid blind dogmatism that this knowledge, or some allegedly better knowledge based on authorities or on our feelings or pure reason, is beyond question and examination. The task is to encourage critical rather than dogmatic use of the conclusions that scientists and others have reached about man and the world, to keep open the path of inquiry, and not to allow inquiry to be stopped at the boundary of present-day science.

---

[13] We certainly do not assert that philosophy has a method that will permit it to give demonstrable certainties beyond the limits of science, as we shall see in Chapter 8; and we have already seen the limits within which mathematics can give demonstrable and indubitable knowledge, in Chapter 3.

Appendix
to Chapter 4

AN EXAMPLE OF SCIENTIFIC METHOD IN BIOLOGY

The preceding sections of this chapter have given a somewhat schematic account of the method of scientific thinking and have illustrated various stages of this method by a variety of examples, each of which was chosen to bring out some specific point. In this appendix we shall use a single example, which has the advantages of being very easily understood in all its details and of illustrating and bringing together all the most important procedures and rules.[1]

Statement of the facts from common observation and statement of the problem—Galambos writes,

Since ancient times the bat has been an object of interest to biologists and laymen alike. The bat flies at night, and this fact has appealed both to mystics, who saw in its nocturnal wanderings collusion with the powers of evil, and to naturalists, who speculated

---

[1] The following simplified account is based on three articles: Robert Galambos, "The Avoidance of Obstacles by Flying Bats: Spallanzani's Ideas (1794) and Later Theories," *Isis*, Vol. XXXIV, Part 2, No. 94 (Autumn, 1942), pages 132-140; Robert Galambos, "Flight in the Dark: A Study of Bats," *The Scientific Monthly*, Vol. LVI (February, 1943), pages 155-162; and Robert Galambos and Donald R. Griffin, "Obstacle Avoidance by Flying Bats: The Cries of Bats," *Journal of Experimental Zoology*, Vol. LXXXVIII, No. 3 (April, 1942), pages 475-90. All quotations, unless otherwise noted, are taken from the first of these three articles, by permission of the Editor of *Isis*.

on how the animal directs itself under conditions where its eyes can be of little or no use.

The first rigorous scientific study of the problem was made by the Italian Lazzarro Spallanzani, who was

> . . . thoroughly familiar with the animals and their behavior, and . . . knew at first hand the nature of the dark subterranean passageways in which they lived. Perhaps it was once when his candle flickered out while he was exploring such a passageway that it first occurred to him to wonder how bats avoid obstacles.

Thus arises a problem: in the "settled area" of our experience, where we are at home with what we observe, men and animals usually guide themselves by sight, but this is unlikely to be the case with bats, which fly in the dark. There is thus an "unsettled area" of experience, a problematical area in which we do not know the explanation of what we observe. Our settled experience is that normal men guide themselves by sight, blind men by touch, all of us sometimes by hearing. Our collateral hypothesis, and the one that Spallanzani used, is that there is some sense organ by which the bat guides its motion. The hypotheses to be tested were hypotheses about the specific sense organ required for this behavior.

First hypothesis to be tested (H_1)—Some animals, such as cats, can see in almost complete darkness; perhaps bats can also. If this is so, bats who have been blinded will be unable to guide their flight. Thus the first hypothesis and the operational hypothesis O_1 ("If we destroy the bat's vision, it will be unable to avoid obstacles") led Spallanzani to perform this experiment. Result: "The animals avoided obstacles as well after the operation as before." In other words, the opposite of the predicted fact is observed, and the hypothesis is inferred to be false by the method of denying the consequent of the hypothesis.

Second hypothesis to be tested (H_2)—The bats might be guided by their sense of touch. But they do not come into actual contact with the walls, but avoid them. Hence this hypothesis does not fit the already known facts and requires no further tests.

Modification of second hypothesis, giving a new hypothesis (H_3) *to be tested*—Perhaps the bats have an extraordinarily acute sense of touch, which would be responsive to slight disturbances in the air near walls and obstacles. Such sensitivity is known to exist in many animals with hair. If this is the correct hypothesis, then destroying the alleged sensitivity should make the bats helpless in avoiding obstacles. So Spallanzani coated a bat with a thick varnish (O_2) and predicted that a "varnished" bat would not avoid obstacles. Yet he observed the opposite; they avoided obstacles as well as unvarnished bats. Thus, H_3 is refuted by denying that its consequent corresponds to the observed facts.

Fourth hypothesis to be tested (H_4)—Taste, in some unexpected way, might be responsible. This is an unlikely hypothesis, for we cannot imagine any mechanism by which the sense of taste could have this effect. But Spallanzani tested it by excising the tongue of a bat (O_3) and observed that the bats retained the ability. Thus this hypothesis is refuted.

Fifth hypothesis to be tested (H_5)—Smell might be responsible. Operational hypothesis O_4: plug up the nose of the bat; then if H, is correct, the bat should not be able to avoid obstacles. The experiment was done on several bats, and the results were scattered. Some animals retained the ability, and in others it was lost or reduced. At any rate, the nose was not completely eliminated as a possible causative factor. Spallanzani believed that his experiment had interfered with the bats' breathing,[2] and that this experimental factor might explain his results. In other words, he believed that here there was an experimental error, which would explain the apparent exception or renegade instance. (But remember that a renegade instance may be especially important if properly understood.)

Sixth hypothesis to be tested (H_6)—Hearing may be involved.

---

[2] This is really an *ad hoc* hypothesis, made to explain a specific exceptional event, and not taken as applying to all cases.

Operational hypothesis O_5: plug up the ears of the animals, and if H_6 is correct, they will not be able to avoid obstacles. Spallanzani performed this experiment, but again his results were not clear-cut. Of 11 bats he used, 10 were unaffected by the experiment. In those ten cases, he observed facts inconsistent with H_6, which tended strongly to refute it. The eleventh bat flew "with difficulty," and thus was apparently a case consistent with the hypothesis. But Spallanzani wrote that this was

. . . an accidental case which, although being negative, does not weaken at all the positive facts advanced, and proves only that in our negative decisions we must never abandon ourselves to a single isolated case.

Here again was a renegade instance, which was not further explored.

Seventh hypothesis to be tested (H_7)—A combination of two or more of these organs is required for guided flight. Operational hypothesis O_6: cover all the head organs of the bat with a hood. If H_7 is correct, the bat will not be able to avoid obstacles. The experiment was done by another scientist, Rossi, and he found that the bats did lose their ability to avoid hitting the walls.

Now, of course, this does not prove H_7. It is a case of affirming the consequent. Moreover, Spallanzani objected to H_7 on the basis of parsimony or simplicity, that is, he did not think it was a *good* hypothesis. He said,

If these senses, separately considered, are insufficient to this purpose, according to my judgment they will be equally so when used together; for the efficacy or power of the whole is finally to be resolved into the value of its component parts, and if these parts be defective, they will transmit their defect to the union of these senses.

The only hypothesis, then, which gives clear-cut results is H_7, but it is poor. How could the bat do something with two or more organs that it cannot do with any of them separately? Spallanzani believed that it could not do so.

Eighth hypothesis to be tested (H_8)—Spallanzani then proposed a new hypothesis on the basis of the following considerations. Since neither eyes, ears, tongue, nose, or touch are separately the condition of guided flight ($H_1 \ldots H_6$ are false), and "all taken together" (H_7) is a poor hypothesis, then there might be "some new organ or sense which we do not have and of which, consequently, we can never have any idea." This is obviously a poor hypothesis, for there is no way to test it; it is fruitless, amounting to no more than an admission that bats do guide themselves in darkness by using a power human beings cannot understand.

And there the problem rested for a century and a half. The established facts that we would not have had if Spallanzani had not used good (but false) hypotheses are: (1) that bats without sight, taste, or touch-sense still have the ability to avoid obstacles; (2) that animals with plugged ears or plugged noses sometimes have this ability and sometimes do not; (3) that animals with none of these senses have lost the ability. The explanation of these facts had to await the twentieth century, when scientists had gained more knowledge of the physics of sound and could thus make use of an hypothesis unthinkable in the eighteenth century.

Ninth hypothesis to be tested (H_9)—An analogy, unthinkable in Spallanzani's time, provided a new hypothesis. Hartridge, an English scientist, "recalled the use of sound-detecting devices used in the War of 1914-1918, and proposed that bats hear reflections of their high-pitched cry and thus inform themselves of the location of obstacles," much in the way that a ship can locate a submarine by sending sound-vibrations into the water and picking up their echoes.

This hypothesis fitted all the facts that were consistent with the other hypotheses, and in addition, it fitted the facts that were renegade instances for H_5 and H_6, for both the respiratory organs and the ears are required by this hypothesis—one to be the transmitter of the signals and the other to be the receiver. In addition, this hypothesis is simpler than H_7 because it restricts attention to only two of the five sense organs, and it is better than H_8, for although Spallanzani could not have imagined such a sensory process, the advance of science had taken this kind of explanation out of the realm of mystery. There was one apparent fact that this hypothesis did not fit: the apparent silence of the bats while flying. But it is known now that there are sounds that are inaudible to the human ear although some other animals can hear them, and such supersonic sounds can be detected by suitable electrical instruments. This objection, therefore, is not serious provided it can be shown that bats do make supersonic sounds that can be detected instrumentally. To test this new hypothesis (H_{10}), which is a modification of Hartridge's, we turn to three experiments of Griffin and Galambos:

O_7: Tie the snout of the bats so that they can emit no sound. This plus H_{10} leads us to expect that the bats will not be able to guide themselves. This is actually observed.

O_8: *Very carefully repeat* the experiment under O_5 on plugging the ears of the bats. If great care is taken to prevent any sounds from being heard by the bat, then this experiment with H_{10} would lead us to expect that all bats would behave like the eleventh bat in Spallanzani's experiment. This was observed. (The renegade instance was the significant one.)

O_9: Use an instrument that will convert inaudible supersonic sounds into audible sounds. This with H_{10} leads us to expect that sounds will be heard while the bats are in flight, and that no sounds will be heard under the conditions of O_7. This is the crucial experiment. Galambos writes,

We found [supersonic sounds] to be emitted by more than one hundred bats of four different species . . . The supersonic cries, moreover, usually appear entirely independently of the audible cry and consist of a band of frequencies in the region of fifty thousand cycles.[3]

---

[3] Robert Galambos, "Flight in the Dark: A Study of Bats," *The Scientific Monthly*, Vol. LVI, No. 2, (February, 1943), pages 155-162, at page 159. Evidence is presented in this article that bats are able to respond to as well as emit supersonic sounds.

And under the conditions of O_7, no supersonic sounds are detected.

Conclusion—H_{10} fits all the observed facts and leads to the discovery of new ones. It is the only hypothesis we know that is consistent with all of them. Hence H_{10} is said to be verified by the process of elimination and convergence of evidence.[4]

BIBLIOGRAPHY

Beck, Lewis White, "The Distinctive Traits of an Empirical Method," *Journal of Philosophy*, Vol. XLIV, No. 13 (June 19, 1947), pages 337-344.

Benjamin, A. Cornelius, *An Introduction to the Philosophy of Science*. New York: The Macmillan Company, 1937.

Bronstein, D. J., Krikorian, Y. H., and Wiener, P. P. (eds.), *Basic Problems of Philosophy*. New York: Prentice-Hall, Inc., 1947. Part 4.

Cohen, Morris R., and Nagel, Ernest, *Introduction to Logic and Scientific Method*. New York: Harcourt, Brace, and Company, Inc., 1934. Chapters 5 and 11.

Dewey, John, *How We Think* (1910). Boston and New York: D. C. Heath and Company, 1933.

Jevons, William Stanley, *The Principles of Science*. London: Macmillan and Company, Ltd., 1877.

Kattsoff, L. O., "The Role of Hypothesis in Scientific Investigation," *Mind*, n.s., Vol. LVIII, No. 230 (April, 1949), pages 222-227.

Larrabee, Harold A., *Reliable Knowledge*. Boston: Houghton Mifflin Company, 1945.

Miller, David L., "Explanation vs. Description," *Philosophical Review*, Vol. LVI, No. 3 (May, 1947), pages 306-312.

Porterfield, Austin L., *Creative Factors in Scientific Research*. Durham, N. C.: Duke University Press, 1941.

Wertheimer, Max, *Productive Thinking*. New York: Harper & Brothers, 1945.

---

[4] Many other simple examples of scientific research that are interesting material for this kind of methodological analysis can be found in James B. Conant's *Science and Common Sense* (New Haven, Conn.: Yale University Press, 1951), and in I. Bernard Cohen's *Science the Servant of Man* (Boston: Little Brown and Company, 1948).

QUESTIONS AND TOPICS FOR DISCUSSION

1. Read selections from Bacon's *Novum Organum*. How does his account of scientific method differ from the one outlined in this chapter.

2. The criticism is made that an experiment affirms a consequent and that science is therefore based upon a logical fallacy.

   (*a*) Show how the argument of the text answers this objection. Do you believe this answer is adequate?

   (*b*) Evaluate the following answer to this criticism: when you say, "If atoms exist, then these and these experimental results will be obtained; and they are obtained; therefore atoms exist," you are indeed affirming a consequent. But that is not what the scientist says. He says, "If you obtain such and such results, then atoms exist, and you do obtain these results; therefore atoms do exist." Therefore he is affirming an antecedent, and this is valid.

3. Comment on the following statements by famous scientists about their method:

   (*a*) "Others will tell you to try to prove you are right, but I say try to prove you are wrong." Pasteur.

   (*b*) "I make no hypotheses." Newton.

   (*c*) "I didn't think; I investigated." Sir Alexander Fleming, describing his discovery of penicillin.

   (*d*) "Students of the natural sciences . . . possess a healthy disbelief in bare logic. They like to see logical deductions verified by experiment." Gunnar Dahlberg, in *The Scientific American*, Vol. CLXXXIV, No. 1 (January 1951), page 49.

   (*e*) "As you will see . . . I have sought to arrive at the truth by a succession of facts, by eliminating, as far as possible, reasoning which is often a deceptive instrument, and by following the torch of observation and experiment." Lavoisier, in a letter to Benjamin Franklin.

   (*f*) "Never accept an experiment until it is checked by a theory." Eddington.

   (*g*) "The evidential value of any fact is an unknown quantity until the fact has been explained." W. D. Bancroft.

4. G. B. Brown (*Science, Its Method and its Philosophy.* New York: W. W. Norton & Company, Inc. 1950) reports that a high correlation was found between the number of children born in a certain region of Germany and the number of storks in that

region. How would a scientist "prove" that this is only a coincidence? What role would hypotheses play in his "proof"?

5. Discuss the obstacles to the use of the method of hypothesis and controlled observation outside the field of the sciences.

6. Compare and contrast explanation and description. Is it true that science does not tell us why things happen, but only how they happen?

7. Describe, as carefully as you can, the role of mathematics and logic in a science that must make use of experiment and observation.

8. "Experiment is observation at its best." Discuss. How is it that one of the most accurate of the sciences, astronomy, is not ordinarily considered an experimental science?

9. Comment on the following:
   (a) "Knowledge is power." Bacon.
   (b) "To know in order to foretell." Comte.
   (c) "Ye shall know the truth, and the truth shall make you free." Jesus.

5

The Laws of Nature

The purpose of the scientist is to discover the laws of nature. Science is inspired by the conception that the universe is a cosmos, not a chaos. The scientist has faith that things and events in the world can be comprehended if he can learn some law or set of laws that "govern" them, and he believes that his methods can lead to the discovery of these laws. The greatest triumphs of science are won when a law is discovered that can be illustrated in case after case and used to predict new and otherwise unexpected facts. Historians sometimes look for laws of history, by which the movements of nations and peoples can be understood and foretold. Psychologists sometimes speak as though they had discovered laws that "govern" all human acts. All such quests for laws and the success that these quests have met in many fields raise profound problems concerning the nature of the universe and of man, especially problems touching on human spontaneity, freedom, and fate. It is therefore an important task of the philosopher to examine the presuppositions, methods, results, and implications of the search for the laws of nature.

THE CONCEPT OF LAW

The scientist searches for truths that are illustrated in many cases, and is interested in a particular case only to the extent that it is an instance of or an exception to some generalization or prediction based upon a hypothesis.

We reach generalizations by abstracting, by a process of selection and neglect. An abstraction is a concept extracted from the complex object that illustrates it. "Red," "hot," and "metallic" are abstractions that I can reach beginning from the perception of a poker in a fire. I do not ordinarily experience red by itself; I experience it only as a quality or adjective of a particular thing. But by selecting the color-quality of the thing and neglecting its other qualities, I obtain the abstraction "red." By combining various abstractions, I can describe particular objects, such as "red, hot, metallic stuff."

As a scientist, I neglect the unique characteristics that an object has and attend to those characteristics that, I believe, apply generally to many other objects. In other words, I am interested in an object as a member of a class of things illustrating the same abstraction over and over again.

A law of nature is a specific kind of combination of abstractions. It is a statement that an instance of some specific abstraction is always associated with, or identical with, an instance of some other abstraction. "This poker is red-hot" is a statement of a particular fact but is not a law of nature. But "All metallic substances, when heated, give off a red light," is a law of nature, for it says that every instance of the abstraction "hot metal" is also an instance of the abstraction "red." (Of course to be quite accurate, we should have to state *how* hot a piece of metal is when it begins to glow red; to do this we must measure the degree to which metal is an instance of the abstractions "temperature" and "emitter of radiation.")

The most important laws of nature are those that mathematically relate measurable instances of one abstraction to measurable instances of another. Such laws are called functional laws, since they treat one measurable quantity as a mathematical function of another. If we have instances of some abstraction and know a law relating this abstraction to others, we can predict instances of other abstractions. To take some well-known examples, Newton's law of gravitation mathematically relates the abstract properties of objects denoted by the terms "mass," "distance," and "force"; Kepler's laws relate the abstractions "distance from the sun" and "velocity of planet"; Galileo's law of falling bodies relates "distance traversed" and "time elapsed"; the Weber-Fechner law relates "strength of stimulus" and "intensity of sensation"; and the law of supply and demand relates the abstractions we call "supply," "demand," and "price."

The scientist searches for those few abstractions whose instances will be most generally or universally correlated with one another. If the scientist could discover several abstractions of which everything in the physical universe was an instance to some degree, and then discover some connection between them such that from his knowledge of the degree to which any one thing illustrated one abstraction he could predict the degree to which it would illustrate the others, he would be in possession of a supreme law of nature. Perhaps Einstein's law relating mass to energy, $E = mc^2$, is such a supreme law.

PRESCRIPTIVE AND DESCRIPTIVE LAWS

It is sometimes asked "Why do things obey the laws of nature?" This question, however, is based upon a serious ambiguity in the words "obey the law." There are some laws that can be obeyed in the literal meaning of the word, and we call them *prescriptive* laws, while other laws can only be *illustrated*. The latter kind of law is called *descriptive* law. So the question must first be answered, "Are the laws of nature prescriptive or descriptive?"

We are all familiar with prescriptive laws, laws that pre-

scribe what we should or should not do. A traffic law is such a
prescriptive law. It tells us that we should not exceed 55 miles
per hour on the highway. It is unfortunately true that such
laws are not always obeyed; men can and do break them.

Descriptive laws, on the other hand, do not tell a thing what
it ought to do, but tell us what has usually or always been
observed to happen. Galileo's law of falling bodies does not
tell the ball what it ought to do, that it ought to reach the
ground in a certain length of time, but tells us what relation
has been regularly observed between instances of the various
abstractions describing its motions. The rolling ball is presumably not the sort of thing that can know the law and then
decide to obey it, as I am the sort of being who can know the
traffic law and decide to obey it.

These two types of laws have not always been distinguished.
It has sometimes been thought that there must be a law-giver
who legislates or dictates the laws to nature, just as government gives law to the citizens. This legislative function has
usually been ascribed to God as the Divine Law-Giver. But
this inference depends upon the mistake of assuming that
because laws as prescriptive do require a prescriber, other
general statements also called laws likewise require a law-giver.
Only prescriptive laws are decreed, and only prescriptive laws
can be broken, for if a descriptive law is "broken," we have
all the evidence we need that what we thought was a law was
actually only a generalization that does not apply to all cases.
Descriptive laws are not decreed, but are "taken," taken from
the facts that illustrate them. We believe them to be illustrated
even by events we have not actually observed.

These two kinds of laws are so frequently confused, and so
many untenable consequences are drawn from this confusion,
that it is worth while to consider how this confusion may have
arisen. The French philosopher August Comte (1798-1857)
formulated the (descriptive) "Law of the Three Stages" in the
development of the human mind. At each stage in the history
of thought, he held, a specific kind of explanation is generally

considered to be suitable and adequate. In the earliest stage, which he calls the theological, "the human mind, seeking the essential nature of beings . . . supposes all phenomena to be produced by the immediate action of supernatural beings." Such a notion originates from an analogy between nature and the kind of social order in which this type of explanation flourishes, namely, one not governed by unchangeable (prescriptive) laws but by the arbitrary and capricious will of an absolute monarch. In such a society, men get ahead by cajolery and flattery; when their understanding of nature is on this level, they practice magic and intercessory prayer. Nature does not seem to them to be uniform; storms and disease and death occur for no known reason; the best protection against them is to propitiate the gods.

The Greeks, so far as we know, were the first people so impressed by the uniformity of nature that they attempted to explain it. Here perhaps their own form of government by law provided the key analogy. Order and harmony in society are brought about through obedience to laws and justice. The order and harmony of nature seem, by this analogy, to require also a natural law or natural justice. This analogy, surely one of the most portentous in the entire history of thought—even though it is a case of the confusion we are now trying to clear up—was drawn by Anaximander, who lived in the sixth century B. C. Another ancient writer, Simplicius, summarized Anaximander's doctrine concerning the events in nature and the changes that things undergo:

And from what source things arise, to that they return of necessity when they are destroyed; for they suffer punishment and make reparation to one another for their injustice according to the order of time, as [Anaximander] says in somewhat poetical language." [1]

Poetical language though it be, it marks a great advance over the more primitive notion that there is no real order in

---

[1] Quoted from *Selections from Early Greek Philosophy*, page 62. (Milton C. Nahm, ed.). New York, F. S. Crofts and Company, 1935.

nature, and that what happens occurs because of the inscrutable will of a god. Anaximander represents the stage of thought
that Comte calls "metaphysical," at which "the mind supposes,
instead of natural beings, abstract forces, veritable entities
[reified abstractions] inherent in all beings, and capable
of producing all phenomena." We are not entirely beyond this
stage of thought when we say, for instance, that an apple falls
to the ground "because of gravity" or that the velocity of the
earth is 19 miles per second "because of" Kepler's law.

We reach the third stage, the positive or scientific, when we
clearly understand the difference between the two kinds of
law and no longer confuse them, when we do not trouble
ourselves about unknown causes of things behind the phenomena we observe, and seek only to describe (preferably in
mathematical equations) what we do observe. A scientific law
reached at this level is only a statement of

. . . invariable relations of succession and resemblance. . . . What
is now understood when we speak of an explanation of facts is simply the establishment of a connection between single phenomena
and some general facts, the number of which continually diminishes
with the progress of science. [2]

According to this conception, a law is only a statement of a
"schedule of observations," as one of Comte's followers called
it. It is like a railroad timetable that tells us that five minutes
after a train arrives from Washington another regularly leaves
for Boston. That is all we need to know about trains in order
to plan a trip; we do not need to know whether the trains are
propelled by steam or electricity, nor do we need to know the
name of the engineer. Comte believed the same thing to be
true of the laws of nature. The schedule of possible observations is all we can know and all we need to know in order to
predict and prepare for future events. *Savoir pour prévoir* was
the motto of Comte's positivism.

---

[2] Auguste Comte, *The Positive Philosophy* (1830) Vol. I, page 2. (Harriet
Martineau, trans., London: John Chapman, 1853).

THE STATUS OF LAWS

This clears up the ambiguity in the question, "Why do things "obey' the laws of nature?" But it does not answer it. We still want an answer to the question, "Why are the specific things in the universe *describable* as instances of general laws?" Laws are statements of specific relations among classes or instances of abstractions, and we still do not know why things, again and again, illustrate the same relations among their properties and actions.

This question has had a long history, and it cannot be said that it has been solved to the satisfaction of many philosophers even today. But we shall consider three possible solutions.

Plato, as we saw in Chapter 3, believed that knowledge is more than perception, which presents only particular objects to the mind. In knowing, Plato believed, we must know how to find and apply and interrelate abstract terms that have many instances presented in perception, and not just sense the one unique, ineffable, and irrepeatable object or event before the individual. The abstract terms, he believed, must also have a denotation. There must be a kind of entity to which they refer, but an entity not given to the senses as a particular. These entities he called "ideas" or "forms," and later philosophers have called them "universals." "Blue" is a universal term applying to all particular blue things. "Blue" is not just an adjective for *them,* but a name for that character by virtue of which blue things are blue and not of some other color. That which is named by the word "blue" might be called "the blue" of "blueness." The blue or blueness is a universal, for some a real being named by the adjective "blue" but not existing as a particular thing at some particular time or place.

According to Plato, the system of universals known by abstraction and reasoning is metaphysically more real than the particular things we know by our senses. The latter change and perish, while the universals are permanent or eternal. The system of universals can be known by reason, and with reasonable knowledge of this system we can understand and explain the particular connections among the instances of universals present in the world of sense experience. Plato seems to have believed that the universals stand in necessary mathematical and logical relations to one another, and that God used this world of intelligible universals as a kind of model in creating the world of changing particular things that illustrate their logical connections with one another. Sometimes he goes so far as to suggest that the intelligible world of ideas or universals is the only real world, and that the world we see about us is only an illusory reflection or shadow of the real world. Other philosophers, and usually Plato himself, did not go this far, but the closest followers of Plato did hold that universals are real and not mere abstractions in our mind, and for that reason they are called "Platonic realists."

It is easy to see that the realist will take a different attitude toward the status of laws in the universe from those who do not believe that there is any "blue" except the blue of particular blue objects. The Platonic realist holds that the laws of nature are parts of reality, superior to the particular things in nature. He can thus consistently hold that there is a legitimate sense in which we can say that the things in nature *obey* and not merely *illustrate* the laws. Things are what they are because of their participation in the realm of universals; the universals stand in logical and mathematical relationships to each other; hence the things we observe must stand in such relations; the abstractions we make from them must be related logically or mathematically to each other.

Other philosophers, both in Plato's time and since, challenged Platonic realism. They held that it was a poor hypothesis; it "duplicated" nature instead of explaining it. One does not understand the connection between the heat of the poker and its color a bit better when told that in the realm of Platonic ideas, "the hot" is related to "the red" universally and necessarily; one should never have known even this if one had not observed specific cases of heated objects beginning to glow. The realm of Platonic universals was attacked by Ockham with his "razor" (see page 84). The philosophers who agreed with Ockham said that the only things that exist are particular or individual objects, and that universals are only fictions we make by abstraction, for the sake of classifying similar things together. A universal, for these philosophers, is only a name, and they are hence called *nominalists* (from Latin, *nomen* = name). For this school of philosophers, only particulars are real, and a law of nature is only a correlation of abstractions that are, as it were, shorthand expressions of a great variety of individual similar objects. A law of nature for the nominalist is what the positivists said it was—a timetable telling us when one particular perception or instance of an abstraction will occur with respect to other perceptions. Laws are not metaphysically real beings explaining what we observe; they are simply logical or mathematical connections found among particular things and holding more or less generally in similar cases.

Nominalism usually appears to us nowadays to be more plausible than Platonic realism, for most people have great difficulty in conceiving how any universal can be objectively real; hence they are easily convinced that nominalism is true, and nominalism is a conviction of our "common sense." But nominalism makes the process of classification and description appear arbitrary and irresponsible, because it does not render intelligible the fact that our perceptions sometimes do and sometimes do not resemble one another. Nominalists cannot even try to explain why the relations among instances of abstractions are constant when the instances themselves vary; they just tell us that they are constant. If the laws are laws connecting universals, and universals are only abstractions in our minds, then the laws seem to be only in our mind, and it becomes rather difficult to see why things outside the mind should even illustrate laws within it.

Philosophers have usually escaped from this quandary either

by becoming idealists [3] or by finding some middle ground between Platonic realism and nominalism. In this chapter we shall consider only the latter route of escape. The middle ground between an extreme form of Platonism and nominalism was worked out by Aristotle, and his theory is generally called *conceptualism*. According to it, there is no such thing as a bare, unique, and ineffable particular, nor is there any such entity as a real universal standing in splendid isolation. Everything that exists is a particular conjunction of content (which Aristotle called "matter") and form or properties. The form does not stand alone, nor is it limited to any particular thing; it may be illustrated in many particular things. A particular thing is a *this*. But with respect to any particular thing, we can always ask *what* it is. The nominalists tended to say that the concrete particularity of a thing (its *thisness*) is all it really is, and everything about it (its *whatness*) is only in our minds. The Platonic realists, on the other hand, tended to say that it is merely an instance of *whatness,* and the *this* is merely a particular manifestation in time of a *what* (or a form).

Consider how a conceptualist would deal with my dog. There is admittedly something unique and ineffable about my dog. She is precisely the dog she is, and not some other dog more or less like her. She has her own history, which is intertwined with my own, and I will accept no substitute for her, however like her that substitute might be. All these unique and particular features are her *thisness,* and they are what I am usually concerned with when I am dealing with her as an individual. They are, in fact, what is denoted by the proper name that I have given her and that I do not use for any other dog. But she also has real characteristics that are not unique to her, her *whatness,* the kind of dog she is. She is an animal, in the generic sense that a starfish is also an animal. She is a Dalma-

---

[3] Idealism will be considered in Chapter 10. But this is the proper place to point out that the idealism discussed there (Berkeley's) is nominalistic in its theory of universals and in its theory of scientific knowledge very close to positivism.

tian, in the specific respect that thousands of other dogs are Dalmatians. In order to "understand" her, I must be acquainted with her as a unique individual; I must know her in the way the French call *connaître* and the Germans call *kennen*. But in order to describe her and explain her behavior or treat her when she is injured, this kind of unique knowledge focused directly and exclusively on her as a *this* does not suffice. I must know the universal terms that apply to other dogs as well as to her, and see and state their connections in ways that others can understand on the basis of their experience with dogs. I must know her in the sense of the French *savoir* or the German *wissen*.

When you know she is a Dalmatian, then all your knowledge of other Dalmatians can be brought to bear to determine your expectations of her future behavior; when you know merely that her name is "Braxza," you do not thereby know anything else about her at all. But when you know that she is a Dalmatian ("Dalmatian" being a universal), the conceptualist rightly says that you do not know the universal in complete isolation from all embodiment in particular objects and specific times and places, nor when you know *her* do you know her merely as a brute fact, a mere *this*. In either case, you know some very important universals, and you know them as applying to her. But you do not know anything about a metaphysical world that includes Dalmatian-ness but, unfortunately, no particular Dalmatians.

The conceptualist answers the question as to how things "obey" laws, then, by saying that there are no absolutely unique, ineffable things, and absolutely universal and transcendent laws that could be impressed upon things perhaps only by an act of God. Rather, a thing, by virtue of being an instance of some specific *kind* of thing, illustrates specific universals and their specific relations to each other by its very nature. By studying particular things, which are instances of groups of universals embodied in a content, we can state the relations between things and the properties and actions of things *as if* these relations held between transcendent real universals and constituted laws that the things must "obey." But, when properly understood, these laws are seen to be what they are because the things behave as they do and regularly evince the same pattern of universals. Far from being isolated from the world of things to which it applies and which it seems to "govern," a law is abstracted from the things that illustrate it.

Laws can, indeed, be stated as definitions of things that "obey" them. To take a simple illustration, consider the notion of force. We have the experience of force when we push on an object, and we notice that the heavier a body is, the more we must push on it to make it move, and that the faster we accelerate it, the more we have to push. There seems to be some rough connection between force, mass, and acceleration. But we may, as the physicist does, *define* force as equal to mass times acceleration ($f=ma$). Thenceforth no one has to ask whether some future force will vary exactly as mass and acceleration and, if so, why things "obey" this law. The law, as it were, has been "built into" the things by definition. If in some case a physical object seemed not to illustrate the law, we should correct our estimate of its mass or acceleration until it did illustrate the law $f=ma$.

INDUCTION AND THE UNIFORMITY OF NATURE

This is all very well, you may say, but we still do not know that future events will be like past cases. Certainly, you may grant, $f=ma$, and if something is not ma, then by definition, it is not f, but that still does not show that we can count on there being future cases of $f=ma$ instead of something different from that, such as a felt force being estimated as m^2a. *What gives us reason to believe that the descriptive statements or laws we made on the basis of our past experience are dependable as a basis for predicting future observations?* This is our final formulation of the ambiguous question, "Why do things 'obey' the laws of nature?"

It does not suffice simply to define things in such a way that if they do not obey laws, they are "renegade instances." This process of definition does nothing to suggest that our definition of force as equal to mass times acceleration or of a Dalmatian as a dog of such and such a kind will be illustrated in the future and that an equally good definition of a unicorn will have no illustrations. Our problem at this point is not solved by rational definition, but by induction.

Bacon reacted perhaps too strongly against the medieval emphasis upon rational thought. He believed that the science of the Middle Ages was long on theory and hypothesis, but short on fact. He proposed, as we have seen, to direct attention to observed facts and to encourage men to gather more and more facts, confident that when enough facts were available, it would be possible to generalize them into universal laws. This procedure is known as induction—the inference from particular cases to general propositions about all cases. It is illustrated, for instance, in inferring that all crows are black from the observation of many black crows and the failure to observe crows that are not black. In common experience we use such inference at every moment of life whenever we act out of habit; Macaulay said that an infant learns by Baconian induction to expect milk from his mother instead of his father. The rules of sound induction were formulated by Bacon and David Hume, and were elaborated by John Stuart Mill in his celebrated *System of Logic* (1843).

Induction alone will not, however, lead to scientific knowledge. Merely observing apples falling in his garden would not have led Newton to the law of gravity. He grasped, as a hypothesis, the notion of a universal force of gravity having a specific relation to mass and distance, and found that the motions of the moon illustrated the law just as well as the fall of the apple. But it may be asked "What gave him the confidence that the motions of apples and the moon would *continue* to illustrate the law?" If they do not, labor is wasted in establishing such a "law."

The answer to this question is: the sound application of an inductive method. He believed that his observations justified applying his law to events he had not yet observed. We know that he succeeded in doing this; the discovery of Neptune was one of the most impressive consequences of the application of Newtonian laws. We also know that if one is careless in making an induction, as in "jumping to a conclusion" or "neglecting negative instances," he will not get generalizations that will bear up in the face of future experience.

But what justification is there for *any* inductive method, even the most careful? Why, or to what extent, does knowledge about the past justify us in making predictions about the future? David Hume wrote the chief philosophical inquiry into this question.

Hume

David Hume (1711-1776) was a Scotch philosopher, historian, and writer on ethics, politics, and religion. While still less than 30 years old, he wrote his *Treatise of Human Nature*, which, as he said, "fell dead-born from the press." Later, in 1748 when he had become famous, he wrote his *Enquiry Concerning Human Understanding*, in which he gave a more popular presentation of some of the central doctrines of the earlier and more technical *Treatise*. We shall discuss his examination of the problem of causation and induction as he presented it in the *Enquiry*.[4]

Kinds of knowledge—Hume begins by distinguishing two kinds of "objects of human reason or inquiry." They are either *relations of ideas*, or *matters of fact*. By the former he means truths "discoverable by the mere operation of thought, without dependence on what is anywhere existent in the universe" (page 116). To use the technical language of philosophy, such

---

[4] The most convenient editions of the *Enquiry* are in *Hume's Theory of Knowledge* (David C. Yalden-Thomson, ed. Edinburgh: Thomas Nelson and Sons, 1951), and *Hume Selections* (Charles W. Hendel, Jr., ed. New York: Charles Scribner's Sons, 1927). Page references are to the Hendel edition.

truths are *a priori*, known in advance of any particular sense experience. Hume does not mean that these truths would be known to us if we had had no experience at all—then we would not even be conscious. He does mean that the knowledge that we have of such truths is not dependent upon our having made any specific observations of a particular object of sense experience. The truths of mathematics, he believed, are known in this way.[5] We can see by logic that a theorem in geometry is true if the axioms are true and if no error is made in deduction; it could not "help" being true. For instance, I know that the interior angles of a triangle are equal to two right angles not because I have ever measured them (if I had, the statement, "All triangles have their interior angles equal to two right angles" would be known as only probably true), but because, given the postulates of Euclid's geometry, the equality logically follows. Hume thinks that the knowledge we get in this way is only abstract and formal; because it does not *depend* on "what is anywhere existent in the universe," it may not *apply* to anything in the universe, either. There may be no real object corresponding to this kind of "knowledge." Reason merely tells us that if the axioms are true, then the theorems are true; it does not tell us that there are things in the actual universe (say, real straight lines) to which the axioms apply. Hence we cannot be sure that this kind of "knowledge" is anything more than an analysis of concepts that are fictional instead of descriptive of things in the actual world.[6]

Matters of fact, on the other hand, are truths that cannot be demonstrated by logic. Our knowledge of them depends upon something more than logic—it depends upon experience. The proposition, "It is now raining," happens at this moment to be

---

[5] Cf. above, pp. 31, 67.

[6] Hume's argument here is relevant to the conception of law mentioned at the end of the last section—that a law *defines* the object and therefore *must* be illustrated or "obeyed" by it. Thus it was suggested that $f = ma$ will always be obeyed because by f we *mean* ma. Hume would say, "Yes, if there *is* a force in the sense defined, it will, by definition, equal ma; but the definition $f = ma$ does not imply that such forces will actually occur in the real universe."

true; but it would not be illogical, in the sense of breaking any rule of formal logic, to say, "It is not raining." The way to find out whether it is raining is not to dispute about logic, but to look out the window. Now, of course, I may be wrong in saying that it is raining; I may make a mistake in perception and see only water dripping from the trees. But if we take the usual precautions against error, looking is better than reasoning when it is a question of the momentary state of observable affairs or matter of fact at the present moment. Observation does not give us the demonstrative certainty we have of the truths of reason, but it gives us something that knowledge of the truths of reason alone could never give us—evidence about the present actual situation in some part of the real world.

We are never satisfied, however, with knowledge merely of the here and now. Knowledge is useful to us only if it can be generalized so that we can count upon it in the future. We are usually interested in momentary matters of fact only as evidence of what to expect in the future. We must then investigate with Hume some sentences that seem to tell us what *will* happen.

Knowledge of the future—Consider the sentence, "The sun will rise tomorrow." This is probably true; we ordinarily say it is certainly true; neither Hume nor any other sane man, perhaps, has ever seriously doubted it. But we cannot demonstrate it merely by the laws of logic. "The sun will not rise tomorrow," is just as certainly false, but it does not in the least infringe any rule of formal logic. Moreover, it is not a fact of observation, either, for our observations are of today, not of tomorrow. How then can we be as sure of it as we seem to be?

Someone might propose to prove it by the following argument:

Events of Kind *a* are always followed by events of Kind *b*.
Sunsets are events of Kind *a*, and sunrises are events of Kind *b*.
Therefore, since the sun has set today, it will rise again.

But how do we know these premises? The first of the premises is the law of causation, and the argument does not show how we can be sure, or whether we can be sure, that there are any classes of events such that a member of the first class *is* invariably followed by a member of another specific class. We also need to understand what ground, if any, there is for asserting the second of the premises. No one doubts that every sunset has, up till now, been followed by a sunrise; [7] but the question is whether sunsets are events of one class and sunrises are events of another class such that members of the latter invariably follow the occurrence of members of the first class. I can often be sure that some events are *not* related in this way. By careful observation and induction I can determine, for instance, that "full moon" and "fair weather" are not related as *a* and *b*; how can I be sure that sunsets and sunrises are related in this way?

We have, then, two questions: Do we know, and if so how do we know, that there are events of Kind *a* and Kind *b*? Do we know, and how do we know, that sunrises and sunsets are respectively of these kinds?

Analysis of the idea of causation—The first of these sentences involves a law of causation. It states what is ordinarily phrased, "Same cause, same effect." The idea of causation is that of necessary connection of events in time. That is, it is the notion that the prior event has not merely been found in the past to be conjoined to a specific kind of subsequent event, but that it is *necessarily* conjoined to it. If this were not so, the idea of causation would not in the least help us to make a transition from the sentence, "Such-and-such events in the past have always been followed by such-and-such other events," to the premise that we need for the argument, namely, "Such-and-such events are necessarily followed by the same kinds of

---

[7] We do not say, of course, that the sunset itself is the cause of the sunrise, but because of their invariant sequence, we believe that they are in some way causally related (that is, as effects of a common cause).

events that have followed them in the past." If a connection is necessary, it will be the same regardless of whether it is about the past, present, or future; only if it is necessary can we be sure it will apply to the future. The causal principle seems therefore to express a necessary truth, for otherwise we would not feel sure, as we do, that it will apply to future cases.

This is the analysis of the idea of causation as it is involved in the first premise we use in predicting or attempting to demonstrate that the sun will rise. How does this idea come to us? Can the premise be proved? These are Hume's questions. And if Hume's classification of knowledge is correct, there can be only two possible sources and justifications of the causal concept: either reason or experience.

What is the source of this idea?—Hume shows first that it does not arise from and is not justified by pure reason. His argument for this is very simple. If, he says, our knowledge of causation came from reason, we could by reason determine what would be the consequence of any given cause prior to any experience of its particular effect.[8] But we cannot do this:

> Present two smooth pieces of marble to a man who has no tincture of natural philosophy; he will never discover that they will adhere together in such a manner as to require great force to separate them in a direct line, while they make so small a resistance to a lateral pressure.[9]

> Were any object presented to us, and were we required to pronounce concerning the effect, which will result from it, without consulting past observation, after what manner, I beseech you, must the mind proceed in this operation? It must invent or imagine some event, which it ascribes to the object as its effect; and it is plain that this invention must be entirely arbitrary. The mind can never possibly find the effect in the supposed cause, by the most accurate

---

[8] Hume has perhaps made an error here. Reason might (in some way Hume did not anticipate) justify the *principle* of causation yet leave the determining of the specific effect of a specific cause to experience. This is, in fact, the conclusion of the German philosopher, Immanuel Kant (1724-1804), whose answer to the question of the justification of induction in many respects resembles the one we shall attempt in the next section.

[9] David Hume, *op. cit.,* page 118.

scrutiny and examination. For the effect is totally different from the cause, and consequently can never be discovered in it.[10]

If this argument is valid (see footnote 8), we are left with only the second alternative. The principle of causation must arise from experience. Following out this alternative, Hume tries to see how experience might have produced it.

But Hume also finds that there is no objective experience that can give us the idea. All that our experience can teach us is that events of a certain kind have usually or always been followed by events of another specific kind. Observe, to take Hume's own example, one billiard ball hit another. We say, "The motion of the first is the cause of the motion of the second." But what do we actually *observe?* Only that the motion of the first billiard ball is followed by the motion of the other when the two come in contact. We do not *see* that the first *makes* the second move. We do not *see* the truth expressed in the subjunctive sentence, "If the first ball had not hit the second, the second would not have moved." We do not *see* that the second *had* to move when the first hit it. We see merely what happens in a given case; we do not see what must invariably or necessarily happen in all cases. We see the conjunction and sequence of events; we do not see causal necessity.

Even common sense tells us that the case we observe might have been simply a coincidence, and that we should not make an induction from one event to all events. Too often we think one event is the cause of another, only to discover later that the connection was a coincidence. To prevent an easy error at this point, one says, "Do it again." So we repeat the experiment. Let us suppose that the same thing happens again. It would ordinarily be said, when this had been done a fair number of times with the same result, that we had proved that the first ball caused the second one to move.

While recognizing that this is what we ought to do before pronouncing a judgment that one thing is the cause of another,

[10]*Ibid.,* pages 119-120.

Hume will not allow us to jump to the conclusion that such an induction proves a necessary connection. For if we could not observe causality in the first instance, how can we observe it in the second or the n-th instance if the second or the n-th is "just like" the first? We obviously could not. And if the succeeding events are *not* "just like" the first, then what is it in the later experiments that makes them different from the first? If there is any difference, that is a sign that the experiment is not being repeated carefully enough, for we should use only repeatable cases in our inductions and generalizations. If they are not alike, we do not make any induction; and if they are alike, we cannot observe anything in the later that we did not also observe in the earlier, and we did not observe causation in the earlier.

Thus we are faced with a dilemma, and we seem blocked in either direction. Yet the fact remains that we do draw the conclusion that one thing causes another when the observations are repeated, while we might not (and usually ought not) do so from a single case. From this fact, Hume draws one conclusion, and asks one question.

The conclusion is this: experiences, no matter how often repeated, cannot give rise to the universal principle necessary for a logical demonstration that the future will be like the past. We cannot in any way empirically justify the inference from, "Up to now this has always happened," to the causal principle, "This will inevitably happen." The causal principle may very well be true, and prudent men like Hume will act as if it is. But experience cannot give us an absolute justification for it.

The question is this: granting that there is no rigorous justification for the belief, why (that is, for what psychological reasons) do we have the belief in the causal principle? In answering this question, Hume points out something that may have been overlooked in saying, "If we cannot infer causation from a single observation, we cannot infer it from a series of observations just like the first." For, he says, the subsequent cases are never *subjectively* just like the first, even if the events observed are as nearly alike as skill in experimentation can make them. Even if the *events* are alike, the *experiences* are not; in fact, the more the events are alike, the less alike are our experiences in one respect—the later experiences include a *difference in expectation.* We see the second case in the light of the first. After several such cases, we fall into the habit of expecting the second billiard ball to move, and the more often we observe this event, the stronger is our habitual or customary expectation. Man, says Hume,

. . . immediately infers the existence of one object from the appearance of the other. Yet he has not, by all his experience, acquired any idea or knowledge of the secret power by which one object produces the other; nor is it, by any process of reasoning, he is engaged to draw this inference. But he still finds himself determined to draw it: And though he should be convinced that his understanding has no part in the operation, he would nevertheless continue in the same course of thinking. There is some other principle which determines him to form such a conclusion. This principle is Custom or Habit. . . . All inferences from experience, therefore, are effects of custom, not of reasoning.[11]

[The belief in causation] is an operation of the soul, when we are so situated, as unavoidable as to feel the passion of love, when we receive benefits; or hatred, when we meet with injuries. All these operations are a species of natural instincts, which no reasoning or process of thought and understanding is able either to produce or prevent.[12]

The uniformity of nature as a hypothesis

"Custom," "faith," "habit," and "instinct" usually connote something emotional. When adduced as a ground of belief, these words suggest that the belief is not quite certain and is held on insufficient grounds. Yet such grounds are those Hume proposes as the only justification for the causal principle and its corollary, the uniformity of nature and the applicability of scientific laws to cases not yet observed.

The assumptions that we need for rendering induction in-

---

[11] *Ibid.,* pages 134-135.
[12] *Ibid.,* pages 136-137.

telligible and defensible are not propositions that men could have stumbled upon by habit or by watching billiard balls, nor can they be demonstrated by formal logic. There are two of these propositions that, taken together, constitute the proposition that nature is uniform. The first is the principle of causation, which may be stated equally well in either of two forms: (1) events of Kind a are usually or always followed by events of Kind b; or (2) any instance of Abstraction a is associated with an instance of Abstraction b. The second is the principle of limited variety: the Kinds of events a and b or Abstractions a and b, are limited in number but unlimited in scope of application or denotation.

Even if in some way we knew with absolute certainty that the first principle were true, it alone would not permit us to say that nature must present uniformities that could be discovered by induction and formulated as laws applicable to future cases, because it *might* be the case that every class of events had few members or only one member (every event absolutely unique), or that every abstraction had only one illustration. In a world in which that was the case, it might still be true that "same causes produce same effects," but the events in the world would be of such infinite variety that the so-called "same cause" would never recur, even approximately. The second of the principles provides the other condition needed for a justification of induction by saying that the classes of events and the classes of properties concerned have many members. Thus the first principle, which states that relations among these classes and properties are constant, has some material for repeated application.

These principles, which constitute the thesis of the uniformity of nature, are not demonstrable by formal logic, nor can we say that experience proves them, although experience does illustrate them (or has, up till now). Let us consider them, therefore, as comparable to the hypotheses we have examined earlier—hypotheses going beyond the facts of experience, yet helping us to explain those facts.

We must examine the hypothesis of the uniformity of nature to see whether it is "good." Does it fit all the facts we have? Yes, in the sense that we have no facts that demonstrate that nature is not uniform. Whenever there is an apparent lack of uniformity, when what we thought was the "same cause" did not produce the "same effect," the hypothesis that nature is uniform occasions further investigation. In such cases, we usually have found and always expect to find that what appeared to be instances of the same abstraction or "same cause" were not actually alike. At least there are no clear-cut facts against the hypothesis.[13]

Is it consistent with other hypotheses? Yes; without it there is no way to test them by making predictions of what will be observed if they are true. A world that is not at least largely uniform is a world in which no predictions could be made; and a world in which no predictions could be made is one in which no hypothesis could be confirmed.

Is it simple? Simplicity is always relative, never absolute; but it is certainly simpler, both logically and psychologically, to say, "same causes, same effects," than to say that the "same cause" will sometimes produce one effect and sometimes, under identical conditions, produce others.

Is it testable, fruitful, and explanatory? Not in the ordinary sense of these words, as we examined them in Chapter 4. Merely reiterating "Nature is uniform" will not, even if it is true, give explicit guidance towards the discovery of any of nature's more recondite uniformities such as those expressed in the laws of nature. By itself, the uniformity of nature does not explain anything; from it you cannot deduce or predict what uniformities may be found. If you tell a scientist who is interested in discovering the cause of sunspots, "Well, you know nature is uniform," you have only told him that there is a cause, but have not in the least enlightened him on the question, "What are the invariable conditions under which sunspots are formed?"

---

[13] Cf. below, page 143.

The hypothesis of the uniformity of nature, therefore, has some of the marks of a good hypothesis, but by itself it is not testable, fruitful, or explanatory. It is a hypothesis that is not put to the test, but is eminently fitted to be a collateral hypothesis. *It is*, in fact, *a member of every family of good hypotheses*, although alone neither it nor any other hypothesis is good in the sense of being testable. It is never the specific member of the family of hypotheses that we can consider proved by the success of some deduction and verification, but is always a collateral for any such hypothesis.

No verification of this hypothesis is possible, in the manner in which we have seen verified the hypothesis about how bats guide their flight. Evidence for it is indirect, and depends upon its position in a system of propositions and a family of hypotheses that we believe represent at least an approximation to the truth.

It is a unique hypothesis. Without it, no hypothesis can be verified. With it, all good hypotheses can be tested, and if it is true, the others that are true can be distinguished from those that are false. If, on the other hand, it is false, no hypothesis can be confirmed. Without it, all hypotheses become poor. There is no way of determining if *it* is false, for whenever it seems to be refuted (that is, whenever some unexpected result occurs under conditions that, we think, would have made an expected result to happen), we modify or reject the hypothesis that the specific expectation of this particular case was true about the specific things in question. To keep inquiry going, we modify or reject the specific hypothesis that led to the false prediction or add some *ad hoc* hypothesis like "experimental error" to explain the apparent lack of uniformity in nature.

Putting the matter succinctly, we cannot experimentally verify or refute the condition without which no experiment is possible. The uniformity of nature is a condition of verification, not an inference from it.

With these unique peculiarities, it does not seem to be merely a matter of "custom" or "instinct" to accept the hypothesis. It appears, on the contrary, to be eminently reasonable even though not required by formal logic. In fact, we have every reason to consider it to be *a priori*, in the sense that it is necessary for there to be scientific knowledge while it is itself not derived *from* scientific knowledge. But we must remember that the specific regularities or uniformities we call laws of nature are discovered only *a posteriori*, by observation.

Some philosophers have regarded the uniformity of nature as a self-evident axiom, indubitable to the natural light of reason or to "common sense." It has been compared to the axioms of geometry, without which nothing in geometry can be demonstrated. There is now reason to believe that not even the axioms of geometry are known by direct intuition, but that they are more properly regarded as postulates—assumptions made within a specific body of propositions not all of which can be proved. Modern geometry does not have to start with propositions that everyone can "immediately see" to be true but indemonstrable; it may and does begin with assumptions that are fruitful for the discovery and demonstration of geometrical propositions that might not have been discovered or could not be proved without them.[14]

The collateral hypothesis of the uniformity of nature resembles the axioms or postulates of modern geometry in one respect, but differs from them in another. It resembles them in that it is not a logically self-evident proposition; we can imagine a chaotic world in which it does not hold. "Nature is not uniform," is no more logically self-contradictory and absurd, and its contradictory therefore necessarily true, than, "A straight line is not the shortest distance between two points," is logically self-contradictory and its opposite therefore necessarily true. And it differs from the axioms or postulates of geometry in that they have alternatives that are logically possible and usable in scientific work. There are non-Euclidean geometries in which the well-known postulates of Euclid are not used. Such geometries, as we have seen, are perfectly valid

---

[14] Cf. above, pages 31, 67 ff.

both mathematically and logically, and only experience can tell whether our universe can better be described by one of these geometries or by the better-known Euclidean system. But the hypothesis that nature is uniform appears to have no good alternative. If you try to formulate a science in which nature is not assumed to be, at least in large measure, uniform and regular, it seems that you destroy the chance to verify any hypothesis about it.

If we assume that induction, when carefully conducted, is invalid, we shall not be able to discover, through verification of any specific hypothesis, whatever uniformities there might be. If, on the contrary, we assume that induction is justified, then we might indeed not be able to verify many hypotheses, but we should have at least an even chance of discovering any uniformities that do occur in nature. Induction, therefore, need not be justified by appealing to faith or instinct, but simply by indicating that it is a good bet. If you make this bet, you may win all the time and you will almost surely win some of the time. But if you do not make the bet, you are sure to lose all the time and miss the truths you might discover.

The principle of indeterminacy

The conclusion we have just reached may be challenged by those who are acquainted with sub-atomic physics. It is said that the motion of a sub-atomic particle is not uniform; given the same conditions in two different experiments, sometimes a particle will behave in one way and sometimes in another. Nature is apparently uniform, we are told, only because these chance variations with no inherent uniformity are statistically cancelled out in our observations of aggregates of uncounted billions of these particles.

This is indeed a serious challenge to the doctrine of the *a priori* character of the assumption of the uniformity of nature. While no one seems quite to know what is the correct interpretation of these facts, which have been summarized in what is known as Heisenberg's "principle of indeterminacy," several points should be carefully noted before we decide to give up the doctrine of the uniformity of nature or to hold that it is only an approximate statistical generalization. First, the facts in question do not show that nature is *not* uniform. They only show that we cannot now, and presumably cannot ever, determine some of the conditions that we should have to know in order to make accurate predictions of single sub-atomic events. Even if nature is completely uniform down to the last electron, the facts described in Heisenberg's principle might well be exactly as they seem to be; we cannot predict where a single particle will be at a certain time because we do not have all the facts we would need for this prediction. We do not have all the facts that we need in order to predict tomorrow's weather, but we believe that we can get them. The Heisenberg principle merely states that, in the case of sub-atomic events, we cannot ever get them.

Second, we must admit the *possibility* that, in the final analysis, nature is not uniform. This is an hypothesis that goes beyond the facts into the realm of the unknown and perhaps the unknowable, because the facts that we should have to have in order to decide this question are, according to Heisenberg and other physicists, forever hidden from us by the conditions of our experiments. If nature is not uniform, then no hypothesis about the future motions of a particular particle can be verified or refuted (or perhaps we should say that all of them can be refuted, so that we are left with no hypotheses at all). Probabilities, applied to large numbers of them, must replace certainties. But the hypothesis that nature is not uniform and that the "blame" for failure to predict the behavior of a particle lies with nature and not with the present limits of human knowledge, could become an invitation to intellectual laziness. It could, though it has not yet, become a block to inquiry. If one believes that there is no uniformity, one will relax in one's effort to find it; this is equivalent to the bad bet mentioned at the end of the preceding section. Such a belief puts a block in the way of investigation just as surely as if some

political power told the physicist, "You can't investigate the
problem of the motions of a particular sub-atomic particle because it conflicts with our ideology."

Third, in the principle of uncertainty we may have reached
an ultimate limit of knowledge. It is only honest to admit this
fact; there is no certainty that we can get the knowledge we
should like to have. But note a very significant fact in this conjecture: it suggests that the limit of knowledge of nature *lies
at the precise point where the uniformity of nature is denied.*
But within the ordinary range of our knowledge, where we are
dealing with aggregates of uncountable numbers of these unpredictable particles, the uniformity of nature is unchallenged
as a condition of any verification and induction. It is like the
situation we meet with in human affairs. We do not have the
information on which to decide when a particular man will
die; but we do know, by induction, that out of a thousand men
his age a certain number will in all probability be dead within
a certain specified length of time. We do not know where a
specific sub-atomic particle will go under the conditions of
an experiment; but we do know where the planets, which contain incredibly large numbers of such particles, will go.

HUMAN FREEDOM AND THE LAWS OF NATURE

The view of the universe as a vast mechanism acting according to inexorable laws has aroused the enthusiasm of scientists,
philosophers, and some poets, and has given them pride in the
intellect of man, which has discovered the pattern of nature.
It has given some of them an enthusiasm for the universe or
its maker, when they see how well ordered and organized it is.
But it has given many men, like Omar Khayyam, the opposite
feelings of helplessness, impotence, and unimportance:

> And that inverted Bowl they call the Sky,
>> Whereunder crawling cooped we live and die,
>> Lift not your hands to It for help—for It
> As impotently moves as you or I.

With Earth's first Clay they did the Last Man knead,
And there of the Last Harvest sowed the Seed:
And the first Morning of Creation wrote
What the Last Dawn of Reckoning shall read.

A world in which everything is caused by something earlier is a world in which human actions are, in principle as predictable as eclipses of the sun and moon. In such a world, men might believe that they are free only because they do not know the hidden causes of their actions and wishes and choices. In such a world there seems to be no place for human freedom and responsibility, and human choice and effort seem illusory and futile.

Perhaps this is the reason why so many people have heartily welcomed Heisenberg's principle of indeterminacy, since it seems to show that not even inanimate nature is as inexorably determined as was formerly believed. It seems to reveal a chink in the armor of cold, impartial, inevitable, natural necessity. But more careful inquiry is likely to shatter these hopes.

The Heisenberg principle does not apply to matter consisting of large numbers of these apparently wayward and free particles; large events are still as predictable with the Heisenberg principle as without it.

But, it has been suggested, the human body is not just the statistically evened-out aggregate of all its atomic constituents, as a block of wood presumably is. Rather, it is said, human behavior is controlled by a kind of trigger-mechanism in the synapses of the brain, where the unpredictable motion of a single electron might open or close a circuit that would cause an arm or leg to move or not to move; hence the larger motions of the body would be as unpredictable as the sub-atomic events that trigger the flow of energy to one or another part of the body. Although this may be true, it is hard to get much comfort from it. For mere unpredictable behavior is caprice, not freedom. Such action, due to the entirely fortuitous motion of a particle in my brain, would be an action for which *I* would not be responsible, for such action might just as well be incompatible with my character, responsibility, and will, as compatible with them.

Still, it has been argued, the mind or the will might exert the deciding force on the motion of the particle in question, whereas if the particle in question were rigidly determined by prior physical conditions, this would not be possible. Hence, in the little area this principle accords to indeterminacy, the will might step in as the decisive causal factor; therefore, man could be free. In such an explanation as this, one would wonder how that which is assumed to be nonphysical could exert a spatial displacement upon that which is physical; and if it can do so, there is no reason to think that this displacement could be effected only on particles whose position is previously *undetermined* by that of others. Such a hypothetical superphysical agent could just as well be an *additional* causal factor in a train of events that would *otherwise* have been exhaustively determined by earlier physical conditions.

The essential feature of this argument is really another assumption that has little to do with the mechanism of brain action and nothing to do with the Heisenberg principle. It is the assumption that the mind of man is not itself completely determined by physical or physiological factors, and that there is thus in the universe some center of indeterminacy other than those considered in the Heisenberg principle. That is to say, the Heisenberg principle neither implies nor is implied by the proposition that the will is free. Something other than the motion of sub-atomic particles must be free if there is to be human freedom.

Of course many philosophers have long agreed with the common belief that the mind is not wholly determined by physical and physiological conditions, or at least that it need not be so determined in every instance of action. Beginning with Socrates, they have said that the physical universe, which they grant is largely uniform and determined, is not the whole of reality, and that man, in his ultimate nature as a mind or soul, is not really a part of the physical universe and hence not "subject" to its laws. They see man as only partially natural, and his soul or will as superior to nature. Thus they can conclude that mind is an effective cause which from time to time can intervene in nature and change its course. By learning to control his propensities and passions, which admittedly have a physiological basis and often a compelling influence upon his thought and decision, and perhaps by availing himself of the help of God, who is the Author of Nature, man, according to this view, can use and control the natural order without becoming subject to its laws.

In this way these philosophers find an escape from the blind necessity of nature through a metaphysical assumption concerning the essence and dignity of man as being supernatural. Man, they say, is a little island of freedom in a sea of necessity. Man is free because he can break the laws of nature, although at the same time, perhaps, he follows some higher (prescriptive) law. Nature is uniform only in those places where supernatural causes issuing from man or God do not interfere with its course.[15]

Still others have held that the fatalistic consequences seen in the "reign of natural law" do not actually follow from it. They argue that man is free not because his actions are uncaused, unpredictable, or capricious, but because and to the extent that his actions follow from his own nature. Freedom, for them, is self-determination under the conditions of the laws of nature, not indeterminacy. They believe that the reign of law seems antithetical to freedom and responsibility only because we ordinarily think of man as merely an effect of alien causes and not also as himself a cause in nature.

Consider, for instance, a man in a quandary trying to decide what to do. Accepting the common view that nature is completely determined by its past states, he might say, "It doesn't matter what I do, because the future is already determined; what must happen will happen." But this view leaves out the

---

[15] This, in general, is the view of the theological dualists. Cf. pages 308-309.

very important fact that the future is determined not by all the past conditions, but by all the *present* conditions, and among these present conditions is the fact that he is now thinking, worrying, and planning. If he does worry and choose, the future will therefore be different from what it would be if he gives up. How he acts will be just as much one of the determining conditions of what happens as some event in the physical world. His feeling of helplessness, for example, may be one of the causes of the dread issue he fears, while a feeling of power might make him act and, in the course of nature, bring about a different effect without in the least infringing any of the laws of nature. When predicting the future under the assumption that there are laws of nature, therefore, we cannot use merely the laws of physics, but must see the individual man with his unique character as one of the determining conditions in spite of the fact—or, indeed, making full use of the fact—that "same causes, same effects." The effective exercise of one's own character is what these philosophers mean by freedom and reponsibility.[16]

But this answer does not seem entirely satisfactory. It amounts to this: a man is free if he can exercise or express his character and thus make a difference to the future course of events, doing so with foresight as to the consequences of his actions. But his character is itself a response to conditions for which he cannot be held responsible, for they lie in his genes, his environment, his training. In the words of Hobbes, men are indeed sometimes free to do what they wish, but they are never free in their wishes.

Another answer to the question of the place of man's responsibility in a universe in which his science is based on the principle of the uniformity of nature calls attention to the fact that the uniformity of nature is a collateral hypothesis made for the purpose of explaining how things (and people) *do* behave. It is not a prescriptive law, saying that they *must* behave this

---

[16] This view is held by many naturalists (cf. pages 442 ff), and some idealists.

way. It is not even a descriptive law, saying that they do *always* behave in this way. It is a hypothesis that we make but cannot demonstrate, and we assume it for the purpose of extending our scientific explanations and for getting along with things practically. While not in the least challenging the usefulness and validity of this principle in the explanation of nature, philosophers who give this answer say that outside the field of science we may legitimately make use of other assumptions, such as those of spontaneity and freedom.[17]

Perhaps the most typical expression of this view is in the doctrine of Kant, who, as we have seen, developed the notion that the uniformity of nature is an *a priori* postulate of science. Kant held that we organize our sense experience by the use of the hypothesis (or what he called the category) of causation, and that the resulting organization of our experience is nature as it can be studied scientifically. Nature is the world of experience, considered as a system of instances of causal laws. But, he held, the world of experience is only a systematic and organized appearance of real things we do not know, and the world of realities may have quite different laws for its own behavior. If this is so, then our entire behavior can be considered from the scientific standpoint as causally necessary in the uniformity of appearances we call nature, yet from another point of view, exactly the same behavior could be considered (although not observed) as a free expression of the reality that is not a part of the system of uniform appearances.

It is thus possible for man to consider himself as a phenomenal part of the realm of nature, and thereby subject to its laws, but also as a real being whose appearances only seem to the scientist to be causally determined.

Thus in respect to mere perception and receptivity to sensations he must count himself as belonging to the world of sense [that is, as a part of causally determined, uniform nature]; but in respect

---

[17] The metaphysical foundations for this view are developed by the idealists. Cf. Chapters 10 and 11.

to that which may be pure activity in himself . . . he must reckon himself as belonging to the intellectual world [of reality].[18]

In morality and in obedience to the (prescriptive) moral law, Kant held that man is not *reacting* to the things in the world, but is manifesting his own spontaneous activity. A man's own activity will appear to the psychologist who examines him as a special case of some uniform law that the psychologist believes the man illustrates; the psychologist will not admit that the man's act is free and spontaneous, because he, like every other scientist, uses the collateral hypothesis of uniformity. But what is good science may not be, in this instance, good morality; for the moral man in making his choice does not act on the assumption, "Whatever I do is simply a response to stimuli over which I have no control." At the moment of moral decision, man feels free. In order to exercise moral choice, he has the right, Kant believed, to make some other postulate or collateral hypothesis than that of the uniformity of nature. He has, in William James' formulation, a right to believe that which is necessary for his moral life, just as the scientist has a right to believe the uniformity of nature and any other indemonstrable postulates required in his work.

But this theory of freedom does not contradict the uniformity of nature, nor does it, like the first two theories examined in this section, say that there are *some* events, namely human actions, that occur without natural causes in a world where everything else is determined. Kant himself says,

The illusion about the contradiction [in the notion that the same behavior is both free and naturally necessitated] rests on the fact that we [do not] think of man in a different sense and relationship when we call him free from that in which we consider him as a part of nature and subject to its laws.[19]

---

[18] Immanuel Kant, *Foundations of the Metaphysics of Morals* (1785) (in *Critique of Practical Reason and other Writings in Moral Philosophy*, Lewis White Beck, trans.), page 106. Chicago: University of Chicago Press, 1949. Quoted by permission of the publisher.

[19] *Ibid.*, page 110.

Putting the same thing in another way: when we consider man scientifically, we must assume that he illustrates all the relevant laws of nature and therefore that he is completely determined; Kant himself says that human actions are, in principle, as predictable as eclipses of the sun and moon. Science is one of the ways in which we organize our experience, and the postulate of uniformity and the laws which are established under the assumption of uniformity apply to man only to the extent that we see him in the context of science, as an effect of earlier causes. Science, however, is not the only way of organizing our experience. There are other ways, which use prescriptive laws, like the laws of morality, instead of descriptive laws, like those of psychology, as integrating principles in terms of which experiences "make sense." Considered in this way, then, man can exercise his freedom in a world that is causally determined, and scientists can seek the putative causes even of the actions for which he takes full responsibility.

BIBLIOGRAPHY

Laws; induction; uniformity of nature

Cohen, Morris R., and Nagel, Ernest, *Introduction to Logic and Scientific Method*. New York: Harcourt Brace and Company, 1934.

Feigl, Herbert, and Sellars, Wilfrid S. (eds.), *Readings in Philosophical Analysis*. New York: Appleton-Century-Crofts, Inc., 1949. Part 5.

Hay, William H. "Bertrand Russell on the Justification of Induction," *Philosophy of Science*, Vol. XVII, No. 3 (July, 1950), pages 266-277.

Hospers, John, "On Explanation," *Journal of Philosophy*, Vol. XLIII, No. 13 (June 20, 1946), pages 337-356.

Lewis, C. I., *Mind and the World Order*. New York: Charles Scribner's Sons, 1927.

Mill, John Stuart, *Mill's Philosophy of Scientific Method* (Ernest Nagel, ed.). New York: Hafner Publishing Company, 1951.

Pearson, Karl, *The Grammar of Science* (1892). London: J. M. Dent & Sons, Ltd., Everyman's Library, 1937.

Poincaré, Henri, *The Foundations of Science* (George P. Halsted, trans.). New York: The Science Press, Inc., 1913.

Russell, Bertrand, *Human Knowledge, Its Scope and Limits*. New York: W. W. Norton & Company, Inc., 1948.

The problem of universals

Aristotle, *Metaphysics*, Book 1, Chapter 9; Book 13.

Carré, M. F. *Realists and Nominalists*. New York: Oxford University Press, 1946.

Dewey, John, *Experience and Nature*. New York: W. W. Norton and Company, Inc., 1929. Chapter 5.

Joad, C. E. M., "Plato's Theory of Forms and Modern Physics," *Philosophy*, Vol. VIII, no. 30 (April, 1933), pages 142-154.

Montague, William Pepperell, *The Ways of Things*. New York: Prentice-Hall, Inc., 1940. Pages 173-188.

Plato, *The Republic*. Books 6 and 7.

―― *Parmenides*. To page 135, standard pagination.

Wild, John, *Introduction to Realistic Philosophy*. New York: Harper & Brothers, 1948. Chapter 19.

Woozley, A. D., *Theory of Knowledge*. London: Hutchinson's University Library, 1949. Chapter 5.

Laws and human freedom

Baldwin, Robert C., and McPeak, James A. S., *An Introduction to Philosophy through Literature*. New York: The Ronald Press Company, 1950. Chapter 9.

Bergson, Henri, *Time and Free Will*. New York: The Macmillan Company, 1921.

Boutroux, Émile, *The Contingency of the Laws of Nature*. Chicago: Open Court Publishing Company, 1920.

Compton, Arthur H. *The Freedom of Man.* New Haven, Conn.: Yale University Press, 1935.

Hartmann, Nicolai, *Ethics* (Stanton Coit, trans.). New York: The Macmillan Company, 1932. Volume 3.

James, William, *The Principles of Psychology*. New York: Henry Holt and Company, Inc., 1890. Volume 2, Chapter 26.

Palmer, George Herbert, *The Problem of Freedom*. Boston: Houghton Mifflin Company, 1911.

Planck, Max, *Where is Science Going?* New York: W. W. Norton & Company, Inc., 1932. Chapters 4 and 5.

Ramsperger, A. G., *Philosophies of Science.* New York: F. S. Crofts & Company, 1942. Chapter 15.
Werkmeister, W. H., *A Philosophy of Science.* New York: Harper & Brothers, 1940. Chapters 8 and 12.

QUESTIONS AND TOPICS FOR DISCUSSION

1. Read an account of the medieval controversy over universals. What were some of the social and religious forces on each side of this controversy? The Renaissance has been called "the triumph of nominalism over realism." Discuss.

2. Does the notion that the laws of nature are only highly probable instead of certain make the problem of induction easier to solve?

3. Does the notion that the laws of social science are only statements of probabilities make the question of human freedom easier to answer? (Discuss the question: If it is truly a law that 80 per cent of the people with a certain personality trait will commit a crime, is human freedom less restricted than if the law stated truly that 100 per cent of the people with this trait would commit a crime?)

4. Set up a series of criteria that an alleged "law of nature" should meet. How do these criteria resemble those for a "good hypothesis"?

5. Some philosophers reject the postulate of the determinism of nature as a foundation for induction, and attempt to base induction on the theory of probability. One of them says, "We find a certain relative frequency for a series of observed events and assume that the same frequency will hold approximately for further continuation of the series." Is this assumption easier to justify than that of the strict uniformity of nature? How would Hume have attacked this point of view?

6. Discuss the statement, "The Heisenberg principle may be true, but it certainly isn't good."

7. Discuss the following statements:
   (a) "The fates guide the willing, but drag the unwilling."
   (b) "The recognition of necessity is the beginning of freedom."

8. The question, "Why do things obey the laws of nature?" is said in this chapter to be ambiguous. It is analyzed into several other less ambiguous questions. Outline the reasons and results of these various "translations" of the original question.

6

The Organization
of Science

THE INTERRELATIONS OF THE SCIENCES

A list of sciences studied in a typical American university will generally include the following departments: astronomy, biology, chemistry, geology, physics, psychology, economics, sociology, and sometimes mathematics.

These sciences are frequently classified in several groups. Astronomy, biology, chemistry, geology, and physics will usually be grouped together as "the natural sciences," and sociology, economics, and usually psychology will be listed as "social sciences." Still further break-downs in the listings may be found. Among the natural sciences, for instance, physics, chemistry, and astronomy may be put together as "exact sciences."

Most of the sciences will in turn be further subdivided. Under biology will frequently be found botany and zoology. Each of these, in turn, will be still further divided. For instance, zoology may be divided into "invertebrate zoology," "vertebrate zoology," and so on.

In such a listing of departments and courses, several things will attract attention. First, there does not seem to be any such thing as "science," but many different sciences. Second, the sciences, although highly specialized, seem to fit together into some general families, such as "natural" and "social" sciences. Third, if you examine and compare many such lists, you will see that there is a great deal of dispute about what the family relations of a specific science are. Psychology, for example, will occasionally be found among the natural sciences; and there seems to be no general agreement as to where mathematics belongs. Fourth, you will see in the courses listed under each department that the lines dividing one special science from another are not very sharp. Under chemistry, for instance, you will find courses in physical and biological chemistry, tying physics and biology respectively to chemistry; courses in social psychology will often be listed under both the department of psychology and the department of sociology.

Before attempting to discover some order in this apparent chaos, we should first consider why there are specialized sciences instead of just one big Science. An obvious reason for this is that the field of scientific knowledge is so vast that no one can survey all or even a large portion of it. To be an expert means to know a great deal about a very small sector of knowledge. This obvious fact is often mentioned contemptuously, but the contempt is not just. We need experts, and the man who is not an expert, even if he knows a great deal about a great many things, cannot build bridges, cure diseases, analyze chemical compounds, or identify bacteria. Although it is true that every man working in any science needs to know something about other sciences, and a great deal about the fundamental principles that underlie all sciences, it is also true that specialization is a condition of progress in inquiry.

There is another answer to the question. The various scientific specialties are distinguished from one another by one or both of two differences in their respective jobs. They differ from each other in *subject matter* or in the *kind of question* they ask. The first is fairly obvious: astronomy deals with the stars, geology with the earth, biology with living organisms, chemistry with chemical reactions. But even these divisions are not sharp. The earth is a planet, and is thus studied also in astronomy; living organisms are the sites of complicated chemical reactions, and are thus studied also in chemistry. Second, the sciences differ from one another in the kind of questions they ask. Biology, for instance, deals with the human organism as an animal, studying its anatomy and physiology, while sociology deals with the relation of the human organism (and occasionally lower organisms) to a group, or of one group to another. Thus both the biologist and the sociologist may deal with man, but they ask different questions about him.

When the sciences do ask questions about the same subject matter, the answers found by one science may be very important to the scientist who is asking a different sort of question. What the chemist has to say about rocks may be very important to the geologist; what the physicist says in answer to his questions about atomic structure is of the utmost importance to the chemist; what the chemist says about the composition of a tissue is essential to the biologist; and so on.

This gives us some picture of the intricate criss-crossings and interrelations of the sciences—they overlap sometimes in subject matter and sometimes in their questions, they borrow from each other, and no sharp lines can be drawn between them. Philosophers have long wished to "tidy up" this confused situation, and some of their efforts should be studied. Philosophers now generally agree that there is a kind of rough hierarchical relation among the sciences, so that we can say that some of them are more basic than the others.

Hierarchy of sciences

The general principle involved in saying that one science is basic to another is that the concepts and methods of one science are presupposed or used in the work of the other. The science that bases its investigations on the methods, concepts, and results of another science is said to be the less fundamental of the two. This does not mean that the less fundamental science is the less important; indeed, the least fundamental sciences are those that deal with human beings, and they may be the most important to us.

As an illustration of the sense in which one science is less basic than another, consider the biologist, who deals with living organism; the living organism is a complex of many organs delicately related and interbalanced by electrical and chemical forces. In order to understand and explain what he observes, the biologist must adduce some of the results of chemistry and physics, but the chemist or physicist does not have to consult the biologist before he formulates a law for his own science. Hence we say chemistry and physics are more basic than biology. (This does not mean, of course, that what the biologist discovers is of no interest to the chemist. Living beings produce many compounds the chemist has not synthesized, and the chemist can often learn much from the biologist about how they are produced and what their reactions are. But that does not mean that the laws or conclusions of chemistry are *logically* derived from the work of the biologist.)

If one science depends upon another, the more basic science is simpler and more general. It is simpler in the sense of being more parsimonious. Physics uses fewer principles and assumptions than chemistry does; it is interested in the mass and motion of objects, for instance, but not (usually) in their complex chemical composition. The laws the physicist derives are laws of motion and energy that will apply to all matter and not just to particular kinds of molecules, which interest the chemist.[1] A basic science is more general in the sense that its laws apply to a wider variety of things. The basic laws of physics are about matter of whatever kind, while the chemist has different things to say about different kinds of matter.

Using the criteria of simplicity and generality, Auguste

---

[1] But the dividing lines cannot be sharply drawn. A physicist working with isotopes, for instance, may be doing work that belongs to chemistry as much as to physics. In general, however, the statement is true.

Comte, in his *The Positive Philosophy,* arranged the sciences as follows:

1. The inorganic sciences: astronomy (including mathematics), physics, chemistry.

2. The organic sciences: physiology and "social physics" (sociology).

There are several things wrong with this classification. For instance, mathematics is certainly no more a part of astronomy than of physics. Moreover, there are serious gaps in the classification. Comte did not believe that there could be a science of psychology different from physiology on one side and sociology on the other, so he omitted it from his list. In spite of its imperfections, however, it is based upon a sound rule:

This classification marks, with precision, the relative perfection of the different sciences, which consists in the degree of precision of knowledge, and in the relation of its different branches. It is easy to see that the more general, simple, and abstract any phenomena are, the less they depend upon others, and the more precise they are in themselves and the more clear in their relations with each other.[2]

An attempt to apply to contemporary sciences the general principle used by Comte would lead, at least approximately, to the following:

1. *The formal sciences:* logic and mathematics. These sciences do not describe particular things but apply generally to all valid inferences and measurements. They deal with the "forms" of propositions and formulae and their logical and mathematical relations to each other, and not with things or their specific and observable characteristics. These sciences are completely rational and *a priori* and borrow nothing from any science of observation or experiment.

2. *The physical sciences:* physics and chemistry. These sciences deal with the energy and material relations among things, physics dealing with them simply as material objects in their energy-relations, and chemistry being concerned with them as matter of differ-

---

[2] Auguste Comte, *The Positive Philosophy,* Vol. I., page 29 (Harriet Martineau, trans.). London: John Chapman, 1853.

ent kinds, capable of being modified and transmuted by chemical reaction.

Under physics and chemistry should be listed those sciences that make use of physical and chemical principles and apply them only to specific subject matters such as the stars or the earth. These sciences are astronomy, geology, and the various branches of physics (optics, mechanics, acoustics, and so on), and of chemistry (for example, inorganic and organic chemistry).

3. *The organic or biological sciences:* biology, with its two subdivisions, zoology (dealing with animal life) and botany (dealing with plant life). There will be other subdivisions under each, according to kind of subject matter (entomology, ornithology, paleontology, and so on), or according to kind of question asked (anatomy and physiology).

4. *The social sciences:* psychology and sociology. Psychology studies the individual's response to his natural environment (where it overlaps with the biological sciences) and to other individuals in a social group (where it overlaps with sociology). Sociology is concerned with the analysis of group relations. In this scheme, economics would be considered a branch of sociology, since it deals with one specific kind of group relationship and behavior.

Some sciences will not clearly fall into any one of these types, but will overlap or be intermediate between two of them. Between Types 1 and 2 might be found some branches of applied mathematics, such as mathematical physics. Between Types 2 and 3 would fall biochemistry and biophysics. Physical anthropology, animal and human ecology, and physiological psychology might be found between Types 3 and 4.

Many scientists and philosophers believe that some one science in this hierarchy, usually physics, is so much more fundamental, universal, and explanatory than the others that all non-formal sciences should be "reduced" to it and their laws regarded as only special cases of the laws of the more fundamental science. They say that the separate sciences are only divisions of labor, that the direction of scientific progress is toward unifying them all in one science. We shall now examine this claim in one field of science.

THE RELATION OF THE BIOLOGICAL TO THE
PHYSICAL SCIENCES

There are three plausible theories of the nature of life, each
one of which has important consequences for the organization of science. The first is *mechanism,* the second *vitalism,* and
the third *emergent holism.* We shall briefly consider each and
trace its implications for the problem of the status of life in the
universe and the position of biology in the family of sciences.

Mechanism

Mechanism is, in biological theory, the view that living organisms can be exhaustively explained in terms of the hypotheses and laws of chemistry and physics.[3] No explanation will
be regarded by the mechanist as valid and complete so long as
there is any term in it (such as life, instinct) that does not likewise belong to chemistry or physics, or any laws (such as the
Mendelian laws of heredity) that cannot be seen as special
cases of, and derivable from, the established laws of chemistry
and physics. Sometimes the mechanist expresses rather a hope
than an ascertained fact with respect to the laws. He may
admit that at present the laws of biology cannot be derived
from those of physics and chemistry, but he asserts as the goal
of science that they should be derived, and he believes that
they can be derived when we have more knowledge.

The mechanist objects to two attitudes frequently taken
toward living beings. He rejects, first, the belief that the concept of purpose is valid or useful in biological inquiry. He

. . . warmly denies that there exists any such thing as purpose in
the Universe, or that events have any ulterior motive or goal to
which they are striving. [He] asserts that all events are due to the
interaction of matter and motion acting by blind necessity in ac-

---

[3] Mechanism as a biological theory is a special case of the more general
metaphysical theory of materialism, which is described and evaluated in Chapter 12. Here we are concerned with it only as a theory of life.

cordance with those invariable sequences to which we have given the name of laws.[4]

The teleological view of things (the belief that "there exists any such thing as purpose" or, more accurately, the belief that concepts of purpose have an explanatory and legitimate place in science and philosophy) is a subjective illusion. It arises from the fact that we generally think of things in relation to ourselves and evaluate them as they affect the accomplishment of what we consider to be "our purposes." But we ourselves act, according to mechanists, under the necessity of nature; not only what we do, but what we will to do, is decided by the inexorable laws of nature; as Mephistopheles, in *Faust,* says, "We believe we push; but we are pushed." What appears to us to be purposive in living organisms—for instance, the exquisite mutual adaptation of the parts of an organism to one another—is the mechanical result of the elimination of those organs or organisms that are not physiologically well balanced. We see only the results, and think that the organism was designed or developed itself for the sake of such adjustments.

Second, the mechanist rejects the idea that there is

. . . any form of existence other than those envisaged by physics and chemistry, that is to say, other than existences which have some kind of palpable material characteristics and qualities.[5]
The existing universe and all things and events therein may be theoretically expressed in terms of matter and energy, undergoing continuous redistribution in accordance with the ordinary laws of physics and chemistry.[6]

A biological organism, for the mechanist, is simply an extremely complex bundle of chemical compounds, so complicated that it is certainly difficult to resolve it into the simple constituents between which chemical and physical relations

---

[4] Hugh Elliot, *Modern Science and Materialism,* page 140. New York: Longmans, Green & Company, Inc., 1919. Quoted by permission of the publisher.
[5] *Ibid.,* page 142.
[6] *Ibid.,* page 143.

can be seen to hold. But analysis is the direction in which the sciences are and ought to be going:

> Differences in the forms of organs are accompanied by differences in their chemical composition, and . . . according to the principles of science we have to derive the former from the latter.[7]

We now know a good deal about the physiological processes of the body; we have detailed information about the chemical composition of foods, and we can trace the various changes of food into living tissue without ever coming across a "biological fact" that is not amenable to chemical explanation; indeed, most of the reactions have been duplicated in the laboratory. The best hypothesis for the biologist, therefore, seems to be that the organism is nothing but an immensely complicated chemical factory or machine. On this assumption, he can discover and has discovered many facts that would otherwise have remained unknown or unexplained. To doubt seriously the truth of this hypothesis in any particular investigation in physiology would block the way of inquiry. As with all collateral hypotheses of this kind, which give valid results only when combined with other specific hypotheses that can be tested, we do not know whether mechanism is ultimately true or not. But indisputably it is a good hypothesis and may be the best available.

Vitalism

The oldest alternative to mechanism is vitalism. This view of life, in fact, is much older than any scientific biological theory, and is probably the view of the nonscientist who uses only his common sense. (Professor C. D. Broad has said that if any man calls his brother or his cat an "ingenious mechanism," we know at once that he is either a "fool or a physiologist.") Developed as a scientific and philosophical theory by Hans Driesch (1867-1941), vitalism is a reaction against mechanism. According to Driesch, a living organism is only partially ex-

---

[7] Jacques Loeb, *The Mechanistic Conception of Life*, page 104. Chicago: University of Chicago Press, 1912.

plicable in terms of the analogy to a machine or a chemical factory; there is something else in the organism that is not describable in terms of chemistry and physics, and the laws of its behavior are not physical or chemical but teleological.

Driesch observed that if the eggs of a sea urchin are cut in two during the early stages of growth, two organisms with all the proper organs are formed. He argued that if the machine theory were correct, imperfect organisms should have been formed (assuming that the egg lived). If you cut an automobile in two, not more than one part of it will still run; usually neither part will. But the organism, at least in the early stages of growth before there is high specialization of function, will continue to live and grow even if large parts of it are removed. (In Driesch's experiments, moreover, it did not seem to make any difference which parts of the dividing egg were removed.) So Driesch argued that the analogy between an organism and a machine was faulty.

In addition to the relatively homogeneous and undifferentiated aspect of the cells (which he admitted were merely a complex of chemical substances), he assumed that there was a non-physico-chemical agent that regulated and directed the growth of the body, teleologically "using" sometimes one part of the protoplasm to make an organ and sometimes another. This agent he called an *entelechy*. It was unobserved and unobservable, but he felt that he had to assume it in order to explain what he did observe, namely the actual difference between the way a machine behaves when divided and the way an organism behaves when divided. He did not believe that this was due merely to a difference in the degree of complexity but was an entirely different type of response. To say that the organism is a machine, he believed, was to omit an important characteristic of the machine, namely that it has an operator or a maker which is not a machine. The proper analogy, he suggested, would be: a machine is to its maker or operator as an organism is to its entelechy. For Driesch, life is physico-chemical conditions plus a teleological agency.

Against this theory, the mechanists had a fairly quick victory. They could readily admit their present inability to explain some of the facts that Driesch had discovered, but they pointed out that if Driesch's explanation were assumed, the facts could *never* be explained. His explanation, they rightly held, was an "explanation only by courtesy," and actually was only a name for our present ignorance of the real physico-chemical conditions. In other words, vitalism was a bad hypothesis. To clinch the point, later mechanists succeeded in explaining in chemical terms many of the peculiar phenomena Driesch had said required the hypothesis of entelechy.

Yet the fact remains that animals do not seem to behave like machines. They reproduce, they repair injuries, they grow, they seem actively to seek goals. Even the term "struggle for existence," which the mechanist and all other biologists invoke as a causative factor in evolution, has more than a shadow of teleological connotation, for machines do not struggle to survive. Driesch's theory, in spite of its explanatory weakness, does call attention to those aspects of life that are too likely to be overlooked by the mechanist.

Teleological conceptions are extremely useful, at least in some stages of biological research. They suggest hypotheses about the direction and function of the underlying physico-chemical processes. To take a simple illustration, suppose a biologist investigates the event ordinarily called "cat chasing a mouse." In purely descriptive terms, he would say, "The mouse ran across the floor; five feet behind the mouse the cat ran across the floor in the same direction." He cannot say that the cat chased the mouse, for the word "chase" is teleological, and when we use it we ascribe a purpose to the cat's behavior. The mechanist could no more literally say that the cat chased the mouse than he could say one meteor chased another across the sky, for to him, the cat is a machine and machines do not seek goals. Yet in explaining the cat's behavior, the mechanist does *take into account* what the cat seems to common sense to be doing, namely, trying to achieve a certain purpose. In the earlier stages of his investigation, at least, the mechanist considers this aspect of the event, and it suggests to him what specific physico-chemical conditions to look for as the explanation of the cat's behavior. (For instance, it might suggest to him that the cat is hungry, which will lead him to investigate the chemical conditions in the cat's blood as the real cause.) In this way the mechanist himself uses the notion of purpose as a *heuristic* hypothesis—as a guiding principle with which to begin, but later to be eliminated as a false hypothesis when he proffers his mechanistic explanation.

While one mechanist criticized vitalism by saying that entelechy was "a comfortable couch where reason was lulled to rest on the pillow of mysterious properties," a vitalist properly retorted, "Teleology is a lady without whom no biologist can live, yet he is ashamed to be seen with her in public."

Emergent holism

In recent years another theory of life and its relation to the underlying physico-chemical conditions has been proposed. Although it cannot be considered clearly superior to mechanism in every respect, it is an interesting alternative. It justifies the use of teleological concepts in biology without basing them upon the weak vitalistic theory. The theory goes under various names, and is most often called holism, organicism, the organismic theory, or the emergent theory of life. It was suggested by Kant and Goethe, and in our own day it has been developed chiefly by Samuel Alexander, Lloyd Morgan, William Stern, Jan Smuts, and Kurt Goldstein. We shall consider only the best known of its proponents, Samuel Alexander (1859-1938), whose *Space Time and Deity* is one of the most important philosophical works of the past 50 years.

The central conception of Alexander's philosophy is that of *emergent quality.* An emergent quality is a quality that belongs to a whole and could not have been predicted from any knowledge of its separate parts. If we could have predicted the quality of a whole from knowledge of the parts (even if we did not actuually do so), the property is called a *resultant quality*. Consider water, for example. Water is a whole comprising oxygen and hydrogen. From a knowledge of the weights of oxygen and hydrogen, the weight of their compound could have been predicted; it is their sum. Weight is thus a resultant property and we can have *a priori* rational knowledge of it if we have knowledge of its conditions. But from our knowledge of oxygen and hydrogen alone, we could not have foretold that their compound would have the properties of wetness, colorlessness, and tastelessness. Such qualities can be learned only *a posteriori*, by observation. (After we have had one experience that oxygen and hydrogen form a wet compound, we can, of course, predict by induction that they will do so in the future; but the point that Alexander wishes to make is that we could not do so without some observation of the properties of the whole itself.)

Knowledge of resultant properties is logically derivable from knowledge of the conditions. Such properties can be rationally analyzed into the properties of the conditions, of which they are a mere sum or aggregate. With respect to resultant properties, therefore, the whole is equal to the sum of its parts. But Alexander believed that the emergent properties are new, simple qualities that can be learned only by a fresh observation. The wetness of water is a simple property that must be directly experienced, and upon analysis of the whole, it disappears. With respect to emergent properties, it is sometimes said (very ambiguously) that "the whole is greater than the sum of its parts."

For Alexander, nature comprises "immense complexities of elements, hitherto chaotic, now gathering themselves together and as it were flowering into some undreamed simplicity"—a new quality.[8] He believed that there were at least four such critical levels or turning points in the evolution of the universe: matter, emerging from the complexity of space-time; chemical

---

[8] Samuel Alexander, *Philosophical and Literary Pieces*, page 304. London: Macmillan and Company, Ltd., 1939. Used by permission of The Macmillan Company, publishers.

structure, emerging from the complex interrelations of material particles; life; and consciousness.

A living body is, according to this conception, a physico-chemical body of a certain degree and kind of complexity, whose actions may severally be viewed as physical or chemical, but taken in their integration or entirety have the quality of life. Life is therefore resoluble without remainder into physico-chemical processes; but it cannot be treated as *merely* physico-chemical. Certain of its functions may be referred to physical or chemical laws, but it is not these separable processes which constitute life. Life exists only when we have that particular collocation of such physico-chemical actions which we know as living. It is the special co-ordination which conditions the appearance or creation of the new quality of life. . . . But it is not *merely* physico-chemical because merely physico-chemical processes are not alive, and they do not give us life until the requisite complexity of integration is attained. So important is it to remember that besides elements there is their form or combination, and that the form is as much a reality as the elements and gives them their significance.[9]

Against the vitalist, he says, "While there is no new entity life, there is a new quality life, with which certain combinations of matter may be endowed."[10] And against the mechanist: "But the new quality of life which [matter] possesses is neither chemical nor mechanical but something new."[11]

This theory has enjoyed wide popularity in recent years. In biology such views have been influential in directing attention to the study of the organism as a whole. It has had repercussions in psychology, which has reacted against the "summative" hypotheses of the association of ideas and separate faculties and reflexes (as in Gestalt psychology). It has played an important part in medical thinking, in what is called "psychosomatic medicine."

But, we must ask, to what extent is it a good hypothesis? Like vitalism, it has been fruitful in calling attention to the

---

[9] *Ibid.*, pages 307-308.
[10] *Ibid.*, page 309.
[11] *Ibid.*, page 311.

facts of organization that tend to be played down by mechanists. Unlike vitalism, it does not explain them with just a magic word like entelechy, for organization or pattern can be observed, modified experimentally, and compared in its diverse manifestations in different organisms. It has put organization and function in the center of attention. It still asserts, moreover, that every biological phenomenon has a physico-chemical base or substratum, so unlike a vitalistic hypothesis it does not have to retreat when the physico-chemical mechanism of some previously unexplained biological process is discovered. Thus it does not block the way of inquiry.

On the other hand, it is probably not as simple as mechanism, for every emergent quality must be accepted as a brute fact, as what Alexander once called a "miracle," accepted with "natural piety." Once a new quality is observed, however, the emergentist does not simply indulge that piety; like the mechanist (and indeed like the practicing vitalist), he begins to investigate the conditions under which it has occurred and thus tries to establish physico-chemical laws for the phenomenon. But it may be a more adequate theory than mechanism, that is, not *too* simple, because it does not minimize the significance of the differences between living and dead matter by saying that the former is only a more complicated case of the latter.

At present there seems to be little purely scientific evidence to justify a choice between mechanism and the emergent theory of life. Some philosophers have, in fact, argued that they are not really two different theories, but only two different "languages" reporting the same set of facts, differing from each other only in vocabulary and emphasis. In the future the mechanist may be able to show that what we call emergent properties, including life itself, are really resultant properties when more adequate knowledge of the parts is available. That is to say, the distinction between emergent and resultant is not an absolute distinction but is relative to the state of knowledge available in the more fundamental sciences. Such a reduction of emergent to resultant properties has occurred in the past, as we see in the physical explanations that can now be given for chemical phenomena. It is possible, with further advances in physics and chemistry, that the emergent property of life will be reduced. If this happens, purpose and organic wholeness will still be useful as heuristic hypotheses. But until and unless this happens, biology may be considered an autonomous science, not merely a branch of chemistry and physics. The real difference between mechanism and the organismic theory of life is probably to be found in the diverse expectations they arouse concerning the future course of biological inquiry.

SOCIETY AS AN OBJECT OF SCIENTIFIC STUDY

The social sciences are the youngest of the sciences. While social problems have concerned men far longer than problems of understanding nature, the difficulties in the way of studying them scientifically are so great that social questions for centuries were considered a part of the art of the statesman or were left to common sense; when they were seriously studied, the studies were carried on by philosophers, who were frequently more interested in reforming society than in understanding it. At most it is only in the past two centuries that there has been very much work deserving the name of social science, if by social science we mean an effort to accumulate facts and test general hypotheses about societies, comparable to the procedure of the natural scientist in observing facts and formulating and testing hypotheses about the world of astronomy, physics, chemistry, and biology.

The scientific study of social facts is enormously difficult. The difficulty lies in part in the social order itself. All scientific discoveries, especially those in the social sciences, disturb and upset previously held beliefs. Many institutions in society, which have a great hold on the loyalties of individuals and groups, simply do not favor the questioning and inquiring attitude when it is directed to them and to the society that supports them. There is social pressure against the scientist who tries to keep an open mind and to ask searching questions about capitalism, or patriotism, or race relations, or religious activities. Large-scale research on society is among the most costly of investigations, and it is a sad fact, but fact nonetheless, that funds for support of it are hard to get, while it is comparatively easy to obtain funds for significant research in physics, chemistry, and biology. Probably every nation in the world spends more in one hour for research on scientific methods of killing large numbers of people than it does in a year on research into the social conditions for the prevention of war.

But leaving this great practical obstacle aside, there are plenty of difficulties in carrying out significant social science research even if funds are available and if the social climate is favorable to such work. We shall discuss briefly three such difficulties. The first is eliminating bias from research; the second is deciding what to investigate; the third is finding a way to test hypotheses about society.

Bias

The social scientist is a member of society, occupying a particular position in it. He is asked to look at society from the inside, much as if one asked Jonah to study the anatomy of the whale. He is not just a scientist driven by curiosity, but a man who has interests in specific individuals, classes, and institutions in the society; he sees it from his own point of view, which is social and political long before it is scientific. Seeing it from a point of view within it introduces a perspective that may distort what is seen.

Putting this in another way, the "facts" of social science are not "clean" and purified "facts of science." They are not "value-free." They may be biased. In observing the economic system, if the scientist approves of it, he will tend to see its "good aspects" and describe as facts only those aspects that are congenial to him; if he is opposed to it, he will hardly be able to keep from emphasizing its weaknesses. The number of facts available is so tremendously large that he cannot cover them all; thus his likes and dislikes will almost inevitably determine which ones he will observe, and will color his reports on his observations. Bacon's Idols are ever-present in our thoughts on society. So long as bias is present, just so long will the "facts" for one social scientist be to some extent different from the "facts" for another.

Much of the training of a social scientist is, or ought to be, training in suspecting and suspending his tenaciously held beliefs so that he can guard his observations from their distorting effect. The well-trained social scientist is able, to a very considerable extent, to eliminate these influences. He wears corrective lenses, as it were. Even so, however, it is extremely hard to be sure whether the perfectly natural desire that the scientist has for one outcome rather than another affects his choice of facts and his manner of weighing and evaluating them.

Some of the worst biases are not those that are private to one or a few social scientists, but those that are shared by the whole community of social scientists. The former kind of bias can usually be detected and eradicated by seeing the different results several social scientists get when dealing with the same field. The latter kind of bias has the insidious effect of appearing to be "objective" because it is shared. Bias thus infects common sense and the entire universe of discourse of a group of cooperating scientists.

What facts are important?

One effect of bias and prejudice is to select facts that will be congenial. No objective science can be based on facts chosen in such a subjective way. But when we reduce the bias of the observer, we open his eyes to an almost immeasurable expanse of new facts that no one man can survey. Hence there must still be selection. What is its basis?

Actually the same problem is faced by the natural scientist, as we have seen (page 119). He makes observations from which he can draw abstractions whose relationships will be in the form of laws. Physics did not get on a firm footing until it was found that the abstractions of mass, position, and velocity were those that could most readily be related to one another by simple mathematical formulae. Then and only then did the physicist have an objective principle of selection, which could tell him, for instance, that the color or smell of a body was not a relevant fact for mechanics, while motion and weight were relevant.

In the social sciences the number of laws that have been discovered is so small that we simply do not know in general what facts are important. Technical journals of sociology or social psychology contain table after table relating abstractions to one another—height to weight of children, intelligence of children to income of parents, frequency of sexual intercourse to estimated degree of satisfaction in marriage, profession of father to professional ambition of children, distance of residence from center of city to number of children in family, and so on. This kind of study has been going on for decades, yet no or few simple laws have been formulated relating results of one set of observations to results of a large number of other sets.

This is not said in criticism of the social scientist. He is not like the astronomer, who can in the nature of the case observe only those characteristics of his objects that happen to be lawfully related to other characteristics. The social scientist is so close to the society, which has such an infinity of puzzling things to observe in it, that he must simply guess that one aspect of social behavior might be related to another and then undertake observations to learn whether they are actually interrelated. But with so large a number of things to observe, it is no surprise that he has not yet hit upon many observables that are found to be important and revealing. The social sciences are therefore rich in descriptions but poor in explanations, for explanations require a few important abstractions related to each other in general laws.

Hypotheses and their verification

The guesses the social scientist makes that such and such a characteristic might be related to another (for instance, that the education of parents might be correlated with the education of their children) are, of course, based on hypotheses about the way people act. (In this case we have the plausible hypothesis that the more educated the parents are, the more they will be interested in the education of their children.)

Without hypotheses, we have seen, there is no way to get from one fact to another. Most of what we said earlier about hypotheses and their use is relevant to the hypotheses of the social sciences; but there are a number of problems concerned with social science hypotheses that require additional attention.

It is easy to think of hypotheses about society. Every man gets along with his fellows every day by the use of hypotheses about them and about why they behave as they do. Most of these hypotheses are so much a matter of common sense, or shared social beliefs, that they are not even thought of as hypotheses; they are *called* facts. But every man goes beyond the actual observable facts whenever he engages in the affairs of life. Whether he is investing in stocks, waiting for a traffic signal, returning a call, making love, preparing for an examination, or disciplining his children, there are behind the facts hypotheses that he uses with such confidence that he is frequently inattentive to the facts themselves. That most men get along as well as they do probably indicates that their hypotheses are useful guides to action and represent at least the approximate truth about some of the social forces and conditions at work.

But every man frequently acts on hypotheses and gets unexpected results, or he finds others acting on different hypotheses and getting along just as well as he does. If he has a critical mind, he cannot be very confident of his social hypotheses when he thinks about them, even though he may continue to act upon them. Common sense and *savoir faire* are certainly the root of most hypotheses with which the social scientists begins his work; but they are no substitute for the scientific testing of these hypotheses. To establish any of the hypotheses as more than a mere rule of thumb for practical behavior in given and stable circumstances requires a procedure somewhat like that explored in Chapter 4.

In order to test any hypothesis, we found that at least two additional hypotheses have to be employed. There must be some previously elaborated hypothesis of great generality (collateral hypothesis) and an operational hypothesis to tell the experimenter or observer what to do and what to expect if the hypothesis he wishes to test is correct. A prime difficulty in the social sciences lies in making these two other kinds of hypotheses, without which no particular hypothesis can be confirmed with certainty.

In the social sciences there are few established collateral hypotheses that can be appealed to as solid ground for testing doubtful hypotheses. Consider, for instance, a social scientist who wishes to test the hypothesis, "Capitalism is a cause of imperialism." He must have a collateral hypothesis about the economic conditions of political changes in general, before he can discuss the specific economic condition of a specific political phenomenon. Can he appeal to the Marxist philosophy to validate his collateral hypothesis that the causes of political changes *in general* are economic? He cannot by any means say that the collateral hypothesis of the economic determination of political and social change has been so well established that he can treat it as anything more than one among many possible and usable postulates. It might equally well be the case that "the martial temper of the people," or the "will of a great man," or climate, or sunspots are determining factors, each of which would establish a different family of hypotheses for the explanation of imperialism.

What a man believes about the collateral hypotheses will usually depend upon, and be expressed in, his "ideology" or philosophy of life, and will not usually be subjected to scientific test at all. Hence the social scientist, even when he is unbiased about "facts," often chooses an untested collateral hypothesis because it is congenial to him, or because he has been trained to accept it, or because most of his fellow scientists seem to accept it.

Now assume that the social scientist can get around the difficulty we have just mentioned, and is in possession of sound collateral hypotheses as a background for testing the hypothesis about the relation of capitalism to imperialism. How will he be able to test his family of hypotheses? In the natural sciences, he does so by affirming the antecedent of an operational hypothesis and observing the result (see pages 95 ff.). That means doing an experiment: holding constant all but one of the factors mentioned in his hypothesis, and varying that one to see whether the expected result occurs. But the scientist's opportunity to do this with respect to social hypotheses is practically nil. The economic institutions of his society will not allow him to "vary the amount of capitalism" in order to see if "the amount of imperialism" varies also.

In some parts of social science, experiments can be and have been done. A classroom or a prison or a group of families on relief have sometimes been used for such experiments, and a combination of experimental and statistical controls can be used. Even in these cases, however, there are great difficulties, and one seldom knows whether the results obtained can validly be applied to other groups that are not included in the experiment (see pages 102, 105). In many social science experiments, it must also be admitted that the mountain has labored and brought forth a mouse; and some of the most "beautiful" experiments reported in technical journals have only confirmed what we already knew by common sense. Inasmuch as experimental social science is a very new field of endeavor, however, the comparative triviality of many of the results thus far obtained should be no cause for despair; in fact, the wisest among the social scientists regard the experiments performed thus far as "trial runs," more important in instructing us on techniques of social experimentation than valuable for the discoveries that have been made.

The hypotheses of history, which would be the most explanatory hypotheses for understanding all sorts of social change, cannot be tested in this way. For centuries there has been a search for "laws of history" that would be sociological laws of changes of social groups (the rise and fall of states, revolutions, development of colonies, spread of culture from one group to another, and the like). But although many such laws have been propounded by historians and philosophers like Montesquieu, Hegel, Marx, Nietzsche, Spengler, Toynbee, Kroeber, and Sorokin, and each of them has been interesting and valuable for the light it has thrown on the otherwise dead facts of history, validation of any of the proposed laws and underlying hypotheses has been lacking. All that the historian can do is to survey the past, formulate an induction such as, "In every society, religion reaches the climax of its development before philosophy does," and then submit his induction to test by his colleagues. His colleagues then try to find exceptions to the induction by a further study of history.

Such testing of laws of history, however, is never very decisive one way or the other. Often the social scientists and historians cannot agree (either because of the lack of needed facts, or remnants of bias) as to whether a specific series of events is an example of or an exception to a proposed law! Just when, for instance, was the climax of religion in our culture— in the thirteenth or the sixteenth century? Side by side we can see many of the same events paraded as evidence for the theory that economic causes are determining factors in social change, and for the theory that emphasizes the dominant role of ideas in history. As illustrations, consider the diverse theories that have been formulated to account for the French Revolution or World War I—some find them to be illustrations of the laws of economic determination, and those at the other extreme find that they illustrate the social consequences of the thoughts of philosophers like Rousseau or Nietzsche.

The difficulties we have examined, difficulties that are freely recognized by the less doctrinaire social scientists and historians, have caused discouragement especially among those who are in a position to aid financially in the support of research in the social sciences. But the considerable successes that have been obtained in experimental social psychology in studies of morale, leadership, and cooperation should give encouragement to the hope that the study of society by scientific methods can progress. We must remember that the social sciences are younger than the physical sciences, that they are less well supported, and that they are dealing with a much more complicated subject-matter than the sciences of physical nature. We should not invidiously compare contemporary social science with contemporary physical science—that is like comparing the strength of an infant with the strength of his father. The social sciences are now in the stage of the physical sciences 400 years ago, yet many critics of the social sciences seem impatient with them because they have not yet had a Newton to reduce most of their discoveries to some simple mathematical form.

Can the social sciences be scientific?

In view of the inherent difficulties in the scientific study of society, especially in applying experimental techniques to social phenomena, there have been arguments aimed at showing that society requires an entirely different kind of study. It is said that the concepts of social science cannot be "reduced" to those of the natural sciences; that one must "understand" a society instead of trying to "describe" and "explain" it; that there is a kind of intuition needed for a "pattern of culture," which could never be known merely by impartial observation; that one must "empathize" into a social situation instead of trying to observe it in a detached way. Sometimes these arguments have gone so far as to say that society is, or at least is very like, a living being that cannot be analyzed, or that there is a "social mind" or "group-mind" that is different from the minds of the individuals within the group.

Our previous discussions of the hierarchy of sciences led to conclusions that might seem compatible with such arguments. We have said that although the more complex sciences depend upon the simpler, they cannot now, and perhaps may never, be reduced to them. If life is a new quality of complex physico-chemical wholes, it is perhaps not unreasonable to suppose that "culture" is a name for an entirely new and unpredictable emergent from wholes consisting of many organisms. If this is so, we should expect that the abstractions drawn from the subject-matter of the natural sciences would not fit and explain the facts of social life. Yet at the same time we should not have to admit that the emergence of culture implies that society is something different from the individuals in their complex interrelations; we should not have to speak of a "social organism" or a "group-mind" in any way other than *analogically*.

The theory of emergent qualities would incline us to say that the facts of social life require new modes of observation and that they can not be deduced from the facts of the biological life of the individuals comprising the society. It would lead us to anticipate that there would be unexpected qualities of social groups that could not have been predicted from a knowledge of the isolated individuals. It would suggest that these qualities would be found only by a kind of "social understanding" or "intuition" or "empathy" that would not be called for when we deal with their separate parts, although the mode of knowledge would have some analogies to the kind of intuitive grasp of the wholeness and togetherness of a biological organism. An attempt to make the social sciences too much like the natural sciences would blind the social scientist to the specifically social facts. Given this kind of social insight or intuitive grasp of the social emergent qualities, we could then use the results of the insight in interpreting the individuals in the social group, who are certainly modified and conditioned by their status in the whole.

This philosophical theory applied to society, however, does not in the least imply that we must go "beyond science" in our social inquiry. For the essential characteristic of science is not that the hypotheses and laws shall take an abstract mathematical form, as in physics or chemistry, or that they shall arise only as a consequence of measurement, induction, and laboratory experimentation, or that they shall have no teleological implications. The essential characteristic of scientific method is that hypotheses, however they originate—whether in induction, intuition, inspiration, or experiment—are submitted to the test of impartial observation. It is of no decisive importance where the hypotheses originate, whether from the manipulation of mathematical symbols or from a "social insight" gained only after months of living with a primitive tribe. It does not matter whether the facts used to check a hypothesis are found in a physics laboratory, an observatory, the dusty archives of a historian, or the field work of a comparative anthropologist. The essential thing is that there be testable hypotheses and an earnest and impartial attempt to test them by seeing to what extent they render observable facts intelligible.

A sufficiently sensitive scientific method, free from the illusion that nothing is scientific unless it is reduced to the laws or hypotheses of physics, should be as capable of dealing with a "pattern of culture" or the "spirit of the times" as with any other hypothesis or alleged fact. There is no doubt that it is difficult. But in an age of science, that admitted difficulty should not be allowed to block the way of inquiry and lead to obscurantism about the most important and least understood of human problems.

BIBLIOGRAPHY

Classifications of science

Benjamin, A. C. *An Introduction to the Philosophy of Science.* New York: The Macmillan Company, 1937. Chapter 18.

Bliss, H. E., *The Organization of Knowledge.* New York: Henry Holt and Company, Inc., 1929.

Carnap, Rudolf, *The Unity of Science* (Max Black, trans.). London: Kegan Paul, Trench, Trubner, 1934.

Flint, Robert, *Philosophy as Scientia Scientiarum, and a History of Classifications of the Sciences.* New York: Charles Scribner's Sons, 1904.

Biology and the physical sciences

Bergson, Henri, *Creative Evolution.* New York: Henry Holt and Company, Inc., 1911.

Cassirer, Ernst, *The Problem of Knowledge* (W. H. Woglom and C. W. Hendel, trans.). New Haven, Conn.: Yale University Press, 1951. Chapter 11.

Driesch, Hans. *The Science and Philosophy of the Organism,* second ed. London: Black, 1929.

Goldstein, Kurt, *The Organism. A Holistic Approach to Biology.* New York: American Book Company, 1939.

McDougall, William, *Modern Materialism and Emergent Evolution.* New York: D. Van Nostrand & Company, 1929.

Morgan, C. Lloyd, *Emergent Evolution.* London: Williams and Norgate, Ltd., 1923.

Nagel, Ernest, "The Meaning of Reduction in the Natural Sciences," *Science and Civilization* (C. R. Stauffer, ed.). Madison, Wisc.: University of Wisconsin Press, 1949. Pages 99-138.

———, "Mechanistic Explanation and Organismic Biology," *Philosophy and Phenomenological Research,* Vol. XI, No. 3 (March, 1951), pages 327-338.

Robinson, Daniel S. (ed.), *Anthology of Recent Philosophy.* New York: Thomas Y. Crowell Company, 1929. Pages 553-575.

Smuts, Jan Christian, *Holism and Evolution.* New York: The Macmillan Company, 1926.

The scientific study of society

Beck, Lewis W., "The 'Natural Science Ideal' in the Social Sciences," *Scientific Monthly*, Vol. LXVIII, No. 6 (June, 1949), pages 386-94.

——, "The Limits of Skepticism in History," *South Atlantic Quarterly*, Vol. XLIX, No. 4 (October, 1950), pages 461-468.

Chapin, F. Stuart, "The Experimental Method in the Study of Human Relations," *Scientific Monthly*, Vol. LXVIII, No. 2 (February, 1949), pages 132-139.

Greenwood, Ernest, *Experimental Sociology. A Study in Method*. New York: King's Crown Press, 1945.

Kaufmann, Felix, *Methodology of the Social Sciences*. New York: Oxford University Press, 1944.

Lundberg, George A., *Can Science Save Us?* New York: Longmans, Green & Company, Inc., 1947.

Lynd, Robert S., *Knowledge for What? The Place of Social Science in American Culture*. Princeton, N. J.: Princeton University Press, 1939.

Northrop, F. S. C., *The Logic of the Sciences and the Humanities*. New York: The Macmillan Company, 1947. Chapter 14.

Ogburn, W. F., and Goldenweiser, Alexander (eds.), *The Social Sciences and Their Interrelations*. Boston: Houghton Mifflin Company, 1927.

QUESTIONS AND TOPICS FOR DISCUSSION

1. Study the system of classification used in a library for arranging the books on science. What underlying theory of the organization of the sciences seems to be involved?

2. If a chemist discovered the process for the synthesis of living protoplasm from inorganic matter, what effect, if any, would this have on the theory of vitalism? Organicism?

3. In this chapter, vitalism is criticized as a poor hypothesis. But E. Cassirer (*The Problem of Knowledge*. New Haven, Conn.: Yale University Press, 1950, page 210) says: "It has been rightly emphasized that in the history of biology the greatest vitalists [Harvey, for example] have always rendered outstanding service towards the explanation of the mechanism within the living organism." Discuss, assuming that Cassirer's statement is historically true.

4. Cassirer (*Ibid.*, page 213) says, "To employ a teleological method in the study of living organisms means only that we examine the processes of life so as to discover to what extent the character of preserving wholeness manifests itself." Does this suggest a way of reconciling the vitalistic and the holistic theory?

5. "In the social sciences it is necessary for the scientist to empathize the situation. He must be able to put himself into the shoes and the frame of mind of the people he studies. The social scientist must be more an artist than a cut-and-dried observer. The methods of natural science do not fit the work of the social scientist." Discuss.

6. In 1824, Comte said, "I shall bring factual proof that there are just as definite laws for the development of the human race as there are for the fall of a stone." Estimate the extent to which this promise has been fulfilled.

7

Intelligence
in the Choice of Values

FACTS AND VALUES

The world we see around us seems very different from the world described by the sciences. The scientific world is one of "cold fact," discovered by the most rigorous attempt to eliminate the personal element from observing and thinking. The facts of science are just what they are, and our liking or disliking them seems to be an impertinence in the face of their impartial truth. The onward march of science constricts the area of ignorance and illusion; it also sometimes seems to make man himself merely accidental, his interests superficial, and his ideals imaginary:

> Science! true daughter of Old Time thou art!
> Who alterest all things with thy peering eyes.
> Why preyest thou upon the poet's heart,
> Vulture, whose wings are dull realities?
>
> How should he love thee? or how deem thee wise,
> Who wouldst not leave him in his wandering
> To seek for treasure in the jewelled skies,
> Albeit he soared with an undaunted wing?

> Hast thou not dragged Diana from her car?
> And driven the Hamadryad from the wood
> To seek a shelter in some happier star?
> Hast thou not torn the Naiad from her flood,
> The elfin from the green grass, and from me
> The summer dream beneath the tamarind tree? [1]

What matters most to man seems to matter not at all to the universe. Whatever makes life worth living seems to be but a subjective human illusion, which the universe itself will indifferently thrust aside.

Yet the world we see does not seem to be put together out of just cold facts. Some parts of the world are suffused with beauty; some actions of men are not mere conditioned reflexes but are moral deeds. The aspects of the world we value *seems* as real as the aspect we know in an objective, impartial way.

Moreover, the world we see does not seem to be put together out of cold facts plus something *else* we call values. The world seems to be one world, with values appearing to be as inherent in the things we experience as are the facts and laws that the scientist discovers by analyzing them. Primitive man, and the ordinary man of today, does not first experience a world of brute and valueless facts, and then wonder how it comes about that a world consisting of colorless, odorless, and tasteless molecules seems to have all the beauties and gratifications he can find in enjoying it, or all the evils that beset him as if the world were planned for his woe. He sees the world originally as the site of things that he appreciates or rejects, long before he understands it as a realm of fact and law.

The facts of science are reached by abstraction from the variegated world of experience. Long ago, men learned that in order to understand, explain, and control things, they had to center their attention on those aspects of things about which they could agree with one another. Judgments of the beauty, pleasantness, goodness, or desirability of things vary from individual to individual; hence these judgments were banished

---

[1] Edgar Allan Poe, *Sonnet to Science*.

from the organization of the knowledge of "things as they are." Primitive men learned how to mix pigments and fight wars; their discoveries were probably the ancestors of the kind of knowledge we now call the natural and the social sciences. But they did not learn, and we have not learned, how to get real agreement on whether a specific painting made with these pigments is beautiful, or whether a war fought according to good scientific strategy is morally just. We have established sciences of chemistry and optics and strategy. We have no rigorous science of aesthetics and ethics.

In the early seventeenth century, a resolute attempt was made to banish all thought of the values of things from scientific attention and to concentrate on the measurable, the geometrical, the mechanical aspects of things. Science was to become impartial with respect to value; the facts of science were to be "value-free" facts. When this was accomplished in the physical sciences, and purposes and values were relegated to some not-quite-real world of human desires and fancies, men achieved unprecedented success in discovering laws relating one cold fact to another. From then on, it was natural that the world as understood by scientists should seem quite different from the world as loved or feared. At the very time when the decision to disregard purpose and to investigate only mechanical causes put into men's hands almost unlimited power to achieve their purpose of controlling nature, the concept of purpose and value was declared illusory and subjective.

In our study of science we have already examined one of the consequences of this bifurcation of experience. It was the rapid advance of science in the study of nature, the conception of which was greatly simplified by the vigorous use of Ockham's razor for the elimination of values, purposes, and ideals in the study of fact. We have also seen some of the difficulties in the scientific study of society, where such an elimination of value is more difficult to perform and where it is still a debatable question whether it ought to be attempted.

In this chapter we are to see some other effects of this

bifurcation, the effects it has had on our understanding, choosing, and pursuing values. One of these effects has been to strengthen the notion that disciplined inquiry is out of place in our experience of values. This means that inquiry is limited to "fact," and hence that evaluating the experience of values, especially in aesthetics and ethics, must be left to "instinct," feeling, or desire. It is the correctness or incorrectness of this point of view that we must carefully weigh.

JUDGMENTS OF FACTS AND JUDGMENTS OF VALUES

For reasons just mentioned, a basic distinction has been drawn between two kinds of judgments.

The first are *judgments of fact.* They report on what we suppose to be the case, without expressing any approval or disapproval of it. Competent men can almost always agree about factual judgments. Factual judgments are judgments which, when scientifically examined, can often be confirmed or refuted. Examples of such factual judgments are: "Sodium cyanide is a poison"; "There are no brick houses on Elm Street"; "Beethoven wrote nine symphonies"; "The population of New York is over eight million"; "Hot metals radiate energy." Factual judgments may be incorrect, as when I say, "There is a dog under the table," but we know what we should do to determine whether they are correct or not.

The second are *judgments of value.* They express an appreciation and are either *pro* or *con.* Such judgments are: "You ought not give sodium cyanide to your guests"; "Beethoven's symphonies are the best ever written"; "Elm Street would be prettier if all the houses were not built of wood"; "The population of New York is too large for the people in it to live a good life." Such judgments as these may be agreed to by many individuals, but when there is disagreement, it is difficult to resolve the conflict and show which of the two discrepant judgments is correct. We cannot very well do an experiment or make an impartial observation in which all personal factors are eliminated, as we would in case of a conflict between factual judgments. There seems to be no way of deciding, once and for all, which of two ways of life is the better, or which of two composers' styles is the more beautiful.

For this reason, many philosophers closely associated with positivism have argued that it is incorrect to call value judgments real judgments or propositions at all. One characteristic usually attributed to a judgment is that it must convey information, and another is that it must be *either* true *or* false. But, they say, the sentence, "This picture is better than that," really conveys no information about the picture, and there is no way in which we can verify it or refute it. According to them, the sentence is not so much a judgment like, "This bottle holds more than that," as it is like the Oh's and Ah's of a person walking through a gallery and expressing his personal emotional reaction to the pictures he sees.

These philosophers believe that, in order to understand the real meaning of a value judgment it must be translated into (1) a judgment of fact about the person who makes the judgment, and (2) an exhortation or request. Proponents of this view argue that when I say, "Tea with milk is better than tea with lemon," I am not conveying any information about tea, but I am conveying some factual information about myself and expressing an exhortation to you. I am (1) giving you the information that I like milk in tea better than lemon in tea and (2) seeking, perhaps unintentionally, to persuade you to prefer milk to lemon. The (1) part of this is a real judgment and may be true or false; it will usually be true for sincere people and false for poseurs and hypocrites. But the (2) part is neither true nor false.

Consider another example. When I say, "Lying is wrong," (1) I mean, "I do not approve of telling lies" (even though I may tell them); and (2) I am expressing a hope that you will not tell lies. In this case, the (2) part is perhaps more pronounced than was the (2) part of the analysis of the sentence about lemon and milk in tea. Frequently the tone of voice and choice of words used in value judgments show that they are being employed persuasively rather than informatively. Usually I do not care how you take your tea, and therefore I am as likely to make a factual judgment, "I like milk in tea," as a value judgment, "Milk in tea is good." But I *do* care whether another person tells lies or not, and for this reason I am less likely to say, "I don't like lying" than "Lying is wrong." I may accentuate the exhortation involved in the latter judgment by table-pounding, breast-beating, or spanking.

The exhortatory and persuasive overtones in pronouncing value judgments have led these philosophers to say that value judgments have an *emotive* or *persuasive* meaning, while the factual judgment, "I like so-and-so," may have only the function of communicating information, and thus has a *cognitive* meaning.

During recent years there has been much emphasis upon detecting the more or less hidden emotive meanings that enter into what are apparently factual judgments. The popular fads of "semantics" and "propaganda analysis," like the old-fashioned "debunking," recognize that techniques can be devised to get people to agree to beliefs and to act in specific ways on the supposition that they are responding to the facts of the case, while actually being persuaded by the unctuous suavity of an advertiser or propagandist. From this the conclusion is drawn by propaganda analysts that "prophylactic" techniques can be devised by which people can protect themselves from this kind of delusion. Such techniques are: be vigilant against "glittering generalities," "loaded words," "banner words," appeals to authority and fear, "slanting," and the like.

Propaganda analysis has served a useful function in developing in many people a habit of detecting the intentions of the propagandist and separating the few facts from the many emotional overtones. In this way it becomes easier to be critical of and resistant to the wiles of those who are out to sell us a "bill of goods" by appealing to our patriotism, vanity, or libido. Such a debunking attitude may, on the other hand, have had some unwanted effects [2] through subtly creating a belief that judgments of value are not intellectually respectable and should be omitted altogether or, if that is not possible, at least left to individual caprice and unexamined private liking and disliking. Such an attitude is not justified merely by noting the distinction between two kinds of judgment. It *may* be true that value judgments are not real judgments. But it *may* be true that while the distinction between the two kinds of judgment is useful and valid, judgments of both kinds are quite proper and intellectually defensible. In other words, it may be that if I say, "Every man has some inalienable rights," I am stating a true or false judgment just as surely as if I say, "Every man has some iodine in his body," though the first is correctly called a value judgment.

The obvious fact that we cannot test the former by anything comparable to a chemical analysis or a public opinion poll does not necessarily mean that it is not really a judgment. It may mean only that the methods of scientific observation are not directly applicable to all kinds of judgment. There is nothing in the useful distinction between two kinds of judgment, or in the commitment scientists have made to consider only the factual judgments, that implies that only valueless facts are real and that values are to be "reduced" to them or thrown out altogether. There might be other things in the world besides facts subject to scientific inquiry; if so, they could be studied by some inquiry other than scientific experimentation. At all events, many philosophers believe this, and we should not deafen ourselves to their arguments in advance by equating in our minds "reality" with "scientific fact."

Whatever our decision about the status of values, we should be on our guard against being misled by appeals to our emo-

---

[2] This is one of the theses of the interesting book by Arthur E. Murphy, *The Uses of Reason.* New York: The Macmillan Company, 1943. See especially pages 70ff.

tions ("If values are merely subjective, then life isn't worth living!"), or by the smug certainty that the facts of science are all there are in the world.

CLASSIFICATIONS OF VALUES

Before attempting to weigh the opposing theories of the status of values in the universe, we must examine and summarize some of the myriad *facts* we have about the values we experience. These facts are unaffected by any later decision one may make concerning the place of values in reality. Such a survey of facts will give some useful distinctions and terminology that we shall need in discussing the main questions of the status of values and how they may be intelligently assessed, chosen, and pursued.

There are many kinds of values. We shall mention several ways in which values have been distinguished and classified.

Extrinsic and intrinsic

There are many things and actions we approve of only because we approve of or desire something else. I am willing to take a bitter medicine, for instance, because I value my health; I am willing to save money I would like to spend so that I can later take a trip I think I shall enjoy. In these cases we have instances of the relation of a means to an end. The value of the means is called *extrinsic*, or *instrumental*. It does not even seem to lie in the thing or act itself, but outside it, in the end that can be accomplished by it.

On the other hand, why do I value my health? Or my vacation? It is rather hard to answer such questions. Of course I might say that I want to be healthy or to have a vacation in order that I may be happy. But why then do I value happiness? It is not long before this line of questioning brings us to a statement about a value that is not regarded as extrinsic. The value of happiness or health or of the pleasure of a vacation seems to lie in *them,* and not merely (or not at all) in something else to which they lead. For this reason they are said to have *intrinsic value*.

There are many intrinsic values. Perhaps it is not going too far to say that everything the enjoyment of which is pleasant is an intrinsic value. I drink coffee because I like it "for itself," and I may often drink it when, as a matter of fact, it leads to undesirable consequences. I do not drink it for the good that it will lead to, as I take medicine for the good consequences it is expected to produce.

Many things and actions, of course, have both kinds of value. Eating food, for instance, has an intrinsic value because men enjoy it. But it also has extrinsic value in that it is a condition of health and life. There are many cases, too, that illustrate what has been called the "Law of Preponderance of Means over Ends." According to this, there is a tendency for means, which borrow their value from the ends they serve, to become ends in themselves and thus to gain intrinsic value. The miser is perhaps the best illustration of this; men who enjoy their work are happier illustrations of it. The principle has such wide application that it is sometimes difficult in specific cases to decide whether "the end justifies the means" or "the means justifies the end."

Solving a problem as to what has extrinsic value is, in principle, exactly like solving a scientific problem of fact. In science we ask, for instance, "Does mandelic acid kill such-and-such germs?" This is a factual question about cause and effect. But I can rephrase the question as a question about extrinsic value. Then I get the question, "Is mandelic acid good (extrinsically) as a remedy for such-and-such a disease?" The relation of means to end is the same as that of cause to effect, *when we desire the effect*. The more knowledge we have about the causal conditions of the things we desire, the more able we may be to achieve our ends. It is chiefly because of this fact that science is useful in the pursuit of values.

Answering a question about what intrinsic values are most worthy is much more difficult. Stating the cause of an effect as a means to an end is very different from judging the value of the end. If I believe, for instance, that euthanasia is morally right, the more scientific knowledge I have, the more successful I can be in bringing a painless termination to the suffering of another person. But knowing how to bring painless death is very different from knowing that painless death is desirable. Whether it is or not is a question of intrinsic value, and it cannot be solved merely by learning what are the most efficient means of attaining it.

When anyone says that values are merely matters of opinion or subjective liking, he is speaking *only* of intrinsic values. Questions of extrinsic values are, in principle, scientifically solvable.

Absolute and relative

An absolute value is a value that ought to be appreciated by any person who has the opportunity to do so. A relative value is a value dependent upon someone's actually appreciating it or being interested in appreciating it.

The only values claimed to be absolute are the intrinsic values. No one would say that an extrinsic value is absolute, since extrinsic values depend upon (1) another value that may or may not be absolute, and (2) the circumstances. Extrinsic values are always relative to the situation and goals of someone. The only question is: are there any intrinsic values that are absolute?

This is a matter of dispute. That *some* intrinsic values are not absolute seems clear. The value judgment, "Hot coffee is good," obviously means "good for me." If someone else prefers cool coffee, I may shrug my shoulders and say, "Every man to his taste," and let it go without argument. Whether all intrinsic values are of this kind is debatable, but the physiological and psychological make-up of an individual, or the social circumstances that have determined the individual's aspirations and attitudes, seem so various that it is hard to be sure that there are any values shared by all individuals.

While no one will assert that the "goodness of hot coffee" is absolute, many people will say that the "wrongness of adultery" is absolute. Still, there are societies that do not condemn what we consider adultery. Is what the individuals in such societies do wrong? It is wrong "by our standards," but conversely, what we do is wrong by theirs.

The doctrine that all moral (and aesthetic) values are "culturally conditioned" or dependent upon the social circumstances is known as *cultural relativism*. Cultural relativism implies that there are no absolute values. Values *called* absolute, according to this theory, are absolute only within a limited social context.

It is an indisputable fact that value judgments do vary from culture to culture and, within a culture, from class to class. This is known as the *fact* of *cultural relativity*. But this fact alone does not imply that there is no value that all men *ought* to appreciate and strive for. The fact of ethical relativity is admitted by those who say there are absolute values, realized in different ways by different cultures. For instance, helpfulness to one's fellows seems to be almost universally admired, and will be approved (if not practiced) in perhaps all societies,[3] but it will be expressed in quite different ways in different societies. The differences between what is approved in one society and what is approved in another, however, are so great that we cannot be very confident that there is any standard universally although only tacitly acknowledged.

Against cultural relativism it is argued that there *are* absolute values and that it is irrelevant to point out that there is no value actually acknowledged universally. In order for there to be absolute values, it suffices that there be a value that *ought* to be recognized; it is not necessary that it be actually recognized. Such an argument is certainly sound from a logical point of view, and it depends only upon the distinction between the theory of cultural relativism and the fact of cultural

---

[3] There are exceptions even to this. Cf. Ruth Benedict, *Patterns of Culture,* Chapter V. New York: New American Library, Mentor Books, 1934.

relativity. We ought not to confuse the value statement, "Charity ought to be practiced by all men," with the factual statement, "Charity is practiced by all men." The falsity of the latter statement does not imply the untenability of the former. There is no *logical proof* that there is no absolute value.

Even so, however, if one is to say that there is an absolute value, one might reasonably be expected to state *what* value is absolute. Otherwise the statement is empty and useless in making decisions concerning values. But when anyone states specifically what values he thinks are absolute, it is usually found on examination that he has chosen a value expressing an ideal of his own culture, while others claim their own values as the absolutes. All will be guilty of "moral ethnocentrism," seeing values from the standpoint of one's own ethnic or cultural group.

For these reasons, it seems difficult to justify any confidence in the belief that any specific value is absolute, even though the doctrine that there are absolute values cannot logically be refuted.

Most men do act as if their own values were absolute. This may have the fortunate consequence of making each of them assiduous in striving for what he thinks is valuable, and willing to make sacrifices for its sake—which might not be the case if he felt that values were only the projections of his subjective desires and hence not worthy of sacrifice of other desires or of life itself. But it may have undesirable consequences in making each man or each social group dogmatic and "absolutistic" or intransigent in attitude, so that instead of understanding another's point of view, there will be only recrimination and violence.

It is one of the most difficult problems to know whether our own values are superior to those of others, so that we ought to try to persuade others to accept them or, if necessary, to force their acceptance upon others, or whether it might be better to believe that the way to peace and mutual understanding is to recognize that all ideals, however noble they appear to us, have their root in the soil of natural and social conditions and will vary as these conditions vary. This is a serious problem in all of our interpersonal relations; it achieves gigantic significance in international affairs.

Values classified according to interest

Another principle for classifying values depends upon the kinds of interest in or approval of the things that persons experience. For example, my interest in a cup of tea is of a very different kind, and is expressed in a very different value judgment, from my interest in philosophy. Although the following "types of value" in part overlap and perhaps do not exhaust all possible values, they do cover the most important species of interest:

1. *Biological values.* Values attached to aspects of life as a biological fact. Examples: food, drink, sex, health, survival.
2. *Economic values.* Values attached to material things used or exchanged for other goods and services (other types of value, or other economic values). Examples: money, property, tools, "credit."
3. *Affective values.* Values experienced in sensuously pleasant experiences. Examples: play, sex, delight in food and drink, "excitement," comfort.
4. *Social values.* Values experienced in social intercourse, cooperation, and competition. Examples: friendship, power, status, a "good name."
5. *Intellectual values.* Values experienced in the satisfaction of disinterested [4] curiosity and the intellectual use of the mind. Examples: knowledge, truth.
6. *Aesthetic values.* Values experienced in the disinterested appreciation of natural and artistic beauty. Examples: beauty, the sublime, the comic, the tragic; genius and talent; "good taste."
7. *Moral values.* Values experienced in social or individual conduct with respect to their rightness, goodness, or ideal development. Examples: values of character and good will; virtues.

---

[4] Disinterested in the sense of not being a means to the satisfaction of some other interest. Knowledge, of course, has an economic, biological, and social value.

8. *Religious values.* Values experienced in or aspired to in religious devotion and worship; values based on what is interpreted to be man's relation to God. Examples: the holy, the sacred.

Several points stand out immediately upon examining this list or other comparable lists proposed by various writers.[5] First, many of the values often overlap. It would be difficult to segregate the religious from the moral; the biological and the affective certainly involve each other; the economic values may be a subclass of the social.

Second, conflicts may occur between values of the various classes. Certainly the pursuit of moral values may conflict with the cultivation of the economic; there is often an antithesis between the moral and the aesthetic; the intellectual is often thought to conflict with the religious, and so on.

Third, there is a complicated relationship of dependence among the various classes of values. Some of them depend upon others. Few values can be attained unless some of the biological values are available, and one would be rightly suspicious of a religious value if it were dissociated from moral values. In general, some degree of achievement of one or more of the first four types seems to be a condition of achievement of most of the last four.

There have been attempts to set up such a listing as this as a scale or standard of value, calling the first four the "lower values" and the last four the "higher values." This is itself a value judgment, and it would be difficult to vindicate it in any detail, although something can be said for it if it is not pushed too far. The obviously relative values seem generally to be examples of Types 1 through 5, and most of the values considered to be intrinsic and absolute are of Types 5 through 8. While it is perhaps true that any value can be used as a means to some other end (for example, piety can be a means to

---

[5] Cf. W. G. Everett, *Moral Values* (New York: Henry Holt and Company, Inc., 1918), and Edouard Spranger, *Types of Men* (Halle: Max Niemeyer Verlag, 1928).

achieve social values; intelligence, a means for economic advancement), and while it is probably true that any value can be intrinsic (as in the case of the roué or the miser), the higher human cultures, and not merely our own, have most often professed to regard the last four types as values that make life "worth living," while the first four make it possible simply "to live." [6]

Furthermore, the last four types of value afford a broader base for distinctively human personality to develop. The first, third, and fourth types, and rudiments of the second, are sought by animals as well as man; and the first and third are perhaps achieved more fully by animals than by men. The last four are preeminently or exclusively human and depend upon the "higher powers" of the human being. Moreover, the last five types are more genuinely social than the first three; pursuit of the first three tends to separate and segregate men, for they are not values that are multiplied by sharing, while the latter types reach their fullest fruition in a community of like-minded persons.

Such considerations as these occupy a central position in one of the most important books on values, Aristotle's *Nicomachaean Ethics*. Aristotle thinks that each being in the world has its own end or good, which depends upon its own specific nature. The proper purpose of anything, its prime good, is that which it can do best, or that which it alone can do. For instance, a "good" saw is one that can cut well; a "good" harpist is a person who can play the harp well; it is not necessary in addition that the good saw be beautiful, or that the good harpist, as such, be also a good husband. "Let the cobbler stick to his last," expresses the Aristotelian notion. But what is *man's* last? According to Aristotle, man is an animal, but he is unique among animals in being a "rational animal" and a "political animal." Hence by analogy to the answer to the question, "What is a good harpist?" Aristotle is able to answer that a

---

[6] Cf. W. T. Stace, *What are Our Values?* Lincoln, Neb.: University of Nebraska Press, 1950.

good man is one who has perfected the rational and the political (social) aspects of his personality; he is one who lives with his fellows and uses his reason in choosing and accomplishing social and, in a broad sense, political values.

SOME UNANSWERED QUESTIONS

The foregoing discussion has been inconclusive in many respects. We have had to refrain from deciding two questions: (1) Are there any absolute values? (2) If so, can we decide, in an intellectually responsible fashion, what specific things or acts have absolute value?

We have not been able to answer these questions, because they require a detailed discussion of choice among opposing theories, and our first purpose was to make the facts about value as explicit as we could. To answer the first question requires an examination of some general philosophical (properly, metaphysical) theories about the nature of both facts and values. To answer the second question requires a discussion of the epistemological problem of validating or vindicating value judgments, not unike the discussion in previous chapters on the validation of hypotheses about facts.

Before entering upon these matters, the reader should be warned that the decisions one makes about disputed points in the theory of values will often reflect one's value judgments. We cannot expect the kind of detachment in the examination of theories of value that we could expect and to some degree may have achieved in scientific theory.

Despite this, and fully cognizant of the danger of mere "rationalization" or of giving "good reasons" instead of "real reasons" for beliefs that grow out of the personal and social life of each individual, philosophers have never been content merely to report facts. They aim at a reasonable account of the whole of our concerns, and uppermost in these concerns are value commitments. While no unchallengeable answer to questions about value can be anticipated, a search is worth the effort, for it will help free the thinker from the Idols of the Tribe and Cave. In the elucidation of values, as in the pursuit of truth, there is no substitute for inquiry. But

You must remember also what has been previously stated, and not seek for exactness in all matters alike, but in each according to the subject-matter, and so far as properly belongs to the system.[7]

THE STATUS OF VALUES IN REALITY

In order to answer the question, "Are there any absolute values?" one must decide what is the status of values in the universe. If, for instance, we call values only those acts or things that give us pleasure, it is pretty clear that nothing (except perhaps pleasure itself) has absolute value, because the pleasure a person gets from a thing or action depends to a considerable extent upon his personal make-up, and this is different in different individuals. Granting this, it seems to follow that no good reason could be given as to why another person *ought* to find pleasure in the same things *I* enjoy. But if, on the other hand, we think of value as being a real quality of things or actions, even if not the kind of property that science deals with, then it is reasonable to argue that there are values not actually appreciated by an individual but that he ought to appreciate. The question, "Are there absolute values?" is not a psychological question about this or that person but a question about ultimate reality—a question of metaphysics.

The theory that values are absolute properties of objects or actions is certainly the view that is *prima facie* most plausible. We generally—even when we think we know better—take the beauty of a sunset, the goodness of an act of courage, and the agreeableness of a cup of coffee as though they were qualities of these things. In our ordinary experience, we certainly talk

---

[7] Aristotle, *Nicomachaean Ethics*, 1098 *a*. (D. P. Chase, trans.) New York: E. P. Dutton & Company, Inc., 1934. Everyman's Library.

most of the time as if the values were properties that we experience as being in the *things* and not just in *us*.

It is only after a certain degree of sophistication is reached that one begins to have doubts about this. If we decide that not even the color is really in the sunset or the sweetness in the coffee, but that these are psychological responses to physico-chemical conditions we do not directly experience, it is almost inevitable that we also conclude that values are dependent upon ourselves.

And once we have decided to attribute to objects only those characteristics about which men generally agree, or those characteristics that can be adduced as bases for predicting their future behavior—a decision long ago made by science—the ground for regarding value as an objective property is surrendered, for men quickly find that they often disagree with one another about value judgments. Even if they can agree about the facts relevant to works of art, for instance, they often cannot agree about their values; psychologists often agree about what motives a man has, but as men they disagree about whether the man's action was praiseworthy or blameworthy.

Troubled by these disagreements among value judgments, philosophers have usually taken one of two courses. Either they agree with Plato, and say that the values we seem to experience as qualities or adjectives of things are mere appearances or instances of real values about which we can come to agreement by intellectual inquiry into our diverse experiences; or they agree with Protagoras that each man is the measure and ground and locus of every value. Thus, out of the difficulties in the naive belief that we know values directly by a kind of value-sense, arise objectivism and subjectivism as value theories.

Plato's theory: objectivism

It was variability and dependence upon circumstances that led Plato, as we saw earlier (Chapter 5), to argue that the true realities of the world are not the things and their qualities that

we perceive by our senses. They change and conflict, as Theaetetus saw, and men cannot agree on them sufficiently to derive
any general conclusions or laws.

The same lead is followed here. The Socratic method, which
begins with the things of the senses and rises to the contemplation of Ideas, can start from either the factually described
qualities of things or from their values. Things that we perceive
as valuable will be transcended in the search for the essences
of these values. These essences themselves will be real values,
absolute, eternal, unchanging, and the condition of the lesser
values that we perceive but dimly and variably in the things of
the world. Professor Gilbert writes:

> Beauty Itself is stable. The many beauties come into being and
> pass out again. No concrete object, either physical or spiritual,
> which we might praise by calling it beautiful, could satisfy the test
> of Beauty's permanence. Bodies and ornaments, laws, customs, and
> sciences, however good, fine, or appropriate, are limited and perish-
> able. The contrast for Plato between the ideas or essences and the
> particular existences or instances always implies the opposition be-
> tween an unchanging one and the changing many.[8]

As before, the search begins with these particular and per-
ishable values, and by comparing them, discovers their idea,
then discovers relations among the ideas, until it finally arrives
at a supreme Idea that is the ultimate source of all the values
that things can have.

We may follow Plato's ascent to the idea of value in several
ways. For instance, we can see what it is that valuable things,
such as good characters, well-governed states, and beautiful
works of art, have in common. Plato finds the common principle
in a certain harmony or proportion, a balance of function in
which each part plays its proper role and all are taken up into
some unity-in-complexity.[9] In morality, or what Plato calls

---

[8] Katherine Gilbert and Helmut Kuhn, *A History of Esthetics*, page 49.
New York: The Macmillan Company, 1939. Quoted by permission of The
Macmillan Company.

[9] Cf. Aristotle's closely related view, page 198.

justice, he finds the essence to consist in the proper balance of the various levels of the soul or personality, with the lower levels (the passions and desires) ruled for the sake of the whole by the higher faculty of reason. In works of art, similarly, there is a natural order and articulation that must be preserved; a good state is one in which each social class fulfills its proper role in the commonwealth. In fact, as Plato in various works develops these diverse themes in a common direction, the Good and the Beautiful seem to merge with the Idea of Truth. Hence arises the Platonic trinity of "the Good, the True, and the Beautiful."

But the dialectic leading to knowledge of the Ideas of the Good and the Beautiful is not coldly analytical; at crucial stages of its presentation, Plato turns from argument to parable and allegory. We shall consider two passages in which this occurs; although lacking in logical precision, they seem eminently suited to the high theme on which he is discoursing.

The first passage occurs in the *Symposium*. After several men at the banquet, in the manner of men when they sit together after a good meal, have discussed love and lovers, Socrates tells how the love of the eternally beautiful can lead men beyond the transient world. Most men, he says, love but the appearance of the beautiful and the good; they try to hold on to them amidst the transience of life, but they fail; even their love of children is but a futile desire for a little longer life and immortality in a world of continuous flux. Socrates says that he has been taught the true way to the love and enjoyment of the good and the beautiful, the Ideas that will not be destroyed by time and circumstance:

He who would proceed rightly in this matter should begin in youth to turn to beautiful forms; and first, if his instructor guide him rightly, he should learn to love one such form only—out of that he should create fair thoughts; and soon he will perceive that the beauty of one form is truly related to the beauty of another; and then if beauty in general is his pursuit, how foolish would he be not to recognize that the beauty in every form is one and the same!

And when he perceives this he will abate his violent love of the one, which he will despise and deem a small thing, and will become a lover of all beautiful forms; this will lead him on to consider that the beauty of the mind is more honorable than the beauty of the outward form.

On this "ladder of love" he will rise to contemplate the beauty of laws and institutions and sciences, until "at length he grows and waxes strong, and at last the vision is revealed to him of a single science, which is the science of beauty every-where."

This brings him to the final goal:

When he comes toward the end [he] will suddenly perceive a nature of wondrous beauty—and this . . . is that final cause of all our former toils, which in the first place is everlasting—not growing and decaying, or waxing and waning; in the next place not fair in one point of view and foul in another, or at one time or in one re-lation or at one place fair, at another time or in another relation or at another place foul, as if fair to some and foul to others, or in the likeness of a face or hands or any other part of the bodily frame, or in any form of speech or knowledge, nor existing in any other being . . . but beauty only, absolute, separate, simple, and ever-lasting, which without diminution and without decrease, or any change, is imparted to the ever-growing and perishing beauties of all other things. . . . The divine beauty [is] pure and clear and unalloyed, not clogged with the pollutions of mortality.[10]

The second passage we are to study occurs in the *Republic.* Socrates says that he cannot answer the question of what is the real nature of the Good, but he will try to show it by an anal-ogy. He calls the sun the "offspring which the Good has created in the visible world, to stand there in the same relation to vision and visible things as that which the Good itself bears in the intelligible world to intelligence and to intelligible objects [Ideas]." [11] The sun is not only the source of the visibility of

[10] Plato, *Symposium,* standard pagination pages 210, 211 (Benjamin Jowett, trans.). New York: The Liberal Arts Press, 1948 (The Little Library of Liberal Arts, no. 7).

[11] Plato, *Republic,* standard pagination page 508 (F. M. Cornford, trans.). New York, Oxford University Press, 1945.

things like animals and plants, but is also the source of their life and existence. By analogy, then, the Idea of the Good is the source of the goodness of all other things, of their being known, and of their very existence.

From this all-to-brief glance at the richness of Plato's theory, we can gather several general features of this, the most important argument for objectivism that has ever been presented. Objectivism argues for the complete intelligibility of our experience of value; there is, as Plato says, a "science" (true knowledge) of values just as there is science or true knowledge of reality. It argues that value is a basic category in the world, and that the world cannot be understood in terms of mere fact. The things around us must be understood as vehicles or revealers of value underlying their existence. Nature itself, but especially human beings, strives to realize the values that are only dimly adumbrated in the mundane concerns of men; the wise man will model his life after his vision of the ultimate values in reality itself. The disputes we engage in about values are due to ignorance of true values, to the variability and dependence of the appearances of value upon variable human circumstances. But to know the good is to do it. Reason, then, is or ought to be the guide of life, for it can enable us to know not only what means should be used to make things conform to values, but what the ideals themselves really are. Philosophy, which is the perfection of this kind of reasoning, is or can become a true and rigorous science of the proper goals of mankind.

The appeal of Platonic philosophy has been one of the leading motifs in the history of Western thought. It was congenial to Christianity, which personalized the process by which the supreme values were made to bear upon the world, holding that they were revealed to man in the person of Christ. In the history of literature, later poets found in Platonism an elevation above the kind of despair Poe expressed in finding that scientific knowledge led only to dull fact. The classical tradition in art—painting the ideal rather than imitating the observable with all its blemishes and imperfections—has its philosophical root in Plato's philosophy, which says that such classicism is not an "escape" from reality but is the only true realism. And in their political life, men have always found inspiration in the notion of a value that is dignified above the variable laws of states, and that has held up to them the standard of a "law of nature" that is unchanging and abiding.

Subjectivism

Subjectivistic theories of value are held by those who are impressed with the variety and apparent irresolvability of conflicting value judgments and who are convinced, on metaphysical or epistemological grounds, that the world of actual existence has only the properties attributed to it by the sciences. Combining these two convictions leads to the conclusions: (1) value is only a name that we give to certain kinds of experiences; (2) the specific kinds of experience called valuable differ from person to person; (3) there is nothing outside or above the individual's experience that can be considered valuable; and (4) no specific objective standard binding on all men can be found or appealed to as a basis for evaluating their value judgments.

Subjectivist philosophers differ among themselves about what kinds of experiences (experiences of pleasure, or power, or self-expression, or satisfied interests?) are to be called valuable. But involved in all their views is the recognition that, underlying value judgments, there is always the experience of desire or interest, an experience of "taking sides" with or against some kind of occurrence. Ralph Barton Perry, one of the leading writers on value theory, in his *General Theory of Value* (1926) defines value as "any object of any interest." Just as aiming at anything *ipso facto* makes it a target, so also, he holds, being interested in anything *ipso facto* makes it a value. Others have modified his definition in various ways, suggesting, for example, that value is not the *thing* we are interested in, but the *experience of satisfying the interest*, while still others (hedonists) say that we are only interested in the pleasure we experience when some need is satisfied and therefore the experience of pleasure is the only value. But whatever be the specific definition proposed, the subjectivists all insist that the necessary conditions not merely for the experience of value but for the very being of value are subjective and lie in the individual organism.

Much can be said on both sides of the age-old controversy between objectivists and subjectivists. There are two strong arguments for the subjectivists. First, they make very effective appeal to the principle of parsimony. A value not experienced, they say, is merely an empty hypothesis. Everything important that we can say about value is really said about the *experience* of value. What we are really interested in, they say, is not what things have value, but what experiences have value; and they complain that the objectivist applies the word value to something that has value only in the context of valuable experience.

Second, subjectivists claim credit for directing our attention to the individual person whose experience is the locus of values. Instead of arguing for an "aristocratic" conception of values that only a few seers or philosophers or saints can appreciate, subjectivism looks for the standard of value in the person or group of persons seeking satisfaction for whatever needs they have. The subjectivist says that, in the long run, the question we have to answer in deciding the rightness or wrongness of an action is: will it probably contribute to satisfying human desires and needs? If not, then no matter how much authority or religious faith or transcendental philosophy may recommend it, it does not fulfill the one essential condition that could make it right. Subjectivists insist upon discussing the good and bad, right and wrong, in the context of daily life; they bring inquiries about values out of the clouds and try to free them from the endless disputes of philosophers and theologians. Questions of value that they think are worth disputing about are (1) what are the most pervasive and fundamental human interests? and (2) what are the best means for attaining their maximum satisfaction in the future?

To answer these questions, we need to know precisely what we and other human beings do desire and then find the means by which the desires can be fulfilled. This does not by any means imply, they say, a static or smug conception of human goals. Most of us do not know what we really desire, and we usually settle for a good bit less than we could achieve if we did have more insight. Seeking the most important goals will undoubtedly require sacrifice of some comparatively trivial experiences that we may, in our ignorance, have magnified far beyond their worth.

The two questions that the subjectivists want answered are very practical questions that science and common sense can help us to answer. We can observe the actual consequences of actions, anticipate consequences of actions we now choose, profit by our experience and that of others so that we can more and more successfully seek the goals we have, and gradually accumulate the wisdom we need about what experiences will, in the long run, make life most worth living.

Opposing subjectivism there are also strong arguments. We shall mention two. The first is that the end proposed by subjectivism is ignoble, however cultivated the interest or disciplined the desire. Religious teachers frequently condemn it by calling it secularism, for it places all emphasis upon man as the center of the system of value. But, say these critics, man without some aspiration for that which is higher than himself is a worthless creature, no better than the beasts of the field. Subjectivism circumscribes man's interests too narrowly, they say, and restricts his growth and the full maturing of his potentialities. A typical critic of subjectivism says, in a characteristic passage,

> What provision does such a system make for the maturing of a mind which desires a love that does not end when a cold clod falls upon the object loved, but a love that is abiding and eternal; what provision does it make for the maturing of a mind that desires a

truth which is not fragmentary like one found at the lower end of a microscope or the upper end of a telescope, but a truth that is pregnant with the intelligibility of the mysteries of life and death; what provision does it make for the maturing of a mind which craves for a life that never passes the last embrace from friend to friend, or crumbles the last cake at life's great feast, but a life ever throbbing and aglow with eternal heart beats? . . . It is a morality for the finite reaches of our body, but not for the spiritual reaches of our soul; it supplies a maturity for the man who goes to bed, eats, drinks, plays golf, attends conferences, reads newspapers, buys and sells, but it does not supply a maturity for the man who thinks thoughts beyond these things, who has remorse of conscience, who wonders what is beyond the stars, and who sits up nights pondering on truth and justice.[12]

As a further criticism, much of the trouble of the modern world is said to be due to the fact that subjectivistic or secular philosophy has become regnant during the period of the highest development of science, with the result that our society has the most excellent instruments and tools at its disposal but uses them for cheap, meretricious, and violent ends. While science has extended man's grasp to a most stupendous degree, subjectivism has continuously reduced the level of that for which he strives. Mephistopheles, himself no common advocate of high ideals, recognizes this in speaking to The Lord of His creation, man:

> Life somewhat better might content him,
> But for the gleam of heavenly light which
>   Thou hast lent him:
> He calls it Reason—thence his power's increased,
> To be far beastlier than any beast.[13]

Every person on his own ought to make up his mind about the validity of these objections, and he will decide on the basis of his own philosophy of life. Those who do not regard them

---

[12] From *Old Errors and New Labels* by Fulton J. Sheen, pages 174-175. Copyright, 1931, Century Company. Reprinted by permission of the publishers, Appleton-Century-Crofts, Inc.

[13] Goethe, *Faust*, "Prolog in Heaven," page 10 (Bayard Taylor, trans.). New York: Random House (Modern Library edition), n.d.

as valid will perhaps point out the low ideals and immoral practices that persisted even during periods of history when religious standards and the aspiration for transcendent ideals seemed to be more important than they are taken to be today; they will say that the objections to subjectivism would be more properly aimed against human nature itself than at a system of philosophy of which few people have even heard. They will also point out that the advance of science, which has as its most widespread corollary the common belief that values are subjective, has nevertheless put into men's hands the instruments that *can* be used to wipe out disease and poverty and perhaps crime and war, if men of good will can make effective use of them.

Those who regard these criticisms as valid, on the other hand, will probably take the view that these high ideals of human welfare are likewise held by objectivists, that the objectivists do not in the least despise or criticize the positive use to which science can be put in achieving them, but—and this is the important point—that the status accorded to these ideals by the objectivists is precisely what is needed if the ideals are to be deeply respected and earnestly striven for.

From the standpoint of intellectual or philosophical dispute, the evaluation of these blasts and counterblasts cannot be final. It is a dispute about opposing values; and we long ago noted that in philosophy there is an ineluctable personal element that cannot be eliminated. The sort of man one is and the direction of one's orientation will determine the decision he makes and the philosophy he will accept.

A second objection to subjectivism is perhaps stronger from an intellectual point of view, as it does not make the emotional appeal that many people find objectionable in the first criticism. This objection is based upon the weakness of the underlying nominalism of the subjectivist's theory of value. In our earlier discussion of nominalism (pages 125-126) we found that the consistent nominalist must say that universal terms apply only to our experiences of things, and not to the things themselves or to their real properties, which are always particulars. That raised a serious question: why do we apply a *specific* universal term to some groups of things but not to others? What is it that makes us collect one group of objects under the name "green things" and another under the name "brown things"? In strict consistency with nominalism we cannot say that it is because *they* are similar, for similarity means that there is some property that is identical in each member of a group of objects. That is precisely the thesis of the realist but not of the nominalist; The identical property is what is meant by a "universal," the existence of which outside of the mind is denied by the nominalist.

Every characteristic of a particular thing is for the nominalist as particular, specific, and unique as the thing itself. It was, therefore, very difficult for him to show how any abstractions could be used as a content for a law of nature, for the abstractions named by universal terms and related in laws are only subjective realities.

Similar difficulties are encountered here. If value is only a subjective universal, the strict nominalist or subjectivist cannot establish any laws of value that will prescribe value experiences to others, or give to others a basis for judging that one attitude to values is objectively wiser than another. Furthermore, a strict subjectivist cannot find any common trait among *objects* that give rise to the experience of value, because the value-universal applies only to experiences. That is, the subjectivist has taken the experience of value to be both a necessary and a sufficient condition of value, and therefore he cannot consistently say that some objects or actions ought to be valued or are preeminently suitable for the experience of value.

To revert to the analogy mentioned at the beginning of this section, any object aimed at becomes a target. Marksmen, however, do not just aim at *anything*; they choose their targets not simply by aiming at them, but by some belief about the things themselves. What they do aim at depends, of course, upon their interests and needs, and if they had no gun or no interest in using it, nothing would be a target. But given a gun and an interest in a specific kind of game, then there are characteristics of *things* that make some things targets and other things not targets. The precise kind of bird flying in the air does not depend upon the hunter; but that it becomes a target for the hunter depends upon his interest in that species of bird and his belief in an objective fact, in no way dependent upon the hunter, that the bird in the air is of that kind.

Applying this analogy to values, we could say with the subjectivist that human interests are the *necessary* conditions of the value of anything, and anything that men are interested in has, to that extent, value.[14] The reason why I choose milk for my tea instead of lemon does indeed depend upon my desires, and if I had no desire I would choose neither and would have no reason for saying one is better than the other. But why do I find that one of them satisfies my interest, and is therefore good? What are the necessary conditions for my being more interested in one rather than in the other? Surely they include something besides interest, some characteristic or quality or potentiality of the thing which, as it were, meets my interests half-way.

This is comparable to what the conceptualist said was the ground for the classifications and abstractions we make. We turn, then, to conceptualism in the theory of values, or what is sometimes called "objective relativism" in order to call attention to the way it synthesizes the truths of both objectivism and subjectivism or relativism.

Objective relativism as a theory of value

Objective relativism is a theory claimed by its proponents to synthesize the positive insights of both objectivism and subjectivism. Objective relativists assert that any property of an object is at least in part dependent upon its relations to other things. The weight of an object, for instance, depends not only

---

[14] The limiting condition expressed in the words "to that extent" is very important and will be discussed below, pages 222-223.

on its own mass but on the gravitational field of the earth; its color depends not only on its chemical composition but also on the composition of the light that falls upon it and the functioning of the eye that responds to the light it reflects. Properties of objects are not intrinsic, but relational or relative. This does not imply, however, that properties are subjective, even if one of the entities in the relationship within which qualities or properties emerge is a subject or person.[15] "Relational" does not mean "subjective." A quality belongs to an object only in a context or relationship, and that is what is meant by calling it relational.

According to this theory, values are relational properties. They emerge in the object (or in the action) that is judged to be valuable, in its relationship to the person who has an interest in it or appreciates it. The values of the object or action are in part dependent upon the person's attitude, but they are not values *of* the attitude or *in* the person.

Because this theory insists that values are at least in part dependent upon the person's directing his interest or appreciation to the object said to be valuable, it is in agreement with subjectivism. Human need or interest is a necessary condition for anything to have value. But holders of this theory do not go so far as to say that the value is exclusively subjective and can be considered in isolation from the factual conditions surrounding the experiencing person. Value depends also upon the nature of the thing to which the organism is related, and is properly attributed to *it* in the context of its bearing upon our conduct.

Because it says that the values are values of the object or of the real action, and not just values of states of mind or attitude, the theory of objective relativism does not belie the adjective "objective." Those who adhere to objective relativism agree with the objectivists that values are not exclusively private or personal, but have objective bases and conditions inde-

---

[15] The theory of objective relativism is also relevant to the problem of perception, and as such will be discussed below, pages 425-430.

pendent of the person. They dispute only the belief of the objectivists that the things we experience as having value do have value apart from our experience.

What recommends a philosophical theory, like a scientific hypothesis, is its ability to meet problems that other theories have failed to resolve. Compromise between opposing views is philosophically sound only if it permits us to solve divergent problems by means of a single theory instead of by means of shifting from one theoretical base to another as problems shift and change. Compromise, in the sense of merely borrowing a little from this theory and a little from that, is not fruitful in philosophy because it results in a theory that is more complex than any of the views from which it borrows, and that has less internal integrity than they do.

Objective relativists assert that their theory is not a compromise in the pejorative sense of this word. They do not, they say, take objectivism from one philosopher and subjectivism from another and mix them together. Rather, they hold, objectivism and subjectivism are themselves simply extremes or exaggerations of aspects found within our dealing with values. Objective relativism does not ignore the interrelatedness of all the factors in this experience. For that reason, objective relativists propose their theory as a single answer to two quite different questions that trouble the objectivists and subjectivists, respectively.

The questions are: how shall we account for the diversity of value judgments or beliefs about values if value is a simple property of real beings, open to discovery by intuition and dialectical reasoning? How shall we account for the agreement and near-unanimity on some value judgments, if value judgments are merely expressions of the likes and dislikes of highly variable individuals? Objective relativists claim to have a theory that answers both of these questions on the basis of the same definition of and hypothesis about value, and therefore claim that their theory is logically simpler than its alternatives, which have to appeal to *ad hoc* hypotheses to answer one of these questions. Objectivists have difficulty in answering the first of the questions, and they have to explain disagreement as due to ignorance or "value blindness" or "bad taste." Subjectivists have difficulty in answering the second, and can only regard such agreements as really occur as due only to a fortunate, but by no means expected, similarity in the physiological and psychological make-up of individuals. But if values have two conditions, one subjective and one objective, and if one of these conditions (the subjective) varies, then obviously the value will vary also. These variations, however, will not be as broad, radical, and irreconcilable as they would be if subjectivism were the whole truth, that is, if the subjective condition were the sole condition of value. For the objective relativist recognizes and insists upon the permanent and uniform objective pole and condition of experiences of value.

Objective relativism is able to further a rapprochement between the social sciences and the theory of value. While psychology and sociology attempt to be purely descriptive sciences, dealing with facts as if they were "value-free" and being concerned only in establishing hypotheses and laws about how human beings actually behave, the human situations with which they deal are by no means "value-free." Descriptive sciences are not competent to establish criteria of the values by reference to which some of these situations are considered desirable and others undesirable; usually, scientific workers in the fields of sociology and psychology accept the common-sense decisions of their society on questions of value, and do not evaluate the standards to which the society itself professes to adhere.

The theory of value, which is concerned with these criteria as its chief problem for investigation, is sometimes called a "normative science," in order to distinguish its function from the descriptive functions of sciences like psychology and sociology. While it is true that psychology and sociology do not have the task of establishing and evaluating criteria by which judgments of value are supported or criticized, they are certainly interested in and informative about the conditions under which individuals and social groups do make their choices among values. For that reason, these sciences can make practically important contributions to value theory if the value theory is so organized as to take into account the personal and social factors as relevant not only to the *facts* of value experience but also to the standards of value-judgment.

The social sciences, as descriptive, are interested in the facts about the experience of value, the conditions of success or failure in striving for values to which an individual or social group is committed. If one reads the Lynds' study of Middletown or the Kinsey report on sexual behavior, for instance, one finds how much in the center of scientific interest is the comparative study of the standards of value prevalent in different social classes in America. However, each of these books is a factual study and does not pass value judgments on the experiences and on the value judgments of the people they describe. But in the normative study of values, we need such facts about the actual needs, interests, experiences, and judgments of people, and the scientific study of human motivation and society supplies this important set of facts.

It would be incorrect to say that we can learn from sociology and psychology what is really valuable; it is not the task of the descriptive sciences to give this kind of knowledge. But we too readily make value judgments on what would be good or desirable for men in disregard of the facts of human personality and social organization; all too frequently in our value judgments of ourselves and others, we are ignorant of the facts that would render the value-seeking of ourselves and others intelligible and comprehensible to us. If objective relativists are correct in saying that values are dependent in part upon human motives, then what we can learn from psychology and sociology about these motives and how they actually are expressed and brought to fruition or frustration can rank with the most important practical knowledge we can obtain.

This theory may be able to provide some reasonable criterion of values. It might be argued, in line with this theory, that whatever is truly valuable is not what actually satisfies me or what I actually desire, but what *would* satisfy me or what I *would* desire *if* I had more knowledge about myself and the action or the thing in question, and could see the ramifications and implications of this knowledge for my present and future concerns. In this way we could make use of scientific knowledge as one of the most important factors in deciding questions of value. This theory does not "relativize" values as much as subjectivism does, for it does not equate what I actually enjoy or desire with "the valuable"; it says that what is valuable or desirable is what I *would* desire if I knew my real deep-lying interest and the full facts of the case. On the other hand, it does not "absolutize" values, as objectivism does; objectivism tends toward dogmatism about what one's own values are and what the values of others ought to be, frequently without sound scientific knowledge of what are the needs and circumstances involved in the pursuit of values.

As a corollary of the last sentence, of course, those with absolutistic and objectivistic convictions will consider this theory too individualistic, relativistic, and subjective. Evaluation of this objection requires discussion of the epistemological problem of value judgment: is there any way to know that one value judgment is true or more tenable than another?

THE VALIDATION OF VALUE JUDGMENTS

Consider two judgments: "Studying medicine is what I desire," and "Studying medicine is desirable (or good)." These two judgments look very much alike, and it has sometimes been thought that the former implies the latter; this, in fact, is the only tenable view for a subjectivist. But in the light of what has been said about the distinction between judgments of fact and judgments of value, it is quite clear that the judgments are very different. The former is a statement of fact, about which it is correct to say that it is either true or false;

and we can find out whether it is true or false by introspection. The second judgment, however, says more than, "I desire to study medicine." It intimates, among other things, that even if the man in question does not desire to study medicine, he ought to study it, or at least, he ought to desire to. The second statement is much richer than the first in its implications. To say that a specific action is desired is to say that it is desired, period. To say that it is desirable is to say that it meets a certain standard of approval that is more than desire, and that it has certain characteristics that conform to criteria and norms.[16] But the question is: can the second statement be judged to be true or false, or are truth and falsity irrelevant to it?

In the preceding sections of this chapter we have seen some of the very great difficulties in the validation of a judgment like the second. But our earlier chapters described the way in which we can go about verifying a judgment of fact that goes beyond a momentary observation. That is, we have found ways in which we can justify the statement, "This liquid is acid," although our momentary observation is expressed in a judgment like, "It tastes sour to me." Similarly, a judgment of value such as, "Studying medicine is desirable," goes beyond the momentary judgment of fact, "I now desire to study medicine." Hence it seems worthwhile to see whether the method used in establishing judgments of fact that are more than momentary subjective observations might not also be used in establishing and testing value judgments, which are more than expressions of a momentary desire.

Discussion of this point will show that while there can be no rigorous scientific process for establishing or testing value judgments, the scientific method of examining hypotheses does have some analogy to a sound method of weighing conflicting value judgments.

Let us form a hypothetical syllogism to answer the question, "Why is it desirable to study medicine." The answer, somewhat

---

[16] Cf. John Dewey, *The Quest for Certainty*, page 260. New York: Minton Balch, 1929.

more fully expressed than would usually be the case, would have the following form: *If an action has such-and-such characteristics, it is desirable or valuable. Studying medicine has these characteristics. Therefore studying medicine is desirable or valuable.*

One might put such an argument even to a person who does not actually desire to go to medical school. The argument would be effective and persuasive if the person agreed that actions that have the specific characteristics mentioned in the first premise are really desirable, and that studying medicine does have these characteristics. That is, if the argument is to persuade him, he must accept the value judgment of the first premise and the factual judgment of the second premise. Arguments about value are for the purpose of (1) convincing someone of the truth of the first premise or of persuading him to accept it as a basis of action, or (2) showing him something he had perhaps not fully realized, namely, that the act in question really has the characteristics of which he approved in the first premise.

An argument of the second kind depends simply upon what are the facts of the case. It is often very difficult to know what the facts are. (Will it be possible to enroll in a medical school? Does one have sufficient aptitude for medical work to make it likely that one can become a good physician?) Although extremely difficult to make, and never very certain, decisions on these questions are *essentially* like any other decisions concerning matters of fact, so let us now pass over this part of the problem.

We are concerned, rather, with the first kind of argument, which has as its purpose to show that some particular formulation of the first premise of the syllogism is tenable, acceptable, or true. To make our analysis more specific, let us suppose that we are arguing with a hedonist, who says, "If an act gives me pleasure, then it is valuable." Now we are faced with two sub-questions: (1) What makes him *believe* this statement is true, that is, why (for what psychological reasons) does he accept it? (2) Can we find out if this statement *is* true, and if so, how?

1. *What makes us believe that a specific value judgment is true?*—An answer to this question will be a judgment of fact. The explanation of a man's holding a specific belief about values requires a deep knowledge of his psychological make-up. Is he a hedonist because he is rebelling against parental authority? Or because he read and liked Epicurus? Or because of the psychoanalytic "pleasure-principle"? In most cases we do not know enough about ourselves or others to answer such questions with any great degree of assurance. From the point of view of decisions about what value judgments one *ought* to make, however, our ignorance of these questions of fact is not especially serious. For no psychological explanation of why one has a belief is ever a sufficient reason for saying that the belief is true or false. Whether the belief is true or false cannot be determined by showing what childhood experiences, for instance, led a man to hold it; at most, such knowledge of his psychological make-up may give another person a kind of "handle" by which he can understand and explain the person's value experience, and this, of course, is very important in "correcting" a person's orientation. But how does one justify one's decision that another person's attitude and belief need to be "corrected"? This depends not only on the psychological facts underlying that person's beliefs and behavior, but also upon some standard by which we can decide whether the person's beliefs about value are sound. The question of the standard is not a psychological, factual question.

2. *Can we validate a value judgment, and if so, how?*—This is the question of the standard. It is the problem of testing the first premise of the syllogism, which is the value judgment that now concerns us. Imagine, then, the situation of the person who is certain that he ought not to go to medical school because, he says, "I think a person ought to do only what gives him pleasure, and I know that I would not enjoy that." An adviser, for some reason whose psychological genesis we do not need to

know, is not a hedonist and rightly or wrongly thinks that he ought to go to medical school. If the adviser attempts to persuade him, he may try to show that he probably would enjoy medical work and thus appeal to what seem to be the facts of the case (i.e., attack his second premise); or he may try to show that the value judgment underlying hedonism and this particular application of it is unsound. We are now concerned with the second kind of attempt. Something like the following conversation may ensue:

Q. "You say that you won't study to become a doctor because you wouldn't enjoy it. That means, I take it, that if you thought you would enjoy it, you would agree that you ought to go to medical school?"

A. "Yes, if I thought I'd get pleasure from it, I'd certainly go."

Q. "Does that mean that whatever you could get pleasure from is something that you'd try to do?"

A. "Yes, that's my 'philosophy'—always act so as to get the greatest pleasure."

Q. "Well, frankly I believe that you would enjoy the work if you'd just let yourself. But maybe you know better what you would enjoy than I do. Even so, I wonder if you really mean what you say. Isn't there anything that ought to matter to a person except the amount of pleasure he gets?"

A. "No, that's my philosophy. You ought to get the most pleasure you can."

Q. "How about this, though. Yesterday I heard you say about the professor of philosophy who gave such a boring lecture, 'I'd like to strangle that guy!' If that would have given you pleasure, why didn't you do it?"

A. "That's easy. I don't want to flunk the course or go to jail. I wouldn't get any pleasure out of *that*, though I would like to throttle him before he gives another such lecture."

Q. "But suppose you were sure you wouldn't have flunked or gone to jail. Oh, I know you can't be sure of things like that, but just for the sake of argument suppose you were. Would it then have been right to strangle him because he gave a boring lecture?"

Up to this point, the questions and answers are pretty straightforward. But in answer to this last question, we can imagine at least two replies:

A_1. "Yes. If I were sure I could get away with it, it would be right to do it."

A_2. "Perhaps I ought to say, 'It would be right for me to do what would give me the greatest pleasure provided it doesn't interfere with the rights of others to do the same.'"

Let us consider now the second answer, which is really far more likely to be given than is the first answer. Notice that the hedonist has shifted his hypothesis. He started out by saying that an action is valuable or right if it meets one requirement: that it gives him a maximum of pleasure or a minimum of displeasure. Now he says the action must meet *two* requirements: it must give a maximum of pleasure, but it must not interfere with the rights of another person. Skillful questioning could elicit still further modifications in the hypothesis, but the steps through which we have gone show the essentials of the way in which value hypotheses are modified by application to new cases, just as hypotheses about facts are modified by application to still further facts.

The essentials seem to be these. The man starts out with his belief that anything pleasant is also good. Now his attention is directed to an *apparent* exception to the rule: strangling the professor of philosophy would be pleasant, but it is at least debatable whether it is good or not. He has, therefore, to make a choice: (1) it is good because it is pleasant, and the commonly accepted notion that it is not good is wrong; or (2) it is not good, even though it is admitted to be pleasant. Answer A_2 represents the second alternative. And in giving Answer A_2, the speaker acknowledges that he gives up his hypothesis when it is submitted to a crucial test of choosing between what is required by the hypothesis and what he regards as bad in spite of the hypothesis that would justify it.

A value hypothesis can be considered validated to the extent that it does not lead the individual who holds it to conclusions that he is unwilling to accept as valuable or right, and to the extent that it does lead to conclusions that he is willing to accept as valuable and right even when they do not accord with his momentary interest. Unless inquiry leads to hypotheses that do not require continual modification and are fruitful for rendering choices intelligible and defensible to individuals who could not at the beginning agree on them, then there is no way for inquiry to settle disputes about values. Experience shows, however, that in most cases, agreement on underlying hypotheses or value judgments can be obtained even in the midst of disagreements about particular instances. Many "disagreements about values" are really disagreements about the facts of the case, that is, about the second premise; and we know that, in principle at least, disputes about facts can be settled by investigation and cooperation.

This is not true of all disputes, however. Remember that the speaker might have given Answer A_1 and stuck to his hypothesis, come what may. For this reason, we cannot have very great confidence that agreements about values, or validation of hypotheses about values, can always be attained. Since men disagree about specific value judgments, they may continue obstinately to disagree about the fundamental principles and hypotheses of the theory of value. It would be unjustified to insist that there is any one value judgment that can be validated by showing that all others conflict with the ordinary value judgments a man is willing to make.

Moreover, there is another serious obstacle to establishing any hypothesis about value as universally valid. A specific value judgment that conflicts with a general hypothesis about value may be wrong itself, so that the specific value judgment in the particular case ought to be modified and the hypothesis reasserted; or the specific value judgment or decision in the particular case may be right, so that the hypothesis about values ought to be modified and rejected. In other words, the argument brings out a conflict of judgments that can be made consistent only if *either* the conclusion *or* the premise is changed; but we have no supersyllogism by which, in cases of such conflict, we can decide where the truth lies.

There does not, therefore, seem to be any way by which a

value judgment, either a specific one applicable only to a given case or a general hypothesis about the kinds of things and actions that have value, can be *proved*. Although we have earlier found that the common notion that science proves its hypotheses is generally exaggerated, and that in science, all we can do is to show that up to now such-and-such a hypothesis is superior to any known alternative, not even this limited degree of proof is available in an inquiry into what values may be absolute.

Science gets along very well without being able to reach the stage of proof. Yet because most people desire the comfort of assurance that they are absolutely right and feel dissatisfied with any inquiry concluding that such a degree of certainty in value judgments is unwarranted, they overlook the positive advantages that flow from recognizing that value principles are hypotheses. By searching out from the myriad of often conflicting desires and interests the common and underlying purposes and fundamental value judgments that we previously sought only blindly and gropingly, we may uncover a few ideals of great generality, ideals that would make a fundamental and ultimate appeal to us and to others. These fundamental principles, when acknowledged, become a standard by which our less fundamental and less well integrated desires are to be judged and disciplined. The unity of character is made more intelligible, and the settled disposition in our choices is made more intelligent, when we orient our seeking for values around some critically examined principle. Even if the principle cannot be proved, it can be critically elaborated so that its implications can be applied to new and unexpected situations for which training and tradition have not adequately prepared us.

Because many people have a deep-seated need for certainty in their pursuit of values, it will seem to them that this conclusion is so negative that they are justified in appealing anew to revelation, authority, tradition, intuition, or the "common moral sense of mankind" to guarantee the rightness of their own beliefs. Many therefore now turn their backs on what may be accomplished by reasonable inquiry in the pursuit of values, and fly to individuals or institutions that will answer all their questions by fiat. For peace of mind, a feeling of security, and blind faith that their value judgments are *really* right, they give up the critical attitude of weighing alternatives and attempting to find a common ground of mutual understanding amid divergent desires and interests.

But meeting of minds can be reached, if at all, only by the use of reason, by examining and weighing the conflicting commitments and choices we are pressed into making. Certainly such an exercise of reason in inquiry does not guarantee any individual's or institution's scale of values, nor can it promise that some scale of values can be found that will bring peace and harmony among now-conflicting interests. But it may do two things, neither of which can be accomplished by any substitute for inquiry.

First, the use of reason in conjunction with the facts about our diverse experiences of value may help us to discover that the apparent diversity of value judgments is not so great as it seems. There will, to be sure, always be students who want to go to medical school and students who do not; some who are willing to strangle a teacher for a boring lecture and some who are not. Such diversity is unavoidable; some is desirable. But on a more abstract level we might find that all or most men do fundamentally desire some of the same sorts of things and actions and states of mind, while some seek them in one form and others in other ways. If this is so (and only the future progress of investigations in the psychology and sociology of value experience can show whether it is), then the conflicts among values may be found to lie on a relatively superficial level, and appear to be fundamental and radical only because no deeper level of agreement and cooperation has been suspected or found. In this way, the French proverb, *tout comprendre est tout pardonner,* so often cited as a basis for moral cynicism, indifferentism, and do-nothing-ism, might be found to contain a profoundly significant moral insight of quite another kind.

Whether this level of agreement can be attained is in the realm of conjecture and hope. If it is reached, it will be reached by a serious inquiry into what men do desire and consider valuable and by a reasonable attempt to discover among their desires some common core of what they *would* desire were they more reasonable, impartial, and wise. It will never be found by appealing to intuitions and revelations and authorities, which, because of their own divergencies, tend to divide instead of unite men.

Second, many persons, including the author of this book, believe that the exercise of reason in tolerant inquiry into conflicts of value is *itself* a value. I would indeed even venture to say that I believe it is an absolute value. Quite apart from whether it can eventually produce peace among men—of which I have serious doubts—the attitude of inquiring, questioning, and cutting the suit of belief to fit the cloth of evidence seems to me to be good. A society that permits and encourages it is a more fit place for the development of the distinctive human talents of intellect and good will than a society that buys peace of mind by thwarting the quest for reasonable understanding and criticism of its values. Peace of mind brought about by a dominant ideology, enforced by propaganda and the sword might produce agreement and peace and harmony among men (although it has not in the past). But that peace would not, as I see it, be as valuable as the faltering and uncertain steps of men who are trying to understand what is right and to choose it by their own lights, even if they should never agree.

Those who find peace of mind in some doctrine uncritically accepted on the word of someone else may not believe this. They will say that it is only evidence of "vain pride of intellect," which is inconsistent with their view of what man is and what is his highest destiny. Here is, perhaps, a basic conflict that cannot be resolved by intellectual inquiry. For one side denies the value and validity of the attitude of inquiry itself. But until we are brought to this final and irreparable break between intractable personal differences, there is much for reason to do. And the doing of it is, I believe, good in itself.

BIBLIOGRAPHY

Bahm, A. J., "The Emergence of Values," *Journal of Philosophy*, Vol. XLV, No. 15 (July 15, 1948), pages 411-414.

Brandt, Richard B., "The Significance of Differences of Ethical Opinion for Ethical Rationalism," *Philosophy and Phenomenological Research*, Vol. IV, No. 4 (June, 1944), pages 469-494.

Bronstein, D. J., Krikorian, Y. H., and Wiener, P. P. (eds.), *Basic Problems of Philosophy*. New York: Prentice-Hall, Inc., 1947. Part 1.

Dewey, John, "Theory of Valuation," *International Encyclopedia of Unified Science*, Vol. II, No. 4. Chicago: University of Chicago Press, 1939.

Golightly, C. L., "Social Science and Normative Ethics," *Journal of Philosophy*, Vol. XLIV, No. 19 (September 11, 1947), pages 505-516.

Green, Thomas Hill, *Prolegomena to Ethics* (1883). Oxford: Clarendon Press, 1899.

Hartmann, Nicolai, *Ethics* (Stanton Coit, trans.). New York: Macmillan Company, 1932. Volume 1.

Jenkins, Iredell, "What is a Normative Science?" *Journal of Philosophy*, Vol. XLV, No. 12 (June 3, 1948), pages 309-332.

Kant, Immanuel, *Foundations of the Metaphysics of Morals* (1785), in *Critique of Practical Reason and Other Writings in Moral Philosophy* (Lewis W. Beck, trans.). Chicago: University of Chicago Press, 1949.

Lafferty, T. T., "Empiricism and Objective Relativism in Value Theory," *Journal of Philosophy*, Vol. XLVI, No. 6 (March 17, 1940), pages 141-156.

Lee, Harold N., "A Precise Meaning of Objective and Subjective in Value Theory," *Journal of Philosophy*, Vol. XXXVII, No. 23 (November 7, 1940), pages 626-637.

Lundberg, George A., "Can Science Validate Ethics?" *Bulletin of the American Association of University Professors*, Vol. XXXVI, No. 2 (Summer, 1950), pages 262-276. Cf. Carmichael, Peter A., "Is it Ethics?" *Ibid.*, Vol. XXXVII, No. 1, (Spring, 1951), pages 41-47.

Otto, Max C., *Science and the Moral Life*. New York: New American Library, Mentor Books, 1950.

Parker, Dewitt H., *Human Values*. New York: Harper & Brothers, 1931.

Pepper, Stephen C., "A Brief History of the General Theory of Value," in *A History of Philosophical Systems* (Vergilius Ferm, ed.). New York: Philosophical Library, 1950. Chapter 39.

Plato, *Republic; Protagoras; Euthyphro; Crito*. Many editions.

Romanell, Patrick, and Leake, C. D., *Can We Agree?* Austin, Texas: University of Texas Press, 1950.

Smith, James Ward, "Senses of Subjective and Objective in Value Theory," *Journal of Philosophy*, Vol. XLV, No. 15 (July 15, 1948), pages 393-405.

Stevenson, Charles L. *Ethics and Language*. New Haven, Conn.: Yale University Press, 1944.

Toulmin, Stephen E., *An Examination of the Place of Reason in Ethics*. Cambridge, Eng.: Cambridge University Press, 1951.

Walker, Merle G., "Hartmann and Perry: Complementary or Antithetical?" *Ethics*, Vol. XLIX, No. 1 (October 1938), pages 37-61.

QUESTIONS AND TOPICS FOR DISCUSSION

1. Do you believe that psychological studies of human nature and anthropological studies of the various cultures can help us to solve our own ethical problems?

2. Does the fact that different cultures have different codes of ethics imply that we ought not feel obligated to follow our own culture's codes?

3. "Cultural relativism in ethics depends upon confusing descriptive laws of sociology with the prescriptive laws of ethics." Discuss.

4. What influence has the theory of organic evolution had on ethical beliefs?

5. Is it possible to apply the kind of test proposed for a value judgment to a dispute on the relative merits of two pieces of music?

6. Read Plato's *Republic*, Book I. Compare the method Socrates used against the "might makes right" doctrine with the procedure outlined in this chapter for testing a moral judgment.

7. Discuss the various theories of human freedom (Chapter 6) in the light of the various theories of value discussed in this chapter. Are there any natural "family relations" among them, so that together some of them constitute a "family of hypotheses"?

8. What are some of the historical and cultural consequences of the distinction between fact and value? Could science dispense with this distinction? Could philosophy?

9. Try to formulate and test several value judgments as premises for a value syllogism.

10. Analyze an ethical discussion, showing the differences between the parts concerned with the factual premise and those concerned with the value premise.

8

The Quest
for Final Answers

Philosophy was described in Chapter 1 as critical, speculative, and synoptic. In succeeding chapters there were critical inquiries into the nature and limits of knowledge and standards of value. We saw repeatedly that following out these critical inquiries led to speculative questions about the status of what we know and what we value. It led to questions concerning the most general features of the universe, man, and man's place in the universe. We found that we could not work out the implications of our knowledge of scientific laws and of our quest for values without raising questions and suggesting hypotheses about the nature of reality as a whole. Questions and hypotheses of this kind, when explicitly formulated so that they can be discussed rationally, belong to the division of philosophy known as metaphysics.

Such questions and hypotheses, tacitly formulated to meet specific interests in our study of knowledge and value, have already come up so often in the course of this book that there can be no sharp break between our critical and our speculative inquiries. A "persistent attempt to think things through" has its critical and speculative stages, though, and one merges into the other.

Like Molière's new-rich man, who employed a tutor and was astonished to learn that he had been speaking prose all his life, perhaps some will be horrified to learn that they have been reading a good bit of metaphysics without knowing it. This chapter will try to show why the horror of metaphysics is so widespread today, and to show that there is little justification for this horror.

WHAT METAPHYSICS IS ABOUT

The word metaphysics has a queer history. Aristotle wrote a work that dealt with the basic concepts of the sciences of nature, which he called *Physics*. After his death, editors who compiled his writings collected a group of short and more or less independent treatises and put them, in their edition, after the treatise on *Physics*. They therefore called them the treatises "after physics," which, in Greek, is *meta ta physica*. Whence the name. But Aristotle, who is one of the most important of all writers in the field that *we* call "metaphysics," was innocent of the word.

The treatises collected under the name of *Metaphysics* were more or less independent of one another, and they were probably never intended as a single work. But so strong was the influence of the work of Aristotle on later thinkers that it is almost correct to say, in spite of its apparent silliness and circularity, "Metaphysics is the part of philosophy that deals with all the problems discussed in Aristotle's *Metaphysics*." In that book, Aristotle studies the organization of knowledge, the meaning of explanation, the nature of "being as being," the relation of universals and particulars, the nature of mathematics, causation, the existence of God, the purpose of the world, the unity of nature—all of which have continued to be regarded as parts of the metaphysician's province.

Metaphysics may be roughly described as a serious intellectual attempt to describe the general features of reality, to see them in their relation to our knowledge and experience of values, and to apply inquiry, which is usually directed to particular kinds of events and things, to the whole of everything. Somerset Maugham, with a passion for philosophy, wrote of it:

> Metaphysics never lets you down. You can never come to the end of it. It is as various as the soul of man. It has greatness, for it deals with nothing less than the whole of knowledge. It treats of the universe, of God and immortality, of the properties of the human reason and the end and purpose of life, of the power and limitations of man, and if it cannot answer the questions that assail him on his journey through this dark and mysterious world it persuades him to support his ignorance with good humour. . . . It appeals to the imagination as well as to the intelligence, and to the amateur, much more, I suppose, than to the professional it affords matter for that reverie which is the most delicious pleasure with which man can beguile his idleness.[1]

THE DISTRUST OF METAPHYSICS

In spite of this deserved praise, metaphysics now has a low reputation. Some of this is caused by simple abuse of language. Popular magazines carry advertisements of books on "metaphysics" side by side with treatises on astrology, and they promise everything from uncovering the "hidden powers of your soul," which will enable you to communicate with the dead, to showing how you can bend all things to your will. No intelligent person, of course, will be fooled by such advertisements into ordering a copy of the book (which will be sent C.O.D. "in a plain wrapper"). But serious people may be fooled into thinking that metaphysics is always a name for mere charlatanry. The cure for this kind of distrust can be found by using a good dictionary, or by comparing these spurious "metaphysical" writings with some book that philosophers would agree is authentic metaphysics—Aristotle's *Metaphysics,* Descartes' *Meditations,* Spinoza's *Ethics* (Parts I-III), Schop-

---

[1] Somerset Maugham, *The Summing Up,* pages 238-239. New York: Doubleday & Company, Inc., 1946. Quoted by permission of the publisher.

enhauer's *The World as Will and Idea,* Bradley's *Appearance and Reality,* Dewey's *Experience and Nature,* Whitehead's *Process and Reality,* Royce's *The World and the Individual,* or the like.

Such vulgar misunderstandings aside, there are other more germane objections to metaphysics that we should examine.

Common sense objections to metaphysics

The man of "healthy common sense" is likely to be impatient with what he calls metaphysics, although many of his own beliefs (in free will or against free will, for instance) belong to the subject-matter of metaphysics. Ignoring the metaphysical content of his own uncritical beliefs, he is likely to consider metaphysics fruitless speculation that has more than a little foolishness in it, and a waste of time.

Certainly metaphysics is a waste of time for one who thinks that time is well spent only in building houses, making money, fighting wars, curing disease, or "wine, women, and song." So also, of course, according to this standard, operas, novels, churches, history, and higher mathematics are ways of wasting time. But it might well be argued that the value judgment that metaphysics and these other pursuits are wastes of time is too narrow. It may be very important to an individual (and, if he has a superior mind, to society) to formulate defensible notions about the whole of things and man's place in it. There are, fortunately, some men like Dmitri Karamazov who, as Dostoevski tells us, "did not care about making a million dollars, but did want an answer to his questions."

Metaphysicians are sometimes said to be blind men looking for a black cat at midnight when there's no cat there. Or they are compared to the blind men who felt of an elephant and disputed whether it was more like a rope, a tree, or a wall. The man of common sense is likely to be skeptical of the alleged power of the human mind to understand reality as a whole, especially when it seems to lead to conclusions about reality that are opposed to his own common-sense view of things.

And well may he be skeptical. There is no guarantee that we can discover truth about reality as a whole. Of course, in the beginning there was no guarantee that we could discover the truth about anything; but men tried to learn, and they did learn much about the weather, molecules, stars, germs, and themselves. The common sense attitude, which we have called the dogmatism of ignorant minds, would always block the way of inquiry if it were taken as the final judge of what we can know.

The wisest conclusion would seem to be: use whatever abilities we have for understanding the world, but do not be overconfident that the answers we get are true. Dogmatism has no more place in metaphysics than it has in science, but a narrow skepticism would prevent us from pursuing any kind of inquiry.

Psychological objections to metaphysics

According to one view of psychology, the higher thought processes are merely rationalizations of our instinctive needs. F. H. Bradley, himself one of the greatest metaphysicians, said, "Metaphysics is the giving of bad reasons for what we believe upon instinct." The Freudians say that a metaphysical belief like the belief in God is only the persistence of the infantile need for the love of a father.[2] Some men sublimate their sexual urges by writing poetry; others do so by writing books on metaphysics.[3] There is no more reason to expect the latter to be true than the former.

We shall deal with this objection in just a moment, after we have stated the sociologist's objection to metaphysics.

---

[2] Sigmund Freud, *The Future of an Illusion,* page 34. London: H. Liveright and the Institute of Psychoanalysis, 1928.

[3] Cf. Alexander Herzberg, *The Psychology of Philosophers.* New York: Harcourt Brace and Company, Inc., 1929.

Sociological objections to metaphysics

Metaphysics, according to many sociologists and anthropologists, is a reflection of the social or cultural conditions under which it develops. Men project into their pictures of ultimate reality the kind of laws and structures they find in their society (see page 122) because their thought about the unknown is conditioned by their conventional beliefs about the world around them. The intellectual climate within which metaphysical speculation occurs is not determined by considerations germane to the truth or falsity of a metaphysical theory, it is said, but by the political ideologies, religious outlook, and technological situation of the society. Just as an individual cannot see things except from a point of view determined by his own psychological make-up, so also, it is said, the social situation still further restricts his perspective.

Such an objection can be illustrated by reference to the way a language may incline those who speak it to accept tacitly a certain kind of metaphysics. The European languages, including Greek, in which the first philosophy was written, have what is known as a subject-predicate syntax. Sentences in these languages typically take the form, "The tree is green," "Der Baum ist grün," "L'arbre est vert." In such sentences we verbally separate a thing (tree) from its quality (green), which then seems to be a "universal" that applies to many things (see page 124). This peculiarity of our languages raises a question we have already discussed, the solution of which belongs to the study of metaphysics. The question is: what sort of "being" does the universal possess, and how is the universal related to the particulars it qualifies? This has been one of the central problems of European metaphysics since the time of Plato.

But, according to those who object to metaphysics, it is a "pseudo-problem" that has arisen only because of the peculiarity of the language spoken. Peoples who speak other languages with a different syntactical structure (for instance, Chinese) have developed other metaphysical theories with quite different questions to be answered. "Reality," the critic says, "is indifferent to our gramatical distinctions; metaphysical questions arise from a confusion of such grammatical distinctions with categories of reality."

If we generalize this objection, it comes to the general statement that all metaphysical problems are psuedo-problems arising from the confusion of the linguistic or other peculiarities of a culture with alleged characteristics of "ultimate reality."

Answer to the psychological and sociological objections

These two objections are, in principle, the same. They agree that metaphysical beliefs are caused by conditions that we cannot control and of which we are generally ignorant. The purpose of intelligent inquiry should be to uncover these hidden causes of belief, not to defend the speculations that flow from them.

There are three responses to these objections. First, they properly put us on guard against an easy dogmatism in metaphysics. If their premises are correct, as they undoubtedly are to some extent, they warn us against formulating metaphysical theories with the headlong confidence we might feel if we believed that our desires and our social environment had no influence on our beliefs. In Chapter 6 we have seen how difficult it is to eliminate bias and the "personal equation" in studies of society. Some of these biases are personal, and some are dependent upon the culture in which we live. In discussions of value we found that it is not possible or even desirable to eliminate the personal commitment to some values, although this commitment has its psychological and social causes. It is, however, possible to become aware of biases and to take precautions so that they will not mislead us like a blind man's evil guide. What is true of bias in those fields is even truer in metaphysics proper. It is exceedingly difficult to be sure what our most deep-rooted convictions are. But one of the best ways of finding out what they are is to see what reasonable alternatives to them have been held by others (see pages 43-44). Perhaps our own stock of bias may prevent us from getting to an objective, impersonal truth in metaphysics; but a good dose of metaphysics can often do much to purge us of our bias. What Bertrand Russell says of philosophy in general is especially applicable to metaphysics:

> The man who has no tincture of philosophy goes through life imprisoned in the prejudices derived from common sense, from the habitual beliefs of his age or his nation, and from convictions which have grown up in his mind without the co-operation or consent of his deliberate reason. . . . While diminishing our feeling of certainty as to what things are, it greatly increases our knowledge as to what they may be; it removes the somewhat arrogant dogmatism of those who have never travelled into the region of liberating doubt and it keeps alive our sense of wonder by showing familiar things in an unfamiliar aspect.[4]

The second response to these objections is that they clearly indicate the great importance, personal and social, of metaphysical thinking, at the same time that they claim that it cannot be conclusive or valid. The quotation made earlier from F. H. Bradley, about metaphysics being the giving of bad reasons for what we believe by instinct, continues: "but the giving of these bad reasons is itself a matter of instinct." Even if it sometimes seems that man is not a rational animal, it does appear that he is a "metaphysical animal." He wants answers to the question that his mind puts to him about his place in the world as a whole. This need in many men and women is so strong that they *will* have an answer to it in spite of all objections; they *will* have a metaphysics, even if they are ignorant of the very name of this study.

The present generation of men want answers just as their less skeptical and critical ancestors did. The arguments of psychologists and sociologists have convinced many of the best minds that metaphysics is impossible, a waste of time, or a

---

[4] From *Problems of Philosophy* by Bertrand Russell, pages 243-244. Home University Library, Oxford University Press, 1912.

sign of neurosis, so that they have turned their talents to science (or, if they are philosophers, to the "critical" rather than "speculative" problems). They leave the ordinary person without the benefit of philosophy that was supplied to their ancestors by such stout-hearted metaphysicians as Thomas Aquinas, Thomas Hobbes, Hegel, or Herbert Spencer.

But the consequence is not that the ordinary layman gives up his interest in metaphysics. Rather, it is catered to by uncritical second-rate writers with press-agents. Our age may not be favorable to the development of metaphysics, but it is favorable to the large sale of books on peace of mind, the destiny of man, the origin of the universe, and the purpose of existence. In spite of the sociological and psychological objection to the possibility of metaphysics, there is a "metaphysical vacuum" which, if not filled by competent philosophical thinkers, will be filled by still more unsatisfactory thinkers who do not even know of the valid objections that have been made to metaphysical speculation.

The third reply to these objections is more in the spirit of critical philosophy. The objections are based upon conclusions derived, or believed to have been derived, from a study of science. For instance, it is proposed as a *law* that the higher mental functions of a man are what they are because of his position in a culture, or because of repression and subsequent sublimation of his sexual drive. But we have repeatedly seen that science itself, in its doctrine of law, makes use of some metaphysical hypothesis about universals. To be sure, the psychologist and sociologist do not usually call their basic assumptions metaphysical; they may not even be aware that they have any such basic principles, so blinding is the effect of shared belief. The psychologist and sociologist usually make objections *only* to those metaphysical theories that they do not like and that are not presupposed in their own scientific work—such as the belief in the objectivity of values. But the assumptions they themselves make are not less metaphysical. Hence their objection ought to be directed to some specific metaphysical theory instead of to metaphysical inquiry itself. But even if we grant that the individual's personality and the culture in which it develops determine in part the metaphysical views that will be put forward by one philosopher and accepted by others, it still would not follow that metaphysical speculation and study would be useless. Even if the study of metaphysics does not lead to results that can be established with certainty, its pursuit has been and still is significant in understanding the organization of the knowledge we do have. The study of metaphysical speculation can be valuable for the light it throws on the science, art, religion, morals, and ideology of the culture out of which it grows. This is because every search for value or knowledge depends upon presuppositions that implicitly guide it, but that might guide it better, or be better guarded against, if they were better understood. The study of metaphysics includes the elaboration and criticism of such presuppositions, which are made explicit only in philosophic inquiry.

In earlier chapters we have been examining the presuppositions of science, such as the various theories of the uniformity of nature, of the status of natural laws, of the relation of life to matter, and the like. If we had oriented our study around religion, we should have had to deal with some of these presuppositions and with still others. Had we been writing a thousand years earlier, certainly the presuppositions we would have unearthed would have been different. The highest claim of metaphysics might be to uncover and examine the "presuppositions presupposed in all presuppositions," and they would be formulated in a conceptual scheme that would be a theory about "ultimate reality." But the more cautious metaphysician, who takes seriously the sociologist's and the psychologist's objection, will not stake such a vast claim. He may, however, accomplish more by trying to discern the hidden presuppositions that have been or are now *taken* to be ultimate, but may be superseded by still further developments of knowledge and of our ability to analyze it.

This conception of the role of metaphysics is immune to the sociological and psychological objections. In fact, this kind of work in metaphysics continues the work of the sociologist and psychologist who are interested in the analysis of the intellectual activities of men in the context of the psychological and social factors influencing it. It is the "attempt to find out what absolute presuppositions have been made by this or that person or group of persons, on this or that occasion or group of occasions, in the course of this or that piece of thinking." [5]

The positivistic attack on metaphysics

Positivists argue that all knowledge as it develops tends in the direction of science, which is the perfected stage of knowledge. Metaphysics appears to the positivist to be a stage in the history of thought that we have now transcended. Unlike metaphysics, science, according to this view, has no interest in explaining things; it suffices to describe them. The laws that describe things are only statistical correlations among observed events. The notion of scientific objects, such as atoms, which are commonly thought of as the causes of or realities behind our experiences, is an unfortunate remnant of metaphysical imagery and picture-thinking. Value judgments, for the positivist, are expressions of emotive or persuasive meanings and have no cognitive value or truth. The proper attitude to religion, he says, is one of agnosticism or a humanism that emphasizes the human goals previously sought by or disguised in religious activities, but now attainable through scientific techniques devoted to human welfare.

Positivism was the name given to this combination of beliefs by Auguste Comte in the nineteenth century. But the beliefs, and even the combination of attitudes involved, is much older. Much of it can be found in Protagoras and Hume. But Comte gave it a name and organized its doctrines, which, when taken separately, seem negativistic, into an affirmative philosophy

---

[5] R. G. Collingwood, *An Essay on Metaphysics*, page 47. Oxford: Clarendon Press, 1940.

and program of action. Comte reached his conclusions chiefly from his study of the history of society, science, and technology, but other philosophers after him based their positivism on more strictly epistemological considerations. The leaders of this movement were the Austrian physicist and philosopher, Ernst Mach (1838-1916), and the French mathematician and philosopher, Henri Poincaré (1854-1912).

About 1920, a group of philosophers in Vienna, known as the "Vienna Circle," revived and brought up to date some of Mach's ideas and put a major emphasis upon the function of language in scientific knowledge. Their school, now scattered throughout the world and of world-wide influence, is known as "logical positivism" to distinguish it from the earlier positivism of Comte. We must now briefly examine their view, for they, like all positivists, hold that metaphysics is impossible.

Logical positivists say that the proper task of philosophy is the logical analysis of the language we use to record and transmit our knowledge. Philosophy is not concerned with getting facts, for that is the business of science. The proper job of the philosopher is to analyze the methods and the language of the scientists, so as to give scientific knowledge a rigorous logical presentation free from the illusions of hidden purposes and alleged but unknown realities.

The opposite opinion is that philosophy is the pursuit of synoptic accounts of experience and is thus superior to the departmentalized sciences. The positivist asserts that this view of the task of philosophy has been shown to be unproductive of worthwhile results in the history of philosophy and science. Philosophers have not established any real knowledge. While scientists have been piling up an imposing array of facts and reducing them to simple laws and theories that lead to the discovery of new and useful facts and techniques, philosophers continue to disagree about everything. They still re-hash the intellectual fare of ancient Greece, and after 2,400 years, they have not answered the puzzles Socrates put before his disciples. Since philosophy has so notoriously failed to provide any knowledge that is settled and dependable, the positivists think that philosophers, especially in the metaphysical part of their work, have been on the wrong track. They should no longer waste their efforts on trying to get any "speculative" or "synop-tic" metaphysical knowledge. There is, nevertheless, important work for them. The proper function of philosophy is critical, not speculative:

> I believe Science should be defined as the *"pursuit of truth,"* and Philosophy as the *"pursuit of meaning"*. . . . It is my opinion that the future of philosophy hinges on this distinction between the discovery of sense and the discovery of truth.[6]

What, then, is "sense" or "meaning," which the philosopher should discover in the statements that scientists make and claim to be true? The positivist's answer to this question is known as the "verification theory of meaning." It is formulated by Schlick:

> We know the meaning of a proposition when we are able to in-dicate exactly the circumstances under which it would be true (or, what amounts to the same thing, the circumstances which would make it false).[7]

The meaning of a proposition is what would be observed if the proposition is true, or what we should expect to observe but fail to observe if the proposition is thought to be true but is actually false. Consider an illustration. There is a proposition in chemistry, "The valence of oxygen is two." What does it mean? We do not see an oxygen atom with anything like two little hooks on its side that grasp other atoms, although some-times such a picture as this is used in introductory courses in chemistry. We do not see the outer shell of electrons with its unoccupied positions said by some chemists to "explain" the valence of oxygen. The positivist wants to banish the assump-tion that such hypothetical, unobservable objects exist as

---

[6] Moritz Schlick, "The Future of Philosophy," in *The College of the Pacific Publications in Philosophy*, 1932, page 54.

[7] *Ibid.*, page 55.

causes of what we observe, even though most positivists will grant that they may be useful fictions since they help us in making predictions. What we do see, and what the statement *really* means, is a particular quantitative relationship that can be observed and measured in chemical reactions between fairly large volumes of oxygen and other elements. The proposition means: a given volume of oxygen will combine with twice its volume of hydrogen. This is what we expect to observe if the proposition, "The valence of oxygen is two," is true.

Consider another example, from the biological sciences. "Cancer is caused by a germ." What does it mean? It means what the bacteriologist would observe if the proposition is true, namely, that every cancer would contain some germ. The observation, however, is not made; hence the proposition, "Cancer is caused by a germ," is false, although it does have a meaning.

Now take a third example, one from traditional metaphysics: "The human will is free." What does it mean? We cannot point out any specific experience that we should have if the proposition is true and that we should not have if it is false. How can we test it? We should have to predict how a person would behave if he did have a free will, and this behavior would have to be recognizably different from the way we should expect him to behave if he did not have a free will. But if we say, "He will behave so and so, under the supposition that he has a free will," we are saying: (1) we know that no amount of knowledge that we could get would suffice to predict his action on the basis of his past history, his nervous system, and the like; and (2) the proposition that he has a free will implies that he will behave in this specific way. The facts of the case, however, are that we know neither (1) nor (2), and (2) seems to be inconsistent with what we ordinarily mean by saying that the will is free, that is, that it is *not* determined. There is therefore no way to test this proposition, and therefore, it is not false but meaningless.

The so-called problems of the existence of God, the immortality of the soul, the objectivity of value, the "real existence" of scientific objects that are not observed (for example, electrons), the purpose of the universe, the reality of universals, and the like—all traditional problems of metaphysics—are similarly shown to be meaningless. *Any* proposed answers to them are meaningless. In a very literal sense, they are "nonsense" because they have no counterpart or verification in sense experience. Many questions, such as, "Are values objective or subjective?" *look* like questions, but they are only pseudo-problems and cannot be answered because they have no meaning. They are logically like the question, "Are circles angelic or diabolical?" which does not even *seem* to make sense.

The proper purpose of philosophy is to uncover and expose these pseudo-problems or meaningless questions that have troubled philosophers. One positivist has said, "Philosophy is the disease of which it ought to be the cure." If we find that some traditional problem of philosophy is a real problem, it can be turned over to the scientist for solution; if we find that it is not a real problem, it can be handed over to poets and dreamers to whom it may afford "matter for that reverie which is the most delicious pleasure with which man can beguile his idleness."

Thus the fate of all "philosophical problems" is this: Some of them will disappear by being shown to be mistakes and misunderstandings about our language, and the others will be found to be ordinary scientific questions in disguise. These remarks, I think, determine the whole future of philosophy.[8]

Metaphysics, at least since the time of Hume and Kant, has not been subjected to so subtle and thorough a criticism as this one formulated by the logical positivists. Can metaphysics meet the attack?

Certainly much of metaphysics cannot, and we should be glad to have it so thoroughly eradicated. If one who is familiar with modern positivism and its analytical methods reads some

---

[8] *Ibid.*, page 60.

ordinary (but perhaps not the best) metaphysical books of 30 years ago, he will be annoyed by the lack of precision and the general fuzziness of argument it shows. The positivists have shown how justly we can ignore much of the tedious lucubrations that have appeared under the title of speculative metaphysics. They tempt us to exclaim, with Hume:

> When we run over libraries, persuaded of these principles, what havoc must we make? If we take in our hand any volume; of divinity or school metaphysics, for instance; let us ask, *Does it contain any abstract reasoning concerning quantity or number?* No. *Does it contain any experimental reasoning concerning matter of fact and existence?* No. Commit it then to the flames: for it can contain nothing but sophistry and illusion.[9]

But a little more examination may make the careful thinker suspicious of the great victory claimed by positivism in discovering that metaphysics is nonsense. We shall examine two grounds of suspicion.

1. Is the verification theory of meaning valid? What does *it* mean? It is a decision freely taken by the positivist, announcing that he will use the word "meaning" in a *specific* way. What justifies him in this? No dictionary defines meaning in this way; this is not what most people *mean* by "meaning." Can we test the meaning of the sentence by itself, so that its "meaning" is what would be observed if the sentence is true? Hardly, for its meaning in this sense is nothing but the observed fact that the positivists behave in a certain way when they investigate the meaning of any other sentence. Yet what we want to know is whether this belief of the positivist is true, and the behavior of the positivist, who already believes it, is not a fair test.

The positivist may say that the sentence setting forth his criterion of meaning is not intended to be *true*, but is rather a stipulation or an assumption he makes. It expresses a decision

---

[9] David Hume, *An Enquiry Concerning Human Understanding*, in *Hume Selections*, pages 192-193 (Charles W. Hendel, Jr., ed.). New York: Charles Scribner's Sons, 1927.

concerning how he will act, not a discovery of some already existing state of affairs. But seen in this way, it is clear that if someone else prefers to use some other criterion of meaning, the positivist cannot legitimately object, although he may not *like* the behavior of the other person who insists on using some other "rule of the game." This, however, is a value judgment, which, according to the positivist, can express only a subjective preference.

At some stage in every theory, of course, a decision must be made, and the decision expresses a preference. But conclusions based on such decisions are not valid objections to conclusions made on the basis of other decisions. Thus one may say that, with the positivist's decision concerning meaning, he cannot consistently say anything that is metaphysical; but that is by itself no criticism of metaphysics, nor does it demonstrate that metaphysics is *per se* impossible.

2. It is not certain that the positivist, in attacking metaphysics, has not fallen into metaphysics himself. We saw earlier that many people object to metaphysics in general when they ought to be arguing only against some specific metaphysical theory, for they themselves make universal judgments about man and the world and the limits of knowledge and the status of values—every one of which is a judgment in metaphysics. Although the positivist is careful not to call any of his judgments metaphysical, the discerning reader can often detect, at least between the lines, the predilections of a positivist author which, when consistently worked out, would be a full-fledged metaphysical system.[10]

If metaphysics is considered as the inquiry into ultimate presuppositions, or as a comparative study of presuppositions taken as ultimate by some "person or group of persons, on this or that occasion or group of occasions, in the course of this or that piece of thinking," then it is clear that positivism can be

---

[10] Several works pointing out metaphysical assumptions involved in positivism are listed in the bibliography.

considered metaphysically, just as metaphysics is considered critically by the positivist.

METAPHYSICS AS HYPOTHESIS

The objections that have been made to metaphysics do not destroy either its possibility or its value. But they do make us skeptical of any claims that in metaphysics we can expect to demonstrate final answers to the ultimate problems of human life. This would once have sufficed to make metaphysics seem worthless, for many philosophers (Bergson, for example, and some rationalists) have believed that metaphysics is the most certain kind of knowledge.

Our previous studies, however, have shown that the sciences neither claim nor give ultimate knowledge; yet they give nonetheless valuable knowledge. In view of this, perhaps the metaphysician should not despair when he concludes that metaphysics, too, does not give absolute certainty about the whole of things. He should be more than satisfied if he could get even as much certainty in metaphysics as he has in science; and in fact he has to be satisfied with much less.

When metaphysicians claimed to have some special way of knowing, such as intuition or *a priori* reasoning, they strove for absolute certainty and ended in disagreements and polemics with others who likewise claimed absolute knowledge. If metaphysicians can make use of the method of hypothesis, however, then their claims may be somewhat less extravagant and their accomplishments somewhat more substantial. Our present task is to see how the method of hypothesis can be exported from the field of science and values, where we have already studied it, to the field of metaphysics.

Here our hypotheses will be extremely abstract and general. They will have as their subject matter nothing less than the whole of existence about which they make a conjecture. Cicero tells us that Democritus began one of his books with the modest statement, "I shall discourse about everything." Stephen

C. Pepper has called metaphysical propositions "world hypotheses":

> The peculiarity of world hypotheses is that they cannot reject anything as irrelevant. When certain inconvenient matters are brought to a mathematician, he can always say, "These are psychological [or physical, or historical] matters. I do not have to deal with them." Similarly with other students of restricted fields. But students of world hypotheses can never have that way out. Every consideration is relevant to a world hypothesis, and no facts lie outside it.[11]

A metaphysical or world hypothesis is in the form, "Reality is such that . . . " and the "such that . . . " must include shoes and ships and sealing wax, and cabbages and kings, facts and values, scientific hypotheses and feelings—literally everything.

Of course no man can know everything, so the metaphysical hypotheses will always be based on a small number of the things that are relevant to them. But by observing the work of some of the great metaphysicians, we can see how they went about the job of making their hypotheses on the basis of their experience, which, if small compared with the standard of all that is, was large and broad by human standards. Some philosophers have formulated their hypotheses out of the received tradition of their church or the ideology of their government, or have taken the facts of science as their raw material, or have had a mystical experience in which they "saw" the truth. In spite of great differences of technique and disposition, however, all the great systems of metaphysical hypotheses seem to owe their birth to a procedure that, when properly understood, is seen to be that of formulating and elaborating a hypothesis.

Let us look at several different descriptions of the way in which metaphysical hypotheses originate and are used. The first is from Dorothy Emmett:

> Metaphysics is an analogical way of thinking. . . . It takes concepts drawn from some form of experience or some relation within

---

[11] Stephen C. Pepper, *World Hypotheses*, page 1. Berkeley and Los Angeles: University of California Press, 1942. Quoted by permission of the publisher.

experience, and extends them either so as to say something about the nature of "reality," or so as to suggest a possible mode of co-ordinating other experiences of different types from that from which the concept was originally derived.[12]

The second is from Pepper:

A man desiring to understand the world looks about for a clue to its comprehension. He pitches upon some area of common-sense fact, and tries if he cannot understand other areas in terms of this one. This original area becomes then his basic analogy or *root metaphor*. He describes as best he can the characteristics of this area or . . . discriminates its structure. A list of its structural characteristics becomes his basic concepts of explanation and description. We call them a set of categories. . . . Since the basic analogy or root metaphor normally (and probably at least in part necessarily) arises out of common sense, a great deal of development and refinement of a set of categories is required if they are to prove adequate for a hypothesis of unlimited scope.[13]

The third is from an English philosopher, Bernard Bosanquet. He describes the method of philosophy in general, but what he says has primary reference to metaphysics:

What philosophy needs as its material is the sort of thing that is in a sense obvious, and yet is hard to make plain and distinct. The very greatest things are of this kind—simple examples are, what the painter perceives when he represents a wood, and not merely a number of trees, or the sociologist, when he understands a crowd and not merely a number of persons—both late in being learnt, though the things are so obvious. The *central facts* should be in the centre. This needs a continuous arduous effort, as opposed to resting upon fixed points here and there.[14]

Our last quotation is from Whitehead:

[12] Dorothy Emmett, *The Nature of Metaphysical Thinking*, page 5. London: Macmillan and Company, Ltd., 1949. Used by permission of The Macmillan Company, publishers.

[13] Stephen C. Pepper, *op. cit.*, page 91 (italics supplied).

[14] Bernard Bosanquet, *The Principle of Individuality and Value* (1912), page xvii. London: Macmillan and Company, Ltd., 1927 (italics supplied). Used by permission of The Macmillan Company, publishers.

The true method of discovery is like the flight of an aeroplane. It starts from the ground of particular observation; it makes a flight in the thin air of imaginative generalization; and it again lands for renewed observation rendered acute by rational interpretation.[15]

One might think that this is Whitehead's account of scientific method; it is, in fact, his description of his philosophical or metaphysical procedure.

What stands out clearly in all these accounts is that metaphysics begins by our taking something in the world seriously, regarding it as a synecdoche or analogy for the whole or as a microcosm that reflects the macrocosm, and using it as a metaphor for the whole. These central facts are generally highly charged with value; hence a system of metaphysics will to some extent carry to the end the marks of its birth in a particular personality and cultural milieu. A metaphysical hypothesis is like a great work of art, which is the whole world seen from a particular artist's point of view and fashioned by his genius working within, or slightly beyond, the style of his culture.

Unlike a work of art, however, a metaphysical hypothesis is supposed to be factually true. It must pass some tests that we do not usually apply to a poem. It must justify itself not by its beauty or style, but more in the way in which a scientific theory is justified: by comprehending, explaining, and rendering integral and intelligible a mass of otherwise chaotic experiences.

Metaphysical hypotheses, however, cannot be verified by scientific test. We cannot search for the purpose of the universe in order to verify a teleological metaphysics by looking for it through a telescope or microscope. The hypotheses of metaphysics are so general that they do not have specific consequences that can be predicted in detail and tested in the laboratory. This was the reason the logical positivists said they had no meaning at all.

[15] Alfred North Whitehead, *Process and Reality*, page 7. New York: The Macmillan Company, 1929.

But there is another test: that of dialectic. Given a metaphysical hypothesis, apply it again and again to the broader and ever-widening reaches of experience to see if it "holds its own" or to see what modifications must be introduced in it to enable it to integrate experience and make experience intelligible. The process is essentially like the Platonic dialectic (pages 202-204), but it will lead to Platonic conclusions only if it begins with the root metaphors with which Plato began.

Just as a scientific hypothesis is judged by the degree to which diverse evidence converges around it, a metaphysical hypothesis must be judged by the degree to which all of our experiences—and not just those in a certain sector of science—point to and converge around it. It may be that no metaphysical hypothesis can serve to bring all our experience into this kind of focus. It is possible that there is some truth about "everything," but that it is so obscure that it cannot be discovered by the human mind; in this case, the best we can do is to try to get a hypothesis that will fit as much of our experience as possible. Or it may indeed be true that the universe is not all of a piece—that the most penetrating analysis will discover contradictions and incongruities in existence that no synthesis can overcome.

Although a philosopher may conceivably be forced to some such conclusion as one of these, they are conclusions to which he should adhere only after he has done his best to discern whatever intelligible order there is. And though he may confess that he cannot find a final answer that is demonstrable and wholly adequate to all parts of experience, he must also acknowledge that the metaphysical theories we have are not all *equally* impotent and inadequate. Some metaphysical theories break down under comparatively little critical inquiry. Others hold their own much better under dialectical scrutiny. Some metaphysicians believe that they have found the one hypothesis that requires no revision. But alternative metaphysical hypotheses cannot be tested so as to eliminate all but one, leaving that one perfect hypothesis standing.

The consequence of this is that metaphysical hypotheses that start from a pregnant root metaphor or a rich central fact or analogy may be developed side by side with other theories, having their origin in different metaphors and analogies. No one of them may be strong enough to eliminate all the others. For this reason, dogmatism about final answers is unjustified in metaphysics.

In the succeeding chapters, we shall study three types of metaphysical hypotheses that have been shown to be sufficiently comprehensive and coherent to hold their own under careful analysis, and that have therefore appealed to serious thinkers both past and present. These hypotheses, or more properly, theories or families of hypotheses, have provided frameworks for the organization of the experience and aspirations of many generations, and each has its adherents at the present time.

The first to be discussed is known as theological dualism, and is defined by the belief that reality consists of two kinds of being, nature and that which transcends nature, or God. This theory takes as its central experience the sphere of religion.

The second is the group of theories known as idealism, which emphasize the ultimate position of mind in the universe.

The third is the group of theories known as naturalism, characterized by their emphasis upon the unity of nature and the adequacy of the scientific method for the discovery of metaphysical truth.

BIBLIOGRAPHY

Ballard, Edward G., "Metaphysics and Metaphor," *Journal of Philosophy*, Vol. XLV, No. 8, (April 8, 1948) pages 208-214.
Barnes, Winston H. F., *The Philosophical Predicament*. London: Adam & Charles Black, 1950.
Bergson, Henri, *An Introduction to Metaphysics* (1903) (T. E. Hulme, trans., with an introduction by T. A. Goudge). New York: Liberal Arts Press, 1949. (The Little Library of Liberal Arts, No. 10.)

Blanshard, Brand, "Current Strictures on Reason," *Philosophical Review*, Vol. LIV, No. 2 (March, 1945), pages 345-368.

Carnap, Rudolf, "On the Character of Philosophical Problems," *Philosophy of Science*, Vol. I, No. 1 (January, 1934), pages 5-19.

Erickson, R. W., "Metaphysics of a Logical Positivist," *Philosophy of Science*, Vol. VIII, No. 3 (July, 1941), pages 320-328.

Hall, Everett W., "Metaphysics," in *Twentieth Century Philosophy* (Dagobert D. Runes, ed.), pages 145-194. New York: Philosophical Library, 1947.

———, "Of What Use is Metaphysics?" *Journal of Philosophy*, Vol. XXXIII, No. 9 (April 23, 1936), pages 236-245.

Hartshorne, Charles, "Metaphysics for Positivists," *Philosophy of Science*, Vol. II, No. 3 (July, 1935), pages 287-303.

Hocking, W. E., Lamprecht, Sterling P., and Randall, John Herman, Jr., "Metaphysics, its Function, Consequences, and Criteria," *Journal of Philosophy*, Vol. XLIII, No. 14 (July 4, 1946) pages 365-78, and No. 15 (July 18, 1946), pages 393-412.

Hoernlé, R. F. Alfred, *Idealism as a Philosophy*, pages 299-306. New York: George H. Doran Company, 1927.

Kant, Immanuel, *Prolegomena to Any Future Metaphysics* (1785) (Lewis W. Beck, ed.). New York: Liberal Arts Press, 1950. (The Little Library of Liberal Arts, No. 27.)

Lee, Harold N., "Metaphysics as Hypothesis," *Journal of Philosophy*, Vol. XLIV, No. 13 (June 19, 1947), pages 344-352.

Mannheim, Karl, *Ideology and Utopia. An Introduction to the Sociology of Knowledge.* New York: Harcourt, Brace and Company, Inc., 1936.

Phillips, Bernard, "Logical Positivism and the Function of Reason," *Philosophy*, Vol. XXIII, No. 87 (October, 1948), pages 346-360.

Werkmeister, W. H., "Seven Theses of Logical Positivism Critically Examined," *Philosophical Review*, Vol. XLVI, No. 3 (May, 1947), pages 276-297, and No. 4 (July, 1937), pages 357-376.

Whiteley, C. H., *An Introduction to Metaphysics*. London: Methuen & Company, Ltd., 1950.

Wick, Warner Arms, *Metaphysics and the New Logic*. Chicago: University of Chicago Press, 1942.

Wiener, P. P., "Some Metaphysical Assumptions and Problems of Neo-Positivism," *Journal of Philosophy*, Vol. XXXII, No. 7 (March 18, 1935), pages 175-181.

QUESTIONS AND TOPICS FOR DISCUSSION

1. What is an analogy? How is an analogy related to a hypothesis? Compare the use of analogies and hypotheses in the sciences and in metaphysics.
2. What characteristics of a good hypothesis are lacking in metaphysical hypotheses?
3. A frequent objection to metaphysics is that metaphysicians cannot agree with one another. Evaluate this objection.
4. What are some of the assumptions underlying the various objections to metaphysics. Are these assumptions themselves metaphysical?
5. "By the very word, metaphysics has to come after physics. Until the physicists get answers to all their questions, metaphysics is premature." Discuss.
6. What are some of the ways in which one metaphysical theory might be judged to be better than another?
7. Read Bergson's *Introduction to Metaphysics*. How does Bergson believe metaphysics differs from science? Does he avoid the use of hypotheses in metaphysics?

9

Theological Dualism

THE "CENTRAL FACT"

The central fact for the theological dualist is the religious experience. His basic analogy is that there is a being who stands to the entire universe in a relation like that in which man stands to some parts of it that he cares for and controls. The fundamental thesis of theological dualism is that in order to understand the world of nature and man and history, it is necessary to see them in relation to that which is higher than nature or man or history. For this reason the theory is sometimes called *supernaturalism*, for it holds that nature, as it is studied in the sciences, can be fully understood only in the light of something not a part of nature, something above nature.

The doctrines of religion, therefore, have preeminent significance in the thinking of theological dualists. Experience as a whole can be understood, they say, only when interpreted in a context of metaphysical principles that a religious person accepts on faith. It follows that there may be various metaphysical theories that are species of theological dualism, depending upon the specific religious doctrines that are accepted and elaborated as metaphysical theses. We shall be concerned primarily with the kind of theological dualism that grows from

255

the conviction that some form of Christian theology is true, and that the truths of this theology are truths that any adequate metaphysics must accept and elaborate.

The basic *philosophic* beliefs of Christianity are:

1. There are some experiences of great and permanent value that cannot be fully understood if seen only as results of physiological, psychological, or social causes. Their understanding requires an acknowledgement that they are evidence of a being above or beyond the realm that can be understood scientifically, that is, nature. (This is the connotation of the word "dualism" in the name of this theory. Dualism indicates any theory that the world is not all of a piece, but that there are two basic categories. The specific dualism asserted here is that the two categories are nature and that which is above nature.)

2. That which is above nature, and is the cause of nature and the object of man's religious experience, is God, a personal being who created the world. Evidence for the existence of God is to be found in the study of both nature and human nature, and in the interpretation of religious experience considered as a revelation of God.

3. Man, in addition to his animal nature, is also a spiritual being. Man is to be understood both in his relation to other natural beings and in his relation to God. God's purpose in human existence is more fundamental than the individual's purposes, which are usually vain, and God sustains man's ethical and religious conduct.

4. Man's spiritual being makes him superior to his position in the natural course of events in time. This suggests that the essential spiritual element in man, his soul, is immortal.

5. Man's spiritual being is not completely determined by events in the course of nature, whether physical, psychological, or social. Man is more than "the sum of his yesterdays," and is not wholly a victim of natural circumstance. He has real freedom to seek out and to fulfill the purposes of God, which

are implicit in his creation. Man can make use of this freedom in a religiously significant way, however, only with the help or grace of God.

6. Values, especially moral values, are inherent and central characteristics of reality. In acting morally or in pursuing the higher values, man attunes himself to the ultimate reality in things, but in acting selfishly or immorally, he alienates himself from God and falls below his proper status in reality.

7. Man's growth in the experience of values is incomplete if it is restricted to secular values, even if it includes the highest moral, aesthetic, and intellectual values. There is a positive value in religious activity itself, in which man comes to acknowledge God as the supreme value of existence and to see that whatever worth he and his concerns have is derived ultimately from the supreme value of God.

8. There is justifiable faith that God as the maker of the universe and as its moral governor will establish His Kingdom in which the earnest pursuit of the supreme value will be made consonant with felicity or blessedness.

These philosophical propositions have been formulated in many ways. In the form just given, they are not restricted to Christianity, or even to the Judaeo-Christian tradition. Theologians of some of the other higher religions could subscribe to them; they do not state what is *specifically* Christian in the religion we are discussing. In order to distinguish the theological from the philosophical content of Christianity, and Christianity from other religions which have many of the same philosophical foundations, it is necessary to add to these philosophical statements some other statements having a more explicitly doctrinal content. Such statements of the dogmas of the Christian churches concerning the divinity of Christ and His mission in the world are formulated in the various "creeds," "confessions," and "articles of faith," which most sects take as the foundation of their specific religious rites.

Development of the theses of religion

Unlike specifically religious beliefs, which seem to be present even among the most primitive men, philosophical theses expressing in full generality the basic tenets of a philosophical world view based on religion were slow in arising in the history of thought. Religious beliefs, although accepted as referring to something eternal, "the same yesterday, today, and forever," do change with the changes in the intellectual and moral atmosphere of a society. The earliest conceptions of God and of His relation to man are very different from the refined metaphysical doctrine the theses of which we have just listed.

In primitive religions, man's belief in the *numinous,* or the sacred, included belief in impersonal power, such as *mana,* individual personal spirits in things, such as *anima,* and individual personal beings who transcend natural objects, or *gods.*[1] The activity of the divine or numinous reality was evidenced chiefly in unusual events, which men feared, or in any portentous events (such as birth and death, war, harvesting) where men felt their own impotence. Men believed that the divine reality could be coerced by magic as well as solicited and propitiated by prayers and religious rites. Many anthropologists believe that both religion and science, as we know them, descended from primitive man's concern with the numinous, the control of it by the technique of magic being gradually replaced by control through the techniques of applied science, and the solicitation and persuasion of it by prayer and ritual being the germ of the later development of religions as we know them.

The numinous was originally thought of as a superior natural force, frequently inimical to man or at least indifferent to his aspirations. Evidence for the divine was found in storm and earthquake, famine and plague. The gods, which were only

---

[1] For the meaning of some of these terms, see V. F. Calverton (ed.), *The Making of Man,* Part V. New York: Random House, Modern Library edition, 1931.

one species of the numinous reality, were thought of as having human form (the doctrine known as *anthropomorphism*). They were originally distinguished from man not by their virtues, but by their superhuman power. They were regarded as having both human vices and virtues in a magnified degree.

Only later does this narrow anthropomorphism give way to the notion that God has only the highest human characteristics in a magnified degree, without the baser human characteristics of anger, lust, and caprice. In the later parts of the Old Testament, we see this change in the conception of God from that of a rather irresponsible and jealous oriental potentate to that of God as the wise and just father of the human family; and in the New Testament, this refinement is carried still further until it is said, simply, that "God is love."

Primitive gods were not only capricious and often inimical to man, but also strictly limited in scope. Each place had its own god (*numen loci*), and each tribe its own tutelary deity. Belief in these local, tribal gods is known as *henotheism*. (Henotheism differs from monotheism in that the former refers to a group's belief in the god supreme *for it*, while the latter refers to a group's belief in a god not only supreme for it, but for all men.) Under henotheism, each god was a deity whose care was limited to a very small portion of the human race. When the Old Testament says, "Thou shalt have no other gods before me," it does not mean that Jehovah is the only god; it does not assert monotheism so much as henotheism, warning the Children of Israel to remain true to *their* god and not to worship the gods of the surrounding tribes.

As the narrowly anthropomorphic aspects of the primitive conception of gods were gradually replaced by a more elevated spiritual conception, henotheism and polytheism gave way to monotheism, the belief that there is only one god. Monotheism is the basis of two important characteristics of higher religions. First, it frees the conception of God from any narrow limitation to a particular social group or geographical region. It thus brings an element of universalism into religion, inspiring the belief that "our God" is the real God of all men and that it is our religious duty to spread His gospel to all men. Thus, tribal religion is replaced gradually by an ideal of one religion for all mankind. And second, in freeing the conception of God from tribal limitation, monotheism makes the conception of the individual's relation to God more direct and personal. God is not the god of this or that tribe or even of all tribes, but is the god of *each person*, who can and ought to seek him individually so as to comprehend his own religious and moral duty.

This pattern of change from physical anthropomorphism to the conception of God as a divine personality without human form, from polytheism to monotheism, from tribal to universal religion, and from the religion of social group-activity to religion as the individual's path to God, can be traced through most of the higher religions. Although men think of their gods as eternal, their thoughts about gods reflect their time and circumstance. They give up one conception of God for a better one. In Whitehead's words, "The progress of religion is defined by the denunciation of gods. The keynote of idolatry is contentment with the prevalent gods." [2]

If the existence of God is thought of as a hypothesis for metaphysics, this continuous change in details of the conception is precisely what we should expect. Although men do not begin to philosophize about God until fairly late in the history of a religion, philosophy then refines and clarifies the conception in two ways. First, it performs a critical examination of the religious practices current in a society. One sees this, for instance, in Plato's criticism in the *Republic* of the popular religious myths and practices of his day. Second, it integrates the concept of God with other concepts of metaphysics, so that the concept of God becomes a category for metaphysics as a whole, not just a conception restricted to the language and outlook of religion itself. This can be seen in many philosophical systems that use the concept of God as an explanatory

---

[2] Alfred North Whitehead, *Adventures of Ideas*, page 12. New York: The Macmillan Company, 1933.

principle without any religious overtones except the name itself.

One instance of a widespread religious doctrine holding that a conception of God as traditionally formulated is the ultimate and final truth is sometimes called *fundamentalism*. This is the belief that the Bible is the true and final revelation of God to man, that the Bible is the divinely inspired and dictated word of God, that the Bible is equally and uniformly inspired in all its parts, and that any revision or modification of the conception of God presented in the Bible is sacrilegious and heretical. Diametrically opposed to fundamentalism is the doctrine of *modernism*. It holds that the conception of God is subject to hypothetical interpretation, because whatever knowledge of God man possesses is mediated through the changing forms of human experience. As our experience grows, says the modernist, we become cognizant of the limitations of the formulae and doctrines of theology that an earlier period has passed down to us. We can then improve the more primitive conception by modifying the theological hypotheses so as to render them more adequate and significant for our own experience.

One of the chief factors favoring the development of modernism has been the comparative study of religions. Comparison of the religious beliefs of different peoples shows that each people forms its own conception of God, suitable to the social and cultural conditions prevalent in that society, or going beyond them in specific directions determined by the aspirations of the seers and prophets of that people. Comparison of the various conceptions of God and of the religious cultus of each people also reveals which elements of belief appear in all or almost all religions, and this provides some basis for the generalization of the philosophical content of religion beyond the specific religious content which distinguishes one sect from another.

These two conclusions of the comparative study of religion —the specificity of each people's conception of God, and the generality of certain fundamental traits in various conceptions of deity—suggest to the modernist that the wise attitude to our own and to other religions is to see each of them as a partial but to some extent distorted view of what God really is. Thus while modernists hold that Christianity is the most adequate of the various representations of God, they believe that Christians can nevertheless learn much of value about the nature of God and about valid religious practices from seeing what aspects of man's relation to Him have been emphasized and perfected in other religions.

Fundamentalists, of course, cannot take this attitude of tolerance, since they hold that they possess a view of God that is directly and infallibly given them by a special dispensation of God Himself, and thus have a view that cannot and need not be corrected in any detail.

The "conflict of science and religion"

Another factor favoring the development of modernism is the interaction of science and religion. What is often referred to as the "conflict of science and religion" is to a great extent misnamed. There is, undoubtedly, a conflict between science and fundamentalism, just as there is a conflict between science and any body of doctrine claimed to be final truth. Science thrives on the conviction that man does not have final knowledge about anything, and that any doctrine, no matter what its credentials, should be subject to inquiry and correction. When the fundamentalist insists that the world was created in six days, for instance, there is a head-on collision with both the attitude and the tentative conclusions of science. There are many statements in the Bible that are not consistent with the findings of modern science; and because fundamentalism has so often been identified with religion as a whole, it has *seemed* there is a conflict between religion itself and science. This belief has been very widespread, especially since Darwin's *Origin of Species* was published in 1859; but a similar belief in irreconcilable conflict extends all the way back to early Greek religion and science.

Fundamentalism, however, is not equivalent to religion. It is one among various hypotheses. The modernist holds that the concept of God, and the hypothesis of His existence, must be made harmonious with the greatest possible extent of our experience, and this experience includes science. Consider the following analogy. The Greek scientists and philosophers had a conception of the atom, which they thought of as a hard little pebble of matter. One can imagine a kind of "fundamentalist" in science, who would say that the modern conception of the atom is wrong because it does not conform to that presented in the writings of Democritus. The "modernist" in science, on the other hand, would say that the ancient conception of the atom was adequate to the knowledge of nature that the Greeks had, but since our knowledge of chemical and physical phenomena has grown, we must either give up the hypothesis altogether or change it so as to make it adequate to our experience. Similarly with the concept of God. In earlier times men thought of God as a tribal deity with anthropomorphic characteristics, and this represented the most adequate conception available to them. But we now have, or believe we have, a wider knowledge of nature and man. We need a concept that will do the same intellectual and religious "job" for us that the concept of Jehovah did for the Hebrews; but the concept of Jehovah as it appears in the Old Testament is not competent to do that job today. We shall call whatever is competent to do that job by the name "God," although it will now be represented in a somewhat different concept and hypothesis from what was represented by the concept of Jehovah for them. We can, on this basis, expect that the concept of God will undergo still further changes as our experience and knowledge continue to change.

There is not any conflict between the facts of science and religion. The sciences and religion deal with different things. Science studies the connections of one fact with another; religion is the appreciation of the relation in which men believe they and the whole world stand to something above and beyond nature, a relation transcending those studied in the sciences.

Nevertheless, there may be a conflict between a metaphysics or philosophy based on religion and one based solely on science. A fundamental belief of the philosopher who takes science as his central fact and nature as his root metaphor is that everything in the universe (or above it, if that notion is allowed) can be subjected to scientific study. Such a philosophy does not admit that there is any dualism in the universe, with the facts of science on one side and the objects of religious faith on the other.[3] Such a dichotomy is claimed in the metaphysics of theological dualism. Hence there is a dispute concerning the relative adequacy of a metaphysics based on religion and of a metaphysics based on science.

Metaphysical theories based primarily upon a religious outlook, however, usually do make room for science, just as those based upon science frequently acknowledge the value of the religious experience. But they dispute about the logical structure of the metaphysical system. Those with the religious experience as central explain science in the light of theological dualism, generally holding that science deals with a "lower order" of reality than the divine, and that the study of science contributes at least indirectly to man's awareness of his relation to that which is above the facts of nature. Those who take scientific experience as central attempt to account for the facts and values of the religious experience without appealing to a metaphysical dualism of God and nature as its foundation.

There are other compromises on a less philosophical level. There are many professional scientists who are religious in their personal outlook, and many a religious person who has respect for scientific knowledge. Sometimes the compromise is in the form of "not letting the left hand know what the right hand is doing." For instance, a practicing scientist may believe in the "rigorous and inexorable rule of causal law" six days a

---

[3] This is the thesis of naturalism. Cf. Chapters 12 and 13, especially pages 418 ff.

week but, on the seventh, accept an account of a miracle; he puts on his religion with his Sunday clothes and his science with his laboratory coat. Or a religious person may profoundly believe in the efficacy of intercessory prayer, yet appeal to scientific methods for curing diseases or predicting the behavior of the stock market. Such compromises are usually based upon failure to think beliefs through to their ultimate conclusions—a failure to construct a consistent philosophy of life.

Philosophy and theology

Religion is an attitude of mind and a mode of conduct predicated upon the acceptance of theses or dogmas listed at the beginning of this chapter. Religion is not an intellectualistic attitude of inquiry and tentative acceptance of hypotheses; it is an attitude of active faith, showing itself in willingness to act with enthusiasm in accordance with this faith. Because philosophy is primarily inquiry, questioning, and investigation, the philosophical attitude is quite different from the religious attitude, even though a man can entertain the articles of faith as metaphysical hypotheses when he is deliberately philosophizing, and accept them on faith as dogmas of his religion when he is carrying out his religious devotions.

Religion is quite distinct from theology. Theology is the study or inquiry into the existence and attributes of God and into His relation to man. Theology is an intellectual exposition and defense of theses accepted as articles of faith in religion. Theology is thus much more like philosophy than religion is. To the extent that the theologian is an open-minded investigator of the question of the existence and attributes of God and does not commit himself irrevocably to drawing certain conclusions set before him by a religious institution, the theologian *is* a philosopher.

Theology is divided into at least two parts: natural and revealed. *Natural theology* is concerned with evidence of God's existence and attributes found in a study of nature. It argues that the best explanation of nature is to be found in the hypothesis of the existence of God. *Revealed theology,* on the other hand, is an elaboration of articles of religious faith in the light of the religious experience and religious texts regarded as God's special revelation to man.

If the evidence for the existence of God is drawn largely or exclusively from natural theology, the theological dualism reached is usually some form of *deism*—the belief that God is the creator or designer of the world but not a personal agent who shows His care for man by revealing Himself or intervening in the course of nature or human affairs. If the evidence for the existence of God is found in revealed theology, the theological conclusion most generally reached is *theism*—the belief that God is a personal being in part immanent in the world and in part transcending it, caring for man, and revealing Himself to man in religious experience, scripture, miracles, or incarnation in human form. Deism regards God as the Author of the world, as a kind of "constitutional monarch" of the world, or as an "absentee landlord" for the world; theism considers Him as more adequately represented in the symbol of a loving Father who instructs and guides man.

Natural and revealed theology are usually thought to be consistent with each other, but revealed theology is considered to go further than natural theology in the detail of its conception of God. This view of their relations to each other can be seen best in the philosophy of St. Thomas Aquinas (1226-1275). According to him, the human intellect, by its own powers and without aid of supernatural revelation, can logically assure itself of the existence of God. (In the next section we shall see some of the ways in which Aquinas believed it could do so.) It leads us to sure knowledge of the existence and the metaphysical attributes of God—His omnipotence, omniscience, omnipresence, perfection, and infinity. But only faith and its elaboration in revealed theology can lead to certainty about the theological attributes of God, such as His grace, His trinitarian personality, and the other specific characteristics by which the Christian conception of God differs from those of other religions. The function of philosophy, which for Aquinas is almost equivalent to natural theology, is to be a handmaiden for theology *(ancilla theologiae)* and to prepare the way for faith (to be *praeambula fidei),* which is made perfect only by the acceptance of the revelation God gives to man. What we learn from one is perfectly consistent with what we learn from the other:

> The knowledge of naturally known principles is instilled into us by God, since God Himself is the author of our nature. Therefore the divine wisdom also contains these principles. Consequently whatever is contrary to these principles, is contrary to the divine Wisdom; wherefore it cannot be from God. Therefore those things which are received by faith from divine revelation cannot be contrary to our natural knowledge.[4]

But suppose, as at least sometimes seems to occur, that the conclusions of philosophy are inconsistent with faith claiming to be justified by revelation. Here we have a conflict of theology and philosophy. There are two ways in which such a conflict could be resolved. The Catholic theory, based on St. Thomas Aquinas, would hold that the philosophy was spurious; the theology of modernism would be more likely to conclude that the revelation was spurious. Let us consider each possibility.

According to Catholic theory, reason (as expressed in philosophy) is consistent with revelation, but if in any case it seems to be inconsistent with it, then that is evidence that what claims to be reason is not reason but error. This means, then, that there is only one true philosophy. Consider this statement by Pope Pius XII:

> It is well known how highly the Church regards human reason, for it falls to reason to demonstrate with certainty the existence of God, personal and one; to prove beyond doubt from divine signs

---

[4] From the *Summa Theologica* of St. Thomas Aquinas, translated by the English Dominican Fathers. Part I, page 14. London: Burns Oates & Washbourne Ltd., 1924. Used by permission of the publisher and of Benziger Brothers, Inc., New York, American publishers and copyright owners.

the very foundations of the Christian faith; to express properly the law which the Creator has imprinted in the hearts of men; and finally to attain to some notion, indeed a very fruitful notion, of mysteries. But reason can perform these functions safely and well, only when properly trained, that is, when imbued with that sound philosophy which has long been, as it were, a patrimony handed down by earlier Christian ages, and which moreover possesses an authority of even higher order, since the Teaching Authority of the Church, in the light of divine revelation itself, has weighed its fundamental tenets, which have been elaborated and defined little by little by men of great genius. For this philosophy, acknowledged and accepted by the Church, safeguards the genuine validity of human knowledge, the unshakable metaphysical principles of sufficient reason, causality, and finality [teleology], and finally the mind's ability to attain certain and unchangeable truth.

Of course this philosophy deals with much that neither directly nor indirectly touches faith or morals, and which consequently the Church leaves to the free discussion of experts. But this does not hold for many other things, especially those principles and fundamental tenets to which We have just referred. However, even in these fundamental questions, we may clothe our philosophy in a more convenient and richer dress, make it more vigorous with a more effective terminology, divest it of certain scholastic aids found less useful, prudently enrich it with the fruits of progress of the human mind. But never may we overthrow it, or contaminate it with false principles, or regard it as a great, but obsolete, relic. For truth and its philosophic expression cannot change from day to day, least of all where there is question of self-evident principles of the human mind or of those propositions which are supported by the wisdom of the ages and by divine revelation. Whatever new truth the sincere human mind is able to find, certainly cannot be opposed to truth already acquired, since God, the highest Truth, has created and guides the human intellect, not that it may daily oppose new truths to rightly established ones, but rather that, having eliminated errors which may have crept in, it may build truth upon truth in the same order and structure that exist in reality, the source of truth. Let no Christian, therefore, whether philosopher or theologian, embrace eagerly and lightly whatever novelty happens to be thought up from day to day, but rather let him weigh it with painstaking care and a balanced judgment, lest he lose or corrupt the truth he already has, with grave danger and damage to his faith.

If one considers all this well, he will easily see why the Church demands that future priests be instructed in philosophy "according to the method, doctrine, and principles of the Angelic Doctor [Thomas Aquinas]," since, as we well know from the experience of centuries, the method of Aquinas is singularly preeminent both for teaching students and for bringing truth to light; his doctrine is in harmony with divine revelation, and is most effective both for safeguarding the foundation of the faith, and for reaping, safely and usefully, the fruits of sound progress.[5]

The Catholic theologian thus holds that philosophy and theology are consistent with each other, but in case there is a conflict between what is claimed to be sound philosophy and theology, the philosophy is spurious:

As the superior science, theology *judges* philosophy. . . . It therefore exercises in respect of the latter a function of guidance or government, though a negative government, which consists in rejecting as false any philosophic affirmation which contradicts a theological truth. In this sense, theology controls and exercises jurisdiction over the conclusions maintained by philosophers.[6]

The ground for this conclusion is the central position occupied by religion in this system of thought:

The premises of theology are the truths formally revealed by God (*dogmas* or articles of faith) and its primary criterion of truth the authority of God who reveals it. . . .
Though, as St. Thomas points out, the argument from authority is the weakest of all, where human authority is concerned, the argument from authority of God, the revealer, is more solid and powerful than any other.[7]

The opposite course would be followed by modernism. It would hold that while religion is an attitude of faith rather than of inquiry, it is the business of the theologian to proceed like the philosopher in attempting to formulate a hypothesis

[5] Pius XII, *Humani Generis*, §§29-31. From the English translation published by the National Catholic Welfare Conference, Washington, D. C., 1950.

[6] Jacques Maritain, *An Introduction to Philosophy*, page 126. New York: Longmans, Green & Company, Inc., 1931. Quoted by permission of the publisher.

[7] *Ibid.*, page 125.

that will cover all the facts and values in the most adequate and parsimonious way. Because of the variety of revelations to which different religions appeal, it would prefer to make philosophical reasoning the criterion by which the alleged revelations should be judged. It does not deny that God can and does reveal Himself; but it holds that no alleged revelation is self-supporting or self-evidently valid. Consider the modernist's attitude toward the Bible as the medium of God's revelation to man. Modern critical studies have shown inconsistencies among its various parts; historical scholarship and scientific study have shown inconsistencies between it and other facts established by sound historiographical and scientific procedures. This means to the modernist that we cannot reasonably accept the entire Bible as the dictated word of God. On the other hand, however, this does not mean to the modernist that we must reject the Bible's religious message because of what he believes to be its factual inaccuracies. He takes a middle course; he maintains that the Bible contains an authentic "deposit of faith," but that men must use their God-given reason to judge and weigh the authenticity of the various parts of it, which the fundamentalist regards as all having equal worth as evidence of God's revelation. Usually he comes out with a quite different conclusion from that of the fundamentalist, so different that it is sometimes disputed whether modernism in theology is Christian in anything but name.[8]

---

[8] Fundamentalism and modernism are prominent opposing movements in Protestantism, "Catholic modernism" having been condemned by the Papacy towards the end of the nineteenth century. The official Catholic view, however, is not that the *simplest* and *most direct* interpretation of all parts of scripture is necessarily the correct one; cf. the Encyclical letter *Humani Generis*, just quoted, §§38 and 39, for the Catholic doctrine on free and literal interpretation of scripture.

PHILOSOPHICAL ARGUMENTS FOR THE
EXISTENCE OF GOD

In order to examine the metaphysical theory of the dualism of God and the world, one must take an attitude quite different from that of religious faith. It is necessary, for such an examination, to suspend the normal belief in God's existence that perhaps most people in our society have, to regard the existence of God as a hypothesis, and then to weigh the evidence for and against the hypothesis. Such an attitude is difficult for many people, who feel that true religious fervor and faith are incompatible with such a cold-blooded attitude of suspended judgment.

The religious attitude of faith—"the substance of things hoped for, the evidence of things not seen"—is utterly different from that of philosophical inquiry. Yet many of the greatest theologians, such as St. Thomas Aquinas, have recommended impartial philosophical investigation as a propadeutic or preamble to a still deeper religious faith. They believe that a thorough philosophical appraisal of the doctrine of the existence of God will prevent later doubts that might trouble the serenity of direct religious faith. Most of the classical arguments for the existence of God have been proposed by theologians and religious philosophers who did not require an intellectual proof to convince them that God exists. Most of them have held that the human intellect is capable of attaining logical certainty, by philosophical arguments, that God does exist; and they have held also that faith is compatible with the conclusions reached philosophically. They usually believed that faith also goes beyond the truths that can be established philosophically, and that theology is thus more than sound philosophy but perfectly harmonious with it.

Philosophers and theologians have proposed proofs of the existence of God. It should be noted in advance that most of these arguments have usually been thought of as *proofs*. Most of them originated in an intellectual atmosphere favorable to the notion that it is possible to get metaphysical conclusions with the same or with a greater degree of certainty than rewards our efforts to arrive at scientific knowledge. The preceding chapter pointed out reasons for concluding that what is ordinarily called "proof" is nowhere possible in a speculative field like metaphysics. If the reader forgets this, it may seem to him that the following criticisms of the "proofs" are unduly negative. This would indicate a misunderstanding of the purpose of the following discussion. The purpose in making criticisms is not to refute the hypothesis of the existence of God. That would be as impossible as to give a proof of the existence of God that admitted of no criticism. Nor, on the other hand, is the purpose to make it appear that skepticism (which in religious matters is usually called *agnosticism*) is the only defensible attitude; there is no more and no less reason to be skeptical about metaphysical hypotheses in religion than about any other metaphysical hypotheses. Rather, the purpose is to show that the positive merits of the arguments for the existence of God are insufficient to justify the notion that they can be so conclusively established that theological dualism can be considered absolutely *proved*. In other words, the purpose of the criticism is to show that theological dualism is a hypothesis with reasonable alternatives, a hypothesis which, though reasonable, is not demonstrated. In this respect it is like every other metaphysical theory.

Every metaphysical theory depends upon some particular interpretation of the broad reaches of our experience. No interpretation is the *only possible* one. Whether the arguments or the criticisms of them are the more convincing turns not only upon the evidence cited and the logical validity of the inference, but also upon answers to the questions: is the general intellectual frame-work of philosophy in which the given hypothesis is proposed more acceptable than its alternatives? For example, in the case before us, does a given argument for God's existence, taken in conjunction with the general philosophical system of which it is a part, make our experience as a whole more intelligible than any other hypothesis?

Whether one's answer to these questions is affirmative or negative will depend to a great extent upon one's prior religious orientation and general philosophical outlook. It has been said, probably correctly, that no believer has ever been made an atheist by an argument against the existence of God, and that no atheist has ever been convinced by logic that God exists. Nevertheless, if one does try to suspend faith in God, or predilections against the belief in God, one can then examine, with some fair degree of impartiality, the arguments that have been proposed, and evaluate theological dualism as a metaphysical theory.

The reader is asked to keep this preliminary statement clearly in mind while studying the arguments concerning the existence of God.

The argument from the common consent of mankind
(consensus gentium)

This is one of the most popular arguments for the existence of God. It says that there is no people that does not have some belief in some God; therefore, by the common consent or common sense of mankind, God must be said to exist.

The argument is logically weak. It suffers from the invalidity of any argument from common sense (see pages 26 ff). In the second place, the premise of the argument, that all peoples do have a belief in God, is not true. Although one might admit some exceptions and still say that the existence of God is commonly believed, the differences in the form and content of this belief are far more striking than their similarities.[9] If one argues that all peoples worship the same God, who appears to different peoples in different forms, the question of the existence of God is begged (that is, what was to be proved is assumed).

---

[9] Cf. James G. Frazer, *The Golden Bough*, Chapter VII, page 91. New York: The Macmillan Company, 1940.

But if one grants the premise, the conclusion still does not follow. For the common belief of mankind that God does exist is as likely to show that there is a common need in mankind (say, a so-called religious instinct) as that there is a real being, God, which satisfies this need. A common belief in God might be an important fact in anthropology and psychology, but would not establish any theological conclusion.

Sometimes it is argued that man has a natural longing for God, as shown by the widespread belief in God, and that man would not have been endowed with this longing unless it could be satisfied. This argument is a special case of the argument from design (see page 279). But here it obviously begs the question, since it assumes that God created this longing in man which He alone can satisfy. Such an argument, therefore, takes the existence of God as a premise to justify religious aspiration, rather than taking religious aspiration itself as evidence for the existence of God.

The ontological argument

The second argument is rationalistic. It comes from the belief that pure reason, without any help from sense experience, can demonstrate metaphysical truths, such as the truth of the proposition that God exists. It is called "ontological" because it is based on an analysis of the concept of being itself. It does not presuppose even the existence of the world of nature, considered as a special kind of being.

According to Descartes, we ordinarily make a distinction between the existence of a thing and its essence or definition. I can define a mountain, for instance, without knowing or caring whether there is actually such a thing, because the essence of a mountain (that is, what a geological formation *would* be if it *were* a mountain) is independent of the existence of this particular kind of geological structure. But

I find it manifest that we can no more separate the existence of God from his essence than we can separate from the essence of a [rectilinear] triangle the fact that the size of its three angles equals two right angles, or from the idea of a mountain the idea of a valley. Thus it is no less self-contradictory to conceive of a God, a supremely perfect Being, who lacks existence—that is, who lacks some perfection—than it is to conceive of a mountain for which there is no valley.[10]

The argument defines God as a perfect being, and a perfect being is one that possesses all perfections or positive qualities. These include the property of being real. Hence it follows that reality pertains to the definition of God. To say, "God does not exist," is as self-contradictory as to say, "Mountains exist, but no valley exists." As the contradictory of a self-contradictory proposition is necessarily true, it follows that "God exists" is a necessary truth, demonstrated by logic from the definition or essence of God.

The classical criticism of the ontological argument was given by Kant, who rejected the claim that pure reason could give metaphysical truths. According to Kant, "real" is not a predicate that can be made a part of a definition. If "real" were a logical predicate, the judgment "x is real" would employ the subject-term, x, as having a different meaning from that of the subject-term in the definition, "x is an A which is B." The first x would have a predicate—"real"—lacking in the second x. No matter how many predicates we add to our definition of x, we should never be able to define it in such a way that we could be sure a priori that the x defined is a real x and not merely a concept of an x that might or might not be real. After I have given an elaborate definition of x and stated all its logical characteristics or predicates, I may add, "And x is real." But I am adding something to the definition, not getting something out of the definition as a consequence of it. That which I add (that x is real), I can learn only from experience or from inferences from what I do experience; but this additional bit of information does not belong to the definition of the thing.

[10] René Descartes, Meditations (Lawrence J. Lafleur, trans.), page 59. New York: Liberal Arts Press, 1951 (The Little Library of Liberal Arts, No. 29). By permission of the publisher.

A hundred real thalers do not contain the least coin more [that is, not one predicate more] than a hundred possible thalers [the concept of a hundred thalers].[11]

A hundred real thalers must be conceptually identical with (that is, have the same predicates as) a hundred possible thalers. This could not be the case if "real" were a predicate applying to an existing thing but lacking in its concept; for in this case we could not define an object unless we knew it existed, and this is absurd.

The hundred real thalers and the hundred possible thalers do not have the same metaphysical status, in spite of the fact that logically, with respect to their predicates, they are identical. One is actual, the other is only thought about. However much I think about the thalers, and however many predicates I attach to the concept of them, it still remains an empirical question whether there is anything really existing to correspond to the thought in my mind. Only an experience, or an argument starting from some experience, can show whether I have the right to say that the thalers I have thought about really exist. Precisely the same conclusion, Kant argued, applies to the notion of God. God's real existence can be proved not from a definition but, if at all, from an experience of something actually existing.

Hence Kant concluded that the ontological argument, which tried to avoid the appeal to experience, used a notion that could come only from experience.

Arguments from the impossibility of an infinite series of conditions

A group of more common arguments for the existence of God depends upon the notion that since everything in the world is dependent upon other things, and these upon still others, and so on, there must be one thing above the world

---

[11] Immanuel Kant, *Critique of Pure Reason* (1781) (Norman Kemp Smith, trans.), page 505. New York: The Humanities Press, Inc., 1950. This and subsequent quotations from the *Critique of Pure Reason* are made with the permission of the publisher.

that is not dependent upon anything else but is the condition of all others.

This argument has several types. One may argue from the existence of motion in the world to the concept of a Prime Mover, from the existence of contingent things to the concept of a Necessary Being, and from the existence of causes and effects to a First Cause. Since the logic of the three arguments is identical, we shall discuss only one of the three. We shall take the last of them, which is the most commonly used. It is usually called the "cosmological argument," since it assumes the existence of the "cosmos," or world.

The argument is this. Everything that occurs has a condition that precedes it in time and is called its efficient cause. And the cause has a cause; and the cause of the cause has a cause, and so on. The question is, how far can this series be continued?

In efficient causes it is not possible to go on to infinity, because in all efficient causes following in order, the first is the cause of the intermediate cause, and the intermediate is the cause of the ultimate cause, whether the intermediate cause be several, or one only. Now to take away the cause is to take away the effect. Therefore if there be no first cause among the efficient causes, there will be no ultimate, nor any intermediate cause. But if in efficient causes it is possible to go on to infinity, there will be no first efficient cause, neither will there be an ultimate effect, nor any intermediate efficient causes; all of which is plainly false.[12]

Therefore the series of causes cannot be infinite, and the series of causes must have a first cause, "to which everyone gives the name of God."

Let us put the same argument in a different form. No event can occur unless there is a sufficient reason for it. The sufficient reason for an event is the sum of all its causes, and the causes of the causes, and so on. If the series of causes of causes of

---

[12] From the *Summa Theologica* of St. Thomas Aquinas, translated by the English Dominican Fathers. Part I, page 25. London: Burns Oates & Washbourne Ltd., 1924. Used by permission of the publisher and of Benziger Brothers, Inc., New York, American publishers and copyright owners.

causes is infinite, there is no *sum* of causes, and we could not say that *all* the causes of an event had occurred, for the infinite series is one without a first member and thus without a sum or totality. Therefore if the series is infinite, there is no sufficient reason for anything; hence nothing will occur. But this is false; therefore the series cannot be infinite. Hence, there must be a first cause.

It should be noted that this argument assumes the objective reality and metaphysical validity of the principle of causation; causation is not here understood as simply regularity in sequences of events. This argument, therefore, cannot be employed by anyone who accepts the Humean analysis of causation (see pages 134 ff). This is not said in criticism of the argument, however, for it is quite possible to argue, and the followers of Aquinas do argue, that Hume is wrong. It is mentioned merely to call attention to the fact that the argument is not innocent of metaphysical assumptions. The argument is not a proof based *only* on the admitted fact that something happens.

Let it be granted that the concept of cause implies the concept of first cause. The first cause is a being that must be assumed to be a cause of itself, for by definition, it is dependent upon nothing else for its being. Hence its being depends only upon its own essence or definition. That is, the concept of *first cause* is equivalent to the concept of *necessary being*, the existence of which follows from its definition. But unless the ontological argument is valid, we cannot infer *real* existence from the *concept* of a necessary being. Hence the crucial step in this argument is an ontological argument, and if the ontological argument fails, so also does any argument that includes it as an essential step.[13]

Still, one may say, "There's *got* to be a cause for things!" This is an entirely natural and understandable response. It seems that the human mind cannot form a conception of

---

[13] Immanuel Kant, *op. cit.*, page 509.

causes *ad infinitum*. But can we really succeed any better in trying to form a conception of an absolutely first beginning? Both conceptions are so far removed from the sure ground of experience that we cannot be certain that we have any clearer conception of a first cause than we have of an infinite series of causes.

In spite of this, most persons probably do find it easier to think of a first cause than to think of an infinite series of causes. I shall tentatively suggest two reasons for this: first, each of us is familiar with the experience of feeling our own volition, of our at least seeming to be the cause of our own actions. I seem to myself to be a free agent, a cause of subsequent events but not the effect of previous events. Therefore I seem to myself to be a kind of "first cause," and it is relatively easy to suppose that if there is a God, this is the way in which He acts. (That our volitions and decisions have causes is true but irrelevant here, for we are not attempting to discover whether the concept of a first cause is valid, but only why it seems clearer and more acceptable than the concept of an infinite series of causes.) Second, each of us is familiar with the symbolism of religion. Through it, we have a *name* for the uncaused cause. Although the *concept* of an uncaused cause is difficult to comprehend, the name "God" is easy to pronounce and to surround with the imagery of our religion. But there is no emotionally colored and traditionally accepted name for "an infinite series of causes," nothing to obscure its logical complexity and difficulty. By having a proper name and imagery for the one, but no proper name and imagery for the other, it is psychologically more palatable to accept the concept of an uncaused cause than to accept the concept of an infinite series of causes. It is possible that, by the rich imagery of the name of God, men have been blinded to the logical difficulties of the concept.

The teleological argument, or the argument from design

This argument, unlike the cosmological argument, is based upon the *particular kinds* and *organizations* of things found in the cosmos. It begins with the observation that things in the world seem to be designed for some purpose, and argues from that to the existence of a designer or artificer. Thomas Aquinas writes:

The fifth way [to prove the existence of God] is taken from the governance of the world. We see that things which lack intelligence, such as natural bodies, act for an end, and this is evident from their acting always, or nearly always, in the same way, so as to obtain the best result. Hence it is plain that not fortuitously, but designedly, do they achieve their end. Now whatever lacks intelligence cannot move towards an end, unless it be directed by some being endowed with knowledge and intelligence; as the arrow is shot to its mark by the archer. Therefore some intelligent being exists by whom all natural things are directed to their end; and this being we call God.[14]

Or consider the argument of the eighteenth-century British theologian, Bishop Paley. Paley asks us to imagine a man walking in a desert and suddenly coming upon a watch. He will conclude rightly that some man must have devised the instrument; its parts would not have come together in this purposive form without some plan or design. Then he proposes an analogy: the universe itself is like a vast clockwork, and we must infer that it also was designed and planned by a supreme intelligence.

Kant, while not convinced by this argument, respected it:

This proof always deserves to be mentioned with respect. It is the oldest, the clearest, and the most accordant with the common reason of mankind. It enlivens the study of nature, just as it itself derives its existence and gains ever new vigour from that source. It suggests ends and purposes, where our observation would not have detected them by itself, and extends our knowledge of nature by means of the guiding-concept of a special unity, the principle of which is outside nature. This knowledge again reacts on its cause, namely, upon the idea which has led to it, and so strengthens the

[14] From the *Summa Theologica* of St. Thomas Aquinas, translated by the English Dominican Fathers. Part I, pages 26-27. London: Burns Oates & Washbourne Ltd., 1924. Used by permission of the publisher and of Benziger Brothers, Inc., New York, American publishers and copyright owners.

belief in a supreme Author [of nature] that the belief acquires the force of an irresistible conviction.[15]

With this recommendation, the argument requires more detailed study than we have had space to give to the others. The most thoroughgoing examination of the argument is by David Hume, in his *Dialogues Concerning Natural Religion* (1776), and some of the points to be mentioned are discussed in detail by him. We must ask four related questions about the argument. (1) Is the analogy a good one? (2) Is there really evidence of purpose in the universe? (3) What does the argument do with the evidence of lack of purpose in some parts of the universe? (4) Does purpose, if it is real, require an intelligent designer for its explanation?

Examination of the analogy—An analogical argument is one in which, from the relationship known to exist between two things, we infer a like relationship from one known thing to another, unknown thing. Thus $2:4=6:x$ is an analogy; from it we can infer $x=12$. In doing so, we do not have to raise the question of the degree of similarity between the 2 and the 6. In a nonmathematical analogy, like Paley's, we do have to raise this question. Is the world sufficiently similar to a watch, that we can infer the existence of a being comparable to a watchmaker as its creator? From the world's similarity to a house, can we infer a Divine Architect? From its mathematical order, can we infer, as Sir James Jeans did, that "God is a great mathematician"? A fertile imagination can see similarities amidst all sorts of differences. Shall we think of the world by analogy to an organism, and then infer that it originated sexually? Or that it is like a work of art, so that there must be a Supreme Artist?

We may, or we may not. Whether we do so or not depends upon our prior faith that our particular analogy is a good one, and this depends upon what our central fact is. Each of us sees so little of the universe that we cannot be sure that any

---

[15] Immanuel Kant, *op. cit.*, page 520.

part of the universe—a watch, a house, an organism, a painting, a mathematical equation—is really a typical part of the universe as a whole. If the blind man who felt of the elephant's tail and inferred that the elephant was like a rope had used an analogical argument, he would have supposed that the cause of the elephant was not another elephant but a human ropemaker.

In spite of objections like these, and many more, Hume does not assert that the analogy is worthless. Hume's chief work on religion is in the form of a dialogue, and it is sometimes difficult to decide which of the speakers presents Hume's own point of view. Scholars disagree on what Hume's real attitude was, but there is evidence that he did believe that there was a being that bore a "remote analogy" to mind as we know it in man. But Hume remained critical of any specific analogy by which theologians might try to infer anything in detail concerning the nature and purposes of God.

Is there really purpose in the universe?—It may be argued that the evidence for purposive design in nature is overwhelming, whatever particular sector of it you examine. No one seriously argues, it will be said, that God is *really* an artist or an architect or a watchmaker; but because of the manifold evidences of design throughout the universe it may reasonably be inferred that there is an intelligent creative being. The evidence of purpose in the universe is of three kinds: (1) the rational intelligibility of things, (2) their adaptation to each other; and (3) their suitability to human purposes. We shall examine each.

(1) *Intelligibility as evidence of purpose*—Things seem to be intelligently designed because they "fit" the way the mind works. Nature does nothing in vain—this fits the mind's law of parsimony. Everything that happens does have a cause—this fits the mind's law of causality. Nature is measurable—this fits the mind's mathematical abilities. The laws of nature can be expressed in elegant mathematical formulae, and highly com-

plex computations give us knowledge of facts that have not been observed.

This argument is impressive. We should note, however, that it depends upon a realistic conception of laws—that there are laws that things "obey" and hence there must be a law-giver. We have seen earlier (pages 120 ff) that the words "law" and "obey" are ambiguous, and it might be that the admitted harmony of nature with our ideas of regularity and simplicity is due to the success we have in eliciting statistical generalities from a much larger mass of data that are not themselves dependent upon or obedient to any realistically conceived law. The proponent of this argument will be quite willing to accept the realistic conception of scientific law, and to reject the alternative conception just mentioned. But pointing out his assumption about laws does serve to show that his argument is dependent upon certain debatable metaphysical conceptions and is not a proof dependent merely upon the admitted fact that nature is regular and intelligible.

Another objection can be made to this view. The argument seems to suppose that there is a kind of Procrustean bed of unchangeable "laws of thought," which exist eternally in the human mind, and that if things fit them, it is because they were designed and made so as to fit them. But it is at least as plausible to argue that the mind and its functions developed in a long evolutionary course along with our bodies, which evolved in such a way as to fit them to the conditions of the environment. If one takes this evolutionary argument seriously, then it appears that the intelligibility of things is a consequence of the mind's slow adaptation to things, rather than to the prior design of things so that they will be suitable to mental comprehension.

(2) *Mutual adaptation as evidence of purpose*—There is much mutual adaptation of things. One need consider only our example of how bats guide their flight in darkness, to be impressed with the way different parts of a single organism are integrated with all the others; and a balanced aquarium is an

example of the mutual adaptation of different organisms to each other.

Nevertheless, there is another hypothesis that will explain the adaptation of part to part and organism to environment. This is the hypothesis of evolution. According to Darwin's theory, animals and plants vary accidentally and spontaneously, or at least in random and unforeseen ways. There then ensues a struggle for survival among these organisms, and those whose variations facilitate their adjustment, including the adjustment to each other, will tend to survive and pass on their variations to their offspring, while those less well-adapted will be eliminated. This process, repeated generation after generation, leads to flowers and bees perfectly adapted to each other's needs, or plants and animals in a lake living in balanced harmony with each other. We can discern a direction in evolution toward increase in an animal's control over the environment, increase of interdependence of parts on whole, and increase of internal coordination.[16] But when we understand the process, we do not need the concept of purpose or design in order to account for it.

It is sometimes said, against the sufficiency of this hypothesis, that it explains the "survival" of the fittest, but not the "arrival" of the fittest. That is, it does not explain how fortunate variations occur or how they are preserved during the earliest stages when their contribution to survival must have been insignificant. It is therefore argued that there must be a purposive agent responsible for the occurrence and perseverance of fortunate variations, and that this shows itself in evolutionary progress.

The theory of evolution, it must be admitted, does not explain and does not even attempt to explain the origin of variations. Even so, however, the case for design is not very convincing. One bit of evidence against it must suffice: the great majority of mutations (distinct and inheritable variations

---

[16] Cf. Julian Huxley, *Evolution: The Modern Synthesis,* page 576. New York: Harper & Brothers, 1942.

of significant magnitude to function as factors in the struggle for survival) are deleterious to the survival of their possessors, whereas on the theory that they are designed or planned, we should reasonably expect the opposite.[17]

(3) *Suitability to human purpose as evidence of design*— There is the common belief that nature is designed especially for human purposes. This view of purposes was more popular in the optimistic eighteenth century than it is today, but nonetheless, men sometimes still argue that all things were put on earth for their benefit. If we think of man as the goal of all things, then we may find much evidence in nature that all things suit his purposes—grass was made for cows to eat, and cows were made to give man milk, butter, and leather.[18] But if we look upon man as himself the product of evolution, we can easily argue that man survived because he took better advantage of the environment and adapted to what he found until he began to use his intelligence in adapting things to himself. It must be said again that such a counterargument does not rule out the hypothesis of design in nature. But it does suggest another good hypothesis, so that we cannot consider the argument from design as *proved* by the natural fitness of the environment to human needs and purposes.

Is everything designed? The problem of evil—While most men prefer to look upon nature's marvelous organization, there is also much evidence of lack of organization. There is not only survival of the few relatively fit; there is extinction of the many less fit. There is degeneration as well as progress. There are things in the world that do not seem rationally explicable by men's minds, constituted as they are. There are mosquitoes and germs, rattle snakes and poison ivy, poverty and pain, which do not seem *prima facie* to indicate that nature was perfectly adapted to be man's home. There are evil purposes

---

[17] *Ibid.*, page 465.
[18] For some amusing eighteenth-century examples of such arguments, cf. Ernst Cassirer, *Rousseau Kant Goethe*, pages 66 ff. (James Gutmann, Paul Oskar Kristeller, and John Herman Randall, Jr., trans.) Princeton, N. J.: Princeton University Press, 1947.

to which human beings subjugate the forces of nature, and one might sometimes wish for instance, that nature were not so organized that atom bombs could work. There are rivalries and aggressions among men that show that they are far from being a happy and harmonious family.

How does the argument from design deal with these undisputed facts? Two ways have been proposed.

First, it is sometimes denied that these so-called evils really are evil. They are parts of a larger system of things of which Pope could say, "Whatever is, is right," and Leibniz could say, "This is the best of all possible worlds." Optimists have shown great ingenuity in explaining evil away. They say that we could not appreciate the good in the world unless there were evil with which to contrast it; that men are made better by having to struggle against evil; that wars are good because they promote national vigor. They are right in saying that at least some evils are disguised goods, and could we but see the whole of things, many other evils might appear to us to be necessary for some greater good that we do not suspect. We might even say, with F. H. Bradley, "This is the best of all possible worlds, for everything in it is a *necessary* evil."

Such optimism, even if justified, does not really meet the logical issue. *If* there is a god, then we might feel some assurance that the evil in the world would be set right in some "far off, divine event, to which the whole creation moves," as Tennyson expressed the optimistic sentiment. But in the argument for the existence of God, emphasis was first placed upon the salient goods and purposes in the world in order to show that the world was designed. Until we show that the design *does* exist, we have no right to discount or neglect the evidence of lack of design or to try to show that it must be interpreted as a part of God's hidden design; we must know that the design exists before we can avail ourselves of these *ad hoc* hypotheses. Whatever may be the recommendations provided by religious faith, we have no logical right to argue from only *part* of the evidence (the part that seems to show design), conclude from this that the *whole* was designed, and only then look at the other part of the evidence in order to explain it away.

Second, a more daring and logically more cogent argument has been formulated by some recent philosophers, acting on a suggestion of Plato's. It is an attempt to resolve the paradox involved in the notion that an omnipotent and perfect God has created less than a perfect world, by denying the omnipotence of God. John Stuart Mill proposed to account for the evidences of design and purpose in the world by the hypothesis of a Designer, and then to take the evidence of lack of perfect design as indicating that the Designer is limited or finite. Mill felt that infinite benevolence joined with infinite power is incompatible with the real evil in the world, and rather than give up the belief in the benevolence of God or close his eyes to the evil in the world, he denied His infinite power. While his hypothesis detracts from the power of God, it need not detract from His infinite worth; the requirement that what is worthy of worship must be omnipotent, he regarded as a vestige of a primitive worship of mere power, an attitude that grows out of fear, not love.

This hypothesis, Mill believed, does not detract from the seriousness with which one can take the religious outlook upon the world. Mill's conception is not dogmatically optimistic, like the previously suggested solutions to the problem of evil, and his view is sometimes called *meliorism*—the belief that the world has a tendency to become better, and that man ought to participate in its betterment. This, Mill believed, strengthened the moral content of religious activity and faith:

One elevated feeling this form of religious idea admits of, which is not open to those who believe in the omnipotence of the good principle in the universe, the feeling of helping God—of requiting the good he has given by a voluntary cooperation which he, not being omnipotent, really needs, and by which a somewhat nearer approach may be made to the fulfilment of his purposes. . . . To do something during life, on even the humblest scale if nothing more is within reach, towards bringing this consummation ever so little nearer, is the most animating and invigorating thought which can inspire a human creature.[19]

Does purpose imply design?—If it be granted that there are purposes in the universe, and that the universe itself has a purpose, does this imply that there is a being that designed the universe? This is one of the most conjectural of all questions in metaphysics, and no sure answer can be given to it. We have evidence in our own experience to indicate that some purposes do imply intelligent design, for the intelligent design in attaining purposes is often our own careful plans. We do not have any absolute evidence, however, that the purposive behavior of animals and even of plants is not due to at least a very low order of consciousness and intelligence on *their* part. But this belief is so speculative that it will not be acceptable to most people.

The more difficult question, however, is whether purposive behavior in *every* case requires intelligence. Unless we assume that it does, then even admitting purposes in nature will not suffice to guarantee that there is a Designer above nature. It might well be that purposiveness requires intelligence and consciousness only in the case of the higher animals and man. Have we any right to regard human purposiveness, at least some of which is predicated upon intelligence and design, as typical of *all* purposiveness that we may believe exists anywhere in the universe?

Here is a question on which all intellectualistic argument must founder. Those who take the root metaphor or central fact on which religious philosophies are based will justify an affirmative answer by their faith that man is a key to understanding the universe. Those who do not have this orientation will be more inclined to think that if there really are purposes in the universe apart from men's freely chosen purposes, they may be explained without the assumption that natural purposes always presuppose intelligent design. In either case, it

[19] John Stuart Mill, *Three Essays on Religion* (1874), Part V, page 256. London: Longmans, Green & Company, Ltd., 1923.

is not a matter to be settled by argument so much as a question of basic orientation or faith.

The argument from miracles

Another common and popular argument for the existence of God is based upon the belief that there are events that occur against the "law of nature" and give evidence of a power "above nature." Just as human beings occasionally break a law in order to do some good, the argument runs, God also breaks the law that He has ordained in order to reward or punish man or in order to give man a vivid awareness of His existence, power, and goodness.

Few things so excite men as the report of a miracle. For this reason, alleged miracles are not uncommon, and they provide a rich field for charlatans to prey upon the gullible. For this reason also, responsible theologians and religious institutions are very skeptical of reports of miracles, and many an alleged miracle has been declared spurious by ecclesiastical authorities, even in cases where the alleged miracle had turned men's minds to religious matters and convinced them of the existence of God. David Hume, in his *Enquiry Concerning Human Understanding*, prescribed tests (like those used by a lawyer in determining the credibility of a witness) that a report of an alleged miracle must meet before it will be accepted by cautious and mature minds. He asks of every alleged miracle:

[Is it] attested by a sufficient number of men, of such unquestioned good-sense, education, and learning, as to secure us against all delusion in themselves; of such undoubted integrity, as to place them beyond all suspicion of any design to deceive others; of such credit and reputation in the eyes of mankind as to have a great deal to lose in case of their being detected in any falsehood; and, at the same time, attesting facts performed in such a public manner and in so celebrated a part of the world, as to render detection unavoidable[?] [20]

---

[20] David Hume, *An Enquiry Concerning Human Understanding* (1748), Section 10. In *Hume's Theory of Knowledge*, page 121 (David C. Yalden-Thomson, ed.). Edinburg: Thomas Nelson and Sons, 1951.

Hume believed that no report of a miracle could pass these tests. But for the sake of argument, let it be granted that some reports of alleged miracles can do so. We still have to raise two questions. The first is the question of the miraculous nature of the unusual and unexplained event *called* a miracle. For an event to deserve this name, it is necessary that it should be inexplicable by the laws of nature. This does not mean that we are not able to explain it with our present knowledge; most events are miraculous, if that is all we mean, and the more ignorant we are, the larger will be the store of miracles. No, the miraculous event is one that is *in principle* inexplicable, *except* on the assumption that its cause is outside the order of nature. It must be an event of such a character that the most complete knowledge of nature will *never* suffice to explain it. Only if we can eliminate the *possibility* of any natural explanation can we be content with the miraculous interpretation of the event, that is, with the belief that the event transcends all laws of nature both known *and unknown* and is due directly to the intervention of God.

Many events that once seemed miraculous are now understood scientifically. Many of the most stupendous and impressive "miracles" performed in perfect good faith by holy men and reported accurately by honest people can now be explained in terms of the principles of psychosomatic medicine, which regards a person's emotional attitude, including his faith, as one of the scientifically relevant conditions for understanding his bodily state. Even in cases where specific explanations of this kind have not been found, most scientifically oriented thinkers would not care to go so far as to say that they will never be discovered; they do not wish to block the way of inquiry.

We have here a conflict between faiths—the faith in a God who can break the laws of nature, and the faith in science, which says that whatever happens can eventually be explained in terms of laws of nature. One might say that unless a man already believes in God, he cannot believe in miracles. The occurrence of events called miraculous is not evidence for the existence of God, but the belief in the existence of God *is* the reason why the unusual events are called miraculous.

Our second question turns upon the religious significance of the belief in miracles. A person who accepts the argument from design, taking as his premise the grand order of nature, cannot argue that evidence for God's existence is found in cases which seem *not* to be under the inexorable laws and beneficent plan of nature. If God's design is real and perfect, then an event that is not consonant with the laws of nature's design is impossible; if the evidence of God's existence is found in the unusual and extraordinary events, then the argument from design is weakened:

> You bring down Heaven to vulgar Earth;
> your Maker like yourselves you make,
> You quake to own a reign of Law, you
> pray the Law its laws to break.[21]

There is one way in which the argument from design might be reconciled with the argument from miracles. It might be said (and it is true) that the appeal of the argument from design presupposes a good bit of intelligence, and the inquiring mind is more likely to be impressed by evidences of design than by alleged miracles. And it might be said (and it is true) that miracles are more likely to impress and arouse the wonder and awe of the man who is ignorant of the subtlety of nature's intricate workings. Hence it has been suggested that God could and would reveal Himself in many ways, adapting His revelation to the mind of the beholder—a miracle here, a law there.

This argument might be a convincing one in theology if we assume as its premise that God exists; then one would expect that "God fulfills himself in many ways." But the purpose of the argument from design and of the argument from miracles

---

[21] The Kasîdah of Hâjî Abdû el-Yezdî (Sir Richard Francis Burton, trans.), iv, 14. Portland, Maine: Thomas B. Mosher, 1908.

is to *prove* the existence of God, not to *assume* it in order to show that there is design or that there are miracles in the world. If neither argument alone can prove it, it might be supposed that each of them would strengthen the other. But this is not true here, because the two arguments start out with incompatible assumptions—one, that nature as a whole is designed, and the other, that it is not.

The argument from the objectivity of values

Under this heading fall one of St. Thomas Aquinas' arguments and several modern arguments that premise that values are objective and infer that there must be some objective supporter for these values.

Aquinas' argument is somewhat similar to his cosmological argument that there cannot be an infinite regress, but it is phrased in the terminology of the Platonic theory of objective value. He says that we observe in the world a hierarchy of perfections or values: this hierarchy cannot be infinite, and therefore there must be a highest member of the series, which must be the cause of all the lower members. This highest member of a hierarchy of values is a Perfect Being, and "this we call God."

The argument from the fact that some things are better than others will perhaps be convincing to anyone who finds it possible to make three assumptions, but unless these assumptions are admitted, the argument fails. The assumptions are: (1) that the ontological argument in its classical form is valid and permits us to infer from the conception of a perfect being to its existence; (2) that value is an objective quality of a thing, and that the more valuable it is, the more real it is. Evil, or the lack of value, on the contrary, must be assumed to be not a positive quality, but mere absence or lack of the good, and to that extent unreal; (3) that the values we observe as the premise of this argument must depend upon or be caused by that which is more valuable. This is the meaning of Descartes' statement (page 62) that the cause must be as perfect as the effect. In support of this view it is argued that if this principle is not admitted, then one must grant that there is more reality in the effect than in the cause, and this is equivalent to admitting that something comes from nothing. This, however, is said to be against a direct logical intuition or common sense.

The third assumption involves a denial of the theory of emergence (page 166). It will be admitted by everyone that from a knowledge of the physical or physiological causes alone we cannot foretell the value of our experiences, and that values therefore appear to be emergents if they are looked at, as it were, from below. But that only shows, according to Assumption (3), that looking at things from below is not adequate; we must not leave the emergent qualities utterly uncaused and without support either from above or below. We must see things and their values in the light of the ultimate causes that must be adequate to account for them and that must therefore be more valuable than the values to be explained.

The fact that the second and third of these assumptions are opposed to subjectivism and the theory of emergence in value theory is not a logical objection to this argument. The proponent of the argument will be quite willing to reject the opposing points of view. If God does exist and does have the qualities attributed to him by the theological dualist, then the opposing metaphysical views are wrong or at least inadequate. But it is important always to be aware of what *other* metaphysical assumptions, not specifically theological, are required in addition to the admitted facts if the arguments for theological dualism are to be cogent.

The moral argument

Like the preceding argument, the moral argument is based upon the experience of values, but it has a somewhat more subjective cast than the previous one and is free of the specifically Platonic elements of the above argument.

This argument states that the existence of God is a necessary, or at least a justified, assumption for understanding and supporting our moral experience. We shall examine three forms of this argument, as presented by Pascal, by William James, and by Kant.

Pascal—Blaise Pascal (1623-1662) was a famous mathematician who contributed to the mathematical theory of probability. He could find no scientific proof of the existence of God, but he believed that the hypothesis that God existed was justified by considerations of probability when we take into account our human concern with our future happiness. It is logically as reasonable to suppose that God exists as that He does not; but it is morally more reasonable to assume that He does. Therefore Pascal makes a wager that God exists, just as a player takes a chance that his partner will do such-and-such things—not because he can prove that his partner will do so, but because his chances of winning are improved by a line of play predicated upon this assumption:

> Your reason is no more shocked in choosing one rather than the other [hypothesis about the existence or non-existence of God], since you must of necessity choose. This is one point settled. But your happiness? Let us weigh the gain and loss in wagering that God is. Let us estimate these two chances. If you gain, you gain all; if you lose, you lose nothing. Wager, then without hesitation that He is.[22]

James—An argument similar to this, but more subtly worked out, is found in William James' pragmatic justification of faith. James, like Pascal, felt that no intellectual proof or disproof of the existence of God is possible. If we look to reason alone, we shall never find any grounds for believing in the existence of a power above nature. But, says James, one must believe or disbelieve, and he must do so in spite of lack of clinching evidence on either side. One cannot really "withold belief," for that is morally and religiously (although not theoretically) equivalent to disbelief. Since, then, one must believe or dis-

[22] Blaise Pascal, *Pensées* (W. F. Potter, trans.), §233. New York: E. P. Dutton & Co., Inc., Everyman's Edition, 1931.

believe, and the grounds for choice are not logically coercive, James says,

> I have preached the right of the individual to indulge his personal faith at his personal risk. . . . If religious hypotheses about the universe be in order at all [that is, if there is no logically clinching evidence against them] then the active faiths of individuals in them, freely expressing themselves in life, are the experimental tests by which they are verified, and the only means by which their truth or falsehood can be wrought out.[23]

James believed that accepting the existence of God was the way to a more vigorous ideal of morality and a way to escape from moral despair in face of the apparent meaningless of human existence in a world of blind causal determinism. Since morality, he believed, cannot be justified on the assumption of atheism, it in turn justifies some form of theism, especially the belief in a limited God, with its melioristic moral implications. This different conduct is moral conduct, which would be meaningless and impossible in a world that was either already perfectly good or wholly indifferent to the pursuit of value.

The great difficulty in James' argument lies in evaluating the morality that follows from this acceptance. How do we know that we can be more moral under the belief that there is a God who supports us, than under the belief that man stands alone and is solely responsible for his virtues as well as his vices? Many philosophers of a Stoical attitude have especially emphasized the moral stamina entailed by the doctrine that man alone must work out his destiny in an unfriendly or indifferent universe; they regard the belief in God as illusory and false comfort that may obscure our true duty—the duty to see things as they are and to persevere in righteousness even if the world is inimical to our highest ideals. Bertrand Russell's

---

[23] William James, *The Will to Believe*, pages xi-xii. Copyright, 1896 by William James. New York: Longmans, Green and Company, 1897, new impression, 1927. Quoted by permission of Longmans, Green and Company. This may be found in H. M. Kallen (ed.), *The Philosophy of William James*, pages 223-234. New York: Random House, Modern Library edition, n.d.

famous essay, "A Free Man's Worship," is typical of this attitude. The religious attitude, Russell says, maintains

> . . . that in some hidden manner, the world of fact is really harmonious with the world of ideals. Thus Man creates God, all-powerful and all-good, the mystic unity of what is and what should be.

But the world of fact, after all, is not good; and in submitting our judgment to it, there is an element of slavishness from which our thoughts must be purged. For in all things it is well to exalt the dignity of Man, by freeing him as far as possible from the tyranny of non-human Power.[24]

In this passage, the conflict between two different philosophies of life is brought to light. The argument between James and Russell is not really an intellectual conflict but an emotional conflict over values, on what constitutes the good life for man. Unless we could establish that James' outlook is morally better than Russell's, we cannot say that James' argument is any better than Russell's. James' argument is not even meant to be a logical proof, having originated in an admission that logic is impotent in this kind of speculation. We are thus left only with faith in God as a basis for moral conduct.

James' argument appears to many philosophers to leave the existence of God exactly where it was without any argument at all—in the realm of faith. If the test for the hypothesis of the existence of God is the effect of its acceptance or rejection on the individual's moral outlook, then it would appear that one person could argue that God exists and another could equally well argue that God does not exist, and they could each appeal to their moral experience as justifying their conclusion. James frankly appeals to our emotions; and as long as our emotions vary from man to man, just so long will the conclusions that men reach by his argument vary from man to man.

Kant—Kant's argument, although somewhat similar to that of James, attempts to avoid this appeal to the emotions. Kant

---

[24] Bertrand Russell, "A Free Man's Worship," in *Mysticism and Logic*, page 49. New York: Longmans, Green & Company, Inc., 1918. Used by permission of W. W. Norton & Company, New York, publishers.

believed that morality was a matter of reason rather than of the emotions. Hence if the existence of God is connected in any way with moral experience, Kant believed that it had to be a logical rather than an emotional connection. Yet we also know that Kant rejected the doctrine that the existence of God could be proved by natural theology. Having rejected the ontological, cosmological, and teleological arguments, Kant devised a moral argument based on reason, not on emotion.

Morality, he held, requires man to strive for the highest good, which is the perfect proportion of happiness to virtue.[25] Man alone cannot attain this highest good, yet it is his duty to strive for it. If we are to take seriously our obligation to try to achieve it, and not explain obligation away as a mere chimera, the highest good must be at least possible of attainment, although not necessarily by man's unaided efforts; it therefore implies that there is some power superior to man that can effect it. The only agency that could make it actual, Kant believed, is God, regarded as the moral governor of the universe. Therefore, if the moral obligation under which man lives is not illusory, man has not only the right but also the duty to assume that God exists.

Our acceptance of this postulate of morality, Kant continues, does not give us any right to claim that we have knowledge of the existence, nature, purposes, and attributes of God. Indeed, it is not knowledge of any kind. God's existence is a matter of faith, but of rational faith rather than (as in James' philosophy) an emotional faith. For this reason, although Kant presents his argument in an *a priori* rational form, he writes in a skeptical vein about all metaphysical theories based upon, or directed toward proving, the existence of God. *Knowledge* that God exists is not available to man; Kant does not even regard such knowledge as desirable from the point of view of the effects it would have on our conduct, for it would make our

---

[25] The argument is given in Immanuel Kant, *Critique of Practical Reason* (Lewis W. Beck, trans.), pages 227-234. Chicago: University of Chicago Press, 1949.

morality merely a calculation of likely consequences (for instance, the consequences of an action in getting us to heaven), and not a ready obedience to what we see as our duty, wherever it may lead.[26] But on the other hand, the postulate that God exists is not the product of "wishful thinking" with all its subjectivity and variability from man to man.

Kant was unwilling to admit that hypotheses, as we have described them, have a legitimate place in metaphysics; since metaphysical knowledge is not *a priori,* with demonstrative certainty, he believed that there is no metaphysical knowledge at all, and he believed that our *a priori* knowledge does not and can not extend further than our knowledge of the world of appearances. For this reason, he surrendered all claim to speculative metaphysics considered as a kind of knowledge. Because he believed that no logical proof of God's existence is possible, he concluded that belief in it could not be admitted into theoretical metaphysics, but could at most be taken as a postulate of a practical metaphysics of the moral life.

Most recent philosophers hold that while metaphysical propositions cannot be demonstrated, those who believe in the possibility of metaphysics nevertheless hold that metaphysical hypotheses are useful for rendering our experience as a whole intelligible, just as scientific hypotheses cannot be demonstrated yet render parts of our experience intelligible and manageable. Morality is just as much in need of intellectual explanation and defense as any other kind of experience. And if the hypothesis of the existence of God renders moral experience intelligible, that is precisely the kind of credential we require for any metaphysical hypothesis. Kant's rigorous demands on metaphysics, perhaps, made him more skeptical of its results than was warranted.

This last point provides a way of summarizing the discussion of the moral argument. If metaphysics is to throw intelligible light on our experience, the moral experience is certainly a

---

[26] *Ibid.,* pages 247 ff.

sector of the whole that must be rendered intelligible by suitable metaphysical hypotheses concerning the nature of things in general. It is an important and central experience, understanding of which is as important as that of any other kind of experience. If analysis of moral experience shows—as Pascal, James, and Kant believed—that the hypothesis that God exists is required or indicated in any explanation of the hold of moral experience on men's minds and hearts, then morality is evidence for the hypothesis that God exists.

The argument from religious experience

It may seem to the impatient reader that we have been beating about the bush without seeing the bush itself. "Surely," he will say, "men are not first brought to belief in God by such far-fetched arguments as you have been examining. Man is religious much earlier than he is philosophical. Men get their religious beliefs from their specifically religious experience; they believe in God because they have seen Him or felt His presence."

This is an important and honest objection to much speculative theology. It clearly indicates that anyone who argues for the existence of God ought to go directly to the root of the matter: to religious experience itself. By the religious experience, one means such experiences as mysticism, prayer, devotion, and worship. Mysticism claims that there is an experience that is direct and intuitive evidence of a God in whom the mystic and perhaps the whole world merge; there is unification into the perfection and oneness and splendor of a supreme and eternal God. Such an experience can be brought on by religious ritual and ceremony, or by fasting and ascetic practices; sometimes it seems to come without any preparation, and simply to overwhelm the person who has it. When such an experience occurs, it is usually considered by the person who has it to be a real and vivid revelation of God and to be the most worth-while and pregnant experience of which man is capable. It is often followed by a complete revolution in one's general mode of life, so that one says he has been "born again."

Psychologists have often proposed explanations of these experiences.[27] They point out similarities between them and some of the symptoms of hysteria found in the psychiatric patient. Anxiety, a strong but not entirely successful repression, and, perhaps, a lively imagination tending toward hallucination, play a part in both the hysterical and religious experience. But all such explanations of why people have religious experiences, even if true, are irrelevant to the main question: are the experiences sources of knowledge? It does not matter really whether the people who have them are "normal and healthy" or "hysterical" or "saintly." All that matters is the answer to the question: does the experience give knowledge of the existence and attributes of God?

The psychologist who discusses and investigates these experiences, of course, is interested in their causes and not in what they mean, except in so far as they can be interpreted as symptoms from which he can learn something about the personality of the religious person. The philosopher, however, cannot ignore the fact that *every* experience has its psychological causes, while at least some experiences supposedly also have reference to something objectively real outside the person. Certainly, then, psychological conditions can be found for religious experience; but the philosopher wants to know whether the religious experience *also* has any validity with respect to what it seems to reveal, not about man, but about God. The philosophical question is: is the religious experience of such a kind that it can be more plausibly interpreted, in a system of metaphysics, as evidence of the reality of the *object* of the experience (God), or only as evidence of some abnormal psychological state?

We must be careful not to beg this question by making an assumption that will require us to interpret the religious expe-

---

[27] Cf., for instance, J. H. Leuba, *The Psychology of Religious Mysticism.* New York: Harcourt, Brace and Company, Inc., 1926.

rience as merely a psychiatric symptom. If we assume, for example, that there is no God, then obviously it will be easy to interpret the religious experience as hallucinatory. But the question is precisely whether there is a God or not, and the proponent of this argument asserts that the best evidence for an affirmative answer is found in the religious experience. The religious experience may be hallucinatory; but we cannot say that it *must* be unless we already know on some other ground that what is said to be revealed in it, God, is unreal.

The argument from religious experience may take one of two forms. It may be based on the interpretation of one's own religious experience, or upon a comparative study of religious experiences.

Argument from the individual religious experience—The former is usually something like this: "I have had an experience in which I find that I am in contact with a Being whose manifest characters show it to be God." C. C. J. Webb says that in the religious experience there is felt to be

. . . an excitation in our souls by the Reality by which we find ourselves confronted and environed, of perceptions and sentiments which, apart from such an object as Theism assigns to them, must be regarded as essentially illusory and incapable of satisfaction.[28]

This experience is of a Person who, as it were, meets us "half-way." The experience is felt to be ultimate and intimate to a higher degree than our ordinary experiences of other persons.

By itself, of course, the experience proves nothing; but it is sufficiently impressive evidence to convince the person who has the experience that there is a God. Then, the person who accepts this evidence as sufficient for himself says, "You do such-and-such things and you will have the experience I am speaking of; then you will see that what I said is true. But you have to have the experience yourself." The experience is in-

---

[28] C. C. J. Webb, *Religion and Theism*, page 134. London: George Allen & Unwin, Ltd., 1934.

communicable, although it may be suggested by symbols, art, and imagery. But the way to have such an experience can be communicated and taught; the proponent of this argument therefore invites us to have the experience he has had and to see if we do not find it most reasonable to interpret it the way he does.

Certainly no one will challenge the efficacy of this procedure. The best way to know God—assuming He exists—is to have the experience in which He is supposed uniquely to reveal Himself. The absence of the experience of the "vision of God" cannot be made up for by any amount of intellectual argument. Nevertheless, the skeptic will not be convinced. Suppose that the skeptic goes through the preparatory exercises and tries to have the "vision of God" but that it does not come. What can be done about this apparent failure of the empirical test? There might be two replies, neither of which quite suffices. (a) It might be argued that the "preparation" for the experience does not "force the hand of God." The vision of God is not a purely human achievement, to be attained by rigorous adherence to minute prescriptions, but essentially is a gift of God, which God gives or withholds. This is the usual theological position, but it does not meet the logical issue. It begs the question, for it presupposes the existence of God. (b) It might also be said, "You did not get yourself in the proper frame of mind; there is some lurking skepticism that shuts you off from God." Perhaps the typical answer to the person who says that he does not "get anything out of" the experience of worship or devotion is, "you did not completely surrender yourself." But this answer reveals a question-begging definition of the religious experience. It defines the religious experience not in terms of religious practices that can be observed impartially, but as one that does reveal God; any experience that does not do so is, by definition, not a religious experience. Such an argument decides in advance which of the various experiences men have are to be considered evidence for the existence of God, and ignores the negative result of any experience that does not seem to reveal the existence of God. Hence, it falls into the fallacy of neglect of negative instances.

Sometimes this kind of proof is called an "empirical argument" for God, because it appeals to experience. But it is different from the kind of empirical argument that would be used elsewhere in science and philosophy, because here the experience is defined in such a way that, by definition, it must lead to a certain conclusion, and any other experience that does not lead to that conclusion is declared spurious. A valid empirical argument would say that we should put ourselves in such-and-such a condition to observe, and then *whatever* we observe would have equal worth in deciding questions of fact.

Argument from comparative studies of religious experience —This argument recognizes that each individual has his own form of experience, which depends not only upon his personality but also upon the religious tradition in which he is trained. It has therefore been proposed that we should compare various experiences called religious to determine if there is some "common core" that seems to be independent of the individual circumstances. The comparative study of various religions, William James believed, does reveal such a core, which appears in different forms in different religions. But stripping away the accidental and variable, James found a nucleus of religious experience, consisting of two parts:

1. An uneasiness; and 2. Its solution.

1. The uneasiness, reduced to its simplest terms, is a sense that there is *something wrong about us* as we naturally stand.
2. The solution is a sense that *we are saved from the wrongness* by making proper connection with the higher powers.[29]

James reached this nucleus by inductively comparing a great many reports of religious experiences. Other philosophers have made comparable studies and have reached more or less the

---

[29] William James, *The Varieties of Religious Experience*, page 508. London: Longmans, Green & Company, Ltd., 1902; in H. M. Kallen, *op. cit.*, page 498.

same conclusions as to the essence of the religious experience. The question still remains, however, whether this common nucleus of religious experience shows us something universal or at least very widespread about *human nature,* or shows us something about the metaphysical status of the *object* of the religious experience.

If we remember the conclusions reached in our earlier study of hypotheses, we shall readily see that no final answer satisfactory to everyone can be given. In science, after the observations are made and everyone agrees about what they are, we still must ask what they mean. That is, we still must ask what hypothesis best accounts for them. We must do likewise with the observations that James has summarized. Can they be better interpreted as evidence of the existence of the "higher powers," or God, who saves us "from the wrongness," or as evidence merely that most men feel that they *need* some higher power to support them and that they believe that they find it in religious experience? It is not a question, "Do men have experiences that they take as evidence of their contact with God?" for the answer to this question is obvious. It is rather a question as to whether the experiences they undoubtedly do have and undoubtedly do interpret in this way require the theological hypothesis.

This brings us to a final mystery. One's prior orientation or sense of values or philosophy of life will determine how central the facts of the religious experiences will be taken to be. If the religious experience is seen as more central than the scientific experience, then one will construct a metaphysics with God as the ultimate category, and use the religious experience as evidence. If one puts emphasis upon the typical scientific experience with a very parsimonious metaphysics built upon it, one will probably prefer to explain the religious experience as indicative of something very important about the vagaries of human nature but as providing no evidence for theological dualism.

Some miscellaneous arguments

In addition to these eight arguments and the various sub-types of several of them, there are a few more arguments that should be mentioned here, although they are discussed elsewhere.

The first of these is Descartes' argument (page 63), which is a special case of the cosmological argument (page 277). It differs from the usual type of cosmological argument in that Descartes tries to prove the existence of God *before* he proves the existence of the external world. Obviously, therefore, the ontological argument is most suitable to his purposes; but he also makes use of a cosmological argument, taking as his premise the *existence* of his idea of God (and not its essence, as in the case of the ontological argument). He finds, as we have seen, that it is certain that he has an idea of God, but that it is not certain that it corresponds to any real object. So he uses the idea of God as simply an effect, and then argues that a perfect being must exist as its cause. The logic of the argument, therefore, is exactly like that of the cosmological argument although it does not start with anything in the objective physical world.

In Chapter 10 we shall find another argument, presented by Berkeley. This argument may be interpreted in somewhat the same way as Descartes' philosophy suggests; that is, the existence of God is taken as a guarantee for the belief that the external world exists. Or it may be interpreted to mean that since the external world does exist, there must be some mind other than our own which experiences it, and this mind is God's.

Many systems of metaphysics that are not examples of theological dualism make use of the concept of God. Sometimes "God" is considered to be a name for the ultimate reality, or ultimate principle, or ultimate value, and not as a personality or individual being. Such metaphysical theories, often combined with other arguments for the justification of the use of the concept of God, are not examples of theological dualism, and we pass over these views, although they may be relevant to the study of other metaphysical theories.

Summary and conclusions

We have now examined in some detail the major arguments proposed as ways of establishing the existence of God and thereby the validity of theological dualism. In each case, the argument failed to *prove* the existence of God in the sense of showing it to be an inescapable logical necessity. The second argument made debatable assumptions about logic, the third about the metaphysical principle of causation, the fourth about purpose, and the sixth, seventh, and eighth about values; moreover, the first, second, and fifth fell into logical or epistemological errors. They could therefore be challenged on grounds that had nothing explicitly to do with the religious belief in God's existence. I therefore conclude that the existence of God is, for metaphysics, no more than a hypothesis, with all the tentativeness that properly attaches to any hypothesis.

The proper test for an hypothesis in metaphysics, as in science, is not, "Can it definitely be proved?" but rather, "How well does the evidence converge around it, as compared with the convergence of evidence around its alternatives?" In answering this question in both science and metaphysics, one cannot simply count the facts in favor of and against a particular hypothesis. Each fact and alleged fact must be weighed; and in metaphysics the weight ascribed to each depends upon the orientation of the thinker, upon what he takes to be the central fact or most pregnant metaphor.

It is important to remember always that there is this personal element in philosophizing, so that one will not permit one's strong and fervent belief in God (or one's equally strong disbelief) to masquerade as cogent logical proof.

From the standpoint of moral and religious concern, perhaps Pascal and James are correct in their insistence that one must believe or disbelieve in God, and that the suspense of judgment for lack of evidence is equivalent to disbelief. But the aim of philosophy and metaphysics is not primarily to make us better men—they may or may not do this—but to give us understanding. And it would be very unfortunate if the practically important concern of man with the ultimate problem of the existence or non-existence of God were to obscure the fact that the existence or non-existence of God is, for philosophy, a hypothesis, not a theorem to be proved from self-evident and inescapable axioms. The man of religious faith will believe the hypothesis that God exists quite independently of any weaknesses the arguments for it may have; and the man who lacks this religious faith will not be convinced by these arguments, however strong they may be.

SOME COROLLARIES OF THEOLOGICAL DUALISM

No hypothesis, either in metaphysics or in science, stands alone. It is always a member of a family of hypotheses with which it coheres, both giving support to them and gaining support from them. In this section we shall consider briefly a few of the hypotheses that appear to be more reasonable if theological dualism is true than if some other world-hypothesis is considered more adequate. These corollary hypotheses may be thought of as collateral hypotheses that give support to theological dualism, if we suppose that there is better evidence for them than for theological dualism itself. Or if we believe theological dualism is a well-established hypothesis, we may think of it as the collateral hypothesis that lends credence to these other hypotheses associated with it. Which supports which is a matter of which we believe has the best independent evidence in its favor; what is not disputable is the coherent family relations among them.

What is man?

Every metaphysical theory involves a theory of the nature of man and of his place in the world. While theological dualism does not dispute any established facts of psychology, it does interpret them in a less mechanical, naturalistic way than is usual among contemporary psychologists. It holds that men differ from animals not merely in degree of intelligence or some other biological way, and that man in his essential being is different from and superior to the things in nature. It argues that the most important dimension for the understanding of man is not that of his relation to nature, but that of his relation to God. We now turn to some consequences of this orientation.

First, the theological dualist is likely to hold that the mind is not a mere accidental physiological offshoot or by-product of the body, but that it is evidence of a soul. The soul is an ultimate and irreducible entity, not to be explained as simply a function or product of the brain and under the laws of natural causation that apply to the brain.

Different religions with their diverse theologies and metaphysical theories have different views of the nature of the soul; in fact, Christianity at various stages of its history has held diverse views in response to the scientific and philosophical theories current at different times. The one most familiar to us nowadays is the theory that there are two kinds of beings in the world—thinking substances or minds, and extended substances, or bodies, and that these interact with each other. This view, espoused by Descartes and often called Cartesian dualism, is in complete opposition to the behavioristic view that human personality can be understood exclusively in terms of physiological mechanisms conditioned by social intercourse.

Second, the theological dualist argues that the human being is to be understood teleologically, not mechanically. The soul is the guiding factor in the behavior of the human being. It controls and uses the body for its own purposes, which are not restricted to the satisfactions of the flesh.

Third, there is usually a strong belief in human freedom, or the "freedom of the will." The limits of human freedom come from God's power (as in the theory of predestination) and not primarily from the power of nature (mechanism). Man has a will that has the power of decision and execution of decision. Nowadays, the will is usually thought of as a kind of system of habits; theological and Cartesian dualism, on the contrary, hold that the body is only one of the conditions of human behavior. Although men frequently "drift along" and fail to exercise their freedom, they *can* exercise it. Theological dualists go even further in saying that man may call upon God for assistance in asserting his freedom from circumstance, so that in the exercise of his true freedom, man is allied with God, a power greater than nature and able to dominate it.

Finally, man is thought of as being the highest manifestation of God's creative power. From this follows the conception that man is a supreme value. He is not an accident of evolution, but in spite of his physical insignificance in a world of cosmic forces and astronomical distances, he is superior to the world of nature. A consequence usually drawn from this is that man's soul, which is thought to be to some extent free from the limitations of the body and of infinitely more importance, will not be sacrificed by its Maker to the vicissitudes of time and the death that time brings to his body. Hence the soul is immortal; man is not merely a citizen of the world and a relative of the animals, but a citizen of the Kingdom of God, which is eternal.

Implications for value theory

According to the theological dualist, the world cannot be adequately understood as only a physical world, the values of which are subjective responses of the human organism. The perfection of God necessarily implies that His work will not be mere brute fact, but will have meaning and value. Thus, the theological dualist is likely to be an objectivist in the theory of values.

The objectivism based on this theory holds that values and the laws of value are divinely instituted. The moral law, for instance, is not to be inferred from men's mundane experience of how best to get along with their fellows, nor is it to be deduced from pure reason. The moral law is revealed to man (as in the Ten Commandments), and it ought to be obeyed because it is the Word of God. While primitive religions put much emphasis upon God's rewarding virtue and punishing vice, conceptions of heaven and hell are not absolutely essential parts of religious belief, and many religions do not have them. These religions tend to emphasize rather the harmony of the world of fact and value, so that the man who loves God and does His will has the Kingdom of God within him.

Primitive religions generally emphasize the arbitrariness and power of God, so that their adherents usually think right is right *because* God commands it. This doctrine seems to underly many of the tabus in the earliest parts of the Old Testament, and is effectively criticized by Plato in the *Euthyphro*. In the more subtle metaphysical theories of the nature of God, as found in later parts of the Old Testament, in the New Testament, and in Greek philosophy, whence it later passed into the Christian tradition, the doctrine is reversed. Instead of an action being right because God commands it, God commands it because it is right, and God is by nature the moral governor and the font of all value.

Theological dualists further hold that the highest values are not the values of morality and beauty and intellect, but that there is a specifically religious value that can be appreciated only through living a life in which one feels himself to be sustained by God in seeking eternal values. The theological moralist says that the love of God will be evidenced in one's moral conduct and in the inward joy of his life; but these moral and hedonistic consequences are not the essential and ultimate values by which religion is to be justified and judged. The ultimate values are above our lives and circumstances, and man must free himself from his involvement in the things of this world in order to reach them. This may end in monasticism and asceticism; but it may also be a stage in our experience that enriches and deepens our appreciation of the world itself and of others who are then regarded as our brothers because all are children of God.

Implications for the philosophy of history

Human life, according to the theological dualist, must be understood in the light of that which is above nature and not merely as a product of blind natural forces. Organic evolution is thought of as manifesting a divine purpose; to an even greater degree, from the dawn of religions, human history has been interpreted as due in large measure to the plans and acts of God in His relation to man. Every religion has its own account of the creation and subsequent history of man. Each account manifests the particular relationship in which human affairs are thought by that religion to stand to God's plan. In the earlier anthropomorphic stages of tribal religion, the agency of God in human affairs was seen in extraordinary and miraculous events and prophecies, in which God was supposed to express His wrath, or vengeance, or care for some particular man or His chosen people. Primitive history usually takes the form of myth, in which gods and men fight alongside one another or fight against each other.

As the religious conception is refined in the direction of a more spiritual, universalistic theology, the agency of God in history comes to expression in subtle philosophies of history. Christian theology is associated with the philosophy of history formulated by St. Augustine (354-430) in his *City of God*. For Augustine, there are really two histories—one, the history of the city of earth, dealing with man as a natural political organism, and one, the history of the City of God, dealing with man as a spiritual being who has fallen from God's grace by sin, and who is predestined to find his way back to the grace of God. The former is secular history, and a study of it will show, according to Augustine, that it is not self-explanatory. It requires interpretation in accordance with the pattern of man's spiritual history of the Fall and Redemption. The destiny of man lies in his discovering that he is not merely a citizen of the city of earth, with its false philosophies and morals, but preeminently a citizen of the City of God. Men seek false and unworthy purposes in striving for status in the city of man; it matters not whether Rome or Carthage wins, for both are doomed to decay in time. Despite Augustine's occasionally generous estimates of the achievements of paganism, only the coming of the Kingdom of God has genuine religious significance and historical value for him.

While many diverse philosophies of history are associated with the theology and metaphysics of Christianity, all have some features common to this Augustinian doctrine. They all see in secular history a higher plan and destiny than can be explained in terms of geography, economics, or politics. The greatest evidence of the contact between mundane history and a theological superhistory (*Heilgeschichte*) is found in the revelation God gives to man in the supernatural and superhistorical teachings of Jesus. Reinhold Niebuhr, who is perhaps the leading philosopher of history in the Christian church today, says,

> There are elements in the "behaviour" of history which point to a "hidden" source of its life. It is in that sense that history is meaningful but pointing beyond itself.[30]
> History after Christ [is] an interim between the disclosure of its true meaning and the fulfillment of that meaning.[31]

The fulfillment of that meaning is not to be found, according to Niebuhr, in some future historical event, such as the establishment of a temporal Kingdom of God on earth; the goal and meaning of history are outside the processes of time. The *Pilgrim's Progress* is only an allegory of man's fall and redemption in history; the man who fully understands the implications of his history does not await "some far-off divine event" or expect that, at some future date, Christ will return to earth to set up His Kingdom. The world of superhistory is eternal,

---

[30] Reinhold Niebuhr, *The Nature and Destiny of Man*, Part II, page 67. New York: Charles Scribner's Sons, 1943.

[31] *Ibid.*, page 49.

and not in temporal passage at all. Man achieves the fulfillment of the meaning of history, and thereby transcends time and history, by seeing it *sub specie aeternitatis*.

Niebuhr believes that the fulfillment of the meaning of history, while it transcends the complexities and ambiguities of all historical processes, is relevant to the processes of historical change. But a more temporalistic interpretation of history, also from a Christian point of view, is found in the works of the English historian, Arnold Toynbee. After surveying the rise and fall of societies, Toynbee believes he finds evidence that justifies the faith that there has been a gradual spiritual progress in mankind, the continuation of which is the only hope of civilization. This, he believes, can be secured only with the help of God:

. . . In the classic version of the myth [*Pilgrim's Progress*] we are told that the human protagonist was not left entirely to his own resources in the decisive hour. According to John Bunyan, Christian was saved by his encounter with Evangelist. And, inasmuch as it cannot be supposed that God's nature is less constant than Man's, we may and must pray that a reprieve which God has granted to our society once [in the incarnation of God in Christ] will not be refused if we ask for it again in a humble spirit and with a contrite heart.[32]

BIBLIOGRAPHY

Brightman, Edgar S., "An Empirical Approach to God," *Philosophical Review*, Vol. XLVI, No. 2 (March, 1937), pages 147-169.

Brownstein, D. J., Krikorian, Y. H., and Wiener, P. P. (eds.), *Basic Problems of Philosophy*. New York: Prentice-Hall, Inc., 1947. Part 7.

Burtt, Edwin Arthur, *Types of Religious Philosophy*, second ed. New York: Harper & Brothers, 1951.

Butler, Joseph, *The Analogy of Religion* (1736) (William E. Gladstone, ed.). Oxford: Clarendon Press, 1896.

Jacobson, Nolan P., "Niebuhr's Philosophy of History," *Harvard Theological Review*, Vol. XXXVII, No. 4 (October, 1944), pages 237-260.

---

[32] From *A Study of History*, by A. J. Toynbee, page 554, abridged by D. C. Somervell. Copyright 1946 by Oxford University Press, Inc.

Macintosh, Douglas Clyde (ed.), *Religious Realism*. New York: The Macmillan Company, 1931.

Martin, J. A., *Empirical Philosophies of Religion*. New York: King's Crown Press, 1945.

Niebuhr, Reinhold, *Faith in History*. New York: Charles Scribner's Sons, 1949.

Santayana, George, *Reason in Religion*. New York: Charles Scribner's Sons, 1905.

Smith, J. D., *The Teachings of the Catholic Church*. New York: The Macmillan Company, 1940.

Sorley, W. R., *Moral Values and the Idea of God*. Cambridge, Eng.: University Press, 1927.

Taylor, A. E., *David Hume and the Miraculous*. Cambridge, Eng.: University Press, 1927.

Temple, William, *Nature, Man, and God*. New York: The Macmillan Company, 1949.

Webb, Clement C. J., *Kant's Philosophy of Religion*. Oxford: Clarendon Press, 1926.

Wieman, Henry N., *Religious Experience and Scientific Method*. New York: The Macmillan Company, 1926.

QUESTIONS AND TOPICS FOR DISCUSSION

1. Comment on the following quotations:

   (a) "He that takes away reason to make way for revelation puts out the light of both." Locke.

   (b) "It is absolutely necessary that one be convinced of the existence of God; but it is not so essential that one demonstrate it." Kant.

   (c) "For Him [Jesus] there was nothing supernatural, because for Him there was nothing natural." Renan.

   (d) "Faith is the substance of things hoped for, the evidence of things not seen." St. Paul.

   (e) "Religion is man's acute awareness of the realm of unattained possibility and the behavior that results from this awareness." H. N. Wieman.

   (f) "Religion is the feeling of absolute dependence." Schleiermacher.

2. Compare the religious beliefs and practices found to be typical in an American city in 1925 with those of 1935. (Cf. Robert S. Lynd and Helen M. Lynd, *Middletown* and *Middletown in Tran-*

sition. New York: Harcourt, Brace and Company, Inc., 1929, 1937.) What do you think such a study would reveal in 1952?

3. Describe the relation between reason and faith in the Catholic philosophy. Comment on Bishop Sheen's statement, "The Church is in love with reason."

4. Why does religious argument so readily tend to use the appeal to authority? Must it do so?

5. Do psychological explanations of religious beliefs have any value as evidence for or against their truth?

6. Which of the various arguments for the existence of God seems to be the strongest? Why? How would you attempt to answer criticisms made of it?

7. Discuss the view that if the soul is not immortal and if God does not reward or punish men, there is no reason for being moral if one can get away with immorality. Do you think that most religious people actually hold this?

8. Discuss the relations between religion and mental hygiene.

10

Idealism

Idealism is a coat of many colors. In common speech, we describe a person as an idealist if he professes and follows high ideals and is not deterred from their pursuit by very real difficulties in attaining them and by the obvious frailty of human nature. Every fortunate person, if really fortunate, knows such persons and is the better for it. Every person with courage, patience, and fortitude has at least a little of this kind of idealism in his make-up. The best parts of history are composed of the acts of such idealists: in art, Michelangelo, Beethoven, Van Gogh; in religion, St. Paul, St. Francis, some great missionaries; in science, Pasteur and the men with Dr. Walter Reed; in social and spiritual reform, George Fox, Florence Nightingale, Susan B. Anthony, Gandhi; and great heroes from Joan of Arc to the countless, nameless men who "serve beyond the call of duty." In literature, where we always find the best exemplars of the various human types, the world has been made better, at least indirectly, by Antigone, Faust (in Part II of Goethe's poem), Alyosha in *The Brothers Karamazov*, Christian Wahnschaffe in Wassermann's *The World's Illusion,* Dinah Morris in *Adam Bede,* Thackeray's Colonel Newcome, and their like.

316

Sometimes we use the word in an opprobrious sense, to refer to an unrealistic and Utopian attitude stultified by impatience with the very practical matter of means for attaining the ideal. The idealist in this sense has been described as "a person with both feet firmly planted on a cloud." If placed in power and endowed with influence over others, the good or evil done by such uncompromising and fanatical idealists can be very great; in the literary examples of such character, we sympathize or are annoyed with the fatuity of Don Quixote, Richard Feverel's father, Père Goriot, Mr. Dombey, and Mr. Micawber.

Technical meaning of idealism

Idealism also means a technical metaphysical doctrine formulated by Berkeley, Leibniz, Hegel, Emerson, Bradley, Royce, Croce, and many other philosophers. Some of the unpopularity of the word "idealism" in our somewhat hard-boiled age has perhaps infected philosophical opinion of the great idealistic systems, and for the past 40 or 50 years, the number of professional philosophers who call themselves idealists has probably declined. But idealism is by no means dead as a system of philosophy. It appeals to many of the best minds of our generation. It is still rewarding to see what idealism means in philosophy and to understand what the idealists say about the world.

There is, of course, a reason why the same word, "idealism," is used as a name both for the personal attitudes we have mentioned and for a system of technical philosophy. Philosophical idealists do emphasize the role of high ideals in conduct; they stress the creative role of ideals in the history of culture; they believe that ideals are not subjective human illusions or inventions but are based upon and give evidence of some profound trait of reality itself. But the philosophical idealists are not the only philosophers who insist upon these points. What is essential to philosophical idealism is not a view of *ideals,* but of *ideas.*

"Idea" and "ideal"

Both etymologically and philosophically, there is a very close connection between these words. We have seen, in Chapter 5, how Plato asserted that the ultimate explanation of things is to be found in universal realities, eternal and perfect, which he called ideas; and in Chapter 7 it was shown how these ideas are, for Plato, not only principles of explanation but also principles and causes of value. Perhaps it would have been better if the word *ideal* had been used as a translation of the Greek term by which Plato referred to these objective and universal realities, values, and purposes. Plato believed, of course, that the mind could apprehend them through a long process of dialectic; but he did not regard them as "in the mind" and subject to psychological explanation. Plato was a realist [1] in his theories of ideas or universals, whereas in modern times we tend to use the word "idea" in a more nominalistic sense, as something that exists as a content of consciousness and dependent upon mind.

When Plato is referred to as the "father of idealism," or idealism is called the "Platonic tradition in philosophy," one should not forget that there is a profound difference between his theory of ideas and the metaphysics of modern idealism. While modern idealism may be compared to platonism in its concern for "eternal values" that cannot be explained in terms of nature, it places much more emphasis than did Plato upon the concept of mind as the ultimate reality.

The emphasis upon mind

The most important concept in modern idealism is neither "idea" nor "ideal," but *mind*. R. F. A. Hoernlé, a leading ideal-

---

[1] For this meaning of realism (Platonic realism), cf. page 125. This kind of realism is not necessarily incompatible with some forms of idealism, and should be contrasted with those forms of realism that are reactions against idealism; cf. pages 422 ff.

ist of the twentieth century, has said, "Mind is, in some sense,
the hero of every idealistic story."

The root *metaphor* of the idealist is that reality is mind, experience, or consciousness. The idealist takes the fact that we
do have experiences as the *central* fact. He regards the fact
that we *have* experiences (or that reality is so constituted that
experiences occur within it) as more important and revelatory
of reality than are the things that we happen to experience.
Instead of explaining how we experience things in terms of
stimuli and responses and the behavior of the nervous system
(which he admits to be an important and valid task of science,
but not adequate for metaphysics), the idealist takes the fact
of experience itself as basic. He points out that all the facts of
science are included in experience, and must be understood as
parts of experience. He takes consciousness of fact and of value
as explanatory of fact and value; he holds that fact and value
taken alone are mere abstractions from the true reality, which
is always concrete *experience* of facts and value. The idealist,
therefore, believes that he alone can gain a truly synoptic philosophy; he believes that he alone does not put the cart before
the horse, does not try the impossible in considering facts in
utter isolation from the mind that experiences them and gives
them their meaning and significance. All other philosophers, he
believes, omit or ignore or de-emphasize the most important
and obvious fact about every experience—every fact or value is
a fact or value only in and for an experiencing, conscious mind.
It is for this reason that the idealist sometimes says that the
world is best described as an idea or system of ideas:

"The world is my idea:"—this is a truth which holds good for
everything that lives and knows, though man alone can bring it into
reflective and abstract consciousness. If he really does this, he has
attained to philosophical wisdom. . . . If any truth can be asserted
a priori, it is this: for it is the expression of the most general form
or all possible and thinkable experience: a form which is more general than time, or space, or causality, for they all presuppose it. . . .
No truth therefore is more certain, more independent of all others,
and less in need of proof than this, that all that exists for knowledge,

and therefore this whole world, is only object in relation to subject, perception of a perceiver, in a word, idea.[2]

The basic analogy that the idealist takes as a guide in metaphysics can be expressed in various ways. He sometimes emphasizes the relation of mind to its objects, in which objects come to have meaning only within consciousness and are to be explained only as aspects of experience. Sometimes the basic analogy is that between a deductive logical system and the world itself considered as a synoptic and systematic whole, in which each part functions so as to contribute to the development of the whole. Sometimes it is found in the experience of value, in which the moral agent grows more self-sufficient and independent of outward things, endowing them with value only as they contribute to the realization of the potentialities of the self. Sometimes it is found in artistic experience, in which the dominance of the creative mind over the material at hand is perhaps most unmistakable. But whatever be the analogy, the idealist thinks reality is a meaningful, intelligible, and valuable whole in which the highest human ideals achieve realization.

The first of the specific forms of idealistic metaphysics to be discussed is based primarily upon the role of the mind and the status of the object in perception. In the next chapter, we shall discuss two other types of idealism that are less narrowly restricted to problems primarily epistemological.

BERKELEIAN IDEALISM

The first representative of modern idealism is George Berkeley (1685-1753), an Irish-born bishop of the Church of England. Because of his daring speculation, his inimitable literary style, his active life, and his attractive personality, Berkeley is one of the most interesting figures in the history of philosophy. He is especially interesting to Americans because he came to this

---

[2] Arthur Schopenhauer, *The World as Will and Idea* (R. B. Haldane and J. Kemp, trans.), Volume I, page 3. London: Kegan Paul, Trench, Trubner Ltd., 1891.

country, in 1729, with "the prospect of planting arts and learning in America."

Locke's theory of knowledge

We must understand the intellectual challenge to which Berkeley's philosophy was a response. This can best be seen in the writings of John Locke (1632-1704). Locke was one of the most important of the English political thinkers; his views on government had a profound effect on the fathers of this country and on the development of constitutional monarchy in England. In 1690, he published his influential *Essay Concerning Human Understanding*,[3] which had as its purpose "to inquire into the original, certainty, and extent of human knowledge, together with the grounds and degrees of belief, opinion, and assent."[4] Locke's reason for undertaking this investigation was not merely his curiosity about matters epistemological; in addition, he had a very practical political interest in determining the sources and validity of men's beliefs which brought them into conflict with each other. He believed that if he could find how men's ideas had their source in their diverse experiences, a great step could be taken in the direction of mutual understanding and tolerance, which was hindered by the dogmatic conviction of most men that their own beliefs (say, their belief in the divine right of kings) were true because they came from God and should not be subjected to critical questioning.

Instead of imagining that we have true beliefs from birth, Locke asks us to trace our ideas back to the experience that engendered them, for it is his doctrine that there is nothing in the intellect that was not first in the senses:

Let us suppose the mind to be, as we say, white paper, void of all characters, without any ideas; how comes it to be furnished?

---

[3] The most convenient abridgement is in Sterling P. Lamprecht (ed.), *Locke Selections* (New York: Charles Scribner's Sons, 1928). Page references are to this volume.

[4] John Locke, *op. cit.*, page 90.

Whence comes it by that vast store which the busy and boundless fancy of man has painted on it, with an almost endless variety? Whence has it all the materials of reason and knowledge? To this I answer, in one word, from experience; in that all our knowledge is founded, and from that it ultimately derives itself.[5]

We have, he goes on to say, two kinds of experience, each of which furnishes us with a specific kind of idea. Our senses are "conversant about particular sensible objects," and give us the ideas of yellow, white, cold, heat, shape, and the like. These he calls the "sensible qualities" that we perceive by our external senses, and the ideas of them he calls "ideas of sensation." We also have an internal sense, which gives us awareness of the operations of our mind when it perceives, thinks, doubts, wills, believes, abstracts, and so on. Our ideas of the operations of our mind, performed on the data of the senses, he calls "ideas of reflection." All that we have in our minds, then, are perceptions or ideas of these two kinds, "having ideas, and perception, being the same thing."

Our minds are able to abstract, separate, compare, and recombine in the same or a different order the ideas that come from the senses. If the mind retains the combinations in which the ideas first arrived, we call them memories; if it separates and recombines them in a different order, we are imagining. Locke then proceeds to show that every idea in our consciousness can be derived from one or the other of the two sources, although the combinations may vary. For instance, our idea of horse is made up of ideas of sensations of color, shape, size, smell, touch, and so on, each of which came from sensation, combined with the idea of reflection caused by the belief that such a thing exists; our idea of a unicorn, on the other hand, is made up of many of the same ideas of sensation, combined with another idea of sensation (a single horn), and with the reflective idea of disbelief. In neither case, however, is there any new, simple idea that does not come from one of the two sources: sensing, and reflecting on our own mental operations.

[5] *Ibid.*, page 111.

How our ideas relate to reality—We have just seen that our mind combines and separates its ideas. It associates them together so that when one idea occurs, we normally expect that other ideas that have occurred together with them in the past will reappear (association of ideas). For example, I have the idea of white, granular, and solid, and I expect to have the idea of sweet; in this way I suppose that these ideas refer to or mean sugar.

Why do my ideas hang together in this way? Locke tells us that our idea of sugar is a "complication of many ideas together; because . . . not imagining how these simple ideas can subsist by themselves, we accustom ourselves to suppose some substratum, wherein they do subsist, and from which they do result." [6] The thing that causes us to have these ideas and that, we suppose, has the qualities of sweetness, solidity, and whiteness is the real sugar. Locke calls it a *substance*. We do not really know or perceive substances, but refer our ideas, which we do perceive, to them as their cause. A substance is merely a "something, I know not what," or "the unknown cause of my sensations."

We infer what the substance is from its effects on us. Locke believes that some of the ideas caused in us by a substance resemble the qualities of the substance itself. Those qualities in a substance that create ideas resembling them he calls the *primary qualities*. They are its shape, size, number, and motion or rest. In other words, they are "physical properties" of the thing, without which it would not exist as a physical thing. In addition, we have other ideas, for instance, ideas of the sweetness of sugar or the yellow we sense when we say, "I see a piece of gold," which do not resemble the qualities of the objects, but are merely the effects of the object on our sense organs and mind. "Yellow" is not really a property of gold, but there is a "power" in gold to produce a sensation of yellow. This power is nothing but the "bulk, figure, texture, and mo-

[6] *Ibid.,* page 176.

tion" of the insensible parts (for example, atoms) of the gold.[7]
These qualities, which we attribute to the object but which do
not inhere in it, he calls *secondary qualities*.

Locke is here saying that the colors, odors, sounds, and tastes
of a thing exist as qualities only in the mind. Like Theaetetus,
he says that they depend primarily on the sense organs and the
mind, and not merely on the substance itself. Most modern
psychologists and physicists agree with Locke and Theaetetus
in this opinion. Nowadays, we say that the object consists of
molecules that we do not see but whose existence we infer
from what we do see; the molecules have chemical and physical (that is, primary) qualities, but no color, taste, or odor; but
the chemical and physical properties of the object have the
power to produce an effect on us that we experience as a color
or taste or odor. Locke and modern physics and psychology
accept the doctrine of epistemological relativism (see page
57) with respect to the secondary qualities, but not with respect to the primary qualities. Locke argued this so well and
with such great influence that this belief has come to be almost
"common sense"; almost everyone who has studied a little
physics or psychology will now say, with Locke, that a tree
falling in a forest where no one can hear it does not make a
sound.

Some skeptical conclusions—In spite of its plausibility, however, Locke's theory has some very unsatisfactory implications.
We shall mention three of them that stimulated Berkeley and
led him to develop an idealistic theory.

The first is the fact that if Locke's philosophy is correct, we
cannot know that there is anything in the world except our
own ideas. The world of nature, for Locke, exists only as the
unknown cause of my ideas; so how do I know that it exists at
all? Causation, we have seen, is at most known to be a relation
among things or events we can observe; how do we know that
it connects what we can observe with what cannot be ob-

---

[7] *Ibid.*, page 206.

served? That is a matter of conjecture or faith. All sane people do feel that there is an external world independent of our experience of it, and most fairly sophisticated people believe, as Locke did, that we experience only its effects on us. But if we accept the thesis that we know only what is in our own consciousness, then we must admit that we do not *know* that there is a common, external, and independent world. Thus, from Locke's eminently plausible starting point, which is accepted by most scientists, a skeptical conclusion is drawn.

Second, let it be granted that there is an external world of objects that affect our minds and produce our experience. Even so, there is an inadequacy in this view that will make a thinking man uncomfortable. For it follows that the world as it is granted really to exist is never a part of our experience and is almost wholly unlike the experiences we do have. The consequence is that *the world we know does not really exist, and the world that really exists is unknown and unknowable.* Here is another skeptical conclusion, one as difficult to accept as the first.

Third, Locke's skeptical conclusions are incompatible with natural theology. Locke believed that the existence of God could be inferred from a study of nature, by an inference from nature to its Author. Berkeley, as a theologian, was naturally interested in such an argument, but he realized that Locke's theory of knowledge weakened or vitiated it, since Locke's premise for it—the existence and orderly arrangement of nature —was not established by his theory of knowledge.

Berkeley, while still in his twenties, wrote his chief philosophical works, in which he discerned and tried to answer the skepticism implicit in Locke's position and shared by most of the scientists of his and our own day. Berkeley never doubted the main features of Locke's psychology and theory of knowledge; he believed that all that we know comes from experience and is only a set of ideas. But what he did was to construct a new metaphysics in which this epistemological and psychological theory would *not* lead to skepticism. This is the purpose

of his books, *An Essay Towards a New Theory of Vision*
(1709), *A Treatise Concerning the Principles of Human
Knowledge* (1710), and *Three Dialogues between Hylas and
Philonous* (1713).[8]

First stage of Berkeley's argument

Berkeley's argument is at first one long criticism of the distinction between primary and secondary qualities.[9] He accepts all of Locke's arguments, which, like those of Protagoras
and Theaetetus, were designed to show that qualities like color
are subjective and dependent upon the perceiver. But then he
goes one step further: he tries to show that if these qualities
are subjective, then the primary qualities are subjective also.
From this he draws the conclusion that if all the properties
attributed to the object are only in the mind, there can be no
object apart from the mind. We shall briefly recapitulate his
arguments:

1. *The distance and size of an object are not directly appre-*

---

[8] Printed in their entirety in George Berkeley, *Essay, Principles, Dialogues,
With Selections From Other Writings* (Mary Whiton Calkins, ed.). New York:
Charles Scribner's Sons, 1929. All page references are to this volume.

[9] Locke says that the secondary quality is a "power in the object" to produce an effect on us, such as the idea of color, which does not resemble the
power in the object, since the power is only a modification of the primary
qualities of the microscopic particles in the object. Berkeley, on the contrary,
understands by secondary quality the quality *of the idea* which does not
resemble anything in the object. Thus Berkeley speaks as if it were admitted
that secondary qualities are subjective, and he is often charged, therefore,
with having misunderstood Locke's distinction. Perhaps he did; and modern
terminology often follows his misunderstanding rather than Locke's own definitions. But if we substitute "sensible qualities" for "secondary qualities" in
the arguments we are about to examine, the validity of the argument is not
affected. To conform to modern usage, however, we shall speak of secondary
qualities as Berkeley did—they are qualities of experienced ideas assumed to resemble nothing independent of the mind and to be subjective; and such qualities are experienced as colors, odors, tastes, sounds, pleasures, pains, and so on.
Cf. Gregory D. Walcott, "Primary and Secondary Qualities," *Philosophical Review*, Vol. XXXV, No. 5 (Sept. 1926), pages 462-472; Reginald Jackson,
"Locke's Distinction between Primary and Secondary Qualities," *Mind*, n.s.,
Vol. XXXVIII, No. 149 (January 1929), pages 56-76; and Winston H. F.
Barnes, "Did Berkeley Misunderstand Locke?" *Mind*, n.s., Vol. LXIX, No. 193
(January 1940), pages 52-57.

hended—We see nothing but patterns of color and light and shade as these are projected upon the retina; every other characteristic we attribute to an object is an interpretation of these, associated with the remembrance of past experiences in which we have found that a certain feeling of strain in focussing the eyes has accompanied a certain degree of effort required to reach so as to get a sensation of touch from the object. (Many of the principles found in modern books on the psychology of perception of distance were clearly formulated by Berkeley.) But Berkeley was not merely interested in the psychology of the perception of size and distance; he wanted also to draw a philosophical conclusion from it. And this was his conclusion: the apprehension of primary qualities depends on, and is psychologically and physiologically more complex than, the perception of secondary qualities; hence, if it be supposed that the secondary qualities are not in the object, we have no good reason for believing that the primary qualities are in the object. There is no more reason to believe that the *perceived* shape of an object (the *image's* shape) is like the *real* shape of the object than to believe that the perceived color resembles some unperceived physical characteristic of the real object.

2. *Primary qualities are not conceivable apart from their relation to the perceiver*—Just as color varies with the eye of the perceiver, so also the size we perceive varies with distance from the perceiver; motion is fast or slow only with respect to the expectations and stream of consciousness of the perceiver. Now variability with respect to the perceiver was one of the reasons why Locke had located the same qualities in the mind; but exactly the same kind of variability attaches to the experience of primary qualities. Hence, to be consistent, they also should be considered as not existing without a perceiver.

3. *Primary qualities attributed to an external object are unthinkable in isolation from qualities that are granted to exist only in the idea*—We cannot frame a conception of an object having size or shape but no quality (like color or hardness) by virtue of which the size or shape could be distinguished

from its surroundings. If I am to think of an object that has shape, I must also think of a difference of quality between the inside and the outside of the boundary of its shape. But if all qualities except size, shape, figure, and motion are in the mind, they are neither within nor without the boundary of the supposedly real external object. Hence, if the secondary qualities are subjective, and the primary qualities are assumed to be objective, then the shape of the object is the disembodied shape of an airy nothing.

4. *Primary qualities are never perceived in isolation from the secondary qualities*—The size we perceive is a size of a tangible body with a certain degree of hardness, or of a colored expanse. We never see secondary qualities that do not have shape, but neither do we see shapes that are not colored or shaded in some way. Now to take the shape of such a figure and imagine that it is in the real world, while leaving the color in the mind, is like trying to imagine the smile of a Cheshire cat without the cat. It is to commit the fallacy of "reifying an abstraction." All our ideas appear in experiences, in which we find them in a relation of "togetherness" and mutual modification; the shapes are shapes of colors, and the colors are colors of shapes. To separate them is to take an abstraction and treat it as capable of existing in isolation.[10]

5. *The conception of a material object having only primary qualities is useless*—Why was it formulated? Only to explain how ideas do arise in the mind. But, says Berkeley, it does not help to explain the origin of our ideas. We have not the least conception of how an idea could arise in the mind from something having only physical qualities; and in terms of Locke's philosophy we are not likely to discover it, since by hypothesis the cause is unknown. Locke's theory that ideas arise as the

---

[10] Cf. George Berkeley, *Principles*, §10, in Mary W. Calkins (ed.), *op. cit.* Here we see Berkeley's nominalism. Actually he went much further and denied that there are any abstract ideas even in the mind. He was surely wrong in this, but the argument as given in the text is independent of his untenably extreme form of nominalism.

effect on us of an unknown object is a case of explaining the obscure by something even more obscure:

> But, though we might possibly have all our sensations without them, yet perhaps it may be thought easier to conceive and explain the manner of their production, by supposing external bodies in their likeness rather than otherwise; and so it might be at least probable there are such things as bodies that excite their ideas in our minds. But neither can this be said. For, though we give the materialists their external bodies, they by their own confession are never the nearer knowing how our ideas are produced; since they own themselves unable to comprehend in what manner body can act upon spirit, or how it is possible it should imprint any idea in the mind.[11] Hence it is evident the production of ideas or sensations in our minds, can be no reason why we should suppose Matter or corporeal substances; since that is acknowledged to remain equally inexplicable with or without the mind, yet to hold they do so must needs be a very precarious assumption; since it is to suppose, without any reason at all, that God has created innumerable beings that are entirely useless, and serve to no manner of purpose.
>
> In short, if there were external bodies, it is impossible that we should ever come to know it; and if there were not, we might have the very same reasons to think there were that we have now.[12]

So much for the argument against an unknown cause of my sensations. Granting that the five preceding arguments have shown the difficulty of the conception that there is a material substance lying wholly outside our experience and having only primary qualities and powers to produce secondary qualities in our minds, we have two questions. How did the conception of an unknown object's existence arise? What is the proper meaning of the statement, "An object exists"?

(a) *What is the origin of the conception of an unknown object?*—Locke himself has already answered this question (see page 323). We find that some of our ideas are so regularly

---

[11] Cf. Locke's admission of this in S. P. Lamprecht (ed.), *op. cit.*, page 188. (Note that Berkeley calls Locke a materialist because he believes in the existence of matter. Locke is not a materialist in the strict sense of the word, because he does not hold that mind is "reducible" to matter.)

[12] George Berkeley, *Principles*, §§19 and 20.

associated with others that we believe they are causally related. But one idea cannot be the cause of another idea; [13] so we suppose that there is something else that is not an idea but is the cause or substratum of our ideas. Common sense, when it gives up the naive belief that things are always exactly as they appear, accepts this conception of the unknown thing behind its appearances.

But if, as Berkeley believes, there cannot be an object having only primary qualities and the power to produce secondary qualities in our ideas, this common notion of an independent material substratum must be in error. If, then, there are no objects independent of the mind, what can we mean when we say an object exists? This is our second question.

(b) *What does it mean to say, "Something exists"?*—All the evidence that we have of the existence of a thing is that we experience it. This is obviously the case when we are speaking of the qualities of a thing; we know that sugar is sweet because we have a sweet taste when we put it into our mouth; we know that the sun is warm by our temperature sense; we know that snow is white by looking at it; we know that this book weighs two pounds by looking at a balance. But what is the sugar, or the sun, or the snow, or the book? It is a complex of qualities, each one of which is in our experience or can be anticipated to be given in some future experience. Each of these qualities, whether primary or secondary, is a quality of an idea, dependent for its nature and its existence upon its being given to consciousness. (For what is a color that cannot be seen? Or a smell that is not given to the sense of smell? Or a sound that we cannot hear?—Nothing.)

If there is nothing in the whole that we call an object except the qualities, and if the qualities are dependent upon experience, it follows, according to Berkeley, that the thing itself is dependent upon experience. Then not only is the *evidence* we have for the existence of a thing found in the fact that we

---

[13] Locke, Berkeley, and Hume agree on this.

perceive it; its very existence itself is nothing but its givenness in experience. If the "being of a color" means its being perceived, and the "being of a sound" means its being heard, and so on for all the other qualities, it follows that the complex of all qualities that we call an object owes its being to the joint perception of some or all of its qualities.

Thus Berkeley comes to his famous thesis: "To be is to be perceived;" "*Esse* is *percipi.*" Whether there are things unperceived or not makes not the slightest difference to what we do perceive; we have no empirical right to assume the existence of things for which we can have no evidence; unperceived and unperceivable matter explains nothing and is a vacuous concept to which we can attach no properties. Hence it is to be rejected as a poor and false hypothesis.

Transition from first to second stage of argument

If Berkeley had stopped his argument at this point, it would have been one of those queer philosophical arguments that seem to be logical enough, but that no one in his right mind could possibly accept. Consider three conclusions that seem to follow from it.

1. *Assuming "To be is to be perceived," it would follow as its converse that "To be perceived is to be"*—But the converse [14] statement is obviously false. I press my eyeball and perceive two lights where previously I perceived only one; but that does not mean there *are* two lights. Or a man in delirium sees pink rats; this is a vivid perception, although no one else believes that the pink rats really exist, and he will not believe it when he recovers. Hence the theory as it now stands cannot account for error or the illusions of the senses. (This was also a fatal objection to the argument as Theaetetus left it.)

2. *Assuming "To be is to be perceived," it would follow that*

---

[14] This is the converse of the original judgment, for the original judgment does not mean that "All that is is perceived" in the sense that some unreal things might also be perceived. The Berkeleian statement is a definition, in which "to be" is asserted to be a synonym of "to be perceived."

"*What is not perceived does not exist*"—This is the contraposi-
tive implied by the original statement, and Berkeley uses it
against the conception of an unknown and unperceivable substratum or cause for our ideas. But no one can really believe
that when we leave this room everything in it will cease to
exist; to be sure, everything in it will "disappear" in the sense
of not being a part of anyone's perceptual consciousness, but
that does not make us think it ceases to be. No one seriously
maintains that things unperceived *ipso facto* do not exist, although in the nature of the case, no empirical proof can be
given that they do exist. The hypothesis of the uniformity and
continuity of nature says that they must continue to exist even
when not perceived; Neptune must have existed before astronomers observed it; and so on. A theory that implies that things
do not exist simply because they are not perceived is *prima
facie* absurd, even though logically irrefutable.

3. *What about other persons?*—Does a person cease to exist
when no one perceives him and when he falls asleep? Or, to
go still further, how do I know that anyone exists when I myself do not perceive him? How do I know that you are not just
an idea in my mind? You may protest that you are not willing
to be just an idea in my mind; but I perceive even this protest
as an idea in my own consciousness. How do I know that my
idea corresponds to anything independent of my own imagination? The doctrine that all that exists is merely the content of
my own consciousness is known as *solipsism;* and even though
no sane person would seriously entertain such a belief, it seems
to follow from "To be is to be perceived."

Berkeley was as sane as the next man, and he had his full
share of the common sense for which the Irish are justly famous. The second stage of his argument shows how he met
these questions.

Second stage of the argument

The second stage of Berkeley's argument involves three
steps. The first shows that Locke's statement that all we know

is ideas is too simple; the second is an analogical argument by
which Berkeley seeks to find the real cause of our ideas; and
the third points out an ambiguity in the word "perceived" in
the thesis, "To be is to be perceived."

1. *Consciousness consists of more than ideas*—Locke believed
that we have ideas of the operations of our own mind, which
resemble but are not identical with these operations themselves. Locke and Berkeley agree that our ideas "are visibly
inactive; there is nothing of power or agency included in
them." [15] Berkeley consistently concludes that we cannot have
an idea of a will or understanding that resembles them, if we
believe that our understanding or will are powers that can act.
But we do have some feeling, or what Berkeley calls a "notion,"
of our own activity. Although Berkeley is often accused of inconsistency in admitting this, he is putting his finger on a very
important aspect of consciousness, an aspect that common
sense has never denied; we feel our own tendencies, impulses,
powers, and activity. When we *analyze* this feeling, perhaps
only sensations "which are visibly inactive" remain; but there
is an air of artificiality about a conception that leaves out all
the active tendencies we inwardly experience. Berkeley is perhaps being faithful to the facts of introspection when he says,

So far as I can see, the words *will, understanding, mind, soul,
spirit* do not stand for different ideas, or, in truth, for any idea at
all, but for something which is very different from ideas, and which,
being an agent, cannot be like unto, or represented by, any idea
whatsoever. Though it must be owned at the same time that we have
some *notion* of soul, spirit, and the operations of the mind, such as
willing, loving, hating—inasmuch as we know or understand the
meaning of these words. [16]

Included in our awareness of ourselves—perhaps constituting
it—is the feeling of active spontaneity, of control over the appearance of some ideas in our consciousness:

I find I can excite ideas in my mind at pleasure, and vary and

---

[15] George Berkeley, *Principles*, §25.
[16] *Ibid.*, §27.

shift the scene as oft as I think fit. It is no more than willing, and straightway this or that idea arises in my fancy; and by the same power it is obliterated and makes way for another. This making and unmaking of ideas properly denominates the mind as active.[17]

By this argument, Berkeley has accomplished two things. First, he has moved away from the representative realism of Locke, the theory that the contents of consciousness are *always* different from the real independent things they represent. Berkeley is saying that there is one being that we know without the intervention of an idea that might veil reality from our consciousness, and that is ourselves considered as minds or spirits. The second thing that Berkeley has accomplished by this theory of self-awareness is to provide a basis for the analogy that will constitute the next step of his argument.

2. *Analogical argument for the theory that mind causes all ideas*—As we have just seen, I know that I, a spirit or mind, can generate some ideas. At the same time, however, I know that I am not the cause of many of my ideas; if my eyes are open, I cannot but see the tree, and I cannot but hear sounds. Where, then, do the ideas originate that I am not the author of? There are three possible hypotheses: (a) from something wholly unlike myself, namely, a material cause having only primary qualities. But the first stage of Berkeley's argument was designed to show that this is untenable; (b) in other ideas. But this is impossible, for one idea does not cause another, as Berkeley and Locke agree; or (c) from something like me, namely, another active mind.

Berkeley chooses the third answer because of the following analogy:

My mind is to ideas of my imagination as x is to ideas over which I have no control. From this analogy, he determines what characteristics x must have. It must be a mind; it must be more powerful than my own so as to force ideas upon me against my own will; it must be permanent in order to account for the existence of things that I do not now perceive; it must

[17] *Ibid.*, §28.

be internally coherent and create its ideas in regular and uniform ways in order to account for what men call the "uniformity of nature." In short, it must be a perfect and divine mind.

The mind of God is the external source of the ideas that we do not spontaneously generate. God is the guarantor and support of the common, permanent ideas we call the external world. Taking the existence of the world as described by science or experienced in our every-day consciousness as his premise, and rejecting the first two hypotheses as inadequate to explain it, Berkeley infers the existence of God:

> It is therefore plain that nothing can be more evident to any one that is capable of the least reflexion than the existence of God, or a Spirit who is intimately present to our minds, producing in them all that variety of ideas or sensations which continually affect us, on whom we have an absolute and entire dependence, in short "in whom we live, and move, and have our being." [18]

3. *Ambiguity in the word "perceived"*—Berkeley is now able to uncover an ambiguity in the word "perceived" that led to the untenable and absurd conclusions in the preceding section. If by "perceived" we mean "perceived by man," then, "To be is to be perceived" does lead to the denial of a difference between error and true perception, to a discontinuous world that ceases to exist when I close my eyes, and to solipsism. But "perceived," in the thesis, "To be is to be perceived," does not have primary reference to human perception; human perception is at most evidence of existence, not the essence of existence. "To be" means ultimately to be an idea in a supreme mind, a mind permanent, eternal, omniscient, and omnipotent.

The ambiguity in the concept of perception is very well brought out in two famous limericks on Berkeley:

> There once was a man who said, "God
> Must think it exceedingly odd
> If he finds that this tree
> Continues to be
> When there's no one about in the Quad."

---

[18] *Ibid.*, §149.

"Dear Sir: Your astonishment's odd,
I am always about in the Quad
And that's why the tree
Will continue to be,
Since observed by Yours faithfully, God."

Berkeley's defense of his conclusions

Because the ambiguity in the word "perceived" is often over-looked, Berkeley's philosophy is sometimes thought of as down-right silly. It seems so far removed from credibility as to be patently absurd, or at most, an amusing *tour de force*. Boswell says that Dr. Johnson praised Berkeley as a "profound scholar, as well as a man of fine imagination," but he must nevertheless have thought Berkeley singularly obtuse to the most common facts. For Boswell writes,

After we came out of the church, we stood talking for sometime together of Bishop Berkeley's ingenious sophistry to prove the non-existence of matter, and that everything in the universe is merely ideal. I observed, that though we are satisfied his doctrine is not true, it is impossible to refute it. I never shall forget the alacrity with which Johnson answered, striking his foot with mighty force against a large stone, till he rebounded from it—"I refute it thus." [19]

Johnson argued in this way in spite of Berkeley's having asked rhetorically, just 50 years earlier: "Do I not know this to be a real stone that I stand on . . . ?" [20]

Berkeley, in fact, anticipated many of the objections that have been naively made to his views, and in this section we shall glance at a few of them and his answers.

1. *Berkeley's philosophy reduces everything to an illusion—* Berkeley answers,

It were a mistake to think that what is here said derogates in the least from the reality of things. It is acknowledged, on the received principles, that extension, motion, and in a word all sensible qual-ities, have need of a support, as not being able to subsist by them-

---

[19] James Boswell, *Life of Samuel Johnson, LL.D.*, page 285. New York: Random House, Modern Library edition.
[20] George Berkeley, *Dialogues*, page 296, in Mary W. Calkins (ed.), *op. cit.*

selves. But the objects perceived by sense are allowed to be nothing but combinations of those qualities, and consequently cannot subsist by themselves. Thus far it is agreed on all hands. So that in denying the things perceived by sense an existence independent of a substance or support wherein they may exist, we detract nothing from the received opinion of their *reality*, and are guilty of no innovation in that respect. All the difference is that, according to us, the unthinking beings perceived by sense have no existence distinct from being perceived, and cannot therefore exist in any other substance than those unextended indivisible substances, or *spirits*, which act, and think and perceive them.[21]

2. *Berkeley's philosophy is impractical; it does not recognize the "hard facts" that we have to take into account*—Berkeley, on the contrary, recognizes that real things in the world do not depend upon *our* perception, and even less on our wishful thinking. Only experience can tell us what is real, so that we can deal practically with the objective ideas and ignore those that are only subjective:

The set rules, or established methods, wherein the Mind we depend on excites in us the ideas of Sense, are called *the laws of nature;* and these we learn by experience, which teaches us that such and such ideas are attended with such and such other ideas, in the ordinary course of things.

This gives us a sort of foresight, which enables us to regulate our actions for the benefit of life. And without this we should be eternally at a loss; we could not know how to act anything that might procure us the least pleasure, or remove the least pain of sense.[22]

3. *Berkeley, in reducing the reality of everything to experience, cannot distinguish truth from error*—Not at all, answers the philosopher. "By whatever method you distinguish *things* from *chimeras* on your scheme, the same, it is evident, will hold also upon mine."[23]

We distinguish between real and illusory things, or what Berkeley calls chimeras, in two ways, according to him. First,

---

[21] George Berkeley, *Principles*, §91.
[22] George Berkeley, *Principles*, §§30 and 31.
[23] George Berkeley, *Dialogues* (Calkins ed.), page 306.

there is the vividness of the experiences of "real things," whereby we find that ideas of "real things" are "more strong, lively, and distinct than those of the imagination." [24] Common sense does tend to use this criterion, although it is often led into error in so doing, for hallucinatory and illusory ideas can be just as vivid as ideas of real objects. Second, there is the regular order and connection of the ideas that we take as evidence for objects, in contrast to the lack of consistency among our mere fanciful ideas. We distinguish dreams from waking consciousness by the greater orderliness of the latter, even though the dream may be intensely vivid; it is in this way that we decide that an idea of water in a desert is a mirage and not a true perception.

> Though [illusory ideas] should happen to be never so lively and natural, yet, by their not being connected, and of a piece with the preceding and subsequent transactions of our lives, they might easily be distinguished from realities.[25]

4. *Berkeley's philosophy would make science impossible*—Berkeley is one of the first philosophers to formulate a positivistic theory of science. As we have seen, positivism restricts scientific knowledge to knowledge of the correlations among perceptions and does not admit any explanation in terms of hypothetical entities that we might suppose exist "behind" the phenomena as their cause. Several times it has been suggested that this theory is inadequate because it is too nominalistic. Regardless of that, however, one should certainly not say dogmatically that a theory like that of Berkeley or the modern positivists would render science impossible. Berkeley gives excellent arguments, that have not been bettered since his day, that scientific objects are really intellectual constructions or syntheses of perceptions; he points out very clearly that scientific explanation is not in terms of unknown and unknowable

---

[24] George Berkeley, *Principles*, §30.
[25] George Berkeley, *Dialogues* (Calkins ed.), page 306.

causes, but in terms of correlations among observables. His own statement is so clear that it should be read:

... You will say there have been a great many things explained by matter and motion; take away these and you destroy the whole corpuscular [atomic] philosophy [science] and undermine those mechanical principles which have been applied with so much success to account for the phenomena. In short, whatever advances have been made, either by ancient or modern philosophers, in the study of nature do all proceed on the supposition that corporeal substance or Matter doth really exist.

To this I answer that there is not any one phenomenon explained on that supposition which may not as well be explained without it, as might easily be made appear by an induction of particulars. To explain the phenomena, is all one as to shew why, upon such and such occasions, we are affected with such and such ideas.[26]

If therefore we consider the difference there is betwixt natural philosophers and other men, with regard to their knowledge of the phenomena, we shall find it consists, not in an exacter knowledge of the efficient cause that produces them—for that can be no other than the *will of a spirit*—but only in a greater largeness of comprehension, whereby analogies, harmonies, and agreements are discovered in the works of nature, and the particular effects explained, that is, reduced to general rules ... which rules, grounded on the analogy and uniformness observed in the production of natural effects, are most agreeable and sought after by the mind; for that they extend our prospect beyond what is present and near to us, and enable us to make very probable conjectures touching things that may have happened at very great distances of time and place, as well as to predict things to come.[27]

5. *Berkeley's philosophy reduces all sciences to psychology, because it deals with the relations among ideas instead of among things—*

... It will upon this be demanded whether it does not seem absurd to take away natural causes, and ascribe everything to the immediate operation of spirits? We must no longer say upon these principles that fire heats, or water cools, but that a spirit heats, and

---

[26] George Berkeley, *Principles,* §50.
[27] *Ibid.,* §105.

so forth. Would not a man be deservedly laughed at, who should talk after this manner?

I answer, he would so; in such things we ought to think with the learned, but speak with the vulgar. They who to demonstration are convinced of the truth of the Copernican system do nevertheless say "the sun rises," "the sun sets," or "comes to the meridian"; and if they affected a contrary style in common talk it would without doubt appear very ridiculous. A little reflection on what is here said will make it manifest that the common use of language would receive no manner of alteration or disturbance from the admission of our tenets.[28]

In a word, this objection is based upon the common usage of "idea" as antonym of "object," while Berkeley, in his technical writings, identifies them.

6. *Berkeley's philosophy is skeptical*—This charge is perhaps the one that Berkeley is most interested in refuting, and he comes back to it again and again. Philonous ("lover of mind"), who represents Berkeley in the *Dialogues,* answers this charge from Hylas (from the Greek *hyle,* "matter"):

I am of a vulgar cast, simple enough to believe my senses, and leave things as I find them. To be plain, it is my opinion that the real things are those very things I see, and feel, and perceive by my senses. These I know; and, finding they answer all the necessities and purposes of life, have no reason to be solicitous about any other unknown beings. . . . Wood, stones, fire, water, flesh, iron, and the like things, which I name and discourse on, are things that I know. And I should not have known them but that I perceived them by my senses; and things perceived by the senses are immediately perceived; and things immediately perceived are ideas; and ideas cannot exist without the mind; their existence therefore consists in being perceived; when, therefore, they are actually perceived there can be no doubt of their existence. Away then with all that scepticism, all those ridiculous philosophical doubts. What a jest is it for a philosopher to question the existence of sensible things, till he hath it proved to him from the veracity of God; [29] or to pretend our knowledge in this point falls short of intuition and demonstration! [30]

---

[28] *Ibid.,* §51.
[29] The allusion is to Descartes; see above, page 63.
[30] The allusion is to Locke; see above, page 325

I might as well doubt of my own being, as of the being of those things I actually see and feel.[31]

The realist's criticism of Berkeley's idealism

In spite of his skillful answers to the objections we have just noted, other and more sophisticated objections have been made to Berkeley's philosophy. We shall here examine one type of criticism. In evaluating it, it should be remembered that metaphysical hypotheses cannot be subjected to "crucial experiments" so as to be either "proved" or "refuted." We cannot, in dealing with Berkeley's idealism, try to "perceive an unperceived object" to see whether it really exists or not; no empirical test for his thesis, "To be is to be perceived," is possible. All that can be done against Berkeley's or any other metaphysician's theory is to point out inadequacies or weaknesses and to try to formulate hypotheses that are free of them. It does not suffice to criticise; one must also reconstruct.

In this section we shall see the objections that some epistemological realists—those who do not believe that "To be is to be perceived"—have made to Berkeley. Later we shall examine in more detail the realists' own theories of perception.[32]

The careful reader will have noticed that Berkeley did not argue for the subjectivity of the secondary qualities; he assumed it, and then showed that in the light of this assumption, it is reasonable to conclude that the primary qualities are likewise subjective. If, however, the secondary qualities are not subjective, his entire argument falls. Attempts have been made to refute him by showing that secondary qualities are not subjective. But most of these attempts have involved such extremely intricate arguments that we cannot pursue them here.[33]

---

[31] George Berkeley, *Dialogues*, (Calkins ed.), pages 299-300.

[32] Cf. below, pages 422-30. The table on page 429 comparing Locke, Berkeley, and recent realists should be consulted.

[33] The most important argument of this kind is G. E. Moore's "The Refutation of Idealism" (1903), reprinted in his *Philosophical Studies*, pages 1-30. London: Kegan Paul, Trench, Trubner Ltd., 1922.

Rather, we shall consider an argument designed to show merely that *there is no reason to affirm* that any content of consciousness or object of perception depends upon the mind. The argument we shall briefly outline is that of the American neo-realist, Ralph Barton Perry.[34] According to Perry, Berkeley commits two fallacies in his argument for the thesis, "To be is to be perceived."

1. *Definition by initial predication*—Berkeley truly argues that it is an initial predicate of anything that I perceive *that* I perceive it. But this does not suffice to establish the conclusion unless it means, "A thing I perceive *must* be perceived by me." That is, "To be is to be perceived," does not follow unless the initial predicate is taken as a defining predicate [35] so that the thing perceived is unthinkable and unreal apart from this predicate.

To see whether this is plausible, consider a simple analogy. Mrs. John Doe is the wife of John Doe, by definition. Although in relation to Mr. Doe she is defined as "wife," Mrs. Doe may stand also in other relations to other people, such as "customer" to Mr. Roe and "bridge partner" to Mrs. Roe. Now if we suppose that Mr. Doe knows her *only* as his wife, and calls her a name (say, "the missus,") that indicates this relation to him, it still does not follow that her *existence* depends on Mr. Doe; only the name that he gives her, or the name others give her because she is married to him, depends upon her relation to him.

Now, apply this analogy to mind (Mr. Doe) and its object (Mrs. Doe). I think my mind knows the table on which I am writing; the table is then, by Locke's and Berkeley's definition, my "idea," because it is a part of my experience. But that does not in the least imply that the existence of the table itself depends upon my experience, for the initial predicate (the predi-

---

[34] In his *Present Philosophical Tendencies,* pages 126-132. New York: Longmans, Green & Company, Inc., 1912.

[35] A defining predicate is one that applies to every instance of the thing being defined and only to the thing defined.

cate "known by me") is not a defining predicate. It only implies a tautology—that I cannot experience a table except as a
table I experience, that is, as an idea. But just as there may be
many things about Mrs. Doe that Mr. Doe does not know and
that do not depend upon him, similarly for the table. Its being
an idea depends upon my experience, and I can experience it
only as my idea; but that does not mean that it is nothing
apart from my experience.

2. *The ego-centric predicament*—But, it may be said, I cannot even think of it or mention it without making it a part of
my "world of thought." Hence the initial predicate, that it is
in my experience (or an idea), is a *universal* predicate. It is
also true that a universal predicate might be satisfactory as a
defining predicate. But in basing idealism upon the fact that
everything even mentioned is *ipso facto* mentioned as part
of someone's thought or experience, Perry holds that Berkeley
fell into an "ego-centric predicament." By this, Perry means
that, from the admitted fact that for every entity experienced
there is an experiencer for whom the entity is an idea, Berkeley
cannot validly infer the conclusion that there are no entities
that are not ideas. For let it be granted for the sake of argument that there *are* entities that are not experienced; by hypothesis, we should not know them. Hence Berkeley's *evidence*
is just the same whether his "To be is to be perceived" is true
or false. "To be is to be perceived" is, therefore, a poor hypothesis, for there can be no *conceivable* evidence against it—
let alone any actual evidence. The evidence seems to be for it
only because the hypothesis is so framed that any evidence
that could *conceivably* be against it is unavailable by the conditions inherent in the empirical test, namely, that what I
experience is what I experience, that is, by *definition* an idea.

Of course neither of these arguments is a refutation of Berkeley's conclusion. They are designed merely to show that the
arguments by which Berkeley believed he had established his
conclusion were weak. Because Perry believed that Berkeley's
thesis was essential to all idealism, he believed that he had

taken the props from under all idealisms; but many idealists admit the validity of his argument against Berkeley, and still maintain that their idealism is not involved in an ego-centric predicament. The next chapter is devoted to two such attempts, those by absolute idealists and by personal idealists.

BIBLIOGRAPHY

General works

Adams, George P., *Idealism and the Modern Age*. New Haven, Conn.: Yale University Press, 1919.
Ewing, A. C., *Idealism. A Critical Survey*. New York: The Humanities Press, 1950.
Hoernlé, R. F. Alfred, *Idealism as a Philosophy*. New York: George H. Doran Company, 1927.
Muirhead, J. H., *The Platonic Tradition in Anglo-Saxon Philosophy*. New York: The Macmillan Company, 1931.
Robinson, D. S. (ed.), *Anthology of Recent Philosophy*. New York: Thomas Y. Crowell & Co., 1929.
Royce, Josiah, *The Spirit of Modern Philosophy*. Boston: Houghton Mifflin Company, 1892.
Sinclair, May, *The New Idealism*. New York: The Macmillan Company, 1922.

Locke

Aaron, R. I., *Locke*. London: Oxford University Press, 1937.
Locke, John, *Essay Concerning Human Understanding* (1690). Especially books ii and iv. Many editions.
Morris, C. R., *Locke, Berkeley, and Hume*. London: Oxford University Press, 1946.

Berkeley

Hone, J. M., and Rossi, M. M., *Bishop Berkeley. His Life, Writings, and Philosophy*. New York: The Macmillan Company, 1931.
Luce, A. A., *Berkeley's Immaterialism*. London: Thomas Nelson and Sons, 1946.
Morris, C. R., *Locke, Berkeley, and Hume*. London: Oxford University Press, 1946.

Wild, John, *George Berkeley. A Study of his Life and Philosophy.*
Cambridge, Mass.: Harvard University Press, 1936.

QUESTIONS AND TOPICS FOR DISCUSSION

1. Do you accept the statement made in the text that Locke's theory of knowledge has come to be accepted as common sense? If so, how does common sense overcome the objections Berkeley made to it?
2. Physical properties of objects, such as their chemical and electrical properties, are sometimes now considered to be "primary qualities." Could Berkeley's arguments be modernized so as to show that even these instances of primary qualities are not independent of mind?
3. Does Berkeley prove the existence of God by an argument based on the existence of nature? Or does he, like Descartes (Chapter 3) prove that the external world exists as a consequence of a *premise* that God exists?
4. Is Berkeley's theory of the cause of our ideas (that is, that they are caused by a mind) able to stand up against Hume's analysis of the concept of cause (Chapter 5)?
5. Read an account of Hume's theory of the self. Compare his criticism of the concept of self with Berkeley's criticism of the concept of material substance.
6. Compare the following statements:
   (*a*) "Berkeley, because he denied that there is any hidden material substance behind our sense experiences, is a forerunner of positivism with its theory that the laws of nature are only statements about our experience."
   (*b*) "Berkeley's metaphysics must be denied by any positivist, because the basic thesis of his work, 'To be is to be perceived,' has no verifiable consequences and hence is, to a positivist, perfectly meaningless."
7. Which of the arguments for the existence of God discussed in Chapter 9 do you think Berkeley could employ?
8. Read some of the philosophical poetry of Wordsworth. Wordsworth is frequently called an "idealist"; was he an idealist in the sense in which Berkeley was an idealist?

11

Idealism — Continued

ABSOLUTE IDEALISM

The metaphysical theory known as absolute idealism was first formulated by the German philosopher, Georg Wilhelm Friedrich Hegel (1770-1831). In discussing absolute idealism, it might seem reasonable to give an exposition of the thought of its founder, as we did in the case of Berkeleian idealism. But Hegel lacks the clarity and conciseness of Berkeley; and his system is so complex and subtle and his terminology so opaque that this is not a suitable way to introduce the philosophy of absolute idealism. It might be reasonable to turn to the thought of one of his greatest followers; but here a different difficulty meets us. Hegel's philosophy was so complex and rich that it was interpreted in different ways by different philosophers, and if we were to take any single man—F. H. Bradley, Bernard Bosanquet, John or Edward Caird, Andrew Seth Pringle-Pattison, Josiah Royce, James Edwin Creighton, or Benedetto Croce—and give an exposition of his views, we should have to neglect others equally important who disagree with him on some important matters.

For these reasons, I shall attempt in this section to give a composite picture of absolute idealism, taking sometimes one man's formulation and sometimes another's. It is my hope that the obvious dangers of such an approach, which might make objective idealism seem "neither fish nor fowl nor good red herring," can be avoided, and that what is lost in historical precision will be outweighed by what is gained in clarity and generality.

Differences between Berkeley's idealism and absolute idealism

There are two central differences between Berkeley's idealism and absolute idealism. They concern the content of knowledge, and the awareness of the self or mind.

Berkeley was an empiricist, who saw in sense experience the archetype and source of all knowledge. This led him to minimize the importance of other forms of consciousness, such as rational thought and the experience of value. The absolute idealists, on the other hand, take a less restricted view of experience. Experience is much more various than the empiricists considered it to be. It includes our moral concerns and struggles as well as the perception of Dr. Johnson's stone, our aesthetic reaction to music as well as our hearing the sensations "in our ears," the march of events in history as well as the association of our ideas. In fact, experience is an all-comprehensive term; everything in any way able to be experienced, whether perceived by the senses or not, is comprised within it. The absolute idealist takes it as he finds it without trying to compress it into an awareness of ideas of sensation and reflection.

Berkeley, you will remember, distinguished between "ideas" and "notions." He thought that notions were a preeminent kind of knowledge of a particular reality, namely, our own minds or "spirits." He believed that ideas are passive and owe their reality to their being perceived; the notions we have of ourselves, on the contrary, give us a direct apprehension of the activity of our own minds. This dichotomy between idea and notion is inconsistent with the definition of the content of experience introduced by Locke and usually accepted by Berkeley. There is some internal evidence in Berkeley's writings that it was introduced as an afterthought. But although it saved Berkeley from skepticism and solipsism, it has always appeared to be an inconsistent part of his system. In Berkeley's philosophy, ideas presuppose a mind for which they are ideas, but the concept of mind presupposes no ideas; it is known directly by intuitive notions. The absolute idealists are in fundamental disagreement with him here, because they assert as one of their principal theses the *mutual* presupposition of mind and object. They hold that neither is conceivable without the other. According to them, we do not first know the mind and only subsequently see how it gets its ideas; rather, we first have experiences of feelings, things, volitions, images, and so on, and out of this complex whole, we gradually segregate and distinguish its two poles, a subjective mental pole and an objective public component we call the object. The Berkeleian conception is that of a mind which, at least in principle, is isolable from its experiences and capable of being known by introspection. The absolute idealistic view is that the mind is not an isolable entity or thing and cannot be known except in contrast and tension with what is not subjective. We do not have minds sharply distinguished from everything else in reality; the mind is not a crystal with sharp edges. We are, says Bosanquet, "individuals with tattered edges," and it is impossible to say exactly where mind ends and the things it does or experiences begin. We find the full content and function of mind only in the whole of experience.

The growth of experience

Every experience, the absolute idealist says, is partially objective and partially subjective. It is subjective because it is "from a standpoint," but it is objective because in its meaning it "transcends" this limited perspective and adumbrates or suggests that which is not included in the momentary consciousness. In its subjective aspect, it is always partial and to some extent distorted. Its partiality, however, entails a growth to larger experience that complements its fragmentariness by covering broader reaches of the objective. The mere fact that we know that our consciousness is at any time limited and partial means that we already, in principle, have transcended these limits; otherwise we should not know that our experience was limited. Some idealists reason from this fact that there must be another mind, an Absolute Mind, in which our own limited minds are imbedded, and that when we look upon our ordinary consciousness as finite and limited, we are already participating in the Absolute Mind.

More cautious absolute idealists are unwilling to make such a leap from our experience to an Absolute Mind. They hold that the slow progress of our consciousness to more and more comprehensive knowledge of objects shadows forth the kind of reality we would reach *if* we could see things from the standpoint of experience made completely synoptic. Let us see, then, how experience grows so that, by extrapolation, we can conceive of the perfect experience or absolute knowledge.

Any experience a subject or a mind has is always partial. The simplest statement, such as, "There is a tree," calls for supplementation before it becomes clear and "really" true. For what does "there" mean? As I turn my head, "there" changes its meaning, and while it was true a moment ago that, "There is a tree," it is now true that, "There is a house." These two statements are both partially true, but because they contradict each other, the absolute idealist argues that they are partially false; and we must define what we mean by "there" in order to remove this contradiction. We must state the objective conditions under which the two sentences are true, and these objective conditions—stated in terms of time, direction, latitude and longitude—are far more elaborate than the simple empirical statement I made when I said, "There is a tree."

This simple, almost trivial illustration, is taken from Hegel's great work, *The Phenomenology of Mind*. Simple as it is, however, it includes an important truth. Knowledge grows by transcending any particular moment of experience, by referring to still more experience that will be less subjective and less contingent upon the particular point of view or "state of mind" than the original experience was. The transcendence involves "saving the appearances" by finding the additional experiences that make our partial report on our experience true, yet prevent us from thinking that it is the whole truth. When we transcend the experience in which we say, "There is a tree," we do not render this statement wholly false; it retains its truth by becoming imbedded in a context of experience within which also, "There is a house," and "There is a dog," can be true without contradiction.

Searching for these additional conditions is the process of "dialectic." We have seen how it goes in our earlier study of Plato; but Hegel and the absolute idealists magnify the dialectic process so that it is no longer merely the structure of philosophical conversation and inquiry—it is for them a real, objective process in the world itself, as it reveals itself in experience. Thus Hegel believed that any sentence, any thought, any historical movement or institution—in fact, anything we experience—contains the seed of its own dissolution. Each thing and each truth is unstable, true or real only within a specific and limited context of experience. The changes in our own experiences, in conceptual thought, and in objects follow a dialectical pattern in which any partial truth or reality (*thesis*) develops its own opposite (*antithesis*) and then produces a new *synthesis* in which both the thing and its opposite are seen to be partially true or real. According to Hegel and most absolute idealists, this dialectical process goes on forever, or until some experience or reality in experience is found in which all the opposing theses and antitheses are reconciled in one comprehensive and synoptic system. Only then is *the* truth attained; according to Hegel, "Truth is the whole."

The dialectic process, in which any partial view or thing (the thesis) generates its opposite (the antithesis) and is then saved in a restricted form in the synthesis, is a central conception in all absolute idealism. This is true even though F. H. Bradley called Hegel's dialectic "an unearthly ballet of bloodless categories," and though there is much artificiality in some of the applications that Hegel made of it. But as a general account of the way in which, in thought and in the world we think about, partiality or partisanship generates opposing partiality or partisanship, with which it is later to be reconciled in a "larger harmony," it does have great merit in exhibiting some aspects of the process and structure of experience and the world.

From the central conception of dialectic, three other closely connected, and in part overlapping principles of absolute idealism are derived. They are: the coherence criterion of truth, the idealistic modification of the ontological argument, and the theory of levels of reality.

The coherence criterion of truth

A criterion of truth is a statement of the general character of knowledge by virtue of which true knowledge can be distinguished from error. It is commonly said that a true proposition is one that "corresponds to reality" or to "fact." "It is raining," is true if and only if it *is* raining, for in some way the sentence designates the state of affairs in which rain is falling, and it is true if that state of affairs actually exists. This conception of a "correspondence" between a proposition and a fact is difficult or impossible to analyze into any simpler terms; "correspondence" is perhaps an underived, basic concept, and if one understands what is meant by "true," he has some grasp of what is meant by "corresponds," and if he understands "corresponds," he understands "true."

Although it seems very simple and obvious to say, "Truth is correspondence of thought (belief, judgment, a proposition, or the like) to what is actually the case," such an assertion nevertheless involves a metaphysical assumption. It tacitly says that there is a fact, object, or state of affairs, independent of our knowledge, to which our knowledge corresponds. The idealist, of course, asserts that mind and its object in some way mutually implicate each other, and that there are not objects on one side, thoughts on the other, and some indefinable relation of correspondence between them. The idealist may be quite wrong in this doctrine, and the realist and the man of common sense may be correct in their belief that it suffices to say that there is an object to which a true judgment corresponds, so that the correspondence constitutes the truth of the proposition or judgment. The idealist, however, attacks this realistic and common-sense view by asking, "How, on your principles, could you know that you have a true proposition?" Or, putting the question in more exact form, "How can you use your *definition* of truth, namely, truth is the correspondence between a judgment and its object, as a *criterion* of truth? How can you know when such correspondence actually holds?"

This is an extremely difficult question. Suppose I have an experience that, I believe, authorizes me to say, "Cats love mice." If this statement is true, then it is a fact that cats do love mice. In order to know that the statement is true, according to the principles of the correspondence theory, I should compare my judgment (or the experience that led to the judgment) with the actual state of the relation of cats to mice to see if they correspond. But, according to the idealist, this cannot be done. For how can I know the actual state of the relation between cats and mice except by having another experience and making another judgment? I cannot, as it were, step outside my mind to compare a thought in it with something outside it; I can never reach *mere fact,* but only other *experienced facts,* and if my experience, "Cats love mice," was in any way wrong, it is quite possible that any fact by which I try to check it may likewise be wrongly experienced or interpreted.

Instead of comparing the judgment, "Cats love mice," with a mere fact to determine whether there is correspondence, I compare one experience and the judgment in which it issues with another experience and its judgment, and if these judgments are incompatible, then I modify at least one of them. For instance, I have had experiences that lead me to conclude,

"Cats love mice"; then I have a perceptual experience of the relations between a particular cat and a particular mouse that makes me conclude that *this* cat does not love *this* mouse. The judgment based on the latter experience is incompatible with the judgments based on the earlier experience; I do not know which of these judgments corresponds to reality, but I discover an incompatibility between my judgments that makes me decide to modify my first judgment, and I change it to read, "Some cats love mice."

If by "fact" one means what is perceived, and if one thinks of the relation of correspondence as holding between relatively abstract true judgments and relatively concrete particular perceived facts, then the illustration about cats and mice may seem to fit the correspondence theory. This is probably what is meant when one says that he tests his beliefs by reference to the facts. But it should not be overlooked that "fact" is always *experienced fact,* that the purported fact may be illusory, and that it must be interpreted and judged before it can serve as a test for other judgments. And we know from our earlier studies, as well as from common sense, that sometimes we do not believe our eyes, and that we are sometimes entirely correct in distrusting the evidence of the senses when it is incompatible with our more abstract, general, theoretical knowledge.

The idealist fully exploits the difficulty of finding a pure case of "correspondence." He says, in effect, that it shows how fruitless is the realist's belief in the independently real object, for when we bring our knowledge to a test, it is not a test before the bar of a Lockean substance, or of a thing that one can claim to know directly, indubitably, and as it actually is. The test in actual cases is precisely what the idealist says it should be: does more experience corroborate or weaken the conclusion formerly reached on the basis of less experience?

According to this test, a belief is true if it coheres with the systematic whole that we seek as an interpretation of experience. Knowledge grows, as we have seen the idealists argue, by bringing the variety and chaos of momentary, fragmentary experiences into a systematic whole. On the very simplest level, we cannot accept contradictory propositions as true, not because we know that metaphysical reality is logically consistent, as the realist might affirm, but because contradictory propositions cannot be brought into a single system of propositions. But coherence is more than mere lack of logical inconsistency: it means the systematic harmony that we demand of diverse experiences before we accept them all as true. In an ideally coherent system, each judgment is not only consistent with the others, but gives the others positive support.

A coherent system of propositions is "a set of propositions in which each one stands in such a relation to the rest that it is logically necessary that it should be true if all the rest are true, and such that no set of propositions within the whole set is logically independent of all propositions in the remainder of the set." [1]

In using the coherence criterion, the ideal of knowledge by which we judge our less-than-ideal knowledge is that of perfectly integrated experience, in which each part is in harmony with all the others and in which the whole encompasses all experience. If we were omniscient, according to this view, we could see the whole by tracing out the ramifications of any part, as Tennyson suggests in his "Flower in the crannied wall." We are not omniscient, but the surest knowledge that we can have is knowledge that is systematically supported by the maximum of experience. In making a choice between two beliefs, the reasonable man chooses the belief that is best supported by the whole of his experience—not merely his present perceptions, but his judgments made on grounds of memory and reason as well. The belief he does not choose can then be "explained away" by showing, for instance, that it is a belief one would expect on the level of experience where it actually arose, but a belief seen to be inadequate on a more comprehensive level.

The idealists argue that the coherence criterion is a corollary of the dialectical growth of knowledge. We hold to a belief until

---

[1] A. C. Ewing, *Idealism. A Critical Survey* (1934), pages 229-230. New York: The Humanities Press, 1950. Quoted by permission of the publisher.

it comes into collision with another belief. Then we modify one or both of the beliefs until they are consistent with each other and with the contexts in which they have originated. We embrace the more comprehensive belief until a new incoherence is found within it or between it and some other parts of our experience. Then the mutual adjustment, choice, or rejection occurs again. All through this process, we are looking for beliefs that we can retain in the face of growing experience. The dialectical correction of any partial experience is founded upon the failure of the partial experience to satisfy the demands of full coherence of experience.

This correction is an endless process. Since we can never have "all experience," we cannot then be sure that any belief is absolutely true. According to the idealist, no belief is incorrigible; even the mathematician is willing to modify his postulates if he finds that a contradiction develops within his system, and it is at least imaginable, as Descartes recognized, that there really is no table here before me. It must not be supposed that the idealist doubts such propositions as, "A straight line is the shortest distance between two points," or, "I am now reading a sentence in the English language." Rather, he is asserting that our certainty of these propositions does not lie in their self-evident indubitability; it lies rather in the fact that without these propositions, almost the whole of our systematically organized experience, indeed sanity itself, would be wrecked. But there remains an outside chance, at least theoretically open, that these beliefs might someday have to be modified in order to save the systematic order we require of knowledge.

The beliefs we call true are those that have developed in a long and searching criticism of other beliefs, and that have held their own in subsequent criticism. Those of which we are most sure are those of which we feel that there is the least reason to fear they will have to be surrendered in the face of new experience. Naturally, then, we can never be absolutely sure that our ideas or beliefs or hypotheses will continue to hold up. "Truth is the whole," said Hegel, but we men can never know the whole, never reach an infinity of experience. Hence there is always room for error in our firmest beliefs; and the coherence criterion is proposed as a way of detecting errors.

An impatient reader, especially if he thinks he is a hard-boiled realist or even endowed with much common sense, may object, "How do you really know that the world itself is a logical whole, so that logically coherent beliefs give knowledge of things as they really are?" He may point out, for instance, the internal coherence of a novel, which does not lead us to suppose that the novel is true, and hold, then, that coherence is not a substitute for correspondence as the meaning of truth.

There are two answers to this objection. The first is that coherence means more than consistency within a limited range of experience. We do require consistency or coherence of action and character in a novel, and if we do not find it, we deny that the novel is "true to life" or "realistic." But that internal coherence or consistency does not make the novel true in the usual sense of the word; it remains a novel, however internally coherent it may be. If coherence is supposed to be a mark of truth, how then *do* we distinguish a coherent novel from a history? Not by discovering incoherences *within* it, nor by comparing it with the "actual fact" that we might claim to know directly and without danger of error. Rather, we test it by checking it against still broader experience. We find events reported in one book for which there is no documentary evidence; we find that the book is written by a man noted as a novelist and not as a historian; we find that the characters portrayed in the book are different from the characters having the same name that we find described, for instance, in an encyclopedia. How then are we to make our picture of the events in question coherent? We do so by calling some of the books "histories" and others "novels"; the experience reported in the book we call a novel can be rendered coherent with the whole of our experience only if we do not take it at its face value.

The second answer to this objection must be considered in detail in a separate section.

The revised ontological argument

The ontological argument, as formulated by Descartes and criticized by Kant (see pages 274 ff), was an argument that from a single concept, that of a perfect being, the existence of a being corresponding to the concept could be inferred. The absolute idealists have developed a modified form of this argument, not for the purpose of proving the existence of God, but for the purpose of defending the objective validity of a coherent whole of experience. In this form, the argument is not refuted by Kant's criticisms of the older argument.

According to the revised version of the ontological argument, by "reality" we *mean* "the object of true knowledge." Ideal or perfect knowledge is the criterion of reality.[2] No one should assert that anything is real unless he has what he considers to be good and sufficient reasons for it, and good and sufficient reasons are characterized by an internal consistency and a coherence with all the evidence at our disposal. To attribute reality to anything when the belief in it is known to be inconsistent with other beliefs we hold is to be incoherent and self-refuting; such incoherence is the mark of mental imbalance, not of sanity.

Consider a simple example. When I believe, "There are mountains on the moon," I do not infer the existence of mountains on the moon from the mere concept I have of "lunar mountains." The reason I have for believing that there are mountains is not, furthermore, that I can compare my belief with the brute fact and see that they agree; even if I were on the moon, it would still be necessary to believe and think as

---

[2] *Cf.* Charles Hartshorne, "Ideal Knowledge Defines Reality: What Was True in Idealism," *Journal of Philosophy*, Vol. XLIII, No. 21 (October 10, 1946), pages 573-582; W. E. Hocking, "The Ontological Argument in Royce and Others," in Clifford Barrett (ed.), *Contemporary Idealism in America*, pages 43-66. New York: The Macmillan Company, 1932.

well as to see and touch. The reason I believe that there are
mountains there is that if I did not believe it, I should not
know how to bring my other beliefs into any kind of coherent
system. I should not know how to interpret pictures I have
seen in astronomy books, or what I have seen through tele-
scopes, or the testimony of astronomers, if I obstinately persisted in saying, "There are no mountains on the moon." Now
this suffices to show me that it is *reasonable* to believe that
there are mountains on the moon.

But the impatient realist may still say, "I don't deny that it
may be reasonable to interpret your experience in this way;
but what I want to know is, what makes you think that
reality, the real moon, corresponds to your experience?" And
in the modified ontological argument we have the answer:
reality is not something outside experience that may or may
not correspond to its logically coherent structure. Rather,
reality is the name that we give to those aspects of our experi-
ence that are most coherent, and there is no other standard
than coherence by which we can justify attributing reality to
anything. It is not only "truths" that are coherent and hold
their own under dialectical development; reality for us is that
maximum sector of our experience that is logically coherent,
and reality itself is total, completely coherent, experience. To
it we are led and by it we remain in the dialectic of experience.

This is the true meaning in Hegel's oft-repeated statement,
"The reasonable is the real, and the real is the reasonable."
By that statement, he meant: in the final analysis, the ground
that we have for believing that anything is real is the superior
reasonableness of the belief in it as compared to disbelief or
doubt. He does not mean the absurd statement that whatever
is abstractly possible because not self-contradictory—a unicorn
on the moon, say—is real. A modern idealist (although he happened not to be an absolute idealist) said the same thing in a
way less liable to such a misunderstanding: "The question,

What is reality? can only be answered by telling how we must think about reality."[3]

In idealism, with its modified ontological argument, we do not begin with an epistemological dualism, with reality on one side and experience or reason on the other, and then ask what guarantees a correspondence between them. Rather, for absolute idealists there is only experience and its movement from the fragmentary and subjective to that which is independent of the particular subjects and centers of consciousness within it. This transition is dialectic, in which the real is that which is able to hold its own in its relation to other aspects of experience. The real is reasonable because only the reasonable is able to preserve itself in dialectical criticism, and because we do not persist in attributing the honorific title of "real" to an object of experience unless it is able to stand up to the questioning of reason.

Reality is not something contrasted to experience. Reality is the system of the most comprehensive, coherent, and synoptic experience we can have. Of course we can and do draw a distinction between "my consciousness" and "things as they really are," and our conception of the latter is the ideal or the norm for judging the adequacy of my own experience. But the distinction is drawn within experience, not between experience and reality. It is drawn between things as I personally and inadequately experience them now and as they would be experienced by my mind if it were free from all limitations. My consciousness fluctuates between the trivial and private and a grasp of things freed from the contingent limitations of myself. The Absolute, which is Bosanquet's name for reality, "is simply the high-water mark of fluctuations in experience, of which, in general, we are daily and normally aware."[4]

---

[3] Borden Parker Bowne, *Metaphysics* (1882), page 3. Boston: Boston University, 1943.

[4] Quoted from G. Watts Cunningham, *The Idealistic Argument in Recent British and American Philosophy*, page 140. New York: The Century Company, 1933.

Levels of reality

Plato's theory involved the notion of "levels of reality." It seems evident that if a thing *exists*, it is as existent as anything else; but he said that some things are more *real* than others if they serve as the foundation and explanation of those others, and those things that are explained are accorded a lower degree of reality. In this sense, Plato's "ideas" are considered by him to be more real than the phenomenal appearances.

Absolute idealists develop the notion of levels of reality as a consequence of their dialectic and their belief that the real is the reasonable. In the coherence criterion, there is a conception of "levels of truth"; beliefs are true according to the wealth of the context of experience with which they cohere. The truer a belief is, the higher its stage in the dialectic. "There is a tree," is true, but in the dialectic it is superseded by another statement, "In 1938 there was a tree at the corner of Fisher's Lane." The second sentence is said to contain "more truth" than the former, because it is less challengeable from variations in the meaning of "there" and "is." When we criticize and modify the former statement, we substitute for it some truth that is more stable and less subject to destructive criticism.

Now consider the objects of our experience. Each thing is related, directly or indirectly, to everything else in the universe, and its character depends upon and is modified by its relation to other things. Some things are highly contingent upon others, and in an unstable environment they are variable and impermanent. Others have such a broad context of relations that they preserve themselves through all sorts of vicissitudes. Those that "hold their own" are more real, according to the levels theory, than those that do not. For instance, the tree is "more real" than the leaf on its bough; the queen is "less real" than the British constitutional system, and so on.

If by reality we mean merely physical existence, of course an electron is as "real" as a star, and the queen is more real than the unwritten English constitution. But by real we mean, paradoxically, also the ideal. A thing is real to the degree that it realizes its ideal nature and full potentialities, and the realization of a thing's nature and potentialities occurs only through a dialectical development. In the final analysis, a thing is real to the extent to which it conforms to the widest context of experience and reality, that is, preserves itself through the most comprehensive experience. For this reason, we can say that the only thing that is wholly real is the whole of the universe considered as a self-explanatory system of experience, internally coherent and absolutely comprehensive and synoptic. This is what the absolute idealist calls The Absolute. The absolute idealist explains things and assigns to them their proper degree of reality by discerning their contribution to the absolute whole of which they are parts. Thus he explains things in terms of that which is "higher" than they are:

. . . The basic principle of the theory of reality of all idealism is that we can explain the lower by including it in the higher but that we can never explain the higher by reducing it to the lower, or by developing a metaphysics in terms of a lower level which precludes the possibility of acknowledging the higher. In some form or other this principle is recognized by all idealists and is the central postulate of all idealism. It follows that idealism reaches a single all-inclusive whole as the highest reality.[5]

This all-inclusive reality is The Absolute.

The proper understanding of the relation of The Absolute to the things within it, and especially to the human beings who have partial experience of it, is one of the moot points that have split the school of absolute idealism. Sometimes the differences between The Absolute and its appearances are so emphasized that the world of human experience is transcended or abrogated; it is appearance, not reality, and to find reality we would have to have a kind of mystic absorption in The

---

[5] D. S. Robinson, *Introduction to Living Philosophy*, page 90. New York: Crowell Publishing Company, 1932. Quoted by permission of the publisher. Actually, the last sentence is a basic principle only of *absolute* idealism.

Absolute, in which all distinctions are blurred in the absolute oneness of things.[6]

Other absolute idealists, on the contrary, hold that The Absolute is "with us when we know it not." For these philosophers, The Absolute *is* experience in its highest dialectical development, and at any stage in the evolution of experience, The Absolute is there as its highest point. "When the Absolute falls into the water," wrote Bosanquet, "it becomes a fish." Hegel expressed somewhat the same notion when, after seeing Napoleon, he wrote, "I have seen the World-Spirit on horseback." This interpretation seeks to preserve the individuality of the minds in the world and to maintain the temporal character of reality, while still insisting that we are "all parts of one stupendous whole."

PLURALISTIC OR PERSONAL IDEALISM

The last of the types of idealism that we shall discuss is pluralistic or personal idealism.[7] Like absolute idealism, it is not a single theory, but a name given to the theories of various philosophers. All personal and pluralistic idealists are more impressed with the plurality of minds in the universe than with the view that there is one single all-embracing Absolute Mind. The pluralist thinks, "Reality may exist in distributive form, in the shape not of an all but of a set of eaches." [8]

The pluralistic idealist holds that the "eaches" are individual selves or minds, comparable to the one that I experience as the context or nucleus in my every experience. He believes that objects must either be ideas in minds, or minds themselves, or

---

[6] Hegel, in criticizing this conception of The Absolute, which he attributes to Schelling, calls it, "The night in which all cows are black."

[7] We shall treat "pluralistic" and "personal" as synonymous adjectives when describing this type of idealism. Some idealists prefer one name and some the other, according to which aspect of this idealism they emphasize. But in this general account, we can ignore most of these differences, and shall use the two names interchangeably.

[8] William James, *A Pluralistic Universe*, page 129. New York: Longmans, Green & Company, Inc., 1909.

at least mind-like. Reality, for him, is a society or community of minds or selves, appearing from the outside like the familiar world of common sense or science, but understood in its real nature as mental through and through.

Pluralistic idealism has had a long history. Perhaps the first philosopher to defend an explicitly pluralistic idealism was Gottfried Wilhelm Leibniz (1646-1716). In the nineteenth century, the view was further developed by Rudolf Hermann Lotze (1817-1881), who had a strong influence on English and American idealists. In England, pluralistic idealism was elaborated by John McTaggart Ellis McTaggart (1866-1925), and James Ward (1843-1925). The tradition of personal idealism has been carried on in the United States by the disciples of Borden Parker Bowne (1847-1910) and George Holmes Howison (1834-1916), and the current leaders among them are Edgar Sheffield Brightman (b. 1884), and Ralph Tyler Flewelling (b. 1871).

The nature and existence of minds

Since the ultimate category of idealism is mind itself, we can best see the distinctive traits of pluralistic idealism by comparing its views of the nature of the mind with the views of the two types of idealism we have already studied.

Pluralistic and Berkeleian idealism—Although Berkeley stated, "To be is to be perceived," his philosophy also entails the view that "To perceive is to be." For if everything that we experience exists only as an idea in the mind, then certainly the mind must be real too. Berkeley, however, was very sparing in his discussion of the nature of the individual mind, and it remained for later idealists to develop this aspect of his theory. We have seen how absolute idealism tended to "explain it away"; we shall now see how the pluralistic idealist emphasizes its irreducible status.

The pluralistic idealist puts awareness of our own minds or selves into the center of discussion. We experience ideas, as Berkeley believed; but I always experience *my* ideas, and you always experience *yours*. Each of us experiences them as ideas of or in his own mind, and each person's experience has his self as a central fact or datum. Berkeley said, "No one ever experiences an object that is not an idea"; the pluralist adds, "and no one ever experiences an idea that is not his own." "The separateness and privacy of each individual," says Brightman, "[is] an ultimate trait of the world." [9]

Berkeley believed that we experience our mind through a specific "notion." The personal idealist says, on the contrary, that awareness of myself is indissolubly given in *every* experience. The mind that Berkeley became aware of in his "notion" was much like the soul of traditional theology. "Soul" is the name generally given to a transcendent entity (existing outside experience) reached only through a debatable inference. Psychology since the time of Hume has successfully attacked the concept of soul as non-empirical and meaningless; it is, for psychology at least, a poor hypothesis. Berkeley, although he dismissed the unknown material object as a support for ideas, kept a spiritual substratum for them.

For transcendent and non-empirical soul as a spiritual substratum of experience, the personal idealist substitutes the "self." The self is the primary datum *in* experience. All experience is experience by and of a self; it is the individual organic unity of experience, of which each of us is always more or less explicitly aware. It has unity in variety, continuity, and purpose; only in relation to it can anything be known to exist, or be experienced, or have any meaning or value.

Pluralistic and absolute idealism—The absolute idealist emphasizes a unity of experience not focused in individual centers of consciousness. The unity he seeks is that of a logical whole or system of experience, which he identifies with the reality of things. The consequence is that the absolute idealist derogates from the reality of the individual consciousness. In seek-

---

[9] Edgar S. Brightman, "The Finite Self," in Clifford Barrett (ed.), *Contemporary Idealism in America*, page 179. New York: The Macmillan Company, 1932.

ing an Absolute, he reduces the individual mind to a mere organ or aspect of the whole; whatever significance it has, he believes, is derived from the degree to which it loses its specific nature and privacy in The Absolute. The absolute idealist is therefore a monist, not a pluralist.

When the absolute idealist deals with an idea without considering it in the context of the individual experience in which it arises and functions, the pluralists say he takes "idea" in an abstract and non-empirical sense.

The pluralistic idealists argue that the monist, in trying to find the mind, loses it. He may gain the whole world, but he loses himself in it. Consciousness is ineluctably individual. There are no "floating ideas"; all ideas are anchored in some individual's experience.

Pluralists have objected to the "block universe" or the "totalitarian state" of the absolute idealist. Its monolithic structure, in which each thing has an assigned place in the eternal order of things, they feel, does not allow elbow-room for individual spontaneity and freedom, no place for individual initiative and action. Everything is necessary. It explains evil away as a necessary part of the good, or makes it an inevitable part of experience about which we can do nothing, instead of giving man a belief in his own spontaneity that will encourage him to exercise his freedom to eradicate it.

The pluralistic idealist considers the universe as analogous to a democratic community, in which each man can freely choose his own goals and freely cooperate with others, exercise his own initiative, and enlarge his experience without losing his identity. The pluralistic idealist reacts against the monism of absolute idealism because he has a "sentiment" in favor of individualism. But it is not entirely a matter of sentiment; he believes that the monism of absolute idealism is intellectually wrong on at least two counts.

First, he says, absolute idealism is not true to the facts. While experience is its central fact, absolute idealism deals with only one aspect of experience. It delineates the logical and dialectical structure of experience with immense skill and subtlety; but it ignores the empirical fact that all the experience we ever have is individual and personal. However comprehensive experience may become through dialectical development, it is still the experience of some individual. The absolutist rightly recognizes that mind is essential for experience, but for the mind of which we are continuously aware he substitutes a mind that none except perhaps a few mystics have ever claimed.

Second, the pluralistic idealist says, absolute idealism is wrong in its epistemology. It identifies experience with reality, and asserts that reality is only experience understood in all its ramifications. According to the pluralists, this view of the relation of experience to reality necessarily leads to The Absolute, for in identifying our experience with part of reality, "our experience" ceases to be ours in any meaningful sense. It becomes just a part of experience—nobody's experience, but absolute experience.

The pluralistic idealist rejects the absolutist's view that experience and what is experienced are identical. For if he granted this, he says, "Self would be merged in its world, and a true plurality of selves would be impossible." [10] He goes back to Locke, and says that our ideas merely represent reality but are not identical with it. He justifies his distinction between experience and what is experienced, the basis of his preserving the plurality of selves, by arguing that the alternative view cannot explain how error can occur or how we are able to know what happened far away and long ago.

Summary—Personal idealists believe with Berkeley and the absolute idealists that the only real things are minds and the contents of experience. They agree with Berkeley (against the absolute idealists) that there are many irreducible and individual minds. But they disagree with both Berkeley and the abso-

---

[10] Edgar S. Brightman, "Personalism and Borden Parker Bowne," *Proceedings of the Sixth International Congress of Philosophy* (1926), page 162.

lute idealists by drawing a distinction between the contents of consciousness and the real objects of knowledge.

The last sentence leads directly to the central thesis of the pluralistic idealism. Granting that the only things that are real are minds and their ideas, and that there is a difference between ideas and the real objects, only one conclusion is possible: *the objects must themselves be minds or parts of some mind not my own.* In either case he asserts a plurality of minds.

The perception of objects

I am, say personal idealists, directly aware of myself as an active being, and I am directly aware of my ideas as *my* ideas. Ideas are not independently real things; their being is their being perceived. But how do we know that there are any things besides our ideas? How do I know that there are any independent objects? How do I know that my experience is not just a consistent dream?

First, the pluralistic idealist points out that ideas have two aspects; their mere being, as psychical events in my mind, brutely given at a particular moment, and their "objective reference," by virtue of which they mean or suggest something other than themselves. We know that one idea can refer to another; there is no reason to doubt that it can refer to other things too. But, a critic may say, the assumption of objective reference begs the question, for what we want to know is, are there any objects except ideas?

The pluralistic idealist replies that the assumption is not arbitrarily made, but is an empirical aspect of our ideas that ought not be neglected. An open-minded and honest analysis of consciousness, he says, cannot omit the character of objective reference, which is as directly felt a part or aspect of the idea as its secondary or primary qualities are. If our analysis deals with the contents of consciousness only as isolated end-products of psychological observation, and is interested only in their intensity, color, and the like, our analysis has distorted the facts of experience. Ideas bear the mark of incompleteness as one of their empirical features.

Not only are our ideas felt as incomplete; my experience of myself is incomplete and fragmentary unless I admit its dependence on something else:

The personalist justifies himself in asserting the existence of this something-beside-me on the ground that I directly experience myself as a limited, hampered self—limited in my perceptual experience to just these special seeings and hearings, and limited also in my personal disappointments and in my baffled purposes. But a direct experience of being limited is . . . a direct (not an inferred) knowledge of something existing beyond the limit.[11]

Brightman attempts to answer the charge of solipsism (the belief that only the individual experiencing mind exists) by putting the burden of proof upon the critic of his position:

The solipsist supposes that whatever is in the mind has no meaning and no explanation beyond the mind in which it is located. But if the solipsist appeals to any meaning, he appeals to reason; and reason is coherence. Now, to suppose that sensations have no explanation beyond the mind in which they are located is to abandon all coherence; for sensations come and go in a most chaotic, formless, and incoherent manner—incoherent, that is, until the reasoning mind takes account of its act of referring beyond itself for its objects and for a rational basis for its existence. The hypothesis that sensations refer to objects of some sort, and that they are produced by some sort of reality other than the mind of the observer, is one that brings order and coherence into the realm of sensation.[12]

In a word, the existence of anything other than ideas and self is a hypothesis, but it is more reasonable than the solipsist's hypothesis. Though Brightman's hypothesis is less parsimonious in kinds of entities assumed, he argues that it is more adequate in explaining the contents of consciousness.

---

[11] Mary W. Calkins, "The Personalistic Conception of Nature," *Philosophical Review*, Vol. XXVIII, No. 2 (March, 1919), pages 125-126. Quoted with the permission of the Editor of *The Philosophical Review*.

[12] Edgar S. Brightman, *Nature and Values*, page 41. Copyright 1945 by Whitmore and Stone. Used by permission of Abingdon-Cokesbury Press.

The nature of objects

Granting, now, that there is an object, what is it? Here, personal idealists are unanimous in their rejection of materialism. They all deny that the real object is to be understood only as matter under laws of mechanics and characterized only by primary qualities. While science may understand nature under the materialistic assumption (although most idealists deny the adequacy of this assumption even in science), a metaphysical understanding of nature must be more synoptic and comprehensive. It must conceive nature in a way that is coherent with the most panoramic view of our experience.

Criteria of adequacy of any theory of objects—To satisfy this requirement, a theory of nature and of the objects of science must meet two criteria. First, it must not conflict with any of the established facts of science (although it may disagree with metaphysical theories based upon belief in the adequacy and incorrigible truth of some scientific hypothesis.) That is to say, even though science may not give us the whole truth, a theory of the object must be such that the scientific conception of it will be at least a "first approximation." The conception of nature adopted in metaphysics must therefore admit the facts of science, the validity of scientific law, and the presuppositions and results of the impartial study of nature.

Second, it must be consistent with the facts of our immediate experience, which is an experience of a knowing, acting, and valuing self and not of a mechanical aggregate of atoms or material parts with only an epiphenomenal mind. In other words, metaphysical theory, in adapting itself to the results of science, should not explain away the teleological search for values that underlies the scientific enterprise itself, and must be adequate to the one reality we directly experience, ourselves.

No materialistic theory, says the personal idealist, can meet both of these criteria. But not all personal idealists agree as to what theory will best meet them. Some have accepted what I shall call a neo-Berkeleian theory and some a panpsychistic theory of objects.[13]

Neo-Berkeleian theory of objects—That which limits our minds and explains the origin and course of our ideas is another mind which is all-comprehending. The "things" that exist in the physical world are manifestations of the creativity of this supreme mind. Thus Brightman writes:

> Every law of nature is a law of God, every energy of nature a deed of God.[14]
> Nature is in the Divine Mind; nature is God's working, his activity, his experience. It is nothing external in which he dwells or on which he acts. It is part and parcel of his very being.[15]

Such a conception is quite compatible with positivism as a theory of scientific knowledge, because both oppose the popular materialistic interpretation of scientific objects. But it goes beyond positivism, because positivism is *only* a theory of science and is not able to meet adequately the second of the criteria mentioned on page 369.[16] When we supplement the positivistic conception of nature with the neo-Berkeleian metaphysical conception, nothing is changed in science itself, so this theory meets the first criterion. The metaphysical supplementation of the concept of a divine mind is harmonious with the scientific interpretation of nature and with the facts of our experience of our own mental reality.

Panpsychistic theory of objects—Panpsychism literally means the view that "all is mind." That is, all reality is psychical and so-called objects are really minds. This view was first devel-

---

[13] It is hard to be entirely sure that any recent personal idealists are neo-Berkeleians; often some of them write as if they were, though occasionally one finds statements by the same writers that are at least seemingly incompatible with this view. But it is a logically possible hypothesis about nature which a pluralistic idealist *could* consistently hold, and therefore I shall describe it briefly; but I would not wish to be interpreted as ascribing this view alone to any particular recent idealist.

[14] Edgar S. Brightman, *Nature and Values*, page 120. Copyright 1945 by Whitmore & Stone. Used by permission of Abingdon-Cokesbury Press.

[15] *Ibid.*, page 124.

[16] Cf. Edgar S. Brightman, *A Philosophy of Ideals*, Chapter II. New York: Henry Holt and Company, Inc., 1928.

oped in modern philosophy by Leibniz, and might well be called the "neo-Leibnizian" view. Leibniz defined a substance, that is, a real entity or monad, as "a being that acts," and the only authentic case of action with which I am directly aware is my own acivity. Thus Leibniz interpreted both objects and himself as monads, and the differences among them as a difference in the degree to which they had experience of the universe as a whole. In recent years a comparable view has been defended by James Ward and Mary Whiton Calkins (1863-1930).

The panpsychist reaches his conception of the object by an analogical argument like that by which Berkeley reached the conception of the mind of God. That is, when I infer beyond my ideas into the world of objects that I do not directly experience, I can interpret them best by analogy to the one reality I know directly: my own mind as a center of experience and action. But the panpsychist, being a pluralist, looks for many realities; everything that exists, he says, is a mind.

No panpsychist means to assert that this book is conscious of you as you are conscious of it. He recognizes that there is a continuous gradation of minds in the animal kingdom, from the subtle consciousness and intelligence of man to the dull restlessness with but a modicum of intelligence found in the lower animals. He is even willing to argue that consciousness may not be a universal characteristic of minds, for what is called our "unconscious mind" shows teleological processes, and we have no evidence by which to decide whether a protozoon, for instance, has any consciousness at all. Believing in the continuity of nature, however, the panpsychist extrapolates beyond the range within which he does have evidence of consciousness and posits mind of a very low order in all existing things.

On the face of it, this view may appear silly to most people in our civilization. But it is a common belief in the Orient, and since it has been formulated and defended by some great thinkers—one of whom, Leibniz, was one of the most penetrating geniuses who ever lived—it merits careful study. Let us suspend what may be a natural repugnance to this view, and see how it meets the two criteria that we have placed upon any theory of the object. On this view, what becomes of causality, mechanism, and the laws of nature?

Here the pluralistic idealist draws a useful distinction between the scientific and the metaphysical interpretation of a concept. Consider the two interpretations of the concept of causation and of the concept of substance. (1) By causation, the scientist, since the time of Hume, has meant only regularity in sequences of events. The laws of nature do not state that one event *makes* another event happen, but only that events of one specific kind are regularly followed by events of another specific kind. (2) By substance, the scientist, since the time of Locke, has understood only a regular congeries of observable traits or phenomena existing simultaneously in a restricted region of space.

The panpsychist leaves these categories untouched as far as science is concerned. Even if panpsychism is true, the scientist should continue to seek for regular sequences or statistical correlations, and to think of an object as the sum or system of all its observed and observable aspects. Hence the panpsychistic theory of the object meets the first criterion.

Now consider the metaphysical interpretation of these concepts. (1) Causation, in my own self-experience, does not mean merely the regular sequence of events; it means activity, initiative, agency. I have direct experience of causal efficacy, when I "exert myself and *make* something happen." (It does not matter that the psychologist can show that many of the actions I think are free are really effects of what he considers to be physiological conditions. The idealist admits this, but insists that something very important is left out of the full experience of causation when it is replaced by the scientifically useful conception of mere regularity of sequence.) When I interpret causation metaphysically, I should make use of this more adequate, more full-bodied experience of causal efficacy.

which is inseparable from the experience of purposing. If the objective connections in the world of nature are to be interpreted metaphysically, then, it will be by analogy to our own experience of purposive causation. Naturally, the object is not supposed to be as free and as purposive in its actions as a higher animal or man is, and hence the laws of nature and of nature's uniformity, expressed in mathematical equations, apply to the relations among those minds we call physical objects.

(2) Substance does not apply, in my own experience, to a mere aggregate of simultaneously existing qualities, such as intelligence, will, feeling of fatigue, sensation of black, perception of typewriter, and so on. Although psychologists analyze the self, in order to understand a mind or self it must be taken as an organic whole, as an active center of an environment with purposes and causal series radiating from it. The person must be understood organically, by a kind of Bergsonian intuition, as a being that exerts causal influences and suffers change, yet teleologically perseveres through the changes and preserves itself.

When positivistic scientists speak of objects, they use substance and causality in the restricted senses established by Locke and Hume. If one develops a metaphysics on the basis of these concepts, the metaphysical view is mechanistic. But when the panpsychist speaks of objects, he attributes to them a self-like character for the sake of rendering the facts of science compatible with the rest of his experience.

It is the belief of many panpsychists, moreover, that the development of organismic or holistic theories of the living organism (see page 166) is in part a scientific vindication of their daring speculation. While most scientists who accept the doctrine of organicism believe that mind is an emergent level based upon the non-mental conditions of matter, the panpsychist believes that mind or selves are not "late arrivals" in the evolution of the universe, but that mind is present throughout. Only after highly integrated organisms with delicately adaptive nervous systems evolved, however, do we find the distinctive traits of mind as we know it.

The human person

Mind as it appears on the human level is characterized by the unity-in-variety of its structure, its temporal transcendence, and its appreciation of ideal values.

By unity-in-variety, we mean that in mind as we know it, there is an organic interrelation among the parts. The whole is what it is because of the parts, but the parts are in turn affected by the whole in which they function. To analyze the mind by removing some part or aspect from the whole and attending to it as if it were an independent thing is not only to deny the integrity of mind, but to change the qualities of the parts themselves. This has been discovered empirically in psychology, and many experimentalists in psychology now insist upon taking the organism or the personality as a whole, not as a sum of isolable parts.[16]

By temporal transcendence is meant the character of mind or of our experience by virtue of which mind is not tied down to its momentary causal reactions to immediately present stimuli. Our consciousness, limited in its existence to the specious present of a few seconds, scans the universe, and thinks at one moment of prehistoric days and at the next of tomorrow's breakfast.

> We look before and after,
> And pine for what is not.

Because our consciousness transcends the physiological conditions that vary from moment to moment, and integrates our experience from moment to moment, we are able to learn from the past and to plan intelligently for the future. We experience not only the pushes and pulls of the physical environment, but we can act intelligently upon it. We can transcend the environ-

---

[16] The most comprehensive scientific study of this is William Stern, *General Psychology from the Personalistic Standpoint.* New York: The Macmillan Company, 1938.

ment itself with all its constraints, and exercise our freedom from its importunities by framing and pursuing ideal values. The personal idealists call a self or mind that can do this a *person*. Persons are pursuers of ideal values and are themselves objective and ultimate values in the universe. Because they are of infinite value in a teleological universe, which the personal idealist believes is friendly to values, most personal idealists believe in the immortality of persons.

Human and divine persons

That which supports the values of the person is not the world of nature. Most personal idealists postulate a higher person than the human as the creator of the world and as the objective support of the highest human purposes. Personal idealists generally take one of three views concerning the relations that exist among the selves that comprise the universe; the first is very uncommon among them, and most personal idealists accept either the second or the third hypothesis.

Atheistic pluralism—This view, held by McTaggart, is that the universe is a "society of persons" integrated by their relations but not united into or under a "cosmic personality." McTaggart argued for this view in many extremely subtle ways, but the most obvious ground for his conclusion is the difficulty of conceiving the possibility that one person can be a part of another person, even God. But his argument is so difficult that it cannot be pursued here.

Pluralism combined with theism—This is the answer given by James Ward. A plurality of self-acting minds of "monads" is ontologically incomplete; the unity and regularity of a pluralistically conceived universe is a fact that metaphysics should explain. Furthermore, in a world that is radically pluralistic, there is no ground for the unification of actions and faith in the attainment of this unification, which is a part of our highest moral goal. Hence for both theoretical and pragmatic or moral reasons (the latter resembling those of Kant [see pages 296 ff]), Ward was led to "a more fundamental standpoint than [that] of the Many, namely, that of the One that would furnish an ontological unity for their cosmological unity [17] and ensure a teleological unity for their varied ends." [18] This One is God who is imminent in the world, yet transcends it. He is not an Absolute, for an Absolute is incompatible with the reality and personality of the individual, which is the most certain fact of all. Ward cannot make clear the exact nature of the relation between God and man, because it is unlike any relation that we can experience; but, he says, God is "a living God with a living world, not a potter God with a world of illusory clay." [19]

Theistic finitism—This theory, which has been developed chiefly by Brightman, takes the view of Plato and Mill (see page 287) that God is finite, and combines it with personal idealism. Brightman defines:

A theistic finitist is one who holds that the eternal will of God faces given conditions which that will did not create . . . If these conditions . . . are within the divine personality, then the position is a variety of idealistic personalism.[20]

Brightman, as we have seen, sometimes expounds what seems to be a neo-Berkeleian theory of the external world; for Brightman that which limits God's will is "the eternal brute facts of [God's] experience." [21] But a more serious ground for attributing finitude of power to God is human personality itself, its freedom and its irreducible status. Man, says Brightman, "cannot be thought of as a part of God, nor as a rearrangement of matter. . . ." [22] He concludes that God created persons and thereby limited himself. In one sense, God is infinite because there is nothing wholly outside the universe of His creation

---

[17] That is, a metaphysical explanation of the uniformity and unity of nature.
[18] James Ward, *The Realm of Ends, or Pluralism and Theism*, page 442. Cambridge, Eng.: University Press, 1911.
[19] *Ibid.*, page 444.
[20] Edgar S. Brightman, *A Philosophy of Religion*, pages 313-314. New York: Prentice-Hall, Inc., 1945. Ward's God is similarly limited.
[21] *Ibid.*, page 321.
[22] *Ibid.*, page 333.

that limits Him, and He is infinite in value and in His support of human valuations. But in another sense, He is limited by the world of free persons that He created and supports. Personal idealism in this theological development obviously has much in common with the theology of absolute idealism.[23]

Summary and Conclusion

With respect to personal idealism, we are in the fortunate position of having a summary statement written by two 'of the leaders of the movement, Calkins and Brightman.[24] Because of its brevity and authoritativeness, it is reproduced in full:

Platform of Personalistic Idealism

1. The universe is completely mental in nature.
2. Every mental existent is either a self, or else a part, aspect, phase, or process of a self. The term "person" is used for selves capable of reasoning and ideal valuations.
3. The physical universe may be regarded as the direct experiencing and willing of one cosmic person,* or as a system of infra-human selves, or as a system of ideas in the minds of finite persons.
4. The total universe is a system of selves and persons, who may be regarded either as members of one all-inclusive person who individuates them by the diversity of his purposing or as a society of many selves related by common purposes.
5. Every self directly experiences itself.
6. The self knows some other selves indirectly, by inference.
7. Any metaphysical theory (except materialism which denies facts of direct experience) about the quality of reality or the number of ultimately distinct beings is compatible with all scientific observations and with scientific laws conceived either (a) as generalizations of observed sequences or (b) as statistical formulations of average behavior. But philosophy is dependent upon the facts revealed by the sciences for its conception not only of the structure of the universe, but also of its values and purposes.
8. Esthetics and ethics are based on psychological doctrines con-

---

[23] Cf. *ibid.*, pages 339-40.

[24] This "platform" was adopted by Professors Calkins and Brightman on May 25, 1929, and published in the *Journal of Philosophy*, Vol. XXX, No. 16 (August 3, 1933), pages 434-435. Quoted with the permission of the Editor of the *Journal of Philosophy*.

cerning the valuing consciousness, but go beyond descriptive psychology both in their normative aspects and in their metaphysical implication of beauty and goodness in the universe. 9. Similarly, the science of religion is primarily a psychological and historical discipline; but the object of the religious consciousness, God, may be identified with a metaphysical object—the cosmic person.[25]

* The term "cosmic person" is understood to include both the God of theism and the Absolute Person.

BIBLIOGRAPHY

General works

Barrett, Clifford (ed.), *Contemporary Idealism in America*. New York: The Macmillan Company, 1932.
Cunningham, G. Watts, *The Idealistic Argument in Recent British and American Philosophy*. New York: The Century Company, 1933.
Ewing, A. C., *Idealism. A Critical Survey*. New York: The Humanities Press, 1950.
Hoernlé, R. F. Alfred, *Idealism as a Philosophy*. New York: George H. Doran Company, 1927.
Muirhead, J. H., *The Platonic Tradition in Anglo-Saxon Philosophy*. New York: The Macmillan Company, 1931.
Robinson, D. S. (ed.), *Anthology of Recent Philosophy*. New York: Thomas Y. Crowell Company, 1929. Part 2.
Royce, Josiah, *The Spirit of Modern Philosophy*. Boston: Houghton Mifflin Company, 1892.

Absolute idealism

Blanshard, Brand, *The Nature of Thought*. London: George Allen & Unwin, Ltd., 1939.
Bradley, F. H., *Appearance and Reality*, second ed. New York: The Macmillan Company, 1902.
Hegel, G. W. F., *Hegel Selections* (J. Loewenberg, ed.). New York: Charles Scribner's Sons, 1929.
Morris, C. R., *Idealistic Logic*. London: Macmillan and Company, Ltd., 1933.

---

[25] Used with the permission of the *Journal of Philosophy*.

Royce, Josiah, *The World and the Individual*, two vols. New York: The Macmillan Company, 1900-1901.

Schopenhauer, Arthur, *Schopenhauer Selections* (D. H. Parker, ed.). New York: Charles Scribner's Sons, 1928.

Stace, W. T., *The Philosophy of Hegel*. London: Macmillan and Company, Ltd., 1924.

Widgery, A. G., "Classical German Idealism," in *A History of Philosophical Systems* (Vergilius Ferm, ed.). New York: Philosophical Library, 1950. Pages 291-306.

Pluralistic idealism

Bertocci, Peter A., "Brightman's View of the Self, the Person, and the Body," *Philosophical Forum* (Boston University), Vol. VIII, (1950), pages 21-28.

Calkins, Mary Whiton, "The Case of Self against Soul," *Psychological Review*, Vol. XXIV, No. 4 (July, 1917), pages 278-300.

Flewelling, R. T., *Personalism and the Problems of Philosophy*. New York: Methodist Book Concern, 1915.

Knudson, Albert C., *The Philosophy of Personalism*. New York: Abingdon-Cokesbury Press, 1927.

Wahl, Jean, *The Pluralistic Philosophers of England and America*. London: Open Court Publishing Company, 1925.

The Personalist is a philosophical and literary magazine published by the University of Southern California; it contains many articles discussing the issues of personal idealism.

QUESTIONS AND TOPICS FOR DISCUSSION

1. In what ways might absolute idealism be considered a suitable metaphysics for a totalitarian ideology? In what ways would it be unsuitable?

2. Do the idealists discussed in Chapter 11 escape from the "egocentric predicament"?

3. Evaluate the following criticisms of the coherence theory of truth:

   (a) "I know there is a table before me. I do not have to wait for the infinite and unattainable 'totality of experience' before I know it. Hence the coherence theory is wrong."

   (b) "What the coherence theory amounts to is this: 'A liar ought to have a good memory.'"

(c) "Coherence is a necessary, but not a sufficient, condition of truth."

(d) "The idealist assumes that reality is a coherent whole, and hence rejects any alleged truth that is not internally and externally coherent. He thereby bases his criterion of truth upon a very shaky metaphysical foundation."

4. Could the coherence theory of truth be formulated as a theory and criterion of value?

5. Why do idealists generally insist upon the validity of teleological explanations in science?

6. Could the theistic personal idealists discussed in this chapter be considered theological dualists?

7. What are some of the conditions in twentieth-century life that make idealism less attractive to most people now than it was 50 years ago? What does this suggest concerning the motives, standards, and "objectivity" of philosophers?

12

Naturalism

INTRODUCTION

A naturalist is a philosopher who takes nature as his central fact. Things usually distinguished from nature he interprets as manifestations of nature. Nature is his basic category; belief that some value or experience or object is contrasted to nature he takes to be evidence of ignorance of the manifold character and complexity of nature itself. Art, religion, science, society, culture, and morality, he believes, have their roots in the world of nature and are to be understood in its terms.

"Nature" is a name for the ultimate reality or totality of things, both human and sub-human, organic and inorganic. "Nature" thus serves a function for the naturalist like that of "mind" for the idealist and "God and the world" for the theological dualist. They are all names given to the whole of reality. It might seem, accordingly, to be utterly trivial to dispute about naturalism and idealism, for such a dispute seems to be about the "best name" to call the universe. If a rose by any other name would smell as sweet, it is reasonable to think that the universe will "smell as sweet" whether we call it mind, or God's creation, or nature.

This is a very superficial criticism, however, for each of the names is used in a metaphorical sense, and each metaphor has its own peculiar suggestive value. The idealist who calls the world a mind does so because he takes as his central fact those things within it that everyone calls a mind, and then from this central fact, he attempts to read off the significant characteristics of the whole. He sees the world as a whole by analogy to the minds within it, which he takes as preeminent instances of those qualities and relations that he believes are most fundamental in the universe itself. He regards mind as being especially typical of the ultimate character of the universe, and hence he does not think that "mind" is merely an empty name for something that would "smell as sweet" if it were called "nature."

Similarly, the naturalist would deny that "nature" is simply an empty name for something that might equally well be called "mind" or "God's creation." He holds that those parts of the universe that everyone agrees to call nature have a central position within experience and illuminate all the rest. Nature, in the naive, common-sense use of this word, suggests the analogy by which he interprets everything; accordingly, he attributes to reality a very different character and structure from that given to it by other metaphysicians.

The theses of naturalism

The characteristics the naturalist attributes to reality are given in three theses:

1. *The anti-dualistic thesis*—The naturalist says, "Everything in the universe is to be understood as parts of or manifestations of nature." Reality does not consist of nature *plus* minds, as Descartes believed, nor does it consist of nature *plus* God, as the theological dualists believe. According to the naturalist, "Nature is considered as the domain in which both knowledge and happiness are pursued." It is "the familiar setting of human history . . . the primary subject matter of all human inquiry." [1]

---

[1] Reprinted from Frederick J. E. Woodbridge, *An Essay on Nature*, pages v, 3, 4. Copyright 1937 by Columbia University Press.

The naturalist believes that the urge many people feel to accept some supernatural entity like God, or some extranatural realm of entities like objective values, springs from a narrow conception of nature that includes only the colorless, odorless, tasteless, and valueless entities of physics. He also believes that a sufficiently broad and comprehensive conception of nature can make room for the sights and sounds and aspirations and ideals that men experience.

Many naturalists admit that there are strata of reality or emergent levels within nature, but they do not sharply segregate the levels they distinguish, as the theological dualist does; they say that the various levels are all aspects of one complex reality, which they call nature in the broadest sense.

2. *The anti-idealistic thesis*—This is the thesis that minds and their experiences are to be explained in terms of nature. The naturalist holds that the things we know or can discover by the use of the mind are more explanatory than the fact that we know them. Minds and their acts are in some sense real for the naturalist; they are observable facts that cannot be explained away. But, says the naturalist, they can be explained if we learn enough about the nature in which they arise and to which they are directed. To be sure, if there were no minds, there could be no process of explanation; but the premises of our explanation, he says, are to be found in the facts we know, not in some transcendental mind whose eternal existence must be presupposed.

Minds, the naturalists usually assert, are relatively late arrivals in the evolutionary process, and we can understand how they evolved and how they now function in much the same way that we understand other complex phenomena of nature and life. While the process of knowing is undoubtedly the most complex of all the known processes of nature, in principle this process is to be explained in terms of nature instead of being taken as a *prius* in the explanation of nature itself. The naturalist feels that the young sciences of psychology, cultural anthropology, and sociology can be scientific, empirical studies of the conditions and processes of consciousness.

3. *The scientific thesis*—The naturalist says: "The best or only sure method of getting knowledge is the method of carefully observing, formulating explanatory hypotheses, and empirically testing them to eliminate the false hypotheses, followed by systematic attempts to generalize observations into laws and hypotheses into theories." This is the method that has worked best in the scientific study of what is ordinarily called "nature," and for this reason it is called the scientific method. In stating that everything real is natural, the naturalist is announcing a *methodological* program, which lays reality open to the careful and strict kind of empirical and rational investigation associated with scientific work. The naturalist does not propose that the philosopher should go into the laboratory or observatory, nor does he think that philosophy can be experimental in the way that physics is; but he does believe that the essential traits of scientific method can be used not only in science but also in history, in practical affairs, and in constructing a metaphysical world-view. In this way he repudiates any appeals to revelation, authority, and intuitive self-evident truths. These have been eliminated from scientific knowledge but are still practiced in some philosophies, and the naturalist proposes to eliminate them from philosophy, too.

The naturalists' respect for science

The scientific thesis is sometimes expressed in a different form. It is said, "The results of scientific study are the surest knowledge we have; therefore, metaphysics should be based upon the results of science." This interpretation of the scientific thesis expresses a very important half-truth, and we should carefully examine its meaning and validity.

Consider first the premise: "The results of science are the surest knowledge we have." While many theological dualists and idealists would not accept this statement, as responsible thinkers they would not challenge, on speculative philosophical grounds, any of the established facts of science (although they might challenge some hypotheses that most scientists would consider well established). One task of the philosopher is to integrate and synthesize facts, and the facts of science must be especially respected because of the meticulous care that has gone into their observation. No responsible thinker, therefore, will profess disrespect for the facts of science; and no competent thinker who loves truth will "try to get around them." He may have what others consider very peculiar ways of interpreting them, but he accepts them as facts. It is therefore unfair to non-naturalists to say, ". . . The naturalist is one who has respect for the conclusion of natural science." [2]

But "respect for natural science'" means one or more of three attitudes. (1) The first we have just described. One can regard scientific facts as facts that must be taken into account in philosophical thinking, so that the philosopher does not make himself ridiculous by challenging the observations and well-founded hypotheses of competent scientists about the facts of nature. Whether a philosopher likes it or not, and however he chooses to interpret it, he must believe that light travels at approximately 186,000 miles a second, that the earth is not in the center of the galaxy, that the earth did not suddenly appear out of nothing in 4004 B.C., that feelings of guilt can frequently be relieved by psychoanalysis, that things that happen in the brain influence a man's thinking and behavior, and so on.

(2) One can take the facts of science as *metaphysically* true. That is, one can take the established results of science as an adequate foundation for metaphysical hypotheses or as "building blocks" in the metaphysical mansion one builds for oneself. If the psychologist says that only the brain can influence consciousness in such-and-such a way, then that is a fact that will be taken into metaphysics and destroy idealism; if the physicist says that everything in nature is a form of energy, that will be

---

[2] Reprinted from John Dewey, "Antinaturalism in Extremis," in *Naturalism and the Human Spirit*, page 2, edited by Yervant H. Krikorian. Copyright 1944 by Columbia University Press.

taken over into metaphysics as a modification of strict materialism.

(3) One can recognize that while scientific facts and generalizations about them are the surest knowledge we have, none of them is "eternally true," and the hypotheses they support may have to be modified in the course of further work. But instead of this attitude being one of distrust of science, it entails acknowledging that beliefs based on science will be corrected and augmented only by a more extensive application of the very same method by which they were established. In this case, the deepest respect is reserved for the procedures of science, and is not given to the present-day results of science as if they were "eternally true."

The first type of respect for science is not the peculiar prerogative of any school of philosophers. The second type of respect, however, is very widespread among naturalists, especially in the past, but its effect on their work has almost always been unfortunate. If a philosopher builds a metaphysical theory in which the latest results of science are used as his foundation, new scientific discovery can suddenly outmode his entire metaphysics. This happened, for instance, in the case of Herbert Spencer, who at the end of the nineteenth century wrote a system of "synthetic philosophy" in which he aimed to integrate and synoptize all the facts of science; yet the facts of science and the best scientific thinking changed so rapidly that he was regarded as old-fashioned even before his death. Because it dogmatizes on the momentary results of science without realizing that more scientific discoveries will be made and will force a revision in the premises of the metaphysician's work, such respect for science is false to the very spirit of science. Metaphysics based on this kind of respect for science can last only until the next fundamental discovery is made.

This kind of respect for science has another drawback in philosophy. The fields of science are so immense now that no one scientist or philosopher can survey them or keep up with all the latest discoveries. Aristotle could do this; to some extent,

Leibniz was able to do so; but Spencer failed, and no one even attempts such a gigantic task nowadays. But that does not mean that science is now regarded as irrelevant to metaphysics; we still have to consider the third type of respect for science.

The third kind of respect for science is that which characterizes naturalism at its best. While not challenging the specific results of science—that is the business of the scientist himself—or dogmatizing about them, the naturalist seeks to understand the world by following a method in philosophy that is continuous with and essentially like that of the scientist. What unites all naturalists, says Sidney Hook, "is the whole-hearted acceptance of scientific method as the only reliable way of reaching truths about the world of nature, society, and man." [3]

A philosopher, although unable to know all the facts of science, can and should learn and practice the method that has made science preeminent as a study of fact. Then the philosopher can apply this method in those fields of value, practical affairs, and metaphysics where Idols of the Mind and powerful forces and ideologies have previously banned open-minded and impartial inquiry. In this respect, the philosopher's admiration for science is an admiration for that which has made science a preeminent way of knowing, and not a parasitical and futile attempt to gather the results of science into some kind of metaphysical theory with a little psychology here, a bit of chemistry there, and a summary of a second-hand report on the latest discoveries in endocrinology and astrophysics somewhere else.

Both the second and the third kinds of respect for science have been current in naturalistic philosophy; sometimes one and sometimes the other has been uppermost. When respect for the facts of science has been predominant, metaphysical theories have usually been speculative and dogmatic materialisms. When respect for the procedures of science has been most

---

[3] Reprinted from Sidney Hook, "Naturalism and Democracy," in *Naturalism and the Human Spirit*, page 45, edited by Yervant H. Krikorian. Copyright 1944 by Columbia University Press.

prominent, there is usually less dogmatism about answers to metaphysical questions, but a strong intention to break down the barriers erected around a narrow conception of nature by belief in the impenetrable mysteries of religion and undisciplined speculation of all sorts. In this and the following chapter, we shall discuss briefly two types of naturalistic philosophy. In the first, materialism, we shall see the acceptance of the results of science as having basic metaphysical significance; in the second, critical naturalism, we shall see the acceptance of the procedures of scientific inquiry applied to the problems of metaphysics.

MATERIALISM

Materialism is the naturalistic metaphysics that regards nature as consisting of matter in motion. Whatever is apparently not matter in motion is to be regarded as "mere appearance" of what is matter in motion. All explanation, therefore, in philosophy as well as in science, is to be phrased in terms of the laws now known or yet to be discovered concerning the relationships among the different kinds of matter and the laws of their motion with respect to each other.

At the beginning of one of the classical expressions of the materialistic philosophy, *Of the Nature of Things*, the Roman poet Lucretius expresses the indebtedness men should feel toward Democritus, the founder of atomistic materialism:

> Whilst human kind
> Throughout the lands lay miserably crushed
> Before all eyes beneath Religion—who
> Would show her head along the region skies,
> Glowering on mortals with her hideous face—
> A Greek it was who first opposing dared
> Raise mortal eyes that terror to withstand,
> Whom nor the fame of Gods nor lightning's stroke
> Nor threatening thunder of the ominous sky
> Abashed; but rather chafed to angry zest
> His dauntless heart to be the first to rend

The crossbars at the gates of Nature old.
And thus his will and hardy wisdom won;
And forward thus he fared afar, beyond
The flaming ramparts of the world, until
He wandered the unmeasurable All.
Whence he comes to us, a conqueror, reports
What things can rise to being, what cannot,
And by what law to each its scope prescribed,
Its boundary stone that clings so deep in Time.
Wherefore religion now is under foot,
And us his victory now exalts to heaven.[4]

The discovery of Democritus, which is said to have emancipated the mind from superstition, was this: reality consists of nothing but empty space and indestructible, minute particles of matter. These particles he called "atoms," from the Greek word meaning "indivisible." The purported effect of this discovery, which Lucretius proclaimed, was to free men from religious hopes and fears, which they feel only because they do not know that nature is infinite in space and time and that all happenings in nature are to be explained in terms of other happenings in nature, according to inexorable laws discovered by patient observation. With this discovery, they can see that in order to understand nature they do not need to know the ways of the inscrutable gods. This discovery encourages them to learn the secrets of nature, and not to live in ignorant fear of the caprice and wrath of the gods.

Materialists for the past two millennia have accepted this as a fair statement of the effect their philosophy can have upon human affairs. But the particular characteristics that they attribute to the world of matter have changed with every advance of scientific knowledge. In spite of the variations in detail, however, there are certain common beliefs found among materialists of all ages.

---

[4] Lucretius, *Of the Nature of Things* (William Ellery Leonard, trans.), pages 4-5. New York: E. P. Dutton & Co., Inc; Everyman's Library edition, 1950.

The theses of materialism

1. *The atomistic thesis*—All materialists think of nature as comprising a large or infinite number of irreducible realities, the nature of each of them being independent of the rest, although the behavior of each is determined by the motion of the others. In ancient philosophy, the atoms were thought of as minute particles differing from each other in size, shape, and (sometimes) mass. Even then, long before the development of modern science, matter—which is to say, reality—was thought of as having only the primary qualities. But as scientific knowledge grew, the details of this conception changed. Now a materialist would say that the atoms of physics and chemistry are not the ultimate building blocks of the universe, but that they consist of more elementary entities having electrical charges, spin, and other physical properties. But they still hold that everything that exists consists of various combinations of relatively few different kinds of things. So although at various stages of science there are different beliefs about the ultimate constituents of things, materialists have always believed that the way to understand anything is to analyze it until one comes to that which is simple, elementary, and unanalyzable, and then to see how these elements can be put together to make up the world's manifold variety.

2. *The reductionistic thesis*[5]—It follows from this that the number of kinds of real things in the world is far less than the number of kinds of apparent realities.[6] Just as millions of different kinds of molecules consist of different arrangements and proportions of about 90 different kinds of atoms, and the different kinds of atoms are merely different complexes of a smaller number of more elementary entities (electrons, protons, neutrons, and so on), so also

---

[5] For reductionism as a theory in science, cf. page 160, above.

[6] Cf. Iredell Jenkins, "The Postulate of an Impoverished Reality," *Journal of Philosophy*, Vol. XXXIX, No. 20 (September 24, 1942), pages 533-547.

> . . . the world, which seems
> To lie before us like a land of dreams,
> So various, so beautiful, so new . . .

is only a reshuffled hand, the same old particles, hurrying
hither and yon, reacting chemically with each other or push-
ing each other about according to the laws of physics. There
is nothing new under the sun:

> The irresistible passion that draws Edward to the sympathetic
> Ottilia, or Paris to Helen, and leaps over all bounds of reason and
> morality, is the same powerful "unconscious" attractive force which
> impels the living spermatozoon to force an entrance into the ovum
> in the fertilization of the egg of the animal or plant—the same im-
> petuous movement which unites two atoms of hydrogen to one
> atom of oxygen for the formation of a molecule of water.[7]

Explanation, therefore, must take the form of reducing the
variety of things apparently real to relations and patterns of
relations among the elementary constituents of matter. No
explanation is ultimate and satisfying unless it shows the thing
explained to be a conjunction of the very simple elementary
facts of physics and chemistry.

3. *The mechanistic thesis*—A philosophical theory is called
determinism if it holds that whatever happens does so of necessity. Determinism is the view that events do not occur by chance.
Determinism can be based upon the laws of the mind in idealism, or upon the predestination by God in theological dualism.
But in either case, it is the belief that whatever happens does
so because of the necessity that the same kind of effect shall
invariably and inevitably result from the same kind of cause.
The special form of determinism held by the materialist is
called *mechanism*.[8] Mechanism is the deterministic theory that

---

[7] Ernst Haeckel, *The Riddle of the Universe*, page 224. New York: Harper
& Brothers, 1901.

[8] There are a few materialists who deny mechanism; Lucretius, for instance,
does so. Cf. also page 143 for a discussion of the principle of indeterminacy in
modern physics. For the materialistic or mechanistic theory in biology, see
above, page 161.

whatever occurs happens because of the *preceding physical events.*

Because the materialist is usually a mechanist, it is sometimes said that he conceives of the universe as a billiard table. Imagine a billiard table with perfectly elastic balls and no friction. By hypothesis, a ball rolling on this table will collide with other balls and set them in motion, and these will hit still others and set them in motion. Though this motion would continue without end, we could, theoretically, predict where all the balls would be at any time if we knew where they are and the force with which they are moving at any instant. Of course we cannot actually do so for any actual billiard table, because the mathematical complexity of the problem is too great and the billiard table is not an isolated system (see page 101). But the materialist believes that the material universe is a closed, isolated system, with nothing outside it (minds or gods) to interfere with its motions. Hence, only the complexity of the calculation prevents us from being able to foretell in the minutest detail every event in the future—not only eclipses of the sun and moon, but also the fall of every sparrow and the rise and decline of cultures and empires:

> If an intelligence should for a given instant be acquainted with all the forces by which nature is animated and with the positions of the beings composing it, and if this intelligence should be vast enough to submit these data to analysis, it would include in one and the same formula the movements of the largest bodies in the universe and those of the lightest atom. Nothing would be uncertain for it; the future as well as the past would be present to its eyes.

Laplace, the great astronomer who wrote these words, is said to have been asked by Napoleon why in his writings in astronomy he did not mention God. He replied, "Sire, I have no need for that hypothesis." The story may be apocryphal, but the answer is the only one that a consistent materialist could have given; everything is to be explained in terms of what occurs in nature, according to the laws of physics.

This conception specifically denies the use and validity of the concept of purpose and design. Whatever happens happens because it must; and it must happen because of what happened just before it. Although men think they act for the sake of purposes, their illusion that they do is itself caused by the nature of their bodies and events that have befallen them in the past. Men attribute purpose and design to the world (and therefore feel impelled to imagine a designer) only because they do not see into the causal necessity of physical things and events.

Materialistic theories of the mind

One of the most difficult questions for the materialist to answer is: what are mind and consciousness? Awareness is indubitably one of the characteristic aspects of human beings, and it is extremely likely that all the higher animals are consciously aware of some things in their surroundings to which they adjust. But if it is true, as the materialist holds, that everything in the world, including human beings, consists only of matter in motion, how can they acknowledge even the existence of "states of mind," awareness, consciousness, feelings, and other so-called mental phenomena?

Because of the difficulty of this question for the materialists, they have attempted to answer it in almost every conceivable way that is at all consistent with their basic theses—and sometimes in ways that are not consistent with their ultimate theory.

As to the nature of mind, we may mention five theories held by various materialists: mind is a particular kind of matter (Lucretius); mind is a form of internal motion (Hobbes, some behaviorists); mind is a property of matter (Diderot, Lenin); mind is a property of certain organizations of matter; [9] and mind is a useless by-product or epiphenomenon of the body.

---

[9] R. W. Sellars, Marvin Farber, and V. J. McGill (eds.), *Philosophy for the Future. The Quest of Modern Materialism,* page viii. New York: The Macmillan Company, 1949.

It is questionable whether the first three of these views really make sense. Certainly they do not if "matter" means what it is ordinarily taken to mean or what the physicist means by it, for such matter is stuff characterized by the primary qualities alone; and if the materialist does not use the word "matter" in the scientific sense, then he has to give up his claims that his is a philosophy supported by science and needing no other support. The fourth theory—that mind is a property not of matter itself but of certain organizations of matter—is hardly consistent with the materialists' emphasis upon the atomistic and reductionistic theses. It is rather hard to see the justification for calling this theory materialistic, and we shall find it easier to explain and evaluate in our discussion of another type of naturalism; [10] I call attention here only to the fact that some contemporary philosophers accept this view of mind *and* call themselves materialists.

The last of the theories mentioned is the one most characteristic of materialism. Epiphenomenalism, as it is called, is the theory that, while admitting that mind *is not* matter or energy, holds it to be a by-product (perhaps a useless emergent) from matter in its living forms. To understand this theory, let us contrast it with the more common-sense view called *psychophysical interactionism* or, in honor of Descartes, one of its chief defenders, *Cartesian dualism*.

According to this widely held view, there are two kinds of reality, minds and bodies. The body is affected by physical stimuli from its environment, and the influences of these stimuli are carried to the brain by nerves. This process can be understood in physical or physiological terms. But somewhere along the line, the nervous excitation affects the mind, which is not a physical entity at all, and produces in it a sensation. The mind decides on some line of action, and affects the body through the mechanism of the brain. A "message" goes out from the brain to the appropriate organ of the body, which

---

[10] Cf. below, pages 430-437.

"executes the command." The process from the sense organ to the brain, and the process from the brain to the muscle or gland, can be understood exactly as the behaviorist or materialist says; but the dualist holds that this account is incomplete, for there is a point in this series at which there is interaction between the physical and the mental.

All materialists reject this view. They say that the mind, as thus contrasted with the body, is a poor hypothesis. Interactionism implies that a physiological or materialistic explanation of behavior is not and cannot ever be adequate and comprehensive, because by this hypothesis the mind, which is not subject to physical study, interferes with the physical process. The interaction of mind and body has all the characteristics of a miraculous intervention, which the scientist cannot countenance. So in place of this hypothesis, which he regards as a poor one, the epiphenomenalist asserts that the only aspect of behavior that we need to consider is the purely physical or physiological; but in the course of a complicated neural process, the epiphenomenalist says, the body creates a by-product that is different from the body and that has no effect upon it. "The mind," says Santayana, "is a lyric cry in the midst of business."

While most behaviorist psychologists profess little interest in metaphysical theory, the theory of epiphenomenalism probably best expresses their tacit opinion. They do not assert that what we all admit is conscious and intelligent behavior is *just like* unconscious and unintelligent behavior; what they do assert is that the physiological conditions of intelligent behavior— conditions of the control of response to a stimulus in the light of the entire state of the organism and the environment—are also conditions of the epiphenomenon of consciousness. Hence if we could get complete knowledge of these physiological conditions, we should be able to explain even intelligent behavior without explaining it in terms of the consciousness correlated with it.

Perhaps an analogy will make this view clearer. Suppose that every time a locomotive begins to move, smoke bellows forth from it. A very stupid person looking on might think that the smoke is the cause of the movement of the engine, for, he says, "Every time the engine moves, I see the smoke, and I never see the smoke except when the engine begins to move." The person who knows more about locomotives, however, understands the true relation; the condition under which the train moves is the movement of the piston, and the piston not only causes the train to move but it also causes a puff of smoke. Now, according to the epiphenomenalist, the mind is like the smoke, and behavior is like the movement of the train. We should no more explain the movement of the train in terms of its smoke than the behavior of an organism in terms of its mind. Behavior is different in cases where there is this epiphenomenon of consciousness just as the behavior of the locomotive changes when smoke begins to come out of its smokestack.

The advantages of such a theory in psychology are obvious. It means that psychology is, or can become, a completely impersonal science without appeal to introspection, about which various investigators might differ. It means that the psychologist need not concern himself with anything except physiological conditions and overt behavior. He reduces all the other alleged causal factors—social, teleological, intellectual, and that of concern with values—to their physiological correlates, and deals only with those.

But the fact that this theory is fruitful as a program of action in the psychology laboratory does not prove that it will be adequate as a metaphysical theory. For a metaphysical theory is supposed to be harmonious with all the facts, and there are at least three considerations suggesting that epiphenomenalism is not harmonious with all the facts.

1. It is objected that epiphenomenalism in some way "degrades" man and robs him of his freedom. The facts of inward experience, especially the process of making a decision, do not seem to be adequately accounted for without some reference to meaning, goal-striving, and evaluation. In reply to this criticism the epiphenomenalist says simply that he is not denying

any facts, but is looking at them from the standpoint of finding scientific explanations for them. If his opponent does not like this way of looking at them, that is no objection to his procedure.

2. A weightier objection is found in the theory of evolution. Evolutionary biology holds that an organ has developed and survived because it is useful to the organism or the species in its struggle to survive. If we think of the mind as an organ that has slowly developed from its beginnings in some variation or emergent from a primitive nervous system—as most evolutionists do—then it is not reasonable to suppose that it would have survived and developed unless it gave the organisms that possessed it some advantage in the struggle for survival. This it could not do according to the hypothesis of epiphenomenalism, for the epiphenomenalist says that the mind is a useless addendum that does not modify behavior. Of course, the evolutionary theory does not disprove epiphenomenalism, but it does suggest that it is not utterly unscientific to suspect and to seek out some real efficacy that mind or consciousness might have in the behavior of the organism.

3. Finally, the most crucial objection to epiphenomenalism is that it is involved in a self-stultifying paradox. Suppose A says, "Epiphenomenalism is true," and B asks him, "Why do you *say* that?" Now if epiphenomenalism is true, the only true answer A can give is, "Because my brain-state produced the belief that it is true and caused my larynx to move in such a way that I pronounced the words, 'Epiphenomenalism is true.' " If B is to be seriously persuaded to believe in epiphenomenalism, however, this is not the kind of answer he requires. A must not merely *explain why he said*, "Epiphenomenalism is true," but must also *defend the statement*, "Epiphenomenalism is true." Defense of the statement, like defense of any statement, requires reference to evidence, reasons, premises, grounds, inferences, arguments, logical principles. Now if evidence, reasons, and so on are not themselves brain-states, the epiphenomenalist cannot adduce them in defense of his state-

ment, for if epiphenomenalism is true, they were not effective in deciding him to make it; and if he does adduce them, brain-states are not the sufficient condition under which he made the statement.

The paradox is this. If epiphenomenalism is true, we cannot consistently argue for its truth. If epiphenomenalism is false, however, we can give an intelligible (although not sufficient) defense of it.

That this paradox is not just a sophism of philosophy can be seen in a typical psychological experiment. Imagine two students, C and D, working together. First C does an experiment on D, and then D does the same experiment on C. In the first experiment, D says, "This light is brighter than that one." C, who is performing this experiment, will say, "D says, 'This light is brighter than that one,' because of the physiological condition he is in, or because of his momentary brain-state as affected by the stimuli and his past training." In other words, C treats D's mind as an epiphenomenon, but at the same time, he is professing to use his own mind in a way that would not be possible if his own mind were an epiphenomenon affected only by his brain but not by objective evidence and principles of inference. Later, D does the experiment on C, and gives the same kind of explanation to C's behavior that C formerly gave of D's. Now D, whose mind C previously regarded as an epiphenomenon, is acting as if his mind were effective in drawing conclusions by logical inference, while assuming that C's mind is a useless addendum to the physiological conditions that "really" determine his behavior. But while a postulate or hypothesis that is useful for explaining someone else's behavior but not for explaining one's own may be very useful in the psychology laboratory (as, indeed, this hypothesis is), it cannot be a synoptic metaphysical hypothesis, of which Pepper says, "Every consideration is relevant . . . and no facts lie outside it." [11]

---

[11] Cf. the quotation on page 248, above.

DIALECTICAL MATERIALISM

Dialectical materialism, as developed by Karl Marx (1818-1883), Frederick Engels (1820-1895), and Vladimir Ilyitch Lenin (1870-1924), is the official philosophy of the communist movement and of the Soviet Union. As such, it is the philosophy professed by a sizeable fraction of the human race, and it behooves us to understand some of its principal tenets.

Dialectical materialism can be considered with restrictions like those involved in our discussion of theological dualism. Theological dualism was studied as a type of metaphysics; we tried to understand it as an intellectual edifice, with little or no attention to the emotions that usually surround it and the institutions that are based upon its acceptance. A comparable plan is to be followed here. We shall not consider the political and economic consequences of the wide acceptance of this set of beliefs known as Marxism. This restriction is made because we are here interested in metaphysical theories *as such*, and not as "patterns of life" or "ideologies" with power to move millions of men to fanatical action.

The "materialism" of dialectical materialism

The dialectical materialists profess to be strict materialists, although in many respects they resemble critical naturalists more than the kind of materialists we have been studying.[12]

Materialism in full agreement with natural science takes matter as the *prius*, regarding consciousness, reason, and sensation as derivative, because in a well-expressed form it is connec' 'c' only with the higher forms of matter (organic matter).[13]

The basic reality of the world is matter in motion (or whatever substitute for it is established by detailed scientific work of physicists). Those aspects of reality that are not apparently

---

[12] Sidney Hook, in his *Toward an Understanding of Karl Marx* (New York: John Day Company, 1933, page 31), calls Marx an "activistic naturalist."

[13] V. I. Lenin, *Materialism and Empirio-Criticism* (1909), from *Selected Works*, Vol. XI, pages 112-113. New York: International Publishers, 1943.

matter in motion are said to be "directly interwoven with material activity." [14] There is in nature a continuous development of quality through quantitative change: vibrations of a certain frequency give rise to heat, and vibrations of a higher frequency appear as visible color; complexity of chemical organization may reach such a degree of elaborateness that the phenomenal quality of life may appear. Thus the dialectical materialist *is* a materialist in his assertion of the fundamental and irreducible character of matter, although he admits something like the process of the emergence of quality (he does not use the word "emergence") from quantitative changes in the levels of integration of material elements.

The Marxist is a materialist also in a more common-sense use of the word. Although the Marxist does not argue—as is commonly believed—that only economic or biological values are real, and that the so-called higher values are to be neglected, denied, or "reduced to" the pursuit of economic goods, the Marxist does believe that, in the final analysis, the determining factor in human behavior is to be found in men's relations to the material productive system of their society. Men stand to each other in a context that is organized with respect to the means of production and distribution of goods. What they believe and aspire to, or at least those beliefs and aspirations that are more than individual vagaries and are able to play a determining role in social change, are subtly determined by their social and cultural organization. Social organization is, at its root, a growth from the material needs of men, and the pattern of their thought and action is impressed upon them by the economic system in which they live. Thus, an agricultural economy will have not only a different form of government from that of an industrial economy, but also different art forms, moral ideals, religious beliefs, and philosophical speculation. Feudalism as an economic institution developed its own ideology or rationalization of the arrangement of power in a

[14] From *The German Ideology*, by Karl Marx and Frederick Engels, page 13. New York: International Publishers, 1947.

feudal community; mercantilism had its peculiar ideology or rationalization; capitalistic nationalism has its own; and all will differ from that of a communistic culture.

This does not imply that men always react automatically and mechanically to the economic arrangements. There are unusual individuals in every social group, and the desires and interests of men cannot be neglected in any study of social organization or historical change. But according to Marx, the economic organization does *largely* determine which ideas and interests will be considered normal and acceptable at any given time, and which ones will be only curiosities without historical efficacy.

Philosophy is a "rationalization" of an economic system. The ruling ideas in philosophy, as in art, morality, and religion, says Marx, are the ideas of the ruling class; and the philosophy that appears to us to be best supported intellectually is actually the one that is most fitting to our place in a social system. Philosophizing may be a protest against the ruling ideas that have tended to dignify a given economic system as "eternally justified," or it may be a "defense mechanism" by which we justify the *status quo;* but in neither case can philosophy be mere contemplation of reality. Philosophy is a weapon in the economic conflict between classes; and for this reason, the dialectical materialist prefers to call both technical philosophy and "philosophy of life" by the name, "ideology."

It is not consciousness that determines life, but life that determines consciousness. . . . With the representation [mere contemplation] of reality, independent philosophy loses the medium for its existence.[15]

The philosophers have only *interpreted* the world in various ways; the point, however, is to *change* it.[16]

In the ideal of an independent philosophy, which shall "sur-

---

[15] From *The German Ideology,* by Karl Marx and Frederick Engels, page 15. New York: International Publishers, 1947.

[16] From *Ludwig Feuerbach and the Outcome of Classical German Philosophy,* by Frederick Engels, page 84. New York: International Publishers, 1941.

vey all time and all existence," there is either conscious or unconscious deception, for the notion of a completely objective
knowledge is an empty and unattainable ideal. Self-deception
is present even in an ideology, but the dialectical materialist
recognizes this also as a necessary consequence of man's nature
as a creature of material needs:

> If in all ideology men and their relations appear upside down, as
> in a camera obscura, this phenomenon arises just as much from
> their historical life-process as the reversal of objects on the retina
> does from their directly physical life-process.[17]

"Dialectic" in dialectical materialism

In our discussion of absolute idealism, we examined the
notion of dialectic as developed by Hegel (see page 351). In
Hegel's dialectic, the dynamics of historical change lie in the
logical instability of any partial scheme of ideas (thesis) that
gives rise to another partial scheme (antithesis), until some
reconciliation or synthesis of the opposition is produced.

Marx accepted the Hegelian dialectic, but "stood it on its
head." That is, in the Marxian dialectic, it is, first, nature as a
material order that undergoes dialectical development, and
then society and social institutions carry on a dialectical conflict because of their inimical economic (material) conditions.
Dialectic is carried on at the ideological level as a conflict between opposing ideas, but these only reflect the opposing material interests that give practical relevance to ideological
conflict. In dialectic and history, Engels said, "Hegel confused
the driving forces [ideologies or philosophical ideas] with the
driving forces *behind* the driving forces [the material or economic factors]." ". . . In direct contrast to German philosophy
[Hegelianism], which descends from heaven to earth, here
[in dialectical materialism] the ascent is made from earth to
heaven." [18]

---

[17] From *The German Ideology*, by Karl Marx and Frederick Engels, page
14. New York: International Publishers, 1947.
[18] *Ibid.*

The dialectical process in nature and society introduces new levels of integration and provides the stage on which qualitative novelty is produced by quantitative changes in the relations of matter. Marx was led to this dialectical consideration through Hegel's philosophy of history, and this, he held, was an entirely new line of departure for materialism. Materialism before this time had been metaphysical and dogmatic, having its origin in a natural science not yet seriously affected by the idea of evolutionary change. Hence, materialism prior to Marx was static. But Engels says,

> With each epoch-making discovery even in the sphere of natural science, [materialism] has to change its form; and after history also was subjected to materialistic treatment, here also a new avenue of development was opened.[19]

In eighteenth-century science, man was still regarded as a machine because of the poorly developed status of chemistry as compared with mechanics; but the development of the biological sciences, and especially the idea of evolution from Kant to Darwin, and the development of chemistry with its emphasis upon the variety of properties of matter, prepared the way for a more comprehensive and activistic materialism that could account for a greater variety of facts than a simple, reductive materialism could.

In fact, Engels traces the development of Marx's materialism from the simple form of earlier metaphysical materialism and idealism as itself an example of dialectic:

> The philosophy of antiquity was primitive, natural materialism. As such, it was incapable of clearing up the relation between thought and matter.[20] But the need to get clarity on this question led to the doctrine of a soul separable from the body [psychophysical interactionism], then to the assertion of the immortality of this soul, and finally to monotheism. The old materialism was therefore negated by idealism. But in the course of the further development

---

[19] From *Ludwig Feuerbach and the Outcome of Classical German Philosophy*, by Frederick Engels, page 26. New York: International Publishers, 1947.
[20] Cf. Lucretius, as an example of this difficulty.

of philosophy, idealism too became untenable and was negated by
modern materialism. This modern materialism, the negation of the
negation [that is, the dialectical synthesis] is not the mere re-estab-
lishment of the old, but adds to the permanent foundations of this
old materialism the whole thought-content of two thousand years
of development of philosophy and natural science, as well as of the
historical development of these two thousand years.[21]

The materialistic philosophy of history

The most important contribution of Marx to theoretical philosophy is his view of history. His theory of history has had
wide influence upon historians, even among those who are
neither Marxists in their general philosophical outlook, nor
political communists. There had been materialistic philosophies
of history before Marx, as in the writings of the historians who
emphasized the role of climate and other natural factors in
historical change. But Marx combined Hegel's dialectical conception of history with an emphasis upon the material conditions of social life and movement.

The essentials of his view are very simple. History is a
struggle between classes, and classes are defined by the relations of their members to the productive system. History is
thus the story of the struggles between masters and slaves,
feudal lords and serfs, capitalists and proletarians. Each of
these classes develops its own ideology, on the basis of its needs
and its relation to the wealth of the society, and the ruling
ideas of any period are the ideas of its ruling class. The ideas
of the privileged ruling class are defenses of its favored position in society, which the rulers and the intelligentsia who support them seek to defend by interpreting the whole of reality
from a standpoint that will make their exploitation and rule
over others appear just and natural.

But opposed to any ruling ideology, there is the ideology of
the exploited majority, who are economically motivated to reject
the ruling ideas and who attempt to justify their dissatisfaction

---

[21] From *Anti-Dühring (Herr Eugen Dühring's Revolution in Science)*, by
Frederick Engels, page 152. New York: International Publishers, 1939.

and to correct its causes by appeal to another set of principles, which constitute an antithesis to the ruling philosophy. Reconciliation between the two, according to Marx, is not effected by a mere logical dialectic that brings out the truth of each and synthesizes them into some "higher truth." Rather, the struggle is on the material level, although it is a struggle in which ideas are weapons along with more direct and violent action.

Consider one stage in the dialectic, the one that the Marxist holds exists in a capitalistic society. In such a society, there are two important classes—the owners of the means of production, and the workers who "own" only their labor. They sell their labor for wages to the capitalist, and use these wages to buy the goods they have themselves produced. (The "middle class," in a pinch, has to side with one or the other of these two classes.) For various economic reasons that we cannot here inquire into, Marx believes that such a society is inherently unstable; it cannot prevent unemployment, depression, and war. Gradually, the lot of the proletariat becomes intolerable, and debate between the capitalistic and the working class ceases to be a war of words and becomes actual revolution. Thus we have:

THESIS: capitalists expropriating the working class.
ANTITHESIS: proletarian reaction through organizations for protection of workers' interests.
SYNTHESIS: a classless society, in which the expropriators are expropriated ("negation of the negation") and every man not only works, but owns the means of production.

In this dialectic, the power of the state is originally controlled by the capitalist and is used for the control of the masses; similarly, ethical ideals, patriotism, and the ruling philosophical and religious [21] ideologies are instruments of oppression and control. But after the revolution, these means of exploitation and control are no longer needed. After a short transition period, the state will be expected to "wither away," religion will no longer be needed as a means of social control,

---

[21] Cf. Marx's statement, "Religion is the opiate of the people."

and each man will enjoy complete independence and freedom. The goods of such a society will be distributed to each according to his need, and labor will be freely given by each according to his ability.

Needless to say, things have not worked out in the way Marx envisaged, and the countries under communist domination are not the Utopias he anticipated. Historians and economists have found many flaws in the details of his argument. In spite of this, Marx's emphasis upon the dialectical structure of social movements, and upon the necessity of tracing each social force back to the economic and material conditions that engender and favor it has done much to take the writing of history out of the realm of chronology and chronicles of courtly intrigue, and to show that many facts previously ignored by historians are relevant to the understanding of historical change.

CRITICISM AND CONCLUSION

There are several points to the credit of materialism. First, materialism is the metaphysical theory that, on the whole, has perhaps been most favorable to the development of rigorous scientific knowledge of reality. It combats any tendency to draw a line anywhere in reality and to say, "Beyond this, science cannot go." These lines have been drawn time and time again; but each time it has been crossed, and the obscurantists have had to retreat still further to draw the next line. Materialists believe that the main obstacle to the advancement of science is not the insufficiency of science itself, but the opposition to science by those who wish to have some sheltered refuge from its progress.

Second, and a corollary to this, is the "hard-headedness" of the materialists. From the earliest times, they have been the philosophical "debunkers" who will not be put off with high-flown ideas and inspirations. They assert, often with acerbity, that the unsolved questions of philosophy are in principle like the solved problems of science, and that only time, effort, and courage are required to reduce speculative answers to scientific test.

Opponents of materialism hold that these attitudes of favoring and fostering scientific work, valuable as they are, are not the exclusive prerogative of materialism, and that the same attitudes can be fostered by a metaphysical theory that is less susceptible to destructive criticism.

Let us consider briefly the weaknesses in materialism pointed out by other naturalists; we ignore here the weighty objections to materialism that have been made by theological dualists and idealists, since they should be obvious from our previous exposition of these theories.

Materialism is not in step with science itself

This objection is often voiced nowadays. It is said, correctly, that matter is no longer the ultimate category of physics, but has been replaced by energy. Matter, it is sometimes said, is only "frozen energy," and it can be converted into energy according to the well-known equation of Einstein; matter is converted into energy every time an atomic bomb explodes. Instead of the universe consisting of little hard pebbles of unchanging matter, the atoms are fields of electrical energy.

It is debatable whether this is really a damaging criticism of materialism, as many idealistically or theologically inclined persons assert. In the past, materialism has always adapted to new advances in science; and if what seems to common sense to be hard matter has turned out to be a dance of electrical charges, there is no reason to believe that in its *philosophical* essentials, materialism would be affected by this change in scientific beliefs. After all, the essential thing in materialism is not that the universe consists of "atoms and the void," but *that reality is made up of an immense number of irreducible and identical or almost identical elements that can be studied by scientific analysis and found to follow laws of physics.*

Perhaps the materialist, in view of this advance in physics, would do well to call himself an "energist" instead of a "materialist," but this change in wording seems to be about all that is required by this objection; the essentials of his root metaphor would be little affected by such a change in terminology.

Materialism is dogmatic

Open a materialistic treatise on philosophy at almost any page, and one of the things that immediately strikes your attention is the over-use of such words as "only," "nothing but," "merely," and the like. Energy is "nothing but" the motion of matter; thought is "only" an inchoate motor response to a stimulus; "Light is *nothing* without, but an apparition *only,* all that is real being the concussion or motion of the parts of [the optic] nerve, from which experience we may conclude that apparition of light is *nothing but* motion within"; [22] life is "merely" a complex chemical phenomenon; and so on. While most metaphysicians, perhaps, tend to become dogmatic in the belief that their own theory is *the* truth, materialists seem particularly prone to take a part of experience that seems to them to have the sanction of science and to universalize and absolutize it. In this respect, although they profess to be followers of science, they do not live up to their ideal by admitting that their metaphysics is, after all, only a hypothesis, and that some of the alternative hypotheses have not been so much refuted as shouted down. The materialist often writes as though the hypotheses of science were eternal verities beyond all criticism and examination; and what is often only a sound methodological principle for the practicing scientist is taken by the materialistic metaphysician as an axiom.

The charge of dogmatism is most easily supported against dialectical materialists. In recent years in Russia, instead of materialism changing (as Marx and Engels said it inevitably would) in step with the advances of science, materialism as interpreted by the rulers has become a dogma used as a standard for the evaluation of scientific work itself. Scientific ideas,

---

[22] Thomas Hobbes, *The Elements of Law* (1650), page 4 (Ferdinand Tönnies, ed.). Cambridge, Eng.: University Press, 1928.

like those in philosophy, art, and literature, have been subjected to tests of metaphysical orthodoxy and political reliabil-
ity. This, of course, is a prostitution of power unworthy of
adherents of a philosophical theory that claims to be based
upon the methods and results of science.

Materialism does not do justice to the consideration of values

According to this objection, which is widely made, materialism degrades everything to a material basis and neglects the
higher values of art, morality, and religion. There is some truth
in this objection, although perhaps not as much as commonly
believed. Antimaterialists, such as theological dualists, hold
that human values depend upon some transcendental spiritual
foundation, and this is denied by the materialist; but that has
not usually led materialistic philosophers to deny that these
spiritual values are important to men. It is not true that materialists in philosophy always, or even usually, are materialists
in the common connotation of the word—men devoted to the
indulgence of the flesh, or the lust for money or power. And
the materialist rejects the charge because he says that only
through increasing our knowledge of the material conditions of
life can we take the pursuit and criticism of value out of the
obscurity to which it has been relegated by idealists and theologians. By studying the material conditions of the experience
and pursuit of value, they rightly say, we may be able to use
scientific knowledge to further the pursuit of ideals more successfully than we can in a society where some men devote
themselves to the "higher spiritual values" with such assiduity
that people in the next street starve to death.

There is a sense, however, in which this charge is justified.
Because the universe is considered by the materialist to be a
realm of "hard fact," with considerations of value extruded into
the limbo of an epiphenomenal mind having a very low status
in the eternal order of things, materialism has probably sometimes had the effect of restricting the use of intelligence to the
investigation of fact, as though consideration of value were not

quite respectable from an intellectual standpoint. If one believes that value is only a subjective, epiphenomenal aspect of hard fact, it is easy to see why one might not be inclined to use much intelligence in studying and formulating principles and laws of value. The consequence of this attitude is that values become intellectual "poor relations" of facts, and that reasonable consideration of the ends of life is neglected in the process of perfecting the tools that might be used as instruments for their attainment. This has to some extent happened in our own culture, which has solved many questions of means to ends but has left the ends of life so unexamined that the means to values are easily prostituted to base purposes. Machines, which result from intellectual genius, are uncontrolled by any widespread and profound grasp of the values they might be made to serve. This has happened to a much greater degree in cultures dominated by a materialistic ideology.

Materialism commits the error of pseudo-simplicity

One of the strongest points in favor of materialism is its simplicity; the world consists of only one kind of thing, and there is only one kind of law in the world. But, it is argued, the simplicity that the materialist finds in matter is spurious, for having defined simple matter as a basic category, the materialist must endow it with "indefinite potentiality" to be and to appear to be all the various things that we find in the world. Thus, matter in the ordinary sense has only the primary qualities and the physical and chemical properties that the scientist ascribes to it; but the world is full of colored things, for instance, so the materialist must attribute to his matter the "potentiality" of producing color under certain psychological conditions. Some of the materialists, as we have seen, even attribute the potentiality of consciousness directly to matter. Hence to matter, simple *in name,* is attributed indefinite complexity and potentiality, so that matter as it is ordinarily understood in science is not adequate as a basis for the explanations predicated upon it.

Materialism commits the fallacy of misplaced concreteness

The adjective "abstract" refers to some aspect or character or part of a thing that cannot exist or be found in isolation from it; thus, "red" is abstract. "Concrete," on the other hand, refers to a thing having many properties and capable of existing in itself. For example, a living animal is concrete, while life is abstract. Whitehead says that the fallacy of misplaced concreteness occurs whenever a philosopher takes some abstract characteristic of a thing and treats it as the concrete reality.

This occurs in materialism. What I see before me is a table, with primary and secondary qualities, sentimental and economic value, aesthetic qualities as well as molecular constitution. But the materialist makes an abstraction from this, and considers only its primary physical and chemical properties, which exist as properties of the concrete object, as being the *real* properties of the *real* table. All the other properties are banished from reality. This is an example of misplaced concreteness, just as damaging in its philosophical consequences as if one were to make the color of the table ultimately real, and say its shape was only an illusory appearance.

Because the world does have, *prima facie,* a great many characteristics that matter, by hypothesis, does not have, anyone who commits the fallacy of misplaced concreteness must find some limbo for the unreal appearances of things. In materialism, this is usually found in the realm of the mind, which is regarded as an epiphenomenon of a low degree of reality. The real world is impoverished, because all values and sensuous qualities are extruded from it. While this impoverishment of reality has been of use in "tidying up" nature so that it can be studied by the parsimonious methods of science, it has produced a metaphysics that does justice to only one part of reality. For in this metaphysics, what appears is not real, and what is real does not appear. The realm of phenomena becomes a kind of limbo containing everything "reality" lacks.

Materialism is self-refuting

To the extent that materialism implies the belief that mind is not an effective agent in the world, it leads to epiphenomenalism. And as we have seen, epiphenomenalism cannot be intellectually defended as a general principle, however useful it may be to the psychologist who takes it as a postulate for his behavioristic or physiological explanations of another's behavior. It is self-refuting, for if it is true, no argument would be able to establish it; and if an argument is given for it, it would have to be based on grounds of rational determination of the behavior of the mind that controls the hand that writes the proof. This is impossible because epiphenomenalism argues that the *only* effective factors are physiological causes.

Hence epiphenomenalism, although useful as a postulate in psychology, is inadequate as a metaphysical thesis.

Materialism's theory of knowledge is inadequate

Even if the materialists, strictly speaking, have no right to speak of ideas and other mental entities that seem to be involved in knowing, they do acknowledge a sphere of consciousness of qualities and feelings. They assert that these qualities do not resemble the qualities of the real objects in the world, but are simply effects that these objects produce upon us. And this is, in essence, the thesis of Locke. We have already seen that it is inadequate as a theory of knowledge. Locke and the materialists make so sharp a distinction between the qualities and status of what we do experience and of what they assert to be real as substance or matter, that it is difficult or impossible to see how we could have any of the knowledge they claim to have about the existence and character of the real world.

Criticism of Locke's theory of knowledge was one of the starting points of idealism, as we have seen in Chapter 10. If a naturalistic metaphysics is to be established, it must have a realistic theory of knowledge that will be able to withstand the criticisms of Berkeley and other idealists, and it can hardly do so by making use of the Lockean dichotomy between the world of substantial reality and a world of insubstantial appearances, ideas, or epiphenomena. Realistic theories of knowledge that may be able to withstand such criticisms will be dealt with in the next chapter, where we shall be concerned with naturalistic theories that are not narrowly materialistic.

BIBLIOGRAPHY

Materialism

Broad, C. D., *The Mind and its Place in Nature*. London: Harcourt, Brace and Company, Ltd., 1925. Chapter 1.

Büchner, Ludwig, *Force and Matter* (1855). New York: Eckler, 1920.

Burnet, John, *Early Greek Philosophy*. London: Black, 1920. Chapters 5, 6, and 9.

Elliot, Hugh, *Modern Science and Materialism*. New York: Longmans Green and Company, Ltd., 1915.

Hobbes, Thomas, *Hobbes Selections* (Frederick J. E. Woodbridge, ed.). New York: Charles Scribner's Sons, 1928.

La Mettrie, Julien de, *Man a Machine* (1748). Chicago: Open Court Publishing Company, 1927.

Lange, Friedrich Albert, *History of Materialism* (1866), third ed. New York: Harcourt, Brace and Company, Inc., 1915.

Montague, William Pepperell, *The Ways of Things*. New York: Prentice-Hall, Inc., 1940. Chapters 13 and 15.

Perry, Ralph Barton, *Present Philosophical Tendencies*. New York: Longmans, Green & Company, Inc., 1912. Pages 57-84.

Sellars, Roy Wood, Farber, Marvin, and McGill, V. J. (eds.), *Philosophy for the Future. The Quest of Modern Materialism*. New York: The Macmillan Company, 1949.

Dialectical materialism

Brameld, Theodore, *A Philosophic Approach to Communism*. Chicago: University of Chicago Press, 1933.

Dewey, John, *Freedom and Culture*. New York: G. P. Putnam's Sons, 1939.

Haldane, J. B. S., *The Marxist Philosophy and the Sciences*. New York: Random House, 1939.

Laski, Harold J., *Communism*. New York: Henry Holt and Company, Inc., 1927.

Marck, Siegfried, "Dialectical Materialism," in *A History of Philosophical Systems* (Vergilius Ferm, ed.). New York: Philosophical Library, 1950. Chapter 24.

Marx, Karl, and Engels, Frederick, *The Communist Manifesto* (1848). Many editions.

Sheen, Fulton J., *Communism and the Conscience of the West*. Indianapolis: Bobbs-Merrill Company, 1948.

Somerville, John, "Dialectical Materialism," in *Twentieth Century Philosophy* (Dagobert D. Runes, ed.). New York: Philosophical Library, 1947. Pages 511-538.

————, *Soviet Philosophy. A Study of Theory and Practice*. New York: Philosophical Library, 1946.

Venable, Vernon, *Human Nature, The Marxist View*. New York: Alfred A. Knopf, 1945.

Zirkle, Conway (ed.), *The Death of a Science in Russia*. Philadelphia: University of Pennsylvania Press, 1949.

QUESTIONS AND TOPICS FOR DISCUSSION

1. Discuss some of the ways in which modern materialism differs from ancient materialism. Ought we to use the same word to describe the Greek belief in material atoms and that of modern philosophers who base their work on modern science?
2. Can a *skeptic* be a materialist?
3. Compare mechanism in biology (Chapter 6) with materialism. Could a biologist be a mechanist, yet reject materialism as a system of philosophy?
4. Some antimaterialists have rejoiced that "materialism is dead" because the physicists now explain matter in terms of energy. Is this rejoicing justified?
5. Many people complain that we live in a "materialistic age." What does this mean? Do you think that they could "reform" the "materialists" by criticizing the metaphysical theory of materialism?
6. Dialectical materialists have claimed that their theory is really a science; others have said that both it and communism are more like theology and religion. Discuss.
7. "Communism is a Christian heresy." Evaluate.
8. What ethical doctrines would you expect to have a "family relationship" with materialism?

9. Can the present situation in Russia—assuming that it is as commonly pictured—properly be interpreted as an "indictment of the theory of dialectical materialism"?

10. Can a man be a Marxist in philosophy and not be a communist in politics?

11. Read one of the following books and point out the human relevance of some of the philosophical theories stated or implied:
    (a) Turgenev's *Fathers and Sons.*
    (b) Hauptmann's *Lonesome Lives.*
    (c) Koestler's *Arrival and Departure.*
    (d) Koestler's *Darkness at Noon.*

13

Naturalism — Continued

About 40 years ago there were forces, both social and intellectual, that brought about a decline in the popularity of the various metaphysical theories we have been discussing, and elicited a "Reconstruction in Philosophy."

Theological dualism, with its tendency to exempt certain areas of experience, such as the religious and the moral, from scientific examination, was challenged by the growing strength of sciences that invaded the precincts of religious thought. The Darwinian theory of evolution, first announced in 1859 and widely accepted by the end of the nineteenth century, not only impugned the accuracy of the Biblical account of creation, but also made many thinkers give up the religious answer to the question, "What is man?" The stability of the religious doctrines that had been the constant ballast for European and American thought for centuries was upset by a growing secularism in all phases of life, and optimism was soon shattered in the cataclysm of war.

Idealism, which had been one of the dominant movements, was challenged and eclipsed by a variety of new interests and doctrines. Its theory of knowledge was attacked by many philosophers, and its belief in the ultimate status of mind seemed unable to cope with new views of mind coming from Darwinian biology and from behaviorism and Freudianism in psychology. Idealism, rightly or wrongly, seemed unable to adjust itself to the empirical discoveries of science and the practical exigencies of a technological civilization. "Ideals are all very well," the representatives of the new century seemed to say, "but we are more interested in realities—in hard facts discovered but not created by mind."

Materialism, however, was unable to exploit the situation brought about by the decline of its old rivals. Had idealism done nothing else, it was important because it had exposed the epistemological superficiality of materialism. Materialism put its own interpretation upon the facts of science and called it metaphysics; but the work of scientists like Einstein and Planck made the materialistic interpretation seem superficial even in its account of the results of science.

While none of these attacks and counterattacks were sufficient to "refute" the metaphysical theories, they did show a general dissatisfaction with the kind of conclusions that metaphysicians had traditionally drawn. Philosophy is always responsive to much more than the demands of professional philosophers for consistency of system and elegance of argument. It is responsive to the needs of men who are not primarily philosophers, but thinkers sensitive to the intellectual and moral currents of their time. The twentieth century, with its confusion and hurry and horrors mixed with stupendous advances in science and technology, has not, on the whole, been satisfied with the thoughts of earlier generations. It has required a new philosophy, or at least, a new emphasis in philosophy that would take account of its peculiar problems.

Any philosophy responsive to the temper of our period must be thought to be "scientific" yet sensitive to the claims of the implicit religious, moral, and political ideals of our culture.[1] It must be tentative in its conclusions and not too sweeping in its claim that it has apprehended the ultimate truths and values.

---

[1] Cf. Joseph Wood Krutch, *The Modern Temper.* New York: Harcourt, Brace and Company, Inc., 1929.

It must not be Utopian, but fully cognizant of the confusions of our life, and patient in its inquiry into their sources and into ways of resolving them. It must, in the common-sense meaning of these words, be realistic and practical. That they are formulating such a *Weltanschauung* is the claim of the philosophers called critical naturalists.

CRITICAL NATURALISM

Nature as the ultimate category

Critical naturalism (frequently called simply "naturalism") is based upon a broader conception of nature than that found in materialism. Materialists begin with a conception of nature as essentially the subject-matter of the natural sciences, and contrast nature to the realm of value, spirit, culture, and mind; then they "reduce" the latter realm to the former and say that the world is ultimately only what it is found to be in physics. Critical naturalists, on the other hand, do not begin with a distinction between what is natural and what belongs allegedly to some other realm of being; they say that the distinction between what is natural and what is not is predicated upon too thin and homogeneous a conception of nature.

If by nature we mean only what is studied in the "natural" sciences, then, of course, distinctions between nature and society, fact and value, body and mind, the secular and the sacred, and the like, must be drawn. For the natural sciences do not study culture, or value, or the more complex human affairs and interests. But, say the naturalists, all of these phases of experience arise in the course of nature and have a legitimate claim to be considered "natural." A conception that identifies nature with matter in motion is not synoptic enough to deal fairly with those parts of experience not already mastered by scientific experimentation. So while the materialist denies their significance or tries to force them into the mold of material nature, the critical naturalist attempts to broaden the concept of nature so that it will contain them without doing violence to their difference from mere matter in motion. Shakespeare recognized the unjustified narrowness of the term "nature" as usually employed. He clearly brought out the need for a more panoramic conception. His characters in *A Winter's Tale* (IV, iv) are discussing some flowers that had been cultivated by the art of grafting, and one of them objects to these flowers as being "unnatural," that is, as not arising in the course of nature understood to be alien to man and his works. But another says,

> Yet nature is made better by no mean
> But nature makes that mean; so, over that art
> Which you say adds to nature, is an art
> Which nature makes.
> . . . This is an art
> Which does mend nature, change it rather, but
> The art itself is nature.

Generalizing on this kind of consideration, the critical naturalist says that we ought not to ascribe to nature merely material, savage, animal, or brutish parts of man, only to have to find some supernatural explanation for his culture, art, science, and religion. Man and all his works appear in nature and are to be best understood as all of a piece, although this is not just a piece of matter in motion.

We can see the contrast between the naturalist and the antinaturalist best, perhaps, in regard to the question of the origin and status of morals. The antinaturalists, from the earliest times, have held that nature is too brutely factual, too indifferent from the standpoint of value, to explain men's experiences of value. Their thesis is summed up in Matthew Arnold's verses "To an Independent Preacher":

> Know, man hath all which Nature hath, but more,
> And in that *more* lie all his hopes of good.

Their only disagreement turns on what this "more" really is.

It may be a revelation of God, or reason, or some transcendental moral sense, or the like. But the naturalist replies,

Moral feelings are not innate but acquired, [but] they are not for that reason less natural. It is natural for man to speak, to reason, to build cities, to cultivate the ground, though these are acquired faculties. The moral feelings are not indeed a part of our nature, in the sense of being in any perceptible degree present in all of us; but this, unhappily, is a fact admitted by those who believe the most strenuously in their transcendental origin. Like the other acquired faculties above referred to, the moral faculty, if not a part of our nature, is a *natural* outgrowth from it.[2]

Thus the naturalist agrees with the materialist in opposing any division between a realm of nature and a realm of mind, or value, or God. But he agrees with the theological dualist that "matter in motion" is not an adequate metaphor for "reality." So he takes the monism of the materialist and combines it with the frank acknowledgement of diversity and value that was insisted upon by idealist and theological dualist. In this way he conceives of nature in the broadest possible sense: it is whatever really is, and this is more than matter in motion.

Why, then, call "reality" by the name "nature"? The reason for this metaphor we have already seen: it is that the naturalist asserts that the whole of reality is subject to the same kind of study that has already gone far toward mastering that part of reality which everyone agrees in calling nature. The critical naturalist says that whatever is claimed as knowledge must be justified by careful empirical enquiry, like that to which the natural sciences are devoted. Whatever any experience offers as insight into reality must be tested before it is accepted; no credence is to be given to intuitions or *a priori* insights. They are, at most, kinds of experiences that must be tested to see if what they suggest is true. As valuable kinds of experience, and as possible sources of knowledge, the naturalist is interested in cultivating, enjoying, and examining them. He does not dog-

---

[2] John Stuart Mill, *Utilitarianism* (1863) (Oskar Piest, ed.), page 32. New York: Liberal Arts Press, 1948 (The Little Library of Liberal Arts, No. 1.) (italics supplied).

matically pronounce them absurd, as the materialists tend to do.

Many beliefs incompatible with strict materialism are able to pass such an empirical test, and the critical naturalist accepts them. For instance, he accepts the reality of purposes in living organisms, while still denying that nature is designed "for a purpose." He finds that he can best explain biological phenomena on the hypothesis that animal behavior is goal-seeking. He therefore refuses to reject, on the basis of a metaphysical dogma of materialism, the evidence of purposes in behavior. Without becoming a vitalist, he broadens the conception of nature to include the phenomena that the vitalist had interpreted as evidence for some supernatural agency. Already, in Chapter 6, we have discussed the theory that life is an emergent within nature from physico-chemical processes. This theory, or others very much like it, would be accepted by most critical naturalists but, of course, denied by materialists.

To consider another example of belief held by naturalists but not by most materialists, take the difference between their conceptions of value. The materialist regards man as merely a complex animal, and his actions as mere reactions to stimuli. Most of the higher value experiences are "reduced" to the subjective pleasures of physiological responses. While the idealist and the theological dualist "denature" values and place them in some realm above that of nature understood scientifically, the naturalist considers men's pursuit of values as perfectly natural, growing out of their natural environment and context. But the naturalist does not "reduce" value experience to mere physiological response to physical stimuli; he holds, on the contrary, that value experience shows that men have potentialities that are neglected or denied if man is understood merely as a reactive mechanism. The critical naturalist seeks to render the ideals and moral rules of men intelligible by interpreting them as empirically established habits or rules that have been found relatively successful in guiding men in their quest for deep and abiding satisfactions.

While many different theories on both these subjects have been held by members of the school of critical naturalism, discussions in previous chapters are fairly typical of the kind of conclusions to which many of them have come. There is no need, therefore, to go into further detail on these topics. The remainder of this chapter is devoted to a brief examination of the views of some naturalists concerning knowledge and its objects, the nature of mind, and the nature and value of religion.

Realistic theories of perception

A naturalist rejects any theory of knowledge and perception, like that of Berkeley and other idealists, that implies that the objects we perceive depend upon the mind or upon consciousness of them. The naturalist has a realistic theory of perception,[3] according to which the objects perceived exist whether perceived or not, and have the properties they are perceived to have.

In previous discussions of the problem of perception (Chapter 10), we have encountered two realistic theories of perception—one, a forerunner of idealism, the other, a reaction against idealism. The first was the theory of John Locke. It is generally called representative realism, because it holds that there is a real object (substance), represented by ideas that it causes; we directly experience ideas, and indirectly know the objects that they represent and, in part, resemble. The second was the theory known as neo-realism, whose thesis is that we directly know an object as it really is, and that the object we directly know is not an idea dependent upon any mind, human or divine.

Neo-realism—According to the neo-realists,[4] some of whom

---

[3] Realism as a theory of perception is different from Platonic realism (page 125), the assertion of the reality of universals. While most naturalists are not Platonic realists, all naturalists are in some sense realistic in their theory of perception.

[4] Cf. the collaborative volume, *The New Realism*. New York: The Macmillan Company, 1912.

were among the most influential American philosophers in the first quarter of the present century, the object I see before me is a physical object, existing in a network of spatial, temporal, and causal relations. I am directly aware of the physical object, and not of a mental duplicate or poor copy of it. The object itself is in my consciousness as it actually is; being in or out of consciousness makes no difference to its properties or its being. It is, when I know it, "in" my consciousness, but it is not "in" my consciousness in the way that a picture is in an album, for consciousness is not a kind of "receptacle" that can hold only one kind of thing, namely, ideas. Rather, consciousness might be compared to a searchlight, illuminating objects without making a photograph of them that it substitutes for the real thing. We should not allow the spatial term "in" to suggest that consciousness is a kind of "place" for a certain kind of thing we call ideas. The neo-realists say that objects can be "in the mind" or "in consciousness" in the very ordinary sense of the words in which I can say to someone, "I have kept you in mind."

The neo-realists agree with Berkeley that we directly perceive what is real, but disagree with Berkeley in denying that what is real is an idea dependent for its existence upon its being in consciousness. They agree with Locke that there are real things in the world apart from and independent of all perception, but disagree with him by saying that we directly perceive them instead of apprehending some copy or representation of them.

Each of these theories has certain weaknesses. We have examined Locke's theory and seen how it cannot consistently remain realistic but easily leads to idealism, since it cannot demonstrate or even show the need of an unknown substratum or cause of ideas.

The problem of error—The neo-realistic theory foundered on another kind of question, the question of how error or illusion is possible. What is the status of the after-image I see when I close my eyes, if what I see exists independently of the perceiving of it? What is the explanation of my seeing a bent stick when a straight stick is put into water at an angle? The question is not how we know that these experiences are illusory if taken to be accurate perceptions of ordinary physical things; it is rather a question of the nature of the thing that we are experiencing when we are having such an illusory perception.

It seems fairly simple to say, with Locke, that illusory ideas are ideas in the mind that do not correspond to anything in external reality. But if one says that, we have seen that a good case can be made for concluding, with Berkeley, that *everything* is in the mind, even the things that we suppose we correctly perceive. The neo-realists refuse to accept Locke's answer, for it would lead to Berkeley's idealism. They take the bull by the horns and assert that illusory objects are not in a realm of mind but in the realm of nonmental being, along with objects of correct perception.

Being, they say, is made up of two kinds of entities: subsistent entities and existent entities. A subsistent entity is anything conceivable, imaginable, or mentionable, but not existing, that is, not having a particular position in space and time, or at least not having a position on which different individuals can agree. Such subsistent entities are universals or imaginary objects, such as a unicorn, a square circle, the sea-coast of Bohemia, the number i, and so on. An existent entity, on the other hand, is one that has a status in space and time and stands in causal relations to others. Thus a horse exists, while a unicorn only subsists. When I see a horse, I see an existent entity; if I think I see a unicorn, I am not seeing a "complex of ideas," as Locke would say, but a subsistent entity, a unicorn that does not exist. Perception is awareness of existent objects; illusion is awareness of merely subsistent entities as though they were existent.

Most philosophers now believe that this is only a "verbal solution" to the problem of illusion. It gives a name to the contents of illusory experience, but it leaves most questions about the occurrence of illusory perceptions unanswered. It immensely complicates the conception of being, by attributing subsistent being to some very queer entities that could not have any place in the world of science or common sense. Realistic philosophers have therefore generally given up this theory. A great variety of realistic epistemological theories have been devised to replace it, some of them resembling Locke's,[5] and others veering perilously close to Berkeley's.[6] It cannot be said that there is a single theory of perception now generally accepted by all or by a clear majority of the members of the realistic school. In the remainder of this section we shall discuss only one of the theories, the one that seems to be particularly suitable to a naturalistic metaphysics. It is the theory generally known as objective relativism.[7]

Objective relativism—According to objective relativism, a thing is what it is in a context of relationships to other things. To consider it to be what it is in only one of its contexts is to commit the fallacy of misplaced concreteness, to confuse an abstract conception of it with its actual being, which is what it is in the totality of its relationships. Indeed, nothing, so far as we know, does exist in isolation from everything else. Certainly, when we know an object, we know it not only in relation to us, but in relation to other objects that environ and affect it. An object is heavy only in a gravitational field that includes other objects attracting it; how heavy it is depends upon its mass in relation to the masses of other things, and an absolutely isolated object would have neither mass nor weight. How large an object is depends upon the ratio of its dimensions to those of some other object; an absolutely isolated object could not be said to be of any particular size. The color

---

[5] Typical of these is the theory of "critical realism" in America and various theories of the "sense datum" in England. For the former, see *Essays in Critical Realism* (London: Macmillan and Company, Ltd., 1920); for the latter, H. H. Price, *Perception* (London: Methuen and Company, 1932), and C. D. Broad, *The Mind and its Place in Nature* (London: Harcourt, Brace and Company, Ltd., 1925).

[6] For instance, Bertrand Russell in some of his books argues that an object is a "construction out of sense data," but holds that sense data are not ideas dependent on minds.

[7] For the comparable theory of values, see above, pages 212 ff.

we attribute to an object depends not only on the functioning of the eye that sees it, but also on the composition of the light that falls upon its surface, and so on, through all the qualities we ascribe to objects.

Theaetetus (see page 57) was saying something like this when he recognized that what we perceive depends not only on *it,* but also on *ourselves in relation to it.* But Theaetetus, as we have seen, relativized all perceptual experience to such an extent that he could not account for the difference between accurate and illusory perception. The modern relativist wishes not to fall into this kind of skepticism, and he points out a very important distinction that Theaetetus neglected. It is the distinction between the relation of an object to the perceiving person and its relation to other objects. While Theaetetus was correct in noticing that the object of perception is related to the perceiver, he did not see that the object's qualities depend not only on this highly variable relation, but also upon its more stable relations to other objects in its context. It is the emphasis upon the latter kind of relation, a relativity among objects, that gives this theory its name, *objective* relativism.

All of the qualities attributed to an object depend upon its relations to its context of other objects. Some depend upon the context that includes the nervous system and mind of the organism that responds to it. The former qualities are the qualities called primary, and because they do not depend upon the relation of an object to a particular organism's nervous system, with all the peculiarities that distinguish it from that of other organisms, they are the qualities about which there can be considerable agreement among individuals. They are the qualities we adduce when we give a scientific explanation of the behavior of objects, the qualities we usually think belong to the object intrinsically, as it really is. But they do not belong intrinsically to the object. They are relational properties in a context of objects that is so easily agreed upon, so easily standardized, so comprehensive in its scope, that its effect is commonly ignored. That is why we ordinarily think of weight as belonging to an object intrinsically, and do not add that its weight is dependent upon the earth and would be different on another planet. We say, "This book weighs a pound"; we do not say, "On the earth, at this latitude, this book weighs a pound." We take for granted the context in which primary qualities are determined; but we should not, in philosophical analysis, allow this to hide the fact that even the primary qualities are contextually determined.

The secondary qualities are more obviously determined by context, because the context in which they appear includes human beings with all their variability. The secondary qualities emerge in relation to a sentient organism,[8] but they do not emerge in a realm of mind set over against the realm of nature. According to the objective relativist, a secondary quality is no more "in the mind" than the weight of an object is "in the earth," although the mind is necessary to the emergence of the former just as the earth is necessary to the phenomenon we call the weight of the object.

For theoretical accuracy, we ought to say, "This book, using a spring-scale, weighs one pound in relation to the earth," and, "This apple is red in relation to me." In each case, there is a context that ought to be stated when we attribute a property to an object. When that context includes ourselves, it is especially important to indicate this, for the personal context varies from individual to individual. In all cases of perception, of course, there is a personal context, but often its effect can be minimized so that social agreement on perception can be reached. Thus, for instance, there is no need to say, "This book weighs a pound in relation to the earth and to me," for the "to me" is probably not a significant factor in determining what the weight of the book is.

---

[8] In this respect, objective relativism as a theory of perception is closest to objective relativism in the theory of value (see pages 213 ff.). If an object is considered in relation to an organism's interest, we attribute value to the object, and if it is related to an organism's sensory processes, we attribute secondary qualities to it. This explains why values are even more variable from person to person than, for instance, the colors they attribute to an object. Values are sometimes called "tertiary qualities" in order to show their similarity to and difference from the secondary qualities.

Everyone on earth can agree on its weight. For this reason, therefore, objective relativists believe that they can escape the skeptical conclusions Theaetetus was made to infer from his relativism. The objective relativist asserts that the most important kind of relativity in establishing the properties of an object is the relativity of one object to another, and not its relativity to us.

Proponents of objective relativism believe that their theory meets the objections brought against the other realistic theories of perception. As against Locke, it does not take secondary qualities "into the mind" in such a way that the real object outside of consciousness becomes a dubious hypothesis. And against neo-realism, objective relativists believe they have a simple and plausible theory of error.

When I look at a straight stick in water and it appears bent, the theory tells us that this is what should be expected in this context. Visual straightness is a property of tactually straight sticks in a context in which rays of light going from it to the eyes or a camera are not distorted by passing from one medium to another. Visual bentness, on the other hand, is a property of tactually straight sticks in a context in which the rays of light going from it to the eyes are refracted by passing from one medium to another. I would be in error if I said that the physical, tactual stick is bent by being put into water; water, fortunately, does not have the property of bending physical sticks when they are put into it at an angle. But I am not in any error if I say that under the conditions of visual observation, it *appears* to be bent, or that the stick in the visual context *is* bent.

It is not that there is a straight stick "in the world" and a bent stick "in my mind" or "in the realm of subsistent entities." Rather, "the shape of the stick" is an ambiguous term, and we must specify the context in which we are speaking of shape. The shape of the stick as a tactual, physical object, in a context of straightedges and compasses, is not affected by its being put into water. But the shape of the stick as a visual object, in the

COMPARISON OF FOUR IMPORTANT THEORIES OF PERCEPTION

Philosopher or Type of View	What Is Directly Experienced	Status of Objects in External World	Status of Illusions	Theory of Mind
Locke, representative realism (pages 321-324)	Ideas of sensation and ideas of reflection (ideas of activity of mind)	Substances, unknown causes of sensation, having primary qualities and power to produce ideas of color, odor, and so on	Complex ideas in mind not corresponding to substance	Mind as thinking substance; Cartesian dualism
Berkeley, idealism (pages 326-336)	Ideas, and notions of spirit or mind	Ideas in God's mind	Ideas in my mind, but not in God's; ideas that are not organized and regular	Mind as active, creative, ultimate reality
Neo-realists (pages 422-425)	Real objects selected by attention and behavior of organism	Existent objects having all properties they are perceived to have, and spatiotemporal and causal relations to others	Subsistent entities without location in objective space or causal relations	Mind as a relation between objects and organism; "searchlight theory"
Objective relativists (pages 425-430)	Objects in a context including other objects and organisms, thereby having both primary and secondary qualities	Objects, considered without reference to the context of the perceiving organism, and thereby having only primary qualities	Objects in a context including the organism or medium of perception as a determining condition, but interpreted without reference to this condition	Mind as an emergent from organism and its purposive relation to environment; mind as functional, or a "way of acting" (pages 430-437)

context of light rays and eyes or cameras, is affected by this context.

We cannot say what the shape of the stick is apart from every context. We are usually interested in how the stick behaves as a tactual, physical object, in causal relation to other sticks, the pressure of the water, and so on. There is, therefore, good practical reason for saying that the stick is "really straight" and only "seems bent." But this is only a statement of a very natural and justified preference for dealing with the stick in those contexts in which its behavior and properties are uniform, simple, and permanent, in which it does not physically bend as it is put into water and straighten out when it is withdrawn, or grow smaller as it recedes from my eyes.

There is a pragmatic or practical element involved in perception, in choosing among the various contexts in which we describe objects, and in choosing which of the various appearances of things (that is, visual rather than tactual) we shall call illusory. We normally say that an object "really" is what it seems to be in the context in which we use it practically or refer to it as a cause of changes in other physical objects. But it would be an error of misplaced concreteness if we regarded its properties in that kind of context as being metaphysically real, and all its other properties as subjective or illusory.

The naturalists' conception of the mind

From the number and variety of theories examined in this book concerning the nature of mind, the reader will rightly infer that this is one of the most perennially baffling problems of metaphysics. All the theories we have examined agree on one point: they all deal with mind as though it were either a thing (in technical philosophical language, a substance) or a property of a thing, and they disagree only about the nature of this thing (is it mental? or physical?), or about the relation of one of its properties to another. The naturalist opposes all of them by saying that mind is not a thing or substance, but a way of acting. Mind is not an occult agency that makes us act in certain ways; it is the name we give to a way of acting. Mind is minding. This view of mind is frequently called the "functional theory."

At first glance, this theory seems either obscure or absurd, or both. We are so in the habit of using "mind" as a noun, as a name for something that seems somehow to be "in our heads" and causally related to our brain, that it takes some effort at reorienting our ways of thinking to grasp the point of this theory. But the naturalist believes it is worth the effort; for although our common language suggests and almost forces us to think of mind as a kind of thing, mind as a thing or substance has never been observed. "Its" workings are all that we observe. "Its" workings are the conscious and intelligent behavior of ourselves or others. The naturalist therefore proposes that we use the word to denote what we *do* observe in intelligent, conscious behavior of ourselves and others, and not speculate about a hidden entity supposed to be the cause of this behavior.

This way of looking at mind is, in fact, very old, but was displaced first by the Christian theory of the soul as a substance created by God, and then by the Cartesian theory of two kinds of beings, extended objects and minds. Aristotle, however, had a functional theory of mind, and compared the relation of body and mind to the relation between an axe and cutting, or between an eye and seeing: "If the eye were an animal eyesight would be its soul." [9] The seeing eye is not an unseeing anatomical entity plus something else existing as a different kind of being—sight; a cutting axe is not a piece of metal plus another being whose faculty is only "to cut." Rather, cutting and seeing are functions of the substances in question, not properties of something else hidden within them. Similarly, Aristotle holds that "mind" or "soul" as applied to human beings is simply a name for certain faculties of action. They are names for potentialities that are manifested in specific ways in specific circumstances. For instance, I have the power to digest food even

---

[9] Aristotle, *De Anima*, p. 412b (R. D. Hicks, trans.). Cambridge, Eng.: University Press, 1907.

when I am not doing so, but the evidence that I have this potentiality is that under specific circumstances I do actually digest it. Aristotle, then, quite consistently (although it sounds strange to modern ears) says that I have a "nutritive" soul, not a *thing* in my stomach that in some way interacts with my body so as to digest food, but a potentiality for action that is actualized when I eat.

In modern times, we use the words "soul" or "mind" in a more specific sense to refer to that which, we commonly believe, *makes* us think, feel, will, be aware, and act more or less intelligently. We do not use the word "soul" to refer to our digestive powers, but, according to the critical naturalist, what Aristotle says about the nutritive soul suggests what modern philosophers and psychologists should say about what is ordinarily called "the mind." Mind is not a thing, but a way of acting. James succinctly describes the kind of action in question: "The pursuance of future ends and the choice of means for their attainment are . . . the mark and criterion for the presence of mentality in a phenomenon." [10]

The mark of intelligent behavior, which is possible only through the integrative action of the nervous system, is the organism's ability to adjust to stimuli impinging upon it in the light of the needs and conditions existing in the body and built up there through past actions and reactions. One of the most obvious differences between the behavior of a machine and that of an organism is that a machine reacts in an automatic, trigger-like way to the forces acting upon it, and does not "take account of" the consequences of its action. An organism, on the contrary, responds sometimes in one way and sometimes in another to objectively identical stimuli. How it reacts depends not only on the stimulus itself, but also on what is going on in various parts of the organism's body as a consequence of past experience that arouses memories and expectations. Animals

---

[10] William James, *The Principles of Psychology*, Vol. I, page 8. New York: Henry Holt and Company, Inc., 1890.

differ greatly in their abilities to choose means for the pursuit of future ends; man has this ability to a preeminent degree.

The difference between the behavior of an intelligent organism like man and one that is merely trained or whose reflexes are thoroughly conditioned is almost as great as that between a machine and an organism. The intelligent organism has a much greater capacity for variable adaptive responses to identical stimuli. My dog "Blue Tooth," who has been conditioned to walk with me, becomes excited whenever he sees me pick up his leash; he will do this as readily in the middle of a stormy night when his master is wearing pajamas as on a sunny spring day. An intelligent person, on the other hand, reacts in one way to a stimulus under one set of conditions and in another way under other conditions, and all these conditions need not be physically acting upon him at the moment. The mark of intelligence is that the person responds not just to stimuli, but to their meanings. Their meanings are not physical properties of the stimuli, but are their interpreted implications for what is not physically present.

An animal can be trained to react to a stimulus in the same way that he has formerly reacted to what follows it. Such a stimulus we call a *signal*. Pavlov's dogs reacted to the sound of a buzzer by secreting saliva, for through training, a connection had been established between hearing the buzzer and the response to the granting of food. Intelligent behavior, however, although undoubtedly dependent in part upon the conditioning of reflexes, is not automatic response to a stimulus. It is response that depends upon an appraisal of a total situation. It may vary greatly even though the overt stimuli are identical from case to case. A stimulus subject to this kind of appraisal is called a *symbol,* and intelligence is response to the symbolic, rather than to the signal, characteristics of stimuli. Both signal and symbolic responses are preparatory to what is coming; but symbolic responses are those in which the organism takes account of alternative possibilities instead of responding automatically to a stimulus.

Consider a simple illustration. I am quietly reading in my home, when suddenly the doorbell jangles. My immediate reaction in one case may be the typical startle response—I give a slight jump; this is a case of mere unconditioned reflex. Blue Tooth jumps up and runs to the door; this is a conditioned reflex, for in the past, when the bell has sounded he has found someone there to bark at or to welcome. His response in this case is anticipatory and preparatory for what is coming, while mine is neither.

Then compare these actions with those in another similar case. I have been reading a newspaper account about a dangerous criminal who has come to several houses in the neighborhood, rung the doorbell, and attacked the person who opened the door. Now my doorbell rings. On this occasion, I do not simply react to it as a physical stimulus affecting my ear. I react in the light of the conditions that are not physically affecting me at the moment, namely, the conditions reported in the newspaper I have read. I cautiously approach the door, and try to see who it is that has rung the bell. On still another occasion, when I am expecting a friend, I respond to the same physical stimulus in the light of that expectation with almost as much alacrity as the dog, and quickly go to open the door. In the latter two instances, I am responding to absent and future events in the light of past events, acting so as to prepare for them, reacting to identical physical stimuli in different ways according to their different "meanings." The dog, however, reacts in the same way to the same stimulus regardless of the differences in their "meaning," of which I am aware.

Such anticipatory or preparatory responsiveness to stimuli is a function of the organism made possible by the complex action of its nervous system. By "distant receptors" my nervous system enables me to deal with an event before it is in physical contact with me, and by its integrative action, to respond to stimuli according to their promised meanings for my needs and tendencies. The nervous system is, as it were, the "cutting edge" of the organism. Although an axe may be used as a hammer and a human organism as ballast in a boat, the "proper function" of the one is to cut and of the other is to respond intelligently and teleologically to stimuli that bear upon its needs. Only if the axe can cut does it have the specific function we ascribe to it; only if a human being can respond to the symbolic aspects of its environment do we ascribe mind and intelligence to it.

The mind is the body's perfected operation and achievement, as Aristotle taught us long ago. . . . [The naturalist] would find it difficult to take the problem of interaction [between mind and body] seriously. For to him it is quite evident that conscious bodies are more efficient than those that are not [conscious]. . . . No one doubts that beings become more efficient by becoming conscious, any more than one doubts that a live man is more efficient than a dead one.[11]

Mind is not a *thing* having efficacious power, something that makes or permits a man to act symbolically. It is, says the naturalist, this way of acting itself. "Mind may be defined as response to the meanings of stimuli . . . as the control of behavior by anticipation.[12]

In Chapter 4 intelligent problem-solving was contrasted to trial and error solutions to problems. Intelligent problem-solving involves acting on a hypothesis that has been tried out symbolically—through anticipation—before it is put into overt practice. A hypothesis is a plan of action. In the case of the dog who runs to the door when the bell rings, the hypothesis has been "built into the nervous system" by training and habituation; he not only leaps before he looks, but he runs before he "thinks." I do neither when I am responding intelligently. Although certainly there are physiological conditions and past training that affect the way I act, the hypotheses I use in intelligent problem-solving are not "built-in" habits. In responding to the symbolic aspects of a stimulus, I suspend action until

[11] Reprinted from Frederick J. E. Woodbridge, *Nature and Mind*, page 333. Copyright 1937 by Columbia University Press.
[12] Reprinted from Yervant H. Krikorian, "A Naturalistic Theory of Mind," in *Naturalism and the Human Spirit*, page 252 (edited by Yervant H. Krikorian). Copyright 1944 by Columbia University Press.

more stimuli arrive to clarify the problematic and unsettled aspects of the situation. The substitute for the overt action is the consciousness of the hypothesis; "To have an idea is to be ready to respond in a specific way to a stimulus; to reason is to rehearse various anticipatory responses in relation to a problem." [13]

Conscious appraisal of a situation, which is reasoning about the meanings of the stimuli, occurs in the period of tension between the occurrence of an unexpected stimulus and overt response to it. My dog does not pause to consider; he acts but does not reason. My organism does not respond automatically. The stimulus arouses in me various alternative reaction patterns that are possible plans for action. Observation of the facts of the situation, followed by anticipatory tracing out of their probable consequences, occurs in me because my nervous system has "built into" it *many* possible plans of action that can be tried out before being put into practice. Reasoning is the process of comparing and interpreting symbols before responding to them overtly.

Reasoning, therefore, need not be interpreted as a transcendental function of an other-worldly entity called mind or pure reason. It is rather a way of acting under the guidance of alternative sets of symbolic interpretations of the stimulus, each of which promises its own anticipated consequences for the future behavior of the organism. Reasoning reaches the highest degree of abstractness or distance from the determinative role of the merely physical characteristics of the stimulus in the use of words and mathematical symbols, which owe little of their meaning for behavior to their specific and unique physical characteristics. Logic, mathematics, and grammar are concerned with the symbolic interrelations among stimuli, and concern only their meanings; but they are meanings of stimuli

---

[13] Reprinted from Yervant H. Krikorian, "A Naturalistic Theory of Mind," in *Naturalism and the Human Spirit*, page 257 (edited by Yervant H. Krikorian). Copyright 1944 by Columbia University Press.

that arise in the natural interaction between a delicately balanced organism and the environment.

Awareness of the symbolical relations constitutes knowledge if the circumstances they imply or suggest are actually met with in the future experience of the organism. In this respect the pragmatic theory of truth fits in with the functional theory of mind.

Pragmatism

The naturalist, as we have just seen, asserts that the mind is a natural phenomenon, not something above or beyond nature. Mind is a mode of behavior, in which the organism seeks goals and anticipates the future. Mind as functionally understood is no epiphenomenon, but an agent in the struggle for survival. The biological theory of evolution, applied to the theory of mind and knowledge, leads to an important conclusion: the test of the value of mental workings is not whether they produce beliefs that in some way "correspond" to reality, but whether they facilitate the adjustment of the organism to its environment or help to resolve the problems presented by the environment. "Knowledge is power," said Bacon; the modern naturalist says, "Knowledge is the fruit of undertakings that transform a problematic situation into a resolved one." [14]

Elaboration of this naturalistic doctrine is the work of the American school of philosophers known as pragmatists. Pragmatism, according to one of its leaders, John Dewey, is "the theory that the processes and materials of knowledge are determined by practical or purposive considerations—that there is no such thing as knowledge determined by exclusively theoretical, speculative, or abstract intellectual considerations." [15] For these philosophers, a meaningful judgment is one that has consequences for our practical experience, one whose truth

---

[14] John Dewey, *The Quest for Certainty*, pages 242-243. New York: Minton Balch, 1929.

[15] John Dewey, quoted in M. H. Fisch, (ed.) *Classical American Philosophers*, page 27. New York, Appleton-Century-Crofts, Inc., 1951.

or falsity "makes a difference" within experience. A true judgment is one that is useful in meeting the practical situation that calls forth the belief as a preparation for dealing with the situation. The true is the useful. The doctrine is not that a true belief is subsequently discovered also to be true, but rather, that the criteria of truth can be shown upon analysis to involve only questions of usefulness in adjustment.

Just as intelligence is a response to a practical situation that is problematical and threatens the on-going of life and inquiry, the criterion of intelligent response guided by a belief, and the criterion of the belief itself, is the degree to which the belief and the action based upon it resolve the problem that elicited it. If a belief aids us in adjusting ourselves to a situation, or resolves the problems presented by the situation, it is useful, and the pragmatists said that this is what we mean when we call a belief true; this is how we discover that it is true, in the only sense of "true" that actually matters. A true belief is one that "works," one that brings about the response that resolves the problem:

> The ultimate test for us of what a truth means is . . . the conduct it dictates or inspires. But it inspires that conduct because it first foretells some particular turn to our experience which shall call forth just that conduct from us.[16]

This test of meaning has been illustrated again and again in our study of hypotheses. An idea, a judgment, a concept, or a hypothesis is not primarily a "copy of reality," judged by its correspondence to reality. It is rather a plan of action, a foresight towards future adjustment. Not the origin, but the application, determines its value or truth. The criterion of its value and truth is whether it produces actions that bring foreseen results.

Pragmatists have differed among themselves in the ways they assess the usefulness and, hence, the truth of a judgment.

---

[16] William James, *Collected Essays and Reviews*, page 412. New York: Longmans, Green & Company, Inc., 1920.

Peirce, for instance, emphasized the usefulness of general or abstract concepts in simplifying and ordering experience. Ideas, according to him, must be tested by their application to, and usefulness in, all conceivable experience, without regard to particular personal interests of the believer. Usefulness meant to him primarily intellectual simplification and integration, and the pragmatic criterion, as he interpreted it, had much in common with the universal coherence sought by the idealists.

William James appealed to two criteria of usefulness. For judgments that could be tested in future experience, James' theory has much in common with Peirce's. He called truth the "cash value of an idea," comparing an idea to a check, which is valueless in itself, but valuable if it can be cashed. An idea is "cashed" at the bank of future experience; if it is "honored" by having our expectations from it fulfilled, we call it true. What was new and distinctive in James' version of pragmatism, however, was his insistence upon the relation of some beliefs to our irrational or "passional" nature. When the "facts of the case" are not sufficient to decide the truth or falsity of a hypothesis, and when the hypothesis is about such an urgent human problem that one must take a stand for or against it, James emphasized that the consequences of *believing* the hypothesis take the place of the consequences of the hypothesis itself. The consequence of the act of belief bears upon our passional nature as acting, desiring human beings. Our passional nature is and, James believed, should be decisive for or against belief in the hypothesis. Thus, for instance, the proposition, "God exists," does not itself have any testable consequences; but the *belief* that God exists does have consequences for our conduct, and these consequences are and should be the determining reasons for choosing whether to believe in God's existence.[17]

John Dewey, most recent of the great representatives of American pragmatism, thinks more in terms of the social con-

---

[17] For James' use of this as an argument for God, see above, pages 294-296.

sequences of beliefs. The conflicts that most concern him are
social in origin, and he insists upon the fact that warranted
beliefs are those that release the potentialities of men and institutions for further free inquiry and growth unhampered by
authoritarianism and dogmatism, which derive the value of
beliefs from their origin rather than their application.

Each of these philosophers is saying, in his own way, that
the true is the useful. Each of them is perhaps inadvertently
illustrating the pragmatic principle that interests determine
outlook. Peirce was a mathematician and scientist and could be
expected to emphasize universality as characteristic of true
and useful beliefs; James was a psychologist with a strong bias
toward religion; Dewey's thought is oriented largely toward
the social setting of intelligent action, and he has devoted himself to educational reform.

While the doctrine that a true belief is a useful belief is
treated differently by each of these men, those outside the
pragmatic movement have criticized it on the basis of the assumption of still another meaning of the "useful." They have
objected to it because they think of "useful" as meaning the
technologically or economically useful. On that basis, of course,
the doctrine can be made to appear absurd. A lie is not true,
however much it helps a man to get out of a scrape, nor is a
false statement in advertising made true by the fact that such
a statement sometimes pays. The writings of the pragmatists
have not always been sufficiently lucid to prevent this kind of
misinterpretation, but the careful reader of the pragmatists,
especially of Peirce and Dewey, can readily see that it is a misinterpretation.

"Usefulness" is not to be interpreted in a narrow sense, as
the personally advantageous in a particular situation. *The kind
of usefulness relevant to the establishment of any truth is determined by the kind of problem that engenders the belief to be
tested.* One would not ordinarily call the proposition, "Caesar
crossed the Rubicon," a useful bit of knowledge, for one generally thinks of the useful as having close relation to overt practical

behavior. But precisely why does anyone think it worthwhile to say, "Caesar crossed the Rubicon"? It would ordinarily be in response to a problematic situation facing a historian who wishes to understand the events of Roman history, and it is a useful belief to the extent that it foretells what he will find if he consults other books, or what he and other historians will conclude if they weigh all the evidence at hand. It is entirely irrelevant whether making this statement is a help or a hindrance in furthering his reputation, although it may indeed be useful in that respect. But the kind of usefulness required for the judgment is usefulness determined by the problem itself. Following out the plan of action (research) dictated by his belief that Caesar crossed the Rubicon and his need for understanding other events in history, this belief shows its usefulness in preparing him for further experiences, and in simplifying and integrating the evidence that this action leads him to uncover.

Because "usefulness" was thus interpreted by the pragmatists, at least when they were writing most carefully, it is unfair of their opponents to say that pragmatism was just a manifestation of American commercialism masquerading as epistemology, or a corollary of the American "philosophy of getting ahead." It might be fairer criticism to go to the opposite extreme, in fact, and to say that the pragmatist has to interpret "usefulness" in such a way that it ceases to have any distinctive meaning other than what everyone has heretofore always meant by "truth," for a true belief is one that satisfies doubt and answers the question that led to it. In other words, it might be said that the pragmatists "trivialized" the concept of usefulness, so that "the useful" denoted primarily what met empirical tests and the requirement of coherence.

Be that as it may, however, pragmatism is an important doctrine because it at least shows how a naturalistic theory of mind, unlike epiphenomenalism, can account for the occurrence and testing of true beliefs. Pragmatism did more than any other movement in modern philosophy to bridge the gap that had opened between behavior and thought, practice and theory, value and fact, interest and objective truth. For doing so, it deserves a prominent place both in modern philosophy and in educational reform.

The freedom of the will

Pragmatism and the naturalistic or functional theory of the mind have thrown new light on the old problem of freedom and responsibility. If their theory of the bearing of foresight upon present behavior is correct, it is not possible to assume that the future is wholly determined by the past. It is not necessary to believe that the world is wound up like a clock, and that man is but a passive spectator of a process that he cannot in the least control. The universe, for the naturalist who is not a materialist, is still "in the making," and among the makers of the universe are the acting human beings whose behavior is guided by their foresight into what might occur but can be prevented, or what might not occur but can be produced. For this to be possible, moreover, it is unnecessary to think of mind as something above nature, intervening in it, as the Cartesian dualist does. Intelligence guiding interest is a factor within nature that introduces novelty, teleology, and new departures.

When it is supposed that the mind is a substance existing outside nature, there is always the troublesome problem of how it acts. If it does not "interfere" with the processes in the body that would have occurred without it, mind seems a useless epiphenomenon. In such a case, it is supposed that the organism is but a machine, and that the will (as an alleged faculty of the mind) is not free. On the other hand, if it is supposed that the will is free, and that the mind is thus able to interfere with and redirect the activity of the body, there is the problem of the uniformity of nature; for this theory seems to deny the possibility of indefinitely extending our understanding of the human body in scientific terms by the discovery of laws describing its behavior.

The functional theory of mind, with its pragmatic emphasis

upon the anticipatory and teleological character of mental behavior, is believed by its adherents to provide a way out of this dilemma, and to make man's claim to be free compatible with the discoveries and postulates of psychology. The functional theory makes the will the active, executive aspect of mind.

Before using the word "will" as the name for a kind of thing in our minds that might be thought to be free or necessitated, the functionalist asks that we analyze the concept of will just as we have previously analyzed that of mind. On what occasions do we say that a person acted voluntarily, that is, as a consequence of an "act of willing"? Not on occasions when he acted capriciously, unpredictably, perhaps inexplicably. If that were the kind of action we call voluntary, "will" would be incompatible with morality and responsibility, for moral actions are actions resulting from a disposition to act in accordance with some principle rather than from the variable impulses that cannot be foreseen from moment to moment. When a man we regard as morally good suddenly does some quite unexpected action, some action that we could not anticipate from our knowledge of his character, we tend *not* to consider this action as one that he has "freely willed," but to interpret it as due to some uncontrollable psychological quirk or overpowering urge for which he is not wholly responsible.

When we say that a man has acted voluntarily or freely, and hold him responsible for his action, we mean, first, that he has not been coerced by another person. No one is twisting his arm when he does a free action. We mean also, in the second place, that he is not acting out of ignorance of the true state of affairs. A man is not "freely" committing suicide when he takes poison from a bottle marked "For headache." And third, we mean, that the action he performs is one that, to use a rather vague expression, "follows from the kind of man he is." A free action, in some sense, "expresses a man's character."

What, then, is character? Character is more than reflex. It is a settled disposition to react to circumstances and needs with due regard to the symbolic value and implications of the stimuli and occasions of the action. A man's character cannot be manifested when he is under overpowering compulsion or coercion, nor is it expressed when he is laboring in ignorance of the important facts that he would be disposed to consider in making his decision. Only those actions that the person performs as a result of insight into the symbolic significance of the occasion are the actions for which he is held responsible; all other actions are his responses to coercion, either overt or subtle (from another person, from fear, from ignorance, and so forth). A free and responsible action is one that flows not from the momentary push of circumstances, but from his settled character based on insight into himself and his situation. Settled character is the moral corollary of insight into the potential ways of responding, combined with a disposition to prefer one kind of outcome to another.

A *good* character is one that is most responsive to the value-implications of each possible line of action, so that its choice is guided by intelligent comprehension of alternative values and a habitual preference for those lines of action that will most. probably lead to approved values.

The actions for which men are rightly held responsible are the actions that could have been otherwise. This does not mean that we cannot find sufficient causal reasons for the acts that took place, for the moral conduct of men may be as determined as any other psychological behavior, and naturalists believe that it is. But the actions are free in the sense that the man who does them is not just a reacting victim of circumstance. Rather, through his insight into the whole situation and himself, integrated through a concept he has of what sort of being he is and hopes to become, he himself becomes one of the effective factors in the decision as to what his action will be. And because human acts are initiators of new causal chains in nonhuman nature and society, the free man is one of the determinants of the future.[18]

---

[18] This theory of freedom has been compared with others and evaluated in our discussion of freedom and the laws of nature; cf. page 148.

Implications for psychiatry and medicine

The theory that mind is a purely natural function to be understood by the methods of science has definite and fruitful implications for psychiatry and medicine. In studying mind, philosophers have frequently thought that they were leaving the world of nature behind them, and they drew a distinction between the "natural sciences" and the "sciences of mind." A comparable distinction was drawn, in the medical sciences, between those parts of the art of healing that were concerned with men's bodies and those parts concerned with their minds. But with the development of the theory that mind is a mode of behavior, the naturalist bridges the gap between these two kinds of medical research and therapy.

The naturalist's functional theory enables us to look upon so-called "mental illness" in a new light. Instead of thinking that there is a "mind" that is sick or abnormal, and that it is just a pity that there is no drug that we can give to cure it as some medicines cure illnesses of the body, the psychiatrist now sees the patient as a single complex unity, not a compound of a physiological body and an immaterial, psychical entity called mind. Abnormal behavior, attributed long ago to possession by evil spirits and later to warped or diseased minds, is now thought of as simply a pattern of behavior "gone wrong" and not effectively adaptive and truly anticipatory. Mental illness is interpreted literally as "behavior disorder," instead of the disordered behavior being looked upon as only a symptom of something wrong in a hidden mind or soul. This revised view has called scientific attention to the physiological conditions of so-called mental illness to a much greater degree than would be justified if it were thought that the body is merely the vehicle or prison of the mind. Psychosomatic medicine, even in its name, signalizes this new outlook.

Not only does this theory have rich suggestions to make concerning the physiological basis of abnormal behavior, which was formerly attributed only to a diseased mind; it also renders intelligible some of the physiological effects of behavior disorders (such as anxiety). And it suggests new lines of therapy for pathological conditions that were once thought of as purely organic in origin. The physician often deals with physiological conditions that are results of behavior that has gone wrong, and frequently, these conditions and symptoms can be righted through aiding the patient to reconstruct the attitudes, habits, and expectations that have issued in this maladjustment. The organismic theory of life (see pages 166 ff), when applied to human beings, provides a basis for understanding these bodily conditions due to "states of mind" without suggesting that the mind is a kind of diseased organ.

Naturalism and humanism in religion

At first glance it might seem that a naturalistic system of metaphysics would be able to provide little or no place for religious values. It might seem that the naturalist, for whom science is the central fact, would have to derogate religion in the manner of Lucretius, who equated it with superstition. Because the religious emphasize the supremacy of faith over critical inquiry, and because Christian orthodoxy has emphasized the conception of a God who stands at least in part above nature, it might be expected that the naturalistic metaphysics would be incompatible with any religious commitment.

Theological dualism and naturalism are indeed incompatible. But the belief that there is *necessary* opposition between religion and science, or between a metaphysics based on religion and a metaphysics based on science as the central fact, overlooks a very important consideration—that neither religion nor science is an eternal and unchanging attitude or set of dogmas. While there are naturalists who are agnostics or atheists, and religiously oriented people and societies who think of religion as simply a way of propitiating a capricious and petulant anthropomorphic god, neither of these narrow views is characteristic of or essential to the religious or the scientific philosophy of life:

The warfare which has been waged between science and religion at certain periods of history has been due to the fact that a premature naturalism or an antiquated religion or both have been current.[19]

Consider these two terms: "antiquated religion" and "premature naturalism." By the former, Lamprecht means religion that has not kept step with knowledge and enlightenment in the pursuit of value. By the latter, he means a naturalism that, like materialism, is too thin and dogmatic in its own way to do full justice to religious values.

Religious conceptions and attitudes, as we have seen, continuously change over long periods of time. Thus they take account of the insights gradually acquired in fields originally quite irrelevant to men's dealings with whatever they consider to be sacred. A narrow anthropomorphism is intellectually dead, but modern religious thinkers do not regard its demise as a loss to religion—it is rather a sign that religion is intellectually responsible and responsive to the facts of life. On the other hand, naturalism and the scientific attitude also change and grow to take account of whole areas of fact and value that were formerly either denied or regarded as transcending nature and the scope of scientific investigation. It is therefore very unrealistic to speak of an opposition between them as though naturalism meant a narrow materialism, and religion meant a narrow anthropomorphism. Redefinition of both is required, before a meaningful analysis of their interrelations can be made.

In this chapter, the concept of nature has been redefined, just as the concept of science and scientific knowledge was broadened to make it more generally applicable. It remains to show how naturalistic philosophers modify some common conceptions of religion so that the alleged opposition between

---

[19] Reprinted from Sterling P. Lamprecht, "Naturalism and Religion," in *Naturalism and the Human Spirit*, page 17 (edited by Yervant H. Krikorian). Copyright 1944 by Columbia University Press.

them and naturalistic views can be replaced by fruitful co-operation.

The naturalist, as we have seen, is interested in many kinds of experience that the materialist is likely to ignore or to deride as mere illusion and wasted effort. Among the experiences that naturalists have analyzed in recent years is the religious experience. Analyzing and being interested in a specific kind of experience, however, are very different from accepting the experience in question as a source of *truth*. The naturalist is committed to a method of constructing and testing hypotheses, a method that makes him unwilling to accept the truth of a religious dogma simply because he has an experience he calls religious. Having any experience is only the first stage of knowledge. Knowledge is a verified interpretation of experience.

No experience, the naturalist says, is necessarily to be taken at its face value. Just as an observation in a laboratory does not explain itself or guarantee its own truth apart from all hypothesis concerning its foundations, validity, and consequences, so also the religious experience—whose existence and value as lifting up the human spirit is not denied—must be investigated before its claim to *truth* is granted.

The naturalist, for reasons already given (page 303), decides that the alleged empirical vindication of dualistic metaphysical beliefs on the basis of the religious experience is invalid. He holds that the religious experience is not really an empirical test for the hypothesis. In spite of that, he admits the *value* of the religious experience just as the theological dualist does; and while the theological dualist proposes one hypothesis to account for the characteristics and value of the experience, the naturalist proposes another. Let us compare them briefly.

The theological dualist finds in the religious experience an awareness of a value transcending the ordinarily narrow values that the individual experiences in his daily life. In the religious experience, he truly says, man feels that he is in personal contact with a being greater than man that (or Who) supports his highest aspirations and saves him from triviality of purpose. In interpreting this experience, the theological dualist asserts that this experience reveals, and is unintelligible without the belief in, a being that metaphysically embodies perfection. The values we experience in religious devotion are held to be mere appearances of another value, eternally realized and fully actual, whose antecedent existence supports man's religious and moral values and guarantees their final triumph in the world.

The belief in the complete antecedent embodiment of religious value in a perfect and eternal God is said by the naturalist, on the other hand, to be an unwarranted interpretation of the experience. This belief, in Santayana's language, is merely comforting poetic imagery to rationalize and dignify the experience itself. Religion is

. . . a symbolic rendering of that moral experience which it springs out of and which it seeks to elucidate. Its falsehood comes from the insidious misunderstanding that clings to it, to the effect that these poetic conceptions are not merely representations of experience as it is or should be, but are rather information about experience or reality elsewhere.[20]

Dewey says essentially the same thing: the values experienced in religion do not

. . . depend upon some prior complete embodiment—as if the efforts of human beings in behalf of justice, or knowledge, or beauty, depended for their effectiveness and validity upon assurance that there already existed in some supernal region a place where criminals are humanely treated, where there is no serfdom or slavery, where all facts and truths are already discovered and possessed, and all beauty is eternally displayed in actualized form.[21]

If such dualistic, perfectionistic hypotheses are rejected, as the naturalist does reject them, what is there in the religious

---

[20] George Santayana, *Reason in Religion* (1905), in *The Collected Works of George Santayana*, Volume IV, page 9. New York: Charles Scribner's Sons, 1936.

[21] John Dewey, *A Common Faith*, page 49. New Haven, Conn.: Yale University Press, 1934.

experience that gives it its value? Not the cognitive claim the theologian makes, but the emotional and moral significance of the experience itself. If the experience has any informative value, the valuable information we get from it is information about ourselves, our potentialities and ideals. The religious experience, says Dewey, is not a foundation for faith in a specific kind of metaphysical truth called theological. It is the experience of a faith valuable in itself as

. . . the unification of the self through allegiance to inclusive ideal ends, which imagination presents to us and to which the human will responds as worthy of controlling our desires and choices.[22]

This kind of experience need not be induced by prayers and fasting or by the act of worship, although it may be. The value of the experience is its consequences for our attitude toward ourselves and others. The religious experience lifts us out of narrow concern with ourselves, and vividly presents ideals and undreamed-of possibilities. The integration and harmonization of our otherwise divisive and dispersive concerns around some central goal of aspiration is its justification and warrant. Because the values that are relevant in the evaluation of the experience are social and human, this view of what is essential in religion is commonly called "humanism."

But why, one may ask, should humanism be thought of as a religion, or why should the experience as the humanist interprets it be considered a religious experience? Anti-religious naturalists, as well as philosophers with a more affirmative appreciation of the usual and typical forms of religion, say that humanists misuse the word "religion" when they apply it to an entirely different kind of activity and experience, having different psychological characteristics, metaphysical presuppositions, and emotional consequences. If by "religious" we refer to an attitude toward transcendent perfect reality, as distinguished from concern with ideals to be achieved by men's working together in nature, it is not religious. Humanism makes

---

[22] *Ibid.*, page 33.

no claim that there is a God who supports our aspirations or rewards our efforts. *God,* says Dewey, is a name for a system of values, not a name for a person or thing. The word *God* "denotes the unity of all ideal ends arousing us to desire and actions." [23]

We are in the presence neither of ideals completely embodied in existence nor yet of ideals that are mere rootless ideals, fantasies, utopias. For there are forces in nature and society that generate and support the ideals. They are further unified by the action that gives them coherence and solidarity. It is this *active* relation between ideal and actual to which I would give the name "God." [24]

Dewey admits that many people will not wish to use the word "God" in this way, and few humanists have followed his usage. Some humanists who join Dewey in rejecting the notion of a transcendent God do not follow him even in discerning forces in nature that support man's ideals. For them, nature is utterly indifferent to men's aspirations. In their view, men should defiantly assert human values without any theological or metaphysical corollaries at all.

Matthew Arnold and Bertrand Russell have pointed out the "indifference" and even "enmity" of nature to man's highest aspirations. Russell sees man as an accident of nature that has, in some unknown way, risen above its source in value and dignity, but not in power. Russell calls on man not to slavishly deify the power of nature and worship it as a god, or to project his yearnings into an imagined god who, he might wish to believe, can secure his triumph over the ruthless natural forces that will destroy him. Russell calls on man "to sustain alone, a weary but unyielding Atlas, the world that his own ideals have fashioned despite the march of unconscious power." [25]

Thomas Henry Huxley, who, a generation earlier, had been

---

[23] John Dewey, *A Common Faith,* page 42. New Haven, Conn.: Yale University Press, 1934.

[24] *Ibid.,* pages 50-51.

[25] Bertrand Russell, "A Free Man's Worship," in *Mysticism and Logic,* page 57. New York: Longmans, Green & Company, Inc., 1918. Used by permission of W. W. Norton & Company, New York, publishers.

one of the men most responsible for the acceptance of Darwin's theory of evolution, likewise rejected the belief that nature supports our highest aspirations, but he also criticized those philosophers who urged a revision of our moral ideas into such a form that they could be promoted by the "blind forces of nature." Many evolutionists believed not only that the theory of evolution could explain the origin of moral codes in the social struggle for survival, but also that in the theory of evolution they could find moral guidance. They argued that right action is action that leads to survival or that helps to prepare the way for a being (such as Nietzsche's Superman) in some way better than man. Adapt and survive, they said, or make way for those who can. Huxley, on the other hand, believed that this was really an excuse for immorality. Instead of the Golden Rule, and the ideal of being one's brother's keeper, it leads to the Nietzschean commandment, "That which falleth, that shalt thou also push." He so opposed the ethical implications drawn from the study of nature that he wrote:

Let us understand, once for all, that the ethical progress of society depends, not on imitating the cosmic process, still less in running away from it, but in combatting it.[26]

Russell and Huxley do not appeal to a being outside of nature, a transcendent God, for help in finding the right and in securing human values, and their essays leave him an orphan in the universe. Nature produced him, but nothing in nature cares for him, and there is nothing in nature that will sustain him. Man is absolutely alone.

This, according to other naturalists who combine a broader conception of nature with modernism in religion (see page 261), is too narrow a conception of both nature and moral value. Man is a part of nature, and it would be unintelligible, they say, to suppose that nature had produced a being with interests

---

[26] Thomas Henry Huxley, "Evolution and Ethics" (1893), in *Selections from the Essays of T. H. Huxley*, page 109 (Alburey Castell, ed.). New York: F. S. Crofts Company, 1947.

and needs wholly unsupported in the natural process in the broadest sense, which includes both the minds of men and their society and culture.

They therefore attempt to formulate metaphysical theories through which they can see man as more at home in nature than Russell and Huxley were willing to concede. For this purpose, they have proposed metaphysical interpretations of religion without theological dualism, insisting rather on the immanence of the divine in nature. Perhaps the most typical of these is the belief that the words "god" or "deity" can be responsibly used for a tendency, a process, or a goal in nature, which is evolving, reaching higher levels of integration on which new and higher values and consciousness of new ideals can emerge. For such a philosophy, God is—as in Dewey's usage—the name given to the tension between the ideal that can come to be and the actual, or God is, in Aristotle's language, the idea or form that activates the movement of nature. God is not only manifested in human striving projected toward something higher than man himself, but is discerned in all the progressive evolutionary processes of nature.

BIBLIOGRAPHY

General works

Dewey, John, *Experience and Nature.* New York: W. W. Norton & Company, Inc., 1929.
———, *Reconstruction in Philosophy* (1921). New York: New American Library, Mentor Books, 1950.
Krikorian, Yervant H. (ed.), *Naturalism and the Human Spirit.* New York: Columbia University Press, 1944.
McCarthy, John W., *The Naturalism of Samuel Alexander.* New York: King's Crown Press, 1948.
Pratt, James B., *Naturalism.* New Haven, Conn.: Yale University Press, 1945.
Sellars, Roy Wood, *Evolutionary Naturalism.* Chicago: Open Court Publishing Company, 1922.

Realistic theory of perception

Adams, E. M., "Primary and Secondary Qualities," *Journal of Philosophy*, Vol. XLV, No. 16 (July 29, 1948), pages 435-442.

Hahn, Lewis E., *A Contextualistic Theory of Perception*. Berkeley, Calif.: University of California Press, 1942.

Klausner, Neil W., "Three Decades of Epistemological Dialectic," *Philosophy of Science*, Vol. XIV, No. 1 (January, 1947), pages 20-43.

Lovejoy, Arthur O., *The Revolt Against Dualism*. New York: W. W. Norton & Company, Inc., 1930.

Miller, David L., "The Nature of the Physical Object," *Journal of Philosophy*, Vol. XLIV, No. 13 (June 19, 1947), pages 352-359.

Montague, William Pepperell, *The Ways of Things*, New York: Prentice-Hall, Inc., 1940. Part 2, Section 3.

Murphy, Arthur E., "Objective Relativism in Dewey and Whitehead," *Philosophical Review*, Vol. XXXVI, No. 2 (March, 1927), pages 121-144.

Oliver, W. Donald, "The Logic of Perspective Realism," *Journal of Philosophy*, Vol. XXXV, No. 8 (April 14, 1938), pages 197-208.

Robinson, Daniel S. (ed.), *Anthology of Recent Philosophy*. New York: Thomas Y. Crowell Company, 1929. Part 3.

Naturalistic theory of mind

Garnett, A. Campbell, "Functionalism and the Intentional Act," *Philosophical Review*, Vol. XLIX, No. 4 (September, 1940), pages 453-464.

Mead, George Herbert, *Mind, Self, and Society*. Chicago: University of Chicago Press, 1934.

Morris, Charles W., *Six Theories of Mind*. Chicago: University of Chicago Press, 1932.

Pragmatism

Dewey, John, et al., *Creative Intelligence, Essays in the Pragmatistic Attitude*. New York: Henry Holt and Company, Inc., 1917.

———, *Studies in Logical Theory*. Chicago: University of Chicago Press, 1903.

Fisch, M. H. (ed.), *Classical American Philosophers*. New York: Appleton-Century-Crofts, Inc., 1950. Parts 1, 2, and 5.

James, William, *Pragmatism*. New York: Longmans, Green & Company, Inc., 1907.

———, *The Meaning of Truth.* New York: Longmans, Green & Company, Inc., 1909.
Leonard, Henry S., "The Pragmatism and Scientific Metaphysics of C. S. Peirce," *Philosophy of Science,* Vol. IV, No. 1 (January, 1937), pages 109-121.
Peirce, Charles S., *Chance, Love, and Logic* (Morris R. Cohen, ed.). New York: Harcourt, Brace and Company, Inc., 1923.
Robinson, Daniel S. (ed.), *Anthology of Recent Philosophy.* New York: Thomas Y. Crowell Company, 1929. Part 3.

Theory of value; philosophy of religion

Burtt, Edwin A., *Types of Religious Philosophy,* second ed. New York: Harper & Brothers, 1951. Chapter 11.
Dewey, John, *Human Nature and Conduct* (1922). New York: Random House, Modern Library Edition, 1930.
Lamont, Corliss, *Humanism as a Philosophy.* New York: Philosophical Library, 1950.
Lippmann, Walter, *A Preface to Morals.* New York: The Macmillan Company, 1929.
Quillian, William F., *The Moral Theory of Evolutionary Naturalism.* New Haven, Conn.: Yale University Press, 1945.

QUESTIONS AND TOPICS FOR DISCUSSION

1. A prominent naturalist has said, "Nature produces spirit, just as soil produces flowers." Do you find this a good analogy?
2. Many naturalists claim that their philosophy is the best foundation for a democratic philosophy of life. Compare it, in this respect, with theological dualism and pluralistic idealism.
3. Is the naturalist, with his functional theory of mind, able to meet the criticisms in Chapter 12 of epiphenomenalism? Is the functional theory merely a disguised form of epiphenomalism?
4. "The naturalist's theory of nature is more like that of the pluralistic idealist than like that of the materialist." Discuss.
5. Materialists deny that naturalists have any right to claim science as a support for their metaphysics, because naturalists use teleological explanations. Discuss.
6. Why would a naturalist be likely to embrace an emergent theory of life?

7. Discuss the naturalist's theory of freedom in the light of the argument of Chapter 5.

8. Does the naturalist have any legitimate right to use the word "God" to denote a natural process?

9. Compare naturalism and theological dualism with respect to their use in the theory of mental hygiene and psychiatry.

10. Of the seven major types of metaphysical theory discussed in Chapters 9 through 13, which one seems to you to be most nearly satisfactory? Why?

Name Index

Subject Index

Inquiry—*Continued*
  as problem-solving, 72 ff, 438
  political obstacles to, 409
  pragmatic theory of, 437 ff
  reason in, 59 ff
  scientific method as model for,
    106 ff
  scientific, in naturalism, 384 ff, 387
  sense experience in, 55 f
  social, 170 ff
  substitutes for, Chapter 2 *passim*
  teleological conceptions in, 166
  uniformity of nature as postulate of,
    138 ff, 141, 145
  vitalism as block to, 165
  and values, 184
  as a value, 225 ff
Intellectual value, 196
Intelligence:
  in epiphenomenalism, 395
  in functional theory of mind, 432 ff
  and purpose, 288
Intelligibility, as evidence of design,
    282 f
Interest, 196 f, 206 f, 213 f
Introspection, 396
Intuition, 40, 179, 247, 373
Isolated system, 101

J

Jehovah, 263

K

Kingdom of God, 257
Kinsey report, 216

L

"Law of preponderance of means over
    end," 192
"Law of three stages," 121 ff
Law, philosophy of, 16
Laws, 238, Chapter 5 *passim* (*See also*
    Nature, laws of)
  descriptive and prescriptive, 120 ff,
    283
  of thought, 87, 283
Life, theories of nature of, 161 ff
Limited variety, principle of, 139
Logic, 16, 32, 69, 87, 159, 437
Logical positivism, 241 ff

M

Magic, 32, 258
Man, vii, 3
  as agent of World-Spirit (Hegel),
    362
  and animal, 433 ff
  as appearance and reality (Kant),
    150 ff
  Aristotle's theory of, 198 f, 431 f
  in "block universe," 365
  Cartesian theory of, 394
  as causal agent, 148, 444
  character of, 443 f
  Christian view of, 311, 416
  in democratic community, 365
  in deterministic universe, 147, 150 ff
  dignity of (Russell), 296
  economic factors in behavior of,
    400 f
  effects of group on, 32
  effects of authority on, 50
  fundamental desires and needs of,
    216 ff
  as God's helper (Mill), 287
  "higher powers" of, 198
  incompleteness of, 349, 368
  and indeterminacy, 146
  in materialistic culture, 409 f
  materialistic theory of, 393
  maturity of (Sheen), 209
  naturalistic theory of, 419 f
  and nature, 145 ff, 188 f, 419 ff
  and need for certainty, 224
  and need for metaphysics, 237 f
  purposes of, 285
  rights of, 190
  Socratic view of, 202 f
  and superman, 452
  as supernatural being, 148, 256
  in theological dualism, 256, 307 ff,
    416
  value commitments of, 195
  "a weary but unyielding Atlas,"
    (Russell), 451
  (*See also* Mind, Organism, Person,
    Self, Soul)
Mana, 258
Materialism, 369, 377, 388 ff, 417
  (*See also* Dialectical material-
    ism)
  criticisms of, 406 ff
  and critical naturalism, 420